Additional Praise for the First Edition

The authors have crammed so much thought-power into the pages of this book it's a challenge to describe or summarize. . . . They explain how the world *doesn't* work, quite remarkably, which helps us see how it *does* work, perhaps. Markets are judgmental, they say, not mechanistic. Amen! They say Japan's decades-long bust proves both the major economic theories are wrong and that the West is destined to follow. They rightly, in my view, claim this is a crisis point in modern history. This book just might help us cope with it. *Worth a try!*

> —*Harry D. Schultz*
> *editor of the* International
> Harry Schultz Letter

Bonner sometimes makes me feel like a house painter staring at a Rembrandt. He is that good. *Financial Reckoning Day* is guaranteed to make you think. It will help you understand why we go from boom to bust and how you can profit from that change. It will open your eyes to a new way of seeing the world and make you a better investor. And it will be one of the most pleasurable reads you have had in a long time.

> —*John Mauldin*
> *Millennium Wave*
> *Advisors, editor of* Thoughts
> from the Frontline

Forward and backward in time, up the alleyways of one theory and down another, often soiled by the sorry sludge of historical missteps . . . the often-disastrous results of the hopes and dreams, needs and wants of all the people in all of history coalesce into a Grand Unified Theory that one cannot adequately define or explain, but by the end of the last sentence, on the last page, of the last chapter, one knows that, surely, this book is something to behold.

> —*Richard Daughty*
> *editor of the* Mogambo Guru
> Economic Newsletter

FINANCIAL RECKONING DAY FALLOUT

FINANCIAL RECKONING DAY FALLOUT

Surviving Today's Global Depression

Fully Revised and Updated
10th Anniversary Edition

WILLIAM BONNER
ADDISON WIGGIN

WITH KATE INCONTRERA

WILEY

John Wiley & Sons, Inc.

For general information on our other products and services or for technical support, please contact our Customer Care Department within the United States at (800) 762-2974, outside the United States at (317) 572-3993 or fax (317) 572-4002.

Wiley also publishes its books in a variety of electronic formats. Some content that appears in print may not be available in electronic books. For more information about Wiley products, visit our web site at www.wiley.com.

ISBN 978-0-470-48327-5

Printed in the United States of America.

10 9 8 7 6 5 4 3 2 1

CONTENTS

FOREWORD

Some people want to buy baseball teams or chase women, but I'm told the number one dream that comes to mind when young people are asked is: "I want to see the world."

I've been around the world twice now: Once on a motorcycle. Once in a Mercedes. So I guess that means I'm crazier than most people.

The reason that I love doing it, other than the sense of adventure, and I certainly love the adventure, is that it's the only way I can figure out what's going on in the world. I don't trust the newspapers, TV stations, or government pronouncements. That's what everyone else knows. I want to see it for myself, close to the ground.

You learn much more about a society by crossing a remote border, finding the black market, and changing money or talking to the local madam than by talking to bureaucrats or economists at the IMF and the World Bank . . . or by watching CNBC.

By the time I cross the border in the jungle, I know 25 percent to 30 percent of what I need to know about a country. I know the bureaucracy. I know the infrastructure. I know the corruption. I know the status of the economy and its currency. And I know whether I stand to make money investing there or not.

The only other way to know what's going on is to study history. When I teach or speak at universities, young people always ask me: "I want to be successful and travel around the world; what should I study?"

I always tell them the same thing: "Study history."

And they always look at me very perplexed and say, "What are you talking about . . . what about economics, what about marketing?"

"If you want to be successful," I always say, "you've got to understand history. You'll see how the world is always changing. You'll see how a lot of the things we see today have happened before. Believe it or not, the stock market didn't begin the day you graduated from school. The stock market's been around for centuries. All markets have. These things have happened before. And will happen again."

Alan Greenspan went on record before he left his post at the Federal Reserve saying he had never seen a bubble before. I know in his lifetime, in his adult lifetime, there have been several bubbles. There was a bubble in the late 1960s in the U.S. stock market. There was the oil bubble. The gold bubble. The bubble in Kuwait. The bubble in Japan. The bubble in real estate in Texas. So what is he talking about? Had he not seen those things, he could have at least read some histories . . . all these things and others have been written about repeatedly.

Alan Greenspan continues to embody the economic mindset of today's policy makers. They have the lunatic idea that a nation can consume its way to prosperity although it has never been done in history.

In the United States, if you have a job, you pay taxes. If you save some money, you pay taxes on the interest. If you buy a stock and you get a dividend, you pay taxes. If you have a capital gain, you pay taxes again. And when you die, your estate pays taxes. If you live long enough to get social security, they tax your social security income. Remember: You paid taxes on all this money when you earned it originally yet they tax it again and again.

These policies are not very conducive to encouraging saving or investing. They promote consumption.

By contrast, the countries that have been doing well the last 30 or 40 years are the countries that encourage saving and investing. Singapore is one of the most astonishing cities in the whole world. Forty years ago it was a slum. Now, in terms of per capita reserves, it's one of the richest countries in the world.

One of the reasons Singapore was so successful is that its dictator, Lee Kwan Yu, insisted that everyone save and invest a large part of their income. There are many other dictators or politicians you can condemn, but they have nothing to show for it, and, in fact, they've been worse. Whatever Lee's policies toward personal freedom, at least he forced people to save and invest.

History shows that people who save and invest grow and prosper, and the others deteriorate and collapse.

As the book you hold in your hands demonstrates, artificially low interest rates and rapid credit creation policies set by Alan Greenspan and the Federal Reserve caused the bubble in U.S. stocks of the late 1990s. Policies then pursued at the Fed made the bubble worse. They changed it from a stock market bubble to a consumption and housing bubble.

And when that bubble burst, it was far worse than the stock market bubble, because there are many more people who are involved in consumption and housing. Millions of people found out the hard way that house prices don't go up forever. Now there are a lot of angry people.

No one, of course, wanted to hear it when the original edition of this book was published. They wanted the quick fix. They still want to buy a stock and watch it go up 25 percent because that's what happened a few years ago, and that's what they say on TV. They want yet another interest rate cut, because they've heard that that's what will make the economy boom.

Bill Bonner and Addison Wiggin wrote me early on to tell me that "a lot of the stuff you write about in *Adventure Capitalist* (Random House) is in our book—except for the travel in the international countries."

I'd go a step further and say it's almost as though they wrote parts of my book and I wrote some of theirs—approaching the same subject from two completely different angles . . . and arriving at the same place. From the lack of government policies encouraging saving and investing to the dramatic effect demography will have on the global economy in the twenty-first century, I kept coming across things in this book that I had seen in my travels. He discovered them by reading history books and studying economics. I saw them up close, on the ground.

"Needless to say, your ideas are genius," I wrote back, "You think like I do, which means we're going to go broke together."

JIM ROGERS

PREFACE TO THE 2009 EDITION:

CONFESSIONS OF A NEWSLETTER MAN

We begin with a question: Was ever there a fairer métier than ours?

The poor carpenter risks cutting his fingers or banging his knee. The used car salesman's hearing goes bad as soon as he takes up his job: "No, I don't hear any rattle," says he. The foot-soldier gets sent to a Godforsaken hole like Afghanistan, where the women are covered up and the liquor stashed away.

But in our trade as newsletter publishers, hardly a day passes without a good laugh. Our only occupational hazard is a rupture of the midriff.

Most people, after all, read the news pages for information. They lack the proper training and perspective to fully enjoy them. The consequence is that they are always in danger of taking the humbug seriously, or worse, finding the people who populate the headlines important.

If you really want to appreciate the media you have to get close enough to see how it works—like a prairie dog peering into a hay bailer—but not so close that you get caught up in it yourself. The investment newsletter business is perfect; it is part of the media, but it wouldn't be mistaken for a reputable part.

More than 30 years ago, we began our career publishing newsletters. Those were the days! They were even more fun than today. Years of television, heavy-handed regulation, and waiting in line for airport security have taken much of the lightheartedness out of American life. In its place, a kind of earnest timidity has settled over the 50 states. Everything is forbidden, or else it is compulsory—especially in the financial markets. You can barely talk about an honest investment without some ambitious prosecutor wanting to make a federal case out of it.

But back in the 1970s, the folks you met in the newsletter trade were even wilder and more disreputable than those who are in it today. At one investment conference, we remember an investment advisor from East Germany. He had escaped the Soviets' grip by stealing a small plane and flying to the west. This alone made him a bit of a hero back in the 1970s. But his talk to investors endeared him further. He gave the following discourse:

"Take a look a zis chart," he would begin, pointing to the bottom of what appeared to be a wave pattern. "Investing is reeelly very simple. You just buy at zee bottom. Heere! Zen, ven ze stock goes up, vat do ve do? Ve sell. Heere! [Pointing to the top of the wave pattern.] It is reeelly verrry simple."

"Well, what if the stock doesn't go up," asked an investor, fresh off the Great Plains and not prepared for patterns or people that weren't perfectly straight.

"Ya . . . ve just keep our eyes on ze chart. If it doesn't go up, ve don't buy it."

We don't recall the man's name. It was something like Dr. Friederich Hasselbauer. We were always a bit suspicious of financial advisors who used the "Dr." title, though many did. Especially when they spoke with thick German accents. We imagined that they had been conducting experiments on Jews before they entered the financial markets.

And then there was the Quack man. His name was "Red Robin." As near as we could figure, he liked ducks. So he called his financial analysis "The Quack Report." He had once made his money paving airport runways. Then, in his fifties or sixties, he decided to devote himself to financial analysis and to save the world from a small group of criminal conspirators known as the Bilderburgers, who were in cahoots with the English government. Once, flying on the Concorde across the Atlantic, Ol' "Red" saw the U.K. Chancellor of the Exchequer, it must have been Lord Barber, on the same flight. He told us that he decided to confront his lordship right then and there, when he had the chance.

"I just went up to him and I said, 'I'm on to you . . . ol' buddy . . . "

It must have been quite a scene. Red Robin was a funny-looking fellow with a paunchy stomach who always dressed in orange coveralls, which made him look a little like a red-breasted sapsucker. Why he wore orange overalls, we don't know; perhaps they were a holdover from his days working on airport runways when he didn't want the cement trucks to run him down.

Red also had funny ideas about publishing investment advice. He offered readers a Lifetime Guarantee—they could have their money back anytime. But then, he added a caveat: "My life, not yours." As it turned out, the guarantee was less valuable than readers imagined—or Red himself had hoped. He was gunned down on a beach in Costa Rica, we were told.

But that was the strange milieu in which we decided to make our career. What was delightful about it were the nuts and kooks, the charlatans and dreamers, the brazen hucksters and earnest geniuses who made up the industry. Here were thinkers whose thoughts were untainted by any trace of advanced doctrinaire theory, let alone rudimentary training of any sort. Here were mountebanks and scalawags galore . . . along with a few saints . . . dispensing market wisdom, stock recommendations, and macro-analysis so far reaching you needed a Hubble telescope to see where it came from.

And here, too, were the sort of men whom rich widows were warned about. And the sort of theorists who made you wonder about the limits of human reason itself.

Y2K AND OTHER TRAGEDIES NARROWLY AVERTED

Our friend, Gary North, somewhat of a legend in the business, began studying the possible consequences of the Y2K computer problem in the late 1990s. The more closely he looked, the more alarmed he became. He began writing about the subject, and the more he explored it . . . the more he thought about it . . . the more convinced he became that it would lead to a complete meltdown of modern society. He looked and he saw commerce coming to a stop. He saw trains that couldn't run without electronic instruction. He saw cash machines frozen up. He saw power plants idled by their computer brains. And what would happen to all that electronic information—bank accounts, trading records, inventories—on which the whole financial world depended? He saw millions of people with no money . . . and then no food. He saw riots in the streets . . . and worse.

Then, he looked around and saw that he and his family were as exposed to the menace as everyone else. He decided to take precautions, moving his family to an isolated rural area where they would be safe from the apocalypse he saw coming.

Maybe he would be wrong, he reasoned. But what if he were right? The cost of being right—and failing to protect himself—could be catastrophic. He moved to a mountain hollow, buried provisions, and began the countdown to the year 2000.

Of course, when the big day came . . . nothing happened. The clocks worked. The trains ran. The power was still on. Apparently, not a single cash machine failed.

People pointed and laughed. But was he wrong? What if the odds of a meltdown had been only 1 in 100 or 1 in a 1,000? Was he not right to give a warning in the strongest possible terms? And wasn't it partly because of him and others like him that billions were spent to correct the problem before January 2000?

Colorful eccentrics, careful analysts, cheerful con men, and self-assured delusionals trying to figure out how things are put together—this is the world of investment gurus.

But guess what? The gurus are often right. True, some financial gurus have gone broke following their own advice. But many have gotten rich.

In the late 1970s, we undertook a study—with Mark Hulbert, who is still at it—of how well these financial gurus actually perform. We wouldn't presume to summarize Mark Hulbert's nearly 30 years of work; we will just tell you what we took from it: There is no right way to invest.

Investment gurus are an original bunch. They come up with all sorts of systems, ideas, and approaches. Almost all of them are successful—sometimes. There are a lot of different ways to invest and to make money. And often one that works spectacularly well in one period may collapse completely when the market changes course. So, too, an approach that often works poorly under certain market conditions will work poorly in other conditions.

But, generally, an investment advisor who works hard to develop and refine a system and who sticks with it can do reasonably well, sometimes. He can be a technical analyst, a chartist, a Graham and Dodd follower, even an astrologer. Almost any disciplined approach, pursued intelligently and steadily, can pay off.

We have a theory that explains why this is so. Investing is, when you get down to the basement of it, a competitive undertaking. If you do what everyone else does, you will get the same returns as everyone else. In order to get better returns, you have to do things differently.

Investment gurus seem to be favored, in this regard, by their own originality and quirky self-reliance.

"Sometimes right, sometimes wrong," they say. "But never in doubt."

Taken together, they are probably the most independent and contrary professional class in the world. And this contrariness, alone, seems to put them at odds with the great mass of *lumpen* investors, allowing them to make more—or, often less—than the common results.

By contrast, what seems to doom the average investor is the same mushy quality that seems to be ruining the whole country. He will wait in line—without a word of protest—while guards frisk girl scouts and old ladies for dangerous weapons. If the mob is large enough, he can't wait to be a part of it and fears being isolated from it. And he will believe any line of guff—no matter how fantastic—as long as everyone else falls for it, too. Dow 36,000? House prices always go up? Interest-only negative amortization mortgage?

A man who follows a newsletter guru has no guarantee of making money . . . but a man who follows the great mass of conventional wisdom is practically guaranteed that he will not.

THE TROUBLE WITH TROUBLE

The trouble with the modern world is that there isn't enough trouble in it. Back when we began in the business, people had real trouble and they really appreciated it. Now, they just toss it off. They're not worried about it because they don't know what it really is.

When we were young, we fully expected that we would never be old. Nuclear war was a very real threat. "We will bury you," said the leader of the Soviet Union, while addressing Western ambassadors at a reception at the Polish embassy in Moscow on November 18, 1956. We thought he meant it. And during the Cuban Missile Crisis, the world was probably only an upset stomach away from annihilation. If either Kennedy or Khrushchev had been in a bad mood, we might never have lived long enough to enjoy the greatest economic boom in human history.

There was also the danger of too many people; India could never feed herself, the experts said. Food production worldwide couldn't keep up with population growth. Hundreds of millions would starve; it was only a matter of time.

As to financial matters, the average family was only a paycheck or two from total disaster. Losing a job could be catastrophic. No one had credit cards. There was no EZ mortgage finance available. Besides, adults back in the 1950s and 1960s were deeply suspicious of debt. It was the lesson they had learned during the Great Depression. That generation knew trouble . . . real trouble.

In the 1930s, one out of every four U.S. workers lost his job—with no unemployment insurance and no welfare system to fall back on. The elder Mr. Bonner had a knack for being in the wrong place at the wrong time. He tried to escape the poverty of his family by joining the army . . . in 1939. Then, he thought he had gotten extremely lucky when he drew the best assignment in the army; they sent him to Hawaii. He said he was recovering from a hangover on the base when Japanese airplanes appeared overhead in December, 1941. They tried to kill him for the next three years.

But Americans had it easy during the war, compared to others. Britain was bombed for months. France was occupied. Italy and France were both battlefields. There were severe financial shocks, too. Britain went broke. France had to form two new governments and replace its currency twice.

But, imagine the time your parents and grandparents would have had, had they lived in Russia, China, India, Germany, Argentina, or Japan: War. Hyperinflation. Starvation. Police repression. Mass arrests. Occupation. Bolshevism. You name it; they lived it.

As long as the generation that had lived through the Depression and WWII were in charge of things, the United States was in pretty good shape. The United States emerged the world's biggest, strongest, most innovative and dynamic economy after WWII.

But, in the 1980s, a new generation took over. It was "morning again in America." During that period, three key events caused trouble—as we had known it—to take a holiday.

First, there was the Crash of 1987. Stocks fell hard. But then, they got right back up again, as though nothing ever happened. As a result, people began to think that crashes were no trouble. Even if stocks fell, they'd soon be on an upswing again. Books began to appear such as *Stocks for the Long Run*. People began to believe you couldn't go wrong in stocks, no matter how much you paid for them.

Second, in 1989, the Berlin Wall was dismantled. Suddenly, we no longer had any enemy worthy of the name. We weren't going to be exterminated in a nuclear war after all. From here on, it would be clear sailing.

Third, the neocons transformed the Republican Party. "Deficits don't matter," said Dick Cheney. They never seemed to matter to Democrats. Now they no longer matter to Republicans either. After the 1980s there was no longer any organized political party in favor of fiscal and monetary conservatism.

Like their federal government, Americans borrowed. And so, their debt increased. Having been the world's leading creditors in the 1950s and 1960s, they became the world's leading debtors in the 1980s and 1990s. Gradually, the consumer economy required more and more debt to produce an extra unit of output. Debtors had to borrow not only to buy . . . but also to pay back, or pay the interest on, previous borrowings. The financial sector boomed by supplying the credit.

America's most profitable businesses shifted from making things to shuffling little pieces of paper back and forth. That's why GM created GMAC and why GE staked its future on GE Finance. And it's why the center of U.S. economic power moved from the manufacturing hinterlands of Detroit and Cleveland to the financial centers on the coast . . . notably the big one in Lower Manhattan.

The Bubble Epoque

By the late 1990s and early twenty-first century, the American economy had entered the bubble epoque. The financial industry—aided and abetted by the Federal Reserve—was providing so much "liquidity" it was causing asset prices to bubble up everywhere. Since then, every warning turned out to be a false alarm. The dot-coms busted and it didn't really matter. The recession of 2001–2002 was so mild few people even noticed. Even terrorists disappeared from North America after the stunning attack in 2001.

Of course, bubbles always blow up—without exception. And when the dot-com bubble exploded in 2000, at first we thought that was the end of the bubble era. But the biggest bubbles were still to come. The bubbles in housing, art, emerging markets, oil, and commodities—all blew up. Then the biggest bubble of all—the bubble in credit—blew up, too, bringing the bubble epoque to a close.

We are now in the post-bubble era. The financial industry has been bombed out. It can no longer create bubbles. Governments all over the world are propping up the walls and shoring up the foundations.

Toward the end of last year, the days were getting shorter and shorter. Darkness covered the land—especially in Iceland, where even in the best of times, late December offers barely enough daylight to smoke a cigarette.

The authorities have gone back to their usual antics. They've bailed out some companies, lowered interest rates to zero, and shored up the financial sector—which just happened to have good representation in the government and its central bank—and saved the bondholders from getting what they had coming.

They've made sacrifices to the market gods, too. Unable to find any virgins in the financial sector, they threw the taxpayers down the well.

And then they went after the savers (admittedly, there weren't many of them) and the next generation, too.

At first, it seemed as if the "stimulus" had failed. Then, gradually, the light increased and the days grew longer. As we write this preface in the spring of 2009, after nine weeks of rising prices, people are beginning to see the world differently, again. To simplify: It doesn't seem nearly as bad a place as it did a few months ago. Even house prices—ground zero of the financial crisis—although not actually rising, they're not falling as fast as they were before. And although people are still losing their jobs, not as many of them are losing their jobs each month as did earlier in the year. This has led many commentators to believe that government's expensive bailout/stimulus efforts are finally working.

And now, the mob screams: "The worst is over!" "We've seen the bottom." "Hoorah for the feds!"

But it is not likely to be so. The bubble epoque cannot be revived.

BASIC TRUTHS ABOUT THE STOCK MARKET, HOUSING, AND THE ECONOMY

So what should you do?

After nearly three decades in the business and writing our daily chronicle of the stock market and economy, *The Daily Reckoning*, for 10 years, we have distilled our advice down to four dicta, a few basic truths to guide you as you navigate your way through the financial news:

Dictum Number 1: People do not get what they want or what they expect from the markets; they get what they deserve.

Of course, people would like the downturn to be over. Many are counting on it. But the market doesn't give a hoot. He's got a "Capitalism at Work" T-shirt on and a sledgehammer in his hand.

What's he up to? He's demolishing a quarter century's worth of mistakes. There are always mistakes made. Investments go bad. Businesses go under. People go broke. When many mistakes are corrected at once, it's called a "recession." And when an entire economic model goes bad, it's called a "depression."

The economic model of the last quarter century caused more mistakes than usual. It encouraged people to spend, borrow, and speculate. And each time the market tried to make some corrections, the authorities came along with more money and easier credit. Businesses that should have gone under years ago kept digging themselves in deeper. Homeowners kept running up more debt. Speculators kept taking bigger and bigger gambles.

Fish gotta swim, birds gotta fly, and bubbles gotta blow. The bubble in the financial sector—including subprime debt, housing prices, bonuses on Wall Street, and derivatives—hit the fan in 2007. And what a mess!

And why shouldn't it be?

Which brings us to the second of our dicta:

Dictum Number 2: The force of a correction is equal and opposite to the deception that preceded it.

The delusions and absurdities of the bubble epoque were monstrous. Naturally, the correction must be huge, too. World stock markets were nearly cut in half. Property prices, too, have been knocked down almost everywhere. The total loss of nominal wealth has been estimated as high as $50 trillion.

In the first quarter of 2009, Warren Buffett's company, Berkshire Hathaway, booked its first loss since 2001. Fifty-nine banks have been shut down over the past 18 months. The United States' leading banks say they need another $75 billion to keep their doors open. And Fannie Mae said it lost $23 billion; it will need $19 billion more to continue jiving the housing market.

Could these losses have been prevented?

Certainly many of them could. If the U.S. Congress had never created Fannie Mae, for example, it never would have distorted the mortgage market as much as it did. And if the feds hadn't created the Federal Reserve Bank, it couldn't have provided so much ready money for so many speculators and borrowers. And if the Fed under Alan Greenspan had done what it was supposed to do—that is, to "take away the punch bowl" before the party got out of control—the bubble in the financial sector probably would have been much more modest.

Of course, people drew all the wrong conclusions. They thought "capitalism failed." They saw the car drive off the cliff . . . but didn't notice how government had twisted the road signs. Instead of warning investors of the dangerous curve ahead, the Fed's low lending rates said: "Step on the gas!" Congress, despite their recent collective cry of disbelief, helped push down the pedal.

Dictum Number 3: Capitalism doesn't always take an economy where it wants to go; but it always takes an economy where it ought to be.

Whoever was responsible for the mistakes, capitalism went about correcting them with its customary élan. It hit imprudent investors with trillions in losses. It knocked down mismanaged corporations. It whacked homeowners . . . and pounded housing-based derivatives to dust.

Capitalism operates by a process that the great economist Joseph Schumpeter called "creative destruction." It destroys mistakes to make room for new innovations and new businesses. Unfortunately, this puts it at odds with government and what most people want. When people make mistakes, they maintain that they are blameless. "Who could have seen this crisis coming?" they ask. "And," they say, "someone else should pay for the loss."

So today the feds, who mismanaged their regulatory responsibilities during the bubble epoque are bailing out mismanaged corporations to protect lenders who mismanaged their money. They are determined to prevent capitalism from making major changes—in the worst possible way.

What's the worst possible way? Simple. Leave the mismanagers in place. Keep the brain-dead companies alive—along with the zombie banks. Let the government take ownership of major sectors of the economy. And stick a debt-ridden society with even more debt!

The federal government is expected to borrow $2 trillion this year alone. From whom? And who will repay it?

Dictum Number 4: The severity of a depression is inversely correlated with government's efforts to stop it.

The more the feds try to delay and distract the process of creative destruction, the longer it takes to get the job done. And the higher the eventual bill.

There are only two fairly clear examples in modern history. After the crash of 1929, the Hoover and Roosevelt administrations tried desperately to stop the correction. They could not make bad debts disappear, or turn bad decisions into good ones. All they could do was to retard the necessary corrections—and cause new mistakes! It wasn't until after WWII, 15 years later, when the New Deal was largely forgotten, that the United States got back to work.

Similarly, when Japan was confronted with a major correction in 1990, its politicians followed the Hoover/Roosevelt model. Over the years, an amount equivalent to almost an entire year's output was applied to recovery efforts. But all they did was to prevent and forestall the needed changes. Now, 19 years later, the Japanese economy is still in corrective mode . . . still fighting deflation.

Is that the end of the story? Not at all. The feds' efforts to stop the progress of capitalism will have some spectacular consequences. The fireworks will start when the bond market cracks sending yields through the roof, for a nation addicted to debt cannot sustain a credit crisis for long. And that is where today's story begins . . .

WILLIAM BONNER
June 2009

ACKNOWLEDGMENTS

We would like to say a few words to thank the many people whose ideas, insights, and dedication helped contribute to the 10th Anniversary edition of this book.

Our thanks go to Kate Incontrera, who in addition to her daily duties as the managing editor of the *Daily Reckoning*, pulled together the research, assembled, and edited many of the ideas you read within. Thanks to Rick Barnard for researching and updating the charts in this edition . . . and to Mark O'Dell, Susanne Clark, and Andrew Ascosi for producing them. Thanks to Joseph Schriefer, Greg Grillot, Ian Mathias, Greg Kadajski, Rocky Vega, Michelle Nickels, Bruce Robertson, Chad Barret, Mike Pizzo, Andrea Michinski, and all the faithful at Agora Financial who keep the lights on while we ruminate.

Thanks again to Rebecca Kramer, without whose persistence this project would never have gotten off the ground in 2002. The first edition of *Financial Reckoning Day* launched a multitome collaboration with John Wiley & Sons. Thank you to Theron Raines for aiding and abetting said collaboration. And special thanks go to Debra Englander, Kelly O'Connor, and Joan O'Neil at John Wiley & Sons for believing in us once again . . . and letting us crash another set of deadlines.

Jennifer Westerfield and Philippa Michel-Finch helped research, write, and edit the original manuscript of *Financial Reckoning Day*. Among other things, they helped us understand the causes and consequences of Japan's boom, bust, and persisting economic malaise. They also waded through the minutiae of details that comprise the area of demographic and aging studies, providing a fertile foundation for our work over the next decade.

Finally, we would like to thank the late Kurt Richebächer, Gary North, James Grant, Marc Faber, Richard Russell, David Tice, Frank Shostak, Richard Daughty, John Mauldin, Doug Casey, James Davidson, Uncle Harry Schultz, George Gilder, Francis Fukuyama, Robert Prechter, Martin Weiss, Porter Stansberry, Patrick Cox, Rob Parenteau, Byron King, Eric Fry, John Forde, Chris Mayer, and Dan Denning for their helpful and entertaining insights; and Thom Hickling for his fine guitar work, may he rest in peace.

WILLIAM BONNER
ADDISON WIGGIN

INTRODUCTION

It had all seemed so logical, obvious, and agreeable in the last five years of the 20th century. Stocks went up year after year. The Cold War had been won. There was a new Information Age making everything and everybody so much smarter—and richer, too. The world was a happy place and Americans were its happiest people. U.S. consumer capitalism was the envy of all mankind. The United States guaranteed the peace and freedom of the entire species, if not with goodness, intelligence, and foresight—at least with its military arsenal, which could blow any adversary to kingdom come. People believed that Francis Fukuyama's *The End of History* had indeed arrived, for it scarcely seemed possible that there could be any major improvement.

But "it's a funny old world," as Maggie Thatcher once remarked. She might have meant "funny" in the sense that it is amusing; more likely, she meant that it is peculiar. In both senses, she was right. What makes the world funny is that it refuses to cooperate; it seldom does what people want or expect it to do. In fact, it often does the exact opposite.

People do not always act as they should. Other people seem irrational to us—especially those with whom we disagree. Nor do we always follow a logical and reasonable course of action. Instead, we are all swayed by tides of emotion . . . and occasionally swamped by them.

This book was written to underline the point that the world is funnier than you think. And the more you think about it, the funnier it gets. Close inspection reveals the ironies, contradictions, and confusions that make life interesting, but also frustrating. A rational person could do rational things all day long, but then how boring life would be. Fortunately, real people are only rational about things that do not matter.

People of action despise thinking of any sort, and rightly so, because the more they think, the more their actions are beset by doubts and arrière-pensées. The more man thinks, the slower he moves. Thought uncovers the limitations of his plans. Exploring the possibilities, he sees yet more potential outcomes, a greater number of problems . . . and he increasingly recognizes how little he actually knows. If he keeps thinking long and hard enough, he is practically paralyzed . . . a person of action no more.

Will the stock market rise?

"I don't know," replies the thinking fund manager.

Can we win the war?

"It depends on what you mean by 'win,'" answers the thoughtful general.

Will house values continue to go up?

"Your guess is as good as mine," responds the honest real estate broker.

This book has been written in a spirit of runaway modesty. The more we think, the more we realize how little we know. In fact, it is a good thing that the book came to an end when it did . . . or we would know nothing at all, or less than nothing.

We are, frankly, in far too much awe of the world, and too deeply entertained by it, to think that we can understand it today or foretell tomorrow. Life's most attractive components—love and money—are far too complex for reliable soothsaying. Still, we can't resist taking a guess.

We may not know how the world works, but we are immodest enough to think we can know how it does not work. The stock market is not, for example, a simple mechanism like an ATM machine, where you merely tap in the right numbers to get cash out when you need it. Instead, the investment markets—like life itself—are always complicated, often perverse, and occasionally absurd. But that does not mean that they are completely random; though unexpected, life's surprises may not always be undeserved. Delusions have consequences. And, sooner or later, the reckoning day comes and the bills must be paid.

In this sense, the investment markets are not mechanistic at all, but judgmental. As we will see, they reward virtue and punish sin.

Our approach in this book is a little different from that of the typical economics tome or investment advisory. Instead, it is an exercise in what is known, derisively, as "literary economics." Although you will find statistics and facts, the metaphors and the principles that we provide are more important. Facts have a way of yielding to nuance like a jury to a trial lawyer. Under the right influence, they will go along with anything. But the metaphors remain . . . and continue to give useful service long after the facts have changed.

What's more, metaphors help people understand the world and its workings. As Norman Mailer put it, "There is much more truth in a metaphor than in a fact." But the trouble with metaphors is that no matter how true they may be when they are fresh and clever, when the multitudes pick them up, they almost immediately become worn out and false. For the whole truth is always complex to the point of being unknowable, even to the world's greatest geniuses.

The world never works the way people think it does. That is not to say that every idea about how the world works is wrong, but that often particular ideas about how it works will prove to be wrong if they are held in common. For only simple ideas can be held by large groups of people. Commonly held ideas are almost always dumbed down until they are practically lies . . . and often dangerous ones. Once vast numbers of people have come to believe the lie, they adjust their own behavior to bring themselves into sync with it, and thereby change the world itself. The world, then, no longer resembles the one that gave rise to the original insight. Soon, a person's situation is so at odds with the world as it really is that a crisis develops, and he or she must seek a new metaphor for explanation and guidance.

Thus, the authors of the present work cannot help but notice an insidious and entertaining dynamic . . . a dialectic of the heart, where greed and fear, confidence and desperation confront each other with the subtle elegance of women mudwrestlers.

In the financial markets, this pattern is well-known and frequently described.

In the late 1990s, those who were sure that stocks would always go up, despite having already reached absurd levels, gave countless explanations for their belief, but the main reason was simply that it was just the way the world worked. But after investors had moved their money into stocks, to take advantage of the insight, few buyers were left and prices had risen so high that neither profits nor growth could support them.

Investors were deeply disappointed in the early 2000s when stocks fell three years in a row. How could this be, they asked themselves? What is going on, they wanted to know?

The answer eluded us when we wrote the first edition of this book in the summer of 2003. And as we write the second edition of this book in the spring of 2009, we still do not know. And even mainstream economists find it difficult to come up with an answer. Paul Samuelson, popularizer of the economic profession for *Newsweek*, admitted that he and his colleagues do not even have words to describe this "baffling economy."

Those who should know the answer to these problems have not been much help. In the late summer of 2002, the most celebrated economist in the world addressed an audience in Jackson Hole, Wyoming. Alan Greenspan explained that he did not know what had gone wrong. He would not know a bubble if it blew up right in front of him; he would have to wait, he told his fellow economists and check the mirror for bruise marks—for only after the event could a bubble be detected.

Almost seven years later, Ben Bernanke and the Obama administration still don't understand where bubbles come from, and what difference would it make anyway? The United States' favorite bureaucrat had explained while occupying the chair at the Federal Reserve that it made none: Even if he [Greenspan] had known where bubbles come from, he said, he could not have done anything about them.

But we did not write this book to carp or complain. Instead, we offer it in the spirit of constructive criticism, or at least in the spirit of benign mischief. We do not know any better than Alan Greenspan or Ben Bernanke or Timothy Geithner or Barack Obama what the future holds. We only guess that we are at one of history's epic crisis points— one of its drawn out reckoning days—where the metaphors of yesterday no longer seem to describe the way the world works today. The financial markets are not the congenial ATM machines of investors' fantasies, after all. Nor is the political world as safe and as comfortable as people had come to believe.

That is another aspect of our book that readers may find unusual. We dip into military history and market history as if passing from a hot tub to a pool. Both illustrate the lively influence of group dynamics; the currents of mass sentiment are similar. Readers will note, however, that political episodes tend to have tragic endings . . . whereas markets typically end in farce. Readers may also be curious as to our focus on European history. We make no excuses or apologies for it. Our office in Paris is surrounded by reminders of Europe's past. Can we not help but learn from it?

Many things have changed, too, since the first edition of this book was published in 2003. Although sales were decent, the book having reached #1 on the *New York Times* Business Bestseller list, we were still considered "mavericks" for pointing out what seemed to us to be painfully obvious: You cannot live beyond your means forever. Policy makers did their best to postpone the inevitable, even driving the stock market to its all-time high in the fall of 2007. But it was a phony prosperity and unsustainable at best, that much is clear to many who were skeptical in the years between our first publication date and today. We provide this updated edition to show that the stock market bubble and the housing bubble were two sides of the same flawed coin.

Not that this edition was easy to get a handle on. The reckoning is still underway as we write. During the final weeks of the update, General Motors, the bellwether of American manufacturing, finally declared bankruptcy; California, the trendsetter state, misread revenues derived from the housing bubble and came up more than $42 billion short; David Walker, the former comptroller general of the country and the protagonist of our film and book, *I.O.U.S.A.*, warned that the United States was in danger of having its Treasury bonds downgraded from AAA status; Rob Parenteau, our chief economist, warned, too, that the United States would likely consider a dual currency regime in order to protect its debt . . . not a good position for the nation that sponsors the reserve currency of the world to find itself in. We point to all these events merely as a way to say we've done our best to stay on top of things, but the story continues . . . wildness lies in wait.

As with the first edition, we have not included the typical formulas or recommendations of an investment book, or the detailed expositions of a book on economics. Instead, we offer only a few simple ideas—including an update of our Trade of the Decade—that readers may well find helpful in the years ahead. Readers who wish to keep up with the progress of the Trade of the Decade or get our most recent commentary are invited to visit us at www.dailyreckoning.com and sign up for free.

CHAPTER 1

THE GILDERED AGE

The real trouble with this world of ours is not that it is an unreasonable world, nor even that it is a reasonable one. The commonest kind of trouble is that it is nearly reasonable, but not quite. Life is not an illogicality; yet it is a trap for logicians. It looks just a little more mathematical and regular than it is; its exactitude is obvious, but its inexactitude is hidden; its wildness lies in wait.

—G.K. Chesterton

Sometime in the late 1990s, Gary Winnick—chairman of the then $47 billion enterprise, Global Crossing (GC)—did something unusual. He decided to take time off from touring art galleries with David Rockefeller, playing golf with Bill Clinton, and enjoying the Malibu beach to learn a little about the business he was in: He bought a video describing how undersea cable was laid. The video was all Winnick needed to know about laying cable. For he understood what business he was really in, and it had nothing to do with ships or optic fiber. Winnick was doing nature's work: separating fools from their money. And he was good at it.

Supposedly, Winnick knew the undersea cable business well. Likewise, the people from whom he raised money were the "best pros" on Wall Street and were supposed to be capable of managing big bucks. After all, if they did not know how to place money to get a decent return, what did they know? And those who provided these "best pros" with money were also supposed to know what they were doing. As it turned out, no one had a clue.

One of the great marvels of life is not that fools and their money are soon parted, but that they ever get together in the first place. Life goes on, we note, for no particular reason other than the vanity of it all. One lie replaces another like cars along a Paris street (where a parking spot rarely remains vacant for long).

Not only does life imitate art, but it slavishly tries to model itself on science, too. Over the course of the twentieth century, a simple idea had become stuck in investors' minds. Everything worked like a machine, they thought, especially the economy. If the economy was growing too fast, Alan Greenspan would "put on the brakes" by raising interest rates. If it was growing too slowly, he would "open up the throttle" by lowering interest rates. It was so simple. The mechanical image seemed to describe perfectly how the Fed worked. There was no experience in the last two decades to contradict it. It had worked so well for so long: It was almost as if it were true.

In his book, *A Random Walk Down Wall Street,* Burton Malkiel popularized the *efficient market hypothesis,* claiming that stock prices moved in a random fashion. The best you can do, he proposed, was to buy the indexes and stay in the market. Over time, the market goes up . . . and you get rich. According to this view, the market is a benign, mechanistic instrument that merely distributes wealth evenly to those who participate: As long as you are "in the market," all the riches of capitalism will flow in your direction.

The trouble is that the market may look mechanistic, but it is not. The market is an unbounded, organic system; mastering it is a human science, not a hard science. The financial markets reflect the activity of the human economy; they are unbounded chaotic systems. The best metaphor for understanding such a system is the nature of which they are a part—infinitely complex and ultimately uncontrollable. Markets are neither kind nor forgiving. If markets do the work of God, as has been suggested, it is the God of the Old Testament, not the New.

But in the late 1990s, we lived in a wonderful world. It was rich and lush . . . the sun shone every day. Progress seemed inevitable and unstoppable, and compiling information in digital form was thought to hold the secret to an ever-increasing abundance of resources for mankind.

It seemed so simple: Computers and telecommunications would provide people with increasing amounts of information, and this in turn would allow goods to be produced faster and at lower costs. Humans, hitherto Neanderthals in a low cave hunched in ignorance and darkness, would now be able to stand upright and edge a little closer to perfection every day. There was no chance that they would slip up, as they had always done in the past, we were told, for this was a more fully evolved species, better adapted to the Information Age. This really was a "New Era," we were assured.

At the dawn of the twenty-first century, a half-century of progress and a 25-year-long bull market had created a race of geniuses. Americans were on top of the world. Their armies were unbeatable. Their currency was accepted everywhere as though it had real value. Dollars were the United States' most successful export, with a net outflow of nearly $1.5 billion per day. And dollars were the product on which the nation enjoyed its biggest profit margin. It cost less than a cent to produce one, and each one was valued at par.

But America's greatest strength was its economy. It was not only the strongest in the world, but the strongest the world had ever seen. The United States had increased its economic lead over the competition in the 10 years running up to the end of the century. In the minds of many, the U.S. economy was unstoppable, and its continued success inevitable. They believed that the nation's leadership position was not merely cyclical, but eternal. It had achieved a state so nearly perfect that improvement was hardly imaginable. American music, art, films, democracy, and American-style market capitalism were everywhere triumphant.

"America is the world's only surviving model of human progress," President George W. Bush told the graduating class of West Point in June 2002. America has its faults, wrote Thomas L. Friedman in the *New York Times* at about the same time, but without it, "nothing good happens."

Oddly, during this golden era of silicon chips and Internet domain names, no one was able to explain why the Information Age never made its way across the Pacific to Japan. No one even bothered to ask the question. But that is one of the comforts of a great boom; question marks disappear. Societies, like markets and individual humans, are infinitely complex. The harder you look, the more you see. When things go well, people are content not to ask questions and not to look too hard. They think they know how the world works and are happy with the jingles and simple metaphors that explain it.

The new information technology, it was claimed, would boost productivity and the growth rate. Few people doubted it. More information would make things better; it seemed as simple as that. For question marks, like winter clothes after Easter, get packed away during a bull market. Not until a chill autumn wind blows do they come back out.

And at the end of September 2001, the drafts of cold weather were just beginning. The Nasdaq was down 73 percent from its high. The Dow was down 32 percent. A recession had begun in March. Although at first it was reported to have ended after a single quarter, later revisions showed that it lasted through the end of the year. Investors had no way of knowing, for they had no crystal balls, but they were in for a spell of bad weather. Yet only a few people began rummaging through their cupboards for their coats and mittens.

We humans understand things by analogy. Indeed, since before Noah built his Ark, humans have tried to understand the world by extrapolating from the known to the unknown. Comparison was the only tool they had to explain what they observed. Once upon a time, a bear might have been said to run "as fast as a lion," for example, or "like a holy hellcat" because it was not possible to time an animal's running speed precisely. After a period without rain, villagers might have remarked that it "was just like the Great Drought" of a few years earlier. They had no way of knowing what might happen, of course, but the analogy warned them to conserve their food. By comparing one thing we don't really understand to another we understand only slightly better, we think we understand both. We imagine Alan Greenspan, for example, pulling levers and turning knobs as if the economy really could be run like a machine.

Yet, strangely, in the new world at the close of the twentieth century, the analogies from years ago or from across the wide Pacific did not seem to matter. Things were different. Not only did the old rules and old lessons no longer apply, analogies themselves were now out of fashion. The New Era was "digital." It was widely presumed that nearly all of life would soon be digitized and that mankind would grow better informed, richer, and morally superior every day. That was . . . until the weather changed.

GURUS OF THE NEW ERA

The history of the New Era will record that it was Robert Metcalfe and Gordon Moore who, like Moses and Aaron, led their followers out of the bondage of the Old Economy and into the land of stock options and caffe lattes. Metcalfe and Moore handed down the laws by which the people of Silicon Valley in the 1990s lived.

Metcalfe described a well-known phenomenon: Each element of a system or collectivity becomes more valuable as it expands. You can see this by thinking about the phone system. When the Bell Telephone Company was founded in May 1877, its products were almost useless. Subscribers could not call anyone because no one had a telephone. But three years later, there were 30,000 phones in use.

This led to the further insight that the company could afford to spend a great deal of money selling and installing telephones because it would earn a profit later on. What's more, it was critical that people purchased Bell telephones rather than a competitor's. Ultimately, the most valuable, and presumably the most profitable, service would be the one that was most ubiquitous.

This insight cleared the way for the popular Internet business plan: Do not worry about profits—fight for market share. Few noticed the flaw: The telephone system was a quasi-monopoly. It made sense to pay a lot of money to put it in place, because the company could expect monopoly-level profits for a very long time. Bell Telephone and its derivatives are still in business. But Amazon.com, the Globe .com, Webvan.com, and thousands of other Internet start-ups had no hope of ever getting a monopoly or anything close to it.

Moore, meanwhile, handed down his own law: He stated that computational power would double every 18 months—which, thus far, it had. This growth rate astonished everyone and led to the other major delusion of Internet investors—that just because computer power increases exponentially, so should Internet businesses and stock prices. Moore's law only applies to the speed at which computers process information. Government quants assumed, wrongly, that this was equivalent to an increase in the nation's wealth, as expressed by gross domestic product (GDP). As we see later on, this in turn led to distortions in other measures, such as productivity and inflation levels.

If Moore and Metcalfe were the Old Testament prophets of the New Era, George Gilder was its messiah. Every revolution needs its intellectuals, its firebrands, its executioners, and its victims. One-third visionary, one-third fool, one-third incomprehensible—Gilder was all of these things, and more. A speechwriter for Romney, Rockefeller, and Nixon, he authored several well-read books, including *Wealth and Poverty* and *The Spirit of Enterprise*. He was quoted more often by Ronald Reagan, the record shows, than any other writer. His book, *Microcosm*, took him farther than anyone had ever gone into the distant reaches of new technology and the enterprising spirit. Since then, some would say he has drifted a bit too far.

Gilder's articles in *Forbes ASAP* were not merely hard to read, they were incomprehensible. But never mind. He was a genius, and he was right about a great many things. His reports were followed by many of the shrewdest investors of our time . . . to such an extent that this "pale, nervous Yankee" was seen as a semi-god or "John the Baptist of the Digital Age," as one article put it. But he had worked himself into such a state of rapture over the possibilities of the Internet that he seemed to have gone a little mad.

One caveat, "I don't do price,"[1] Gilder commented. Too bad. Because, as investors would discover later, prices are important. A technology may be spectacular; the company that owns it may be a great company; but the stock is only a good investment at the right price.

Star-Crossed

"Listen to the technology!" Gilder's Caltech physics professor, Carver Mead, had advised the New Era messiah. Listening carefully, Gilder had believed that, if he strained his ears enough, he could almost hear the cosmos speaking. "Buy Global Crossing!" he thought he had heard.

Gilder did not usually buy, and judging from the press reports, he had little interest in picking stocks. But this Ulysses of the Telecosm had forgotten to plug his ears or have himself lashed to the mast. Thus, the sirens at Global Crossing got him . . . and drove him crazy. Nowhere was this more manifest than in his book, *Telecosm,* in which he announced the emergence of a new economy, "based on a new sphere of cornucopian radiance—reality unmassed and unmasked, leaving only the promethean light." To this day, we do not know what that sentence was supposed to mean. It was all very well to blather about how Global Crossing helped to bring "a new epoch of spirit and faith" with its "majestic cumulative power, truth, and transcendence of contemporary science and wealth." But with a profit/earnings (P/E) ratio of negative 130, an investor would have been a fool to bet money on it. Yet in June 2001, George Gilder continued to praise Global Crossing, qualifying the stock as "no surer bet in the Telecosm."[2]

Oh, but we forgot—Gilder didn't "do price."

Master of the Bandwidth Universe

Gary Winnick had been a former Drexel Burnham bond trader before he got into the fiber-optic business almost by accident. He had seen the possibilities of bandwidth after financing an undersea cable for AT&T in 1997. His first cable took 14 months to lay, but it was extremely profitable.

Thus, did the simple business plan for Global Crossing emerge—raise money and lay fiber-optic cable! Early estimates of construction costs were around $2.7 billion. The money was soon coming into the Hamilton, Bermuda, headquarters of Global Crossing at the speed of light. The stock went public in August 1998 at $9.50. Eight months later, it hit $60 a share, giving the company a market capitalization of $54 billion. Winnick's personal stake in the company rose to $4.7 billion. He was soon having dreams of building an undersea broadband network that would link continents and serve global carriers like Deutsche Telekom and AT&T.

Three years later, in November 2001, Global Crossing "shocked and angered" investors by reporting a loss of $3.35 billion, more than six times greater than the loss from the same quarter a year earlier. Included in the loss was a $2 billion write-down of its stake in another star-crossed company from the Gildered Age, Exodus Communications, then operating under protection of the U.S. Bankruptcy Code. Global Crossing common stock traded at only $1.24 in mid-November—up from the 38 cents rate of October 9, but down from the $13.30 level set in June, when George Gilder believed it to be a sure thing. In a year and a half, investors had lost about $52.9 billion on the stock.

Still Gilder, the New Era hallucinatory, held on. "If you bought Global Crossing in 1998," he had written just a few months earlier (in

June 2001), "you bought one 5,000-mile cable. Today you are buying a 102,000-mile network. If you bought Global Crossing in 1998, you bought $400 million in revenue. Today, you are buying over $5 billion in sales and more than a billion dollars in adjusted cash flow, growing at 40 percent a year. If you bought Global Crossing in 1998, you bought into static transatlantic STM1 sales. Today you are buying an IP backbone with traffic growing at 450 percent a year and 20 percent ownership of Exodus (the Web's key hub for exafloods of content, storage, and services) which almost doubled year-to-year revenues in the March quarter. If you bought Global Crossing in 1998, you bought the dream of a global web of glass and light. Today you are buying that web."[3]

"If you bought Global Crossing in 1998," a cynic might have retorted, "you would have lost 98 percent of your money." (See Figure 1.1 for Global Crossing losses.)

The dream turned out to be a better investment than the web itself. As Global Crossing raised an increasing amount of money and laid ever more cable, it hastened its day of reckoning. Instead of

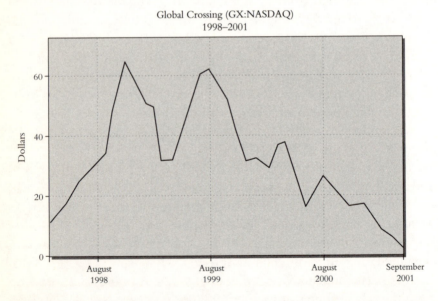

Global Crossing (GX:NASDAQ)
1998–2001

FIGURE 1.1 The New Era's Promethean Light
Global Crossing was George Gilder's favorite stock. Unfortunately for investors, Gilder did not "do price." Global Crossing declared bankruptcy in January 2002. Founder Gary Winnick banked some $700 million before resigning as CEO. On resignation, he stated: "I deeply regret that so many good people involved with Global Crossing also suffered significant financial loss."

Gilder's exaflood of profitable content, the cable companies were soon swamped with excess supply: They were soon so deeply underwater financially that they had no hope of escape. While Gilder watched the stars of the Telecosm, smart industry insiders turned their own eyes earthward and saw the deluge coming.

Thus, in November 2001, investors were not the same warm-hearted, generous naïfs who lent money to Global Crossing and other wunderkinder at the height of the tech boom. After all, lenders had marked Global Crossing's bonds down to a suspicious 18 cents on the dollar. Its secured bank debt traded at 67 cents on the dollar. Preferred shares were priced to yield 177 percent—if they yielded anything at all.

Bandwidth had seemed like a good investment when investors had a lot of money and little bandwidth. But soon, investors had less money and lots of bandwidth to choose from. Prices of bandwidth plummeted. Meanwhile, according to experts, less than 10 percent of fiber-optic cable was used or "lit." And, despite this fiber glut, Global Crossing continued to spend $500 million every quarter to finance more construction. Adding more capacity at this stage was akin to a drunken partygoer opening another bottle of wine.

Not surprisingly, on January 28, 2002, Global Crossing declared bankruptcy, leaving lenders with losses of nearly $4 billion.

More surprisingly, many were those who still believed: A *Fortune* article published June 9, 2002, for example, lamented the collapse claiming that the company had a "decent shot at survival."

Whose fault was it? Winnick who had had the gumption to ask for the money, or the patsies who had given it to him? They might have ponied up the $2.7 billion, and maybe Global Crossing would still be in business. Instead, they kept shoving big bills in Winnick's pockets until he had raised $20 billion. By the time his company had folded, its long-term debt had swelled to $7.6 billion (with total liabilities of $14 billion), and it simply did not have the cash to make its interest payments.

But what happened to the $20 billion that Winnick had raised? He had spread the money around—acquiring other overpriced telecoms, giving Wall Street a way to earn massive fees by keeping the money coming his way. From 1998 through 2001, the top Wall Street firms earned more than $13 billion in telecom underwriting and investment-banking fees.

And so both the juice and hokum whirled around. Salomon's technology analyst, Jack Grubman, talked up the stock. Investors bought it for more than it was worth. Winnick bought other telecoms for more than they were worth. Everybody made money.

But it was an empty vanity. People do not really get rich by spending money on things they do not need and cannot afford, at prices that are too high. All they do is move money around . . . and waste a great deal of it. In the telecom sector alone, far more dark fibers were put down than the world really wanted. And when the end of the bubble finally came, Global Crossing alone had torn a $54 billion hole in investors' pockets.

Yet not all that money disappeared. By the time Global Crossing declared bankruptcy, Winnick had sold $735 million of stock, and received another $15.8 million in other emoluments. Winnick must have felt pretty smart. He had done what he had set out to do: Winnick and family had pocketed more than $600 million by cashing in stock during 2000 and 2002, even as Global Crossing struggled with a severe debt load, falling prices, and an industry in upheaval. Winnick also arranged to sell 10 million shares at $12 in May 2002, a decision wryly qualified by *Forbes* as "good timing" when it saw the company's shares drop below the 2 cent level at the end of 2002.

There are some things, as Mae West observed, of which a man can have too much and suffer no harm. But too much money is a clear and present danger to a man . . . or even to an entire economy. Telecom was not the first, nor will it be the last industry to be ruined by an excess of good fortune.

Moses Returns

Michael Malone, editor of *Forbes ASAP* and author of several books on business and the new economy, grew rich in Silicon Valley by accident. He received founders' shares from both Tom Siebel, founder and CEO of Siebel Systems Inc., with whom he co-authored *Virtual Selling*, and Pierre Omidyar, founder of eBay. He had no idea what the shares were worth and was astonished to find himself a wealthy man. But he lacked faith; he sold his shares as soon as he could.

For the new economy bubble did not seem real or right to him. "Most of us know, intuitively, that these young web companies minted by the hour, will not survive and prosper," he wrote. He predicted moreover that, in the "coming reckoning," investors' money would be lost, retirement funds would be erased, and that the valuations ruling the stock market would come back down to earth from their irrational heights.

By the late 1990s, Metcalfe and Moore shared this sentiment. It was as if they had returned to the Valley and found that their tribesmen had turned the Internet Age into an absurd parody. Instead of using the power of the silicon chip and the Internet to launch real businesses and create real wealth, they found investors dancing recklessly around the graven image of enterprise—the initial public offering (IPO).

Metcalfe described himself as hung up on the stock market bubble: "There's stuff going on out there that I just don't get yet," he explained. He considered the bubble "distorted," and expressed concerns that this distortion would eventually "blow up." His writings show a concern for entrepreneurial obsession with IPOs: "I'm frequently asking [entrepreneurs] the question, 'So, what's your company going to be?' The answer these days usually contains the letters I-P-O. That's the wrong phrase to have in the first five sentences explaining what your new business is going to be about. If you're thinking IPO, you've got your eye on the wrong ball . . . These people think that an IPO is a significant event. I view it as a minor financial event. They view it as what life is all about."[4]

Would there be a day of reckoning coming? "The [venture capitalists] get in on the ground floor," Metcalfe continued, "and they get out early. [But] . . . these poor schmucks in the public markets. They are going to start looking for profits and they're not going to find them. It's all going to come crashing down."[5]

But it was too late. According to the popular thinking of the time, Malone, Metcalfe, and Moore had become out of touch.

Digital Man "Gets It"

In summer 2000, Ed Yardeni categorized humans of the New Era into two different types, the "forward-looking camp" and the "backward-looking crowd."[6] According to Yardeni, the first camp believed that the digital technology revolution was transforming our economy into the New Economy, and the second viewed the New Economy as mostly hype and considered the technology revolution to be a stock market bubble. These views were further explored by the chief economist at Deutsche Bank, Alex Brown, who concluded, "The first group gets it, the second group doesn't." It thus became fashionable for the delusional to refer to their fellow lunatics as those who "get it" and to dismiss everyone else.

Typically, the expression *getting it* described a position considered so hip and correct that there was no need (and little hope) of ever justifying it by appeals to reason or experience. Men who wondered at the extreme claims of radical feminism, for example, were told that they just didn't get it. Likewise, any attempt by a white person to disagree with black racists—such as those who claimed that Cleopatra was black African—was met with a "you don't get it, do you" response.

Whether by checking the bumps on human heads, the activity in their e-mail accounts, or their voting habits, Yardeni identified a whole new subspecies of human—the "digital man": "The first group is composed of digital humans who believe the New Economy's secular trends are overwhelming the Old Economy's business cycles. The second group is mostly analog-type personalities who believe that fluctuations are wired into our brains and collective behavior,"[7] he wrote.

Before this, Yardeni was best known as the man who had made Y2K hysteria respectable. He had predicted that the computer problems associated with the year 2000 would cause a recession. Of all the Y2K personalities, perhaps none was proven more wrong than Yardeni. Not only were there no Y2K problems of any economic significance—the effect of the whole scare created a boom, not a recession. Huge spending on Y2K prophylactics turned into a big balloon in productivity, thanks to the miracle workers at the Bureau of Labor Statistics. Yardeni must have been astounded: Two little digits on the Gregorian calendar—and BOOM! The world's biggest economy took off.

But commentators had conveniently forgotten Yardeni's Y2K fiasco. "The New Economy," wrote David Denby in the *New Yorker,* "seems to be producing a New Man who, in imitation of the economy itself, is going through wrenching changes in the way he lives, works, buys and interacts with other people."[8]

There they were—a new race of humans walking among us. All we knew about them was that they "got it," and they were digital. We also knew something of their whereabouts—there were evidently many digital humans on Wall Street and very few in Japan! "Information wants to be free," they said. "Speed changes the meaning of information." "Our goal is to achieve ubiquity." What they said did not seem to matter; they were the young, hip, plugged-in tech guys. And they got it.

Someone once said that you only make big money from people who are stupider than you. The Digital Men figured this out early . . . and were fortunate in having such a large market. Like the hustlers and chutzpahs who sold modern art to Fortune 500 corporations, they went right for the high ground. Everyone—from top corporate CEOs to cab drivers—wanted to throw money their way. Michael Wolff in *Forbes ASAP* described what it was like when the absurd pretensions of the New Era techies met feeble, empty-headed corporate America:

> I wish I could communicate, however guilty I feel about it now, the sheer joy of sitting in meetings with well-established businessmen representing billions of dollars of assets and multimillion-dollar profit streams and being able not only to high hand them because I got it and they didn't, but also to be able to actually humble them, to flagrantly condescend to them, to treat them like children. On the basis of this knowingness, hundreds of billions of dollars have traded hands.

But why didn't the big money guys get it? Quite simply, because there was nothing to get. The techies had no real knowledge—just a pretense of knowledge—big, hollow ideas that in the end, meant nothing. Granted, they had technology, but they had no more idea of what it might do or what it might mean than anyone else. Probably less—since they tended to have so little real experience. And even the technology they mastered was often shown to be ineffective, or quickly superseded by more, yet newer technology of an impact and significance that was even less certain.

Each revolution seems to demand a New Man to go with it . . . or go along with it. The French Revolution produced the "Citizen" *sans culotte* eager to crucify the priests from whose hands he formerly took the sacraments and chop off the head of the aristocrat whose land he had tilled. The Russian Revolution produced a New Man, too—the new Soviet Man, who not only could do the work of 14 normal men, but was above the reach of normal emotions and body functions.

As Trotsky put it, he would be able to "master even the semi-conscious and unconscious systems of his own body: respiration, the circulatory system, digestion and reproduction."

Those who got it were supposed to know, deep down, an inchoate, indescribable truth that the rest of us could not quite fathom. As a result, Digital Man—a race of mutant *Homo supersapiens*—was supposed to not merely inherit the world, but to take it by adverse possession. But none of the New Men in history (from Russia, France, or elsewhere) ever succeeded in eliminating the weaknesses and sins to which we humans are heirs. And even if there were a New Man for the New Economy, he was apparently very similar to the old one: "Greedy, obsessed, and ignorant"[9] were the words that David Denby, writing in the *New Yorker,* used to describe the New Men he saw around him.

Of all those who "got it," few got it as good as George Gilder.

Gilder's role in the Information Revolution was to justify the dreams of the masses. Like Marx, Engels, or Lenin, he helped convince the *lumpeninvestoriat* that they could get rich without working by buying into technology they did not understand and stock in companies they did not know with money they did not have. What was talk of gigabits of photons flying over glass fiber and multiplexing, pulsating transits other than the information revolution's answer to Marxist claptrap about dialectical materialism? To the average investor, it was all weird and unfathomable. But if it made him rich, why ask questions?

And to those who did ask questions—whether they were the reactionary bourgeois elements of Russia in 1917 or the reactionary conservative investors, such as Warren Buffett in 1999, the answer was the same: They didn't get it. The fault was not so much intellectual, for no one accused Buffett of being stupid. It was deeper than that. The new era demanded investors who understood it in their heart, bones, and guts—with no need for question marks or explanations—investors who just got it.

Like the new Soviet Man, who needed no profits to motivate him to work, the New Man of the digital era needed profits to lure them to invest. How could Global Crossing be worth $60 per share? The question never occurred to him. He could only think about "the new sphere of cornucopian radiance." How could he look closely at

Amazon.com at $200 a share when the "promethean light" was shining in his eyes?

Madmen Get Rich

The information revolution also had its little cells working feverishly to make the world a better place.

"This is real," we recall a lunch companion telling us in early 2000. She had been a commodities trader. But commodities had gone down in price for so many years that it scarcely seemed worth the effort to trade them anymore. What the world craved was intangibles, not tangibles. "No one is interested in commodities trading," she explained. So, our friend gave up commodities trading and followed the money: She was now working as an advisor to dot-com entrepreneurs, providing them with information on how to go public. "These guys work 24/7," she explained. "They think they're building a whole new world."

One of the leading entrepreneurs of the Gildered Age was Michael Saylor, founder of MicroStrategy. Of all the messianic madmen of the era, Saylor certainly stood out—perhaps as the most insane, and certainly as one of the richest. Saylor brought entertainment to millions and helped separate countless fools from their money.

"We're purging ignorance from the planet," Saylor exclaimed, setting a lofty goal for himself. He was on a "crusade for intelligence," he claimed;[10] he wanted to make information free and have it run like water. He planned to write a major book on the subject, to be entitled *Intelligence*.

In a contest between ignorance and stupidity on the one hand, and information and intelligence on the other, we know how to bet. A certain level of madness is often an advantage in the business and entertainment world, but this was too extreme for that. Purging the planet of ignorance? Only a buffoon or mountebank would say such a foolish thing. Saylor was clearly one or the other—maybe both.

After all, he made a public spectacle of himself every time he opened his mouth: "I think my software is going to become so ubiquitous, so essential, that if it stops working there will be riots,"[11] he had told a writer for the *New Yorker*. MicroStrategy had merely developed software that helped businesses figure out who was buying their products. The software allowed McDonald's, for example, to evaluate how many more (or less) Big Macs a Chicago franchise would sell on a winter Friday than a franchise in Miami.

Saylor also had less visible corruptions; he had hidden massive indiscretions in his company's financial statements.

The stock market had gone mad over companies such as MicroStrategy. Shares were offered to the public on June 11, 1998. Nearly two years later, the stock hit $333. Saylor made $1.3 billion that day and $4.5 billion in the preceding week—bringing his personal net worth to $13.6 billion. At the time, MicroStrategy, with sales of only $200 million and a reported profit for 1999 of $12.6 million, was worth more than DuPont. This made Saylor the richest man in the Washington, D.C., area—wealthier even than Oracle founder, Larry Ellison. At $333, the stock price was as insane as the company's CEO.

While we were mocking MicroStrategy, its share price, and its dizzy CEO in our daily e-mails at www.dailyreckoning.com, the rest of the financial press was praising him. Hardly a single report failed to find something flattering to say. The English language has thousands of negative words, but before March 20, 2000, the ink-stained hacks, analysts, and TV presenters could not seem to find a single one that applied to Michael Saylor.

Then came March 20, 2000. That day, the financial reporters opened their dictionaries and Michael Saylor made history. Under pressure from the Securities and Exchange Commission (SEC), he was forced to admit that MicroStrategy had cooked its books for the previous two years. Instead of a profit of $12.6 million in 1999, the company would now show a loss of $34 million to $40 million. Revenue, too, was downsized. Never before had a man lost so much money in such a short time. In six hours, his net worth dropped by $6.1 billion.

From that day on, Saylor's life changed. Instead of being praised by investors and the financial media, he was whacked hard. Investors were out $11 billion. Some of them were angry. Others were suicidal. "I never thought I could lose like this," said one investor on the Yahoo!/ MicroStrategy message board . . . before declaring that he was going to kill himself.

Before March 20, 2000, Michael Saylor could do no wrong; after that he could do no right. Most prominently, *Fortune* listed him as number one in the "Billionaire Losers Club," with total losses of $13 billion.

But a difficult failure does a man more good than an easy success. On the evidence, Saylor was a better man in the fall of 2001 than he had been a few years earlier. According to *Washington Post* reports, he turned to drink to drown his losses.[12] When not drinking, he was tending to his business. The stock was still overpriced, but at $3.36, a lot less overpriced than it had been.

So was he still a visionary? An "older, wiser" one, he replied.

The excesses of the dot-com bubble have been well documented elsewhere. Even in 2001, economists and analysts conceded that the whole Internet thing had gotten out of hand. Of course, they had no way of knowing that Saylor had fudged the numbers. Nor could they be blamed for not realizing how quickly many of the tech companies would collapse, or how far the whole sector would fall. Who could have predicted such things? But, most of those who had seen no reason to resist buying MicroStrategy at more than $110 per share in December 1999, now claimed that they had known all along that there was a bubble in the tech sector. With the wind blowing from a different direction, they found it all too easy to change tack.

We recite the excesses of this era not merely to gawk or scold, but to show how the world really works. It was not just the worst minds in America that were caught up in the bubble delusion, but many of the best. Nor was the bubble a perversion of human nature or an aberration in human history. Episodically, such things happen. People begin to believe that the old lessons no longer apply and the old rules no longer work.

A world of make-believe, the bubble economy comprised virtual companies with virtual revenues and virtual profits. Companies that had never made a dime of profits, and never would, were valued as if they were worth billions. By the fall of 2001, the worst of them had already crashed, and the best were on their way back down to where they had started. Many of the dot-com entrepreneurs had turned to driving cabs or waiting tables. A few of the era's wheelers and dealers were already being hunted down by ambitious prosecutors and locked up. Some had moved into real estate. Meanwhile, many of the intellectuals who directed, rationalized, hyped, and often profited from the Information Revolution were still at large, but poorer and humbler.

A River Runs Through It

In the summer of 2000, *Harry Potter and the Goblet of Fire* arrived (in hardback) on the nation's bookshelves. It was such a hit that many stores quickly ran short of copies. Parents turned to the Internet, and to the Internet's most famous company, Amazon.com, to secure a copy. Amazon was able to take advantage of this success story to bring on 63,550 new customers.

But even the most popular book of the season proved a loss maker for the company. Harry Potter sales resulted in losses for Amazon of about $5 million, or about $78.68 per sale (more than three times the purchase price). Company spokesmen promptly claimed that there was no cause for concern as they would make up for the losses through all the new customers the book had brought. But how, we recall wondering at the time? By selling the next Harry Potter book at four times what it would cost in Barnes & Noble? And how, we wondered again, could you put any reasonable value on these losing Internet companies? But the summer of 2000 was not yet the time for questions. It was still a time of faith.

The value of a stock is determined, ultimately, by the stream of earnings it is expected to produce; the same is true even for Internet stocks. But Amazon, the great big river of Internet reverie, produced no stream of profits. Not even a trickle. Moreover, a report by McKinsey & Company found that the best way to value dot-coms was to return to economic fundamentals with the discounted cash flow approach. But it is hard to discount a flow of cash that does not exist.

Yet it was the nonexistence of cash flow that made Amazon.com (AMZN) and many other Internet companies so attractive. Lacking facts, investors were left to use their imaginations. Cash flow could be anything they wanted it to be. Analysts could imagine any price target that suited them. No company stimulated imaginations more than Amazon.com. The company flowed through the entire landscape of Internet-Land mania. From the glacial melt source high in the Andes of technological innovation and speculative imagination . . . to the murky depths of the Gildered Age and the absurd pretensions of *The Cluetrain Manifesto* . . . to the bug-infested jungle of competition and creative destruction . . . to the frauds of the first-mover advantage and hedonic price measures . . . to the myths of the New Man, New

Economy, New Metrics, and New Era . . . right down to the delta of washed-out dreams, where all those hyped-up humbugs eventually settle in the mud . . .

Amazon.com flowed through it all.

And never, during this entire spell of absurdity, inanity, and chicanery, could anyone say with any assurance what the company was worth. In place of a bottom line that could have been multiplied to produce a meaningful price comparison, AMZN had only a sinkhole.

Looking at its financial details more closely, Amazon might have had sales of $574 million in the first three months of 2000, but it also had a net loss of $308 million and an operating loss of $198 million. Moreover, compared with the same period of the previous year, although sales had doubled, operating losses had come close to quadrupling. Granted, the company boasted $1 billion in cash and securities, but against that, it had $2 billion in debt, an accumulated deficit of more than $1 billion and only $25.6 million in stockholders' equity.

Lacking the fulcrum of profits on which to lever a reasonable price, a number of approaches were used over the years to come up with an unreasonable one. Remember "eyeballs"? These visual portals were once considered a means of establishing the value of an Internet stock. So was "stickiness"—the amount of time the eyeballs stayed glued to the site. Another common approach was multiplying the rate of sales growth. But, finally, the confederacy of dunces that passes itself off as a group of stock analysts went back to fundamentals. They began to value Internet companies in the same way publishers value a subscriber—in terms of lifetime value.

Indeed, both publishing companies and Internet companies operate on the same basic premise: They spend money to bring in customers. Then, they expect a stream of income (sales, renewals, advertising) from each customer. The value of a company can be determined by calculating the net value of each customer over the lifetime of the relationship and multiplying by the number of customers. Amazon had about 15 million customers at the time. But how much was each one worth?

In February 2000, Jamie Kiggen, an analyst with Donaldson, Lufkin & Jenrette, dreamed his way to a figure of $1,905. We wondered how, in an industry noted for aggressive competition and razor-thin margins (so thin, in fact, that Amazon's margin was negative—minus 39 percent—meaning it lost money on each sale), could the company possibly make nearly $2,000 per customer? It couldn't. The idea was preposterous. Still, it gave investors a price target of $140 a share for AMZN. Another analyst, Eric Von der Porten, of Leeward Investments (a California hedge fund, with less of an attachment to the big river), used Kiggen's model and priced the lifetime value of each customer at just $26. Multiply that by the number of customers, and you get a capital value for the company of about $440 million—or a stock price of about $1.25.[13]

Killers of the New Economy

Jeff Bezos, Amazon's founder, would have argued that Kiggen's model was wrong and that it was too early to try to put a value on Amazon because he was not even trying to make a profit. As he explained to *Playboy*, "We are a customer store."[14] He did not mean that AMZN sold customers. He meant that the company focused on the customer instead of on making a profit or even a product. This was another conceit of the Internet Age—that these companies put the customer on a higher plane. What bread did Jeff Bezos eat? What air did he breathe? Were we supposed to be in awe of him and all the other new Digital Men who "got it" and no longer needed profit margins or products? Or should we have been appalled?

He was 35 when *Time* magazine awarded him its "Person of the Year" title in January 2001. When the going was good, *Time* gushed, "Jeffrey Preston Bezos . . . peered into the maze of connected computers called the World Wide Web and realized that the future of retailing was glowing back at him . . . Every time a seismic shift takes place in our economy, there are people who feel the vibrations long before the rest of us do," rattled *Time*, "vibrations so strong they demand action—actions that can seem rash, even stupid." Well, yes. Very stupid.

Sales might have continued rising at the big River-of-No-Returns. But profits? In the fourth quarter of 2000, Amazon lost $545 million, a figure $222 million higher than that of the same period the year before. Cumulative losses for the company almost exceeded $3 billion. For *Time,* Amazon's losses were "a sign of the New Economics of Internet commerce" and "the idea that in the new global marketplace whoever has the most information wins."

"It's a revolution," *Time* exclaimed. "It kills old economics, it kills old companies, it kills old rules."[15]

But all the River-of-No-Returns killed was investors' money. It claimed to be "the planet's" largest virtual store. It had 23 million registered customers, and Jeff Bezos said it would continue getting bigger and bigger—growing at a compound rate of 50 percent for the next 10 years. That would give it more than 1.3 billion customers by the year 2010. Wow. And sales would hit more than $100 billion. It would be the biggest virtual store in the whole blooming galaxy.

But imagine that you had never heard of Amazon, or of the New Economy. Imagine that Jeff Bezos came up to you and offered you his company for $14 billion. It has $2.1 billion in revenue. Assets of uncertain value. Billions in debt. And it loses more than $1 billion a year. What would be your reaction? Would you pay $14 billion for the privilege of losing $1 billion per year? Would you want a piece of that deal? In the heyday of the New Era, many people did. Most lived to regret it.

Some people get rich in a revolution. Some people get killed. By October 2001, it was becoming clear who would be the victims—those who believed in Amazon.com and the Information Revolution.

Bezos was, of course, one of those victims. In 2001, he was awarded the "Fame Is Fleeting Award," by Gretchen Morgenson in the *New York Times,* "for one of the fastest falls from grace in recent history."[16] She considered it sadly ironic that he was facing irate shareholders only a year after being honored as *Time*'s Person of the Year.

For at the end of 2000, Amazon's stock price showed a decline of 89 percent to the $7 to $10 range (from its December 1999 high of $113). Thus, a pin had pierced the bubble in high technology, and those who "got it" were getting it good and hard. Their day of reckoning had come.

The Cisco Kids

Of all the companies that might have been able to harness the new advantage given them by the Information Age, perhaps none was better placed than Cisco. The company was so admired by investors that they gave it a market cap higher than any other company had ever received. Even after the Nasdaq had crashed, Cisco's CEO John

Chambers explained to investors that the company would nevertheless continue to enjoy 30 percent to 50 percent annual sales growth for as far as the eye could see.

But the eye could not see very far. It saw only what it wanted to see. Neither Mr. Greenspan, the world's most celebrated macroeconomist, nor Cisco Systems, recently one of the most envied corporations on Wall Street, really understood what was going on.

As was becoming obvious, it was a capital spending boom—not productivity or New Era information technology—that made Wall Street's numbers look so appealing. In the late 1990s, businesses all over the planet felt the need to get into the swing of the New Era by spending on information technology (IT). In the perverse logic of the late tech bubble, if they could spend enough, fast enough—their share prices would rise.

But sooner or later, companies had all the routers and multiplexers they needed—even more than enough. Business capital investment fell between 2000 and 2001. And unsold equipment piled up on the shelves.

Meanwhile, Cisco sales, which analysts had expected to grow 30 percent per year for the next 10 years, began falling instead. In fact, in 2001 they were down 25 percent on the preceding year. Like an auto dealer in a downturn, Cisco found itself with its lot full of various makes and models that it wanted to unload—new and used.

"Cisco Systems Capital," reported the company's Web site, "now offers refurbished Cisco equipment with the same warranty protection and support as new . . . but at a lower price." Discounts listed at www.usedrouter.com ranged from almost 70 percent to as little as 20 percent.

"I can buy the equipment for 10 cents on the dollar," said one regular customer. "The stuff we are seeing right now is very often less than a year old and still under warranty."

At its peak in early 2000, Cisco (CSCO) was worth nearly half a trillion dollars. This is the equivalent of about $4,000 for every household in America, or about $75 for every Homo sapiens on the planet. Meanwhile, Cisco shares traded hands at about 190 times earnings. This implied a growth rate for the company of about 190 percent according to the conventional analysis. In reality, this figure was about 3.5 times the company's actual growth rate. It was also mathematically unsustainable: the higher the rate of growth, the faster the market opportunity would be exhausted.

Cisco's story is well known. In 1984, Sandy Lerner and Len Bosack got together to solve a problem. They needed to make the computers in Stanford University's business school capable of talking to those in the engineering school. They built routers, cobbled together some software, and solved the problem. Henceforth, Stanford's business students could send dirty jokes to the guys in the engineering department via computer. It was not long before other computer users were showing up at Lerner and Bosack's door to get the communications equipment. The couple got married and set up shop in their home—manufacturing the devices themselves and using credit cards as a source of capital.

By 1990, CSCO was a player in Silicon Valley. The Lerner and Bosack team brought in a venture capital group that took the company to the public markets and then forced the founding couple out. Lerner and Bosack divorced in the early 1990s. So they had neither the company they founded nor each other's company.

But if the marriage did not prosper, the company certainly did, and Cisco figured that it needed to offer more than just routers. So in the mid-1990s, it began purchasing other companies involved in the computer communications trade. Cisco acquired one company in 1993, three companies in 1994, four companies in 1995, and seven in 1996, including the $4 billion acquisition of StrataCom, then the largest purchase in the history of Silicon Valley. It picked up 6 more companies in 1997, 9 in 1998, 18 in 1999, and bought 10 in 2000, for a total of 58 acquisitions.

The Cisco kids were certainly on a buying binge. The idea was pretty simple. Customers did not want routers. They wanted solutions to their communications problems. And since the problems had varied solutions, Cisco needed to offer a variety of products. Cisco, in other words, was not a router company. It was a marketing channel for computer communications. When it bought some small company with a useful, but largely unknown, device, the product was marked with the Cisco brand and launched to the customer base. Negligible sales could go to monster sales almost overnight. One company, for example, that had $10 million in revenues at the time of acquisition, gave Cisco technology that soon generated more than $1 billion in revenues.

This was all very well, but when two new companies a month were being purchased, they were not all likely to produce such spectacular results. In fact, most were likely to be duds. A lot, it turned out, depended on how the accounting was done.

Moreover, Cisco's appetite for acquisitions drove up prices to preposterous levels. It bought ArrowPoint for shares worth $5.7 billion— a lot of money to pay for a company that had a negative book value, had never earned a penny, and had sales of only about $40 million. But what did the Cisco kids care? The company's funds did not represent real money; it was "Cisco scrip"—a new currency provided by delusional investors.

Each share of CSCO stock was thought to be worth about $63. But an investor would earn no dividends, and the company itself earned only 38 cents per share. Even if profits continued to increase at the 1999 rate, Cisco would earn only $3.74 per share in five years. If the stock price had continued apace, the company would have been worth nearly $5 trillion, an amount equal to half of the entire U.S. GDP.

What's more, the process of creative destruction, of which Cisco was such an extraordinary beneficiary, was not likely to stop dead in its tracks the moment the company finally reached a level of profitability that justified its price (if ever). That is the trouble with new technology, after all. There is always newer technology, as well as other Lerner and Bosack teams, just waiting for their moments of fame and fortune.

Icahn of the Old Economy

In contrast to Cisco, there was General Motors. Carl Icahn, corporate raider of 1980s fame, was in the news again at the century's end, attempting to force GM to sell its stake in Hughes Electronics—in order to "unlock shareholder value."

GM had more sales, in dollar terms, than any other company in the world—$177 billion worth. But it earned a profit of $6 billion (3 percent of sales). Not only were earnings low, but the other news was not good. GM was losing market share and its unionized workers seemed ready to revolt.

But GM did have a few things going for it. Even in September 2000, $6 billion was a lot of money. Plus, the company had $10 billion in cash. Its pension plan was overfunded by $9 billion. And it owned a stake in Hughes that was worth $15 billion. Icahn's idea was obvious. He would buy a big enough block of GM stock to be able to force the company to sell the Hughes shares.

The entire company—at its then current stock price—had a value of about $36 billion, less than one-tenth of Cisco's. Imagine that you, personally, could have bought the company. For $36 billion, you would have bought a company with $10 billion in the cash register. So, you would only really be $26 billion out of pocket. And then, you could have sold the Hughes holding for $15 billion, so the rest of the company would really have cost you only $11 billion.

You would have had the world's biggest company (producing cars, trucks, and other things you could put your hands on) as well as a spare 1966 Corvette in a garage somewhere for you to drive around. Factories, real estate, giant machinery . . . you would have got it all. Plus, you would have earned about $6 billion each year. Expressed in conventional terms, the operating part of the world's largest company had a P/E of just 1.83. From your point of view, as owner, you would have gotten back your investment money in about 20 months and have earned about $6 billion every year after that. Or, you could have bought 10 percent of Cisco.

Relying on the slogans and feebleminded dicta of the financial media, you would have avoided GM. GM was "old economy." It was a has-been company that seemed unable to get its act together. Owning GM was definitely not cool.

But Carl Icahn did not worry about being cool. He had a PhD in philosophy from Princeton. In his thesis, he developed the idea that collective thinking is invalid: "Knowledge is based only on what you observe. You talk to me about something, you must relate it to something that's observable."

Of course, George Gilder had no interest in GM. He was interested in GC (Global Crossing), and he couldn't get enough of it when it was trading at 33 times sales and $60 per share. The man must have been beside himself with joy when, in October 2001, he could buy as many shares as he wanted for only 50 cents apiece. Investors had lost 99.9 percent of their money already, but the losses did not stop there. An investor who held on at 50 cents would have lost another 96 percent of his money by the end of the following year, when the stock traded for only 2 cents. But still, maybe the promise of the Information Age would come true at last. Suddenly, late at night, when sensible men had taken to their beds and only techies, terrorists, and teenagers were still awake, the world's dark fibers would light up with data. And maybe then, Global Crossing's stock would rise . . . to 3 cents!

Of course, this does not mark the end of the GM story . . . the car maker would prove to be one of the most prominent victims once the tech bubble morphed, aided and abetted by the feds, into a much larger bubble; a bubble who's detritus—once popped—dripped all over the "real" economy as well as the financial markets More on this in a coming chapter . . .

DREAMERS AND SCHEMERS

We might laugh, but Gilder, the messiah of the New Era, was still in the wilderness, and who can fault him for that? After all he did no harm. As in every revolution, the real mischief was done by the small cadre of cynical gunrunners who followed in their messiah's visionary footsteps. Who can blame Gilder (or Marx for that matter) for his disciples' excesses?

One such gunrunner was Jack Grubman. He hustled stocks to investors—stocks that would later blow up. And the traffic made him a rich man; he earned as much as $20 million per year as Salomon Smith Barney's telecom analyst. Unlike Gilder, he was not dizzy enough to believe in the cause—he realized it was just a way to separate the fools from their money. Instead of buying telecom stocks, he sold them.

According to press reports, Grubman worked closely with Global Crossing's chairman, Gary Winnick, perhaps advising him on his stock selections. Money was the only driving force of their collaboration. A former Global Crossing employee described Winnick and his cronies as "the biggest group of greedheads in an era of fabled excess."[17]

Winnick, like Grubman, made money on Global Crossing—again, by selling rather than buying its stock. When the telecoms blew up, he managed to walk away with $730 million before the bomb detonated. But other investors were not so lucky: They lost $2.5 trillion in market value. Somehow, Grubman forgot to tell them when to sell.

Instead, as late as spring 2001, he wrote about the "historic opportunities to buy world-class assets such as Global Crossing that are evolving into world-class operating businesses at compelling value." On that same day, Global Crossing shares sold for $7.68. If they were "compelling" then, you would think the shares would be absolutely irresistible later on! Alas, after the company went bankrupt, Grubman, who owned a $6 million townhouse in Manhattan, with neither mortgage nor lien, simply "discontinued coverage" of the stock.

All of this did not mean much to Gilder. No, no—he really was not to blame. For he was still staring at the skies, thinking about gigabits, and scribbling away . . . when creditors pulled up in front of his house and wondered how much they could get for it.

But how had it come to this? he asked himself. After all, he had listened to the technology and had begun hearing voices just as the Information Revolution was getting underway. In a better world, things might have gone differently, he convinced himself. After all, he had been earnestly blathering before large crowds . . . and making good money at it: 350 people had paid $4,000 each to attend his Telecosm conference in 1997; and his speeches, heard by thousands, earned him $50,000 a time. Moreover, in 1999, his list of recommended tech stocks had averaged more than 247 percent return, and by the end of 2000, his newsletter boasted 70,000 subscribers paying $295 a year. At the bubble's peak, just one "gildered" word could boost a stock price 50 percent in a single day.

But then, the New Era messiah had stumbled over a bit of bad luck. Techs crashed, and suddenly people were not interested in attending his conferences or reading his newsletters, for they no longer seemed to care how many bits you could crowd onto the head of a silicon chip. Worse, in January 2002, came the news that his favorite corporation—the company he thought would "change the world economy"—had filed for bankruptcy protection. Gilder reflected on his fortunes over those past few years: "You can be just fabulously flush one moment, and then the next, you can't make that last million-dollar payment to your partners, and there's suddenly a lien on your house. . . . For a few years in a row there, I was the best stockpicker in the world. But last year you could say . . . I was the worst."[18] Poor George, very rich when things were going his way, had gone broke when they changed direction.

But to his credit (not his benefit), at least the guru had put his money where his mouth was. He had not merely misled investors; he had misled himself, too. He had bought into everything—Global Crossing, the New Era, his own publishing business.

Still suffering from New Era hallucinations, he continued to have faith in the wonders of technology even after the Nasdaq's crash. He later expressed his belief in the power of his "telecosm," claiming that it was "transforming the world economy and every existing political and cultural arrangement," and could significantly improve productivity: "Its ability to transmit any amount of information, to anyone anywhere, anytime, at a negligible cost, will unleash surges of productivity as yet unimagined."[19]

Behind Gilder's pensée was an even nuttier idea—that information, in the form of digitized data, could make people rich. But then his thinking was very much in the spirit of the times, when a powerful sense of optimism pervaded American civil society.

THE VALUE OF INFORMATION

"Cogito, ergo sum" (I think, therefore I am), wrote France's most famous philosopher, René Descartes. The proposition was self-evidently absurd. If Descartes had thought he was a chipmunk, would he have been one? One could spend a lifetime poking around in the corpus of Descartes' œuvre, but the defect is right there on the surface: proof of existence described only through the dark glass of the mind; that things are whatever you think they are. Not that we humans can know it any other way. But Descartes' self-centered assertion is an invitation to trouble, for it flatters our self-confidence and lures us to destruction.

By the end of the twentieth century, Americans had come to believe that they lived in a benign world. Like Descartes, they believed that whatever they thought was true and that they could think their way to wherever they wanted to go. Information technology was moving as fast as a beer truck through a bad neighborhood and promised similarly heady results. What a wonderful world it was, now that American-style capitalism had triumphed over all competitors! After all, anyone with sense enough to buy and hold stocks could get rich (or at least, that is what they thought). Granted, there would be problems, but none that they could not think through to find a solution.

During the lunatic phase of the great bull market of 1982 to 2000, it was widely believed that the important parts of life could be digitized. Information alone, specifically digitized information, was thought to be a more valuable resource than oil or farmland. The new information technologies were supposed to have the power to bring about a number of improvements, including healing the sick, raising prosperity levels, eliminating the business cycle and ending war forever. Now, everyone would have access to the latest healing information, and everyone would be able to use the Internet to tap into the secrets of wealth that were previously guarded closely by powerful, elite organizations.

Booms, busts, and bear markets, as everyone knew, resulted from imperfect information. Businesses typically overdid it. They borrowed too much and produced too much when times were good. And then, thanks to overdoing it, times went bad, as there were soon too many products on the market and too much debt. Information would eliminate these problems, as businesses would have more accurate and timely data on which to base their projections. Then, with no more down cycles in business, there would be no more falloffs in earnings and no more reasons for bear markets. And war? Wasn't war the result of a failure to communicate? Now that people could connect to the Internet and communicate in this one, vast, new, free market—wouldn't war be a thing of the past, too? For the entire world would now have access to the undeniable superiority of the U.S. model of free elections and a free economy. Surely all nations would put down their weapons, take up computers, and get on with the serious business of life—making money!

People's imaginations ran wild. In their fantasies, they pictured the little 1s and 0s of the digital age marching forward forever in a world of eternal peace, ever-increasing prosperity, and constantly expanding contentment. That is what people wanted; surely the latest information technology would help them get it.

There were, of course, theoretical problems. You could have set down the most powerful computer ever made—with the most complete database of information ever assembled—in front of the smartest man in Plato's Athens. What good would it have done him? Would he have any idea what he had in his hands? Imagine Napoleon shivering in his tent. Give him the price of grain in New York or the number of atoms in a cubic centimeter of cognac and you do him no favor. You might as well ship him a crate of sunscreen. Information out of context is useless.

Information is useless not only when it is unwanted or out of context, but also when it is in too great supply, for then it has to be sorted, rerouted, or thrown away. "Paralysis by analysis" is the popular expression. In any given situation, an infinite amount of information might be brought to bear. Any of it might be relevant and useful. But time is limited.

Napoleon knew full well he could not wait for every possible message to make its way to him. Nor did he have the luxury of weighing every bit of information just in case the optimum course of action should reveal itself. Like every general and every other human on the planet, he had to act based on imperfect information—guessing what was really important and hoping he had the information he needed. Every bit of information beyond what he actually needed was a cost— and potentially an expensive one. For every bit of extra information slowed him down; he had to evaluate it for relevance and authenticity and, ultimately, absorb it into his view of things or reject it.

GRAFFITI ON THE INTERNET

There are many examples from military history in which the quality and integrity of information were decisive. In the middle of World War II, the Allies dressed a dead man in a British officer's uniform. They then fastened to the body a set of plans for their counterattack on Hitler's army in Europe. The plans were, of course, intended to mislead Hitler about Allied intentions. The body was then dumped into the sea, so it would wash ashore where the Germans could find it. Hitler also believed he had a network of spies in England who would be able to fill him in on the coming landings. But these spies had almost all been discovered and "turned," so they were feeding false information reports to the Nazi high command. Thus, the information that Hitler was receiving was worse than no information at all. It lacked integrity. The more of it he had, the worse off he was.

Solzhenitsyn tells us how the Russian army in World War I was commanded by German-speaking officers from Prussia, who would transmit their orders and battle plans in the German language. The enemy often intercepted and read these messages, whereas Russian troops, for whom the plans were intended, found them incomprehensible. In our own War Between the States, Lee's plans at Antietam were betrayed to the Yankees when a Southern officer used them to wrap a cigar—and left them by mistake to be discovered by Union troops.

In the military, the units charged with gathering information and separating fact from fiction are called "Intelligence" units. This screening process is tough work, and it gets tougher the more facts and fictions there are to sift through. Today the Internet, though ultimately just a means of communication, delivers an almost infinite number of facts and fictions. The tough part—the "Intelligence" work—is sorting them out.

Although information is free on the Internet, free information sometimes turns out to be worth a lot less than you pay for it. Barely had the Internet begun working than fraudsters were using it to mislead investors. A typical scheme, such as the one perpetrated by a student at Georgetown Law School, involved buying the shares of some marginal company and then going on the Internet, spreading rumors or outright lies to ramp up the price. This was easier to do than misleading the Wehrmacht. You only had to announce some new breakthrough, some new contract, a rumored buyout, new technology . . . whatever. The whole idea was to create the kind of buzz that got people talking about it. Then supposedly reasonable "investors" would jump at the chance to buy a stock they knew nothing about, on the basis of a recommendation from someone they did not know, founded on information whose accuracy could not be affirmed and whose source could not be traced.

A lawyer defending one of the alleged Georgetown manipulators responded that it was impossible to mislead people on the Internet: According to him, Internet postings were nothing but "graffiti," with no more informational content than graffiti has artistic content. The lawyer's argument was that his client had just used the Internet as a graffiti artist uses the wall of a public building . . . or perhaps as a dog uses a tree. He pollutes it, perhaps vandalizes it, but no serious person would mistake it for useful information. But here, junk life imitates junk art. Pumping and dumping stocks on the Internet did in fact work. In just a few hours, the graffiti artists of the Internet were able to sell their shares at a profit.

Yet while information may be cheap, knowledge is dear. It takes time to learn how to do anything. It can take a lifetime to master a trade—even one that is as rudimentary and analog as woodworking or gardening. And the Internet did nothing to expand the supply of time. On the contrary, it made time more dear. Herbert Simon, winner of the 1978 Nobel Prize in Economics, gave the following reason for this: "In a world where attention is a major scarce resource, information may be an expensive luxury, for it may turn our attention from what is important to what is unimportant."[20]

Internet investors treated every digit as if it had value. In fact, few had any worth whatsoever. Many were not only valueless, but had antivalue, reducing the sum of knowledge or wisdom in whomever took them seriously.

By the end of the twentieth century, America was suffering from information overload. As one commentator put it, "Americans today are literally drowning in information . . . we find ourselves awash in a vast ocean of data, what with the Internet, nonstop cable TV news, e-mail, voicemail, faxes, pagers with stock quotes, cellular phones and an explosion of newspapers, magazines and books and well, you get the idea."

He cites "data glut" as a serious issue in the American workplace, and finds that the average worker now spends more than half his or her day processing documents. Meanwhile, paper consumption per worker tripled (to 1,800 pounds annually), in the 1980s, and "third-class mail" increased at 13 times the population growth rate, he reports. Nowadays, office workers often spend hours reading and answering e-mail, not to mention voicemail, faxes, and the rest. Initially a blessing, e-mail is now a curse to those whose inboxes are inundated with "FYI" messages and other information on a daily basis.[21]

In 1997, author David Shenk found that "information overload fuels stress and promotes faulty thinking." The data glut we all slog through every day at work simply "reduces our attention span" and "makes us numb to anything that doesn't lurch out and grab us by the throat" Shenk concluded.

Having two mistresses is not necessarily better than having one. Nor is eating two lunches an improvement over a single one. But information was supposed to be different, wasn't it? The more you had, the richer and smarter you were supposed to be. Yet, in 2001, people seemed no brighter than they had been before the Information Age began. Most movies seemed no better than those of the 1950s and 1960s; art was becoming more grotesque; the editorials in the *Herald Tribune* were as absurd as ever; and investors appeared to be making increasingly ridiculous decisions.

What was more, markets seemed totally perverse in nature, for while everyone proclaimed the benefits of the Information Age, it was, ironically, the most ignorant who seemed to reap its greatest rewards.

REFILLING THE PUNCH BOWL

The tech bubble of Wall Street in the late 1990s was a lot of things: silly, embarrassing, entertaining . . . and educational. People who should have lost money, did. And they probably would have lost a lot more, but in 2001, the Feds, led by Alan Greenspan, stepped in and did what they do best—they began throwing cash around.

Greenspan's predecessor, William McChesney Martin, once remarked that the real job of the Fed was to "take away the punch-bowl"[22] before the party got out of control. While the country was really beginning to feel the twangs of a hangover headache from the tech bust, instead of taking away the punch bowl, Sir Alan did the exact opposite: he spiked it with the high-proof gin of easy credit.

Every time the head of the Federal Reserve faced a problem, he slunk over to the punchbowl and dumped more in, until Americans were wobbling under the influence of the lowest interest rates in 45 years . . . and a 1 percent key Fed lending rate for only the second time in history.

So, drunk on easy credit, where were the American people to turn? To real estate, of course . . . and with serious conviction.

Housing mania took over the United States—and everyone was getting in on the action. Yale professor Robert Shiller explained the phenomenon as "infectious exuberance."

Speculative bubbles are fueled by the social contagion of boom thinking, encouraged by rising prices. Sooner or later, some factor boosts the transmission rate high enough above the removal rate for an optimistic view of the market to become widespread. Arguments that this boom is unlike past bubbles—I call them "new era" stories—become more prominent and seemingly credible. In the recent housing boom, such optimism was much in evidence . . .

In this sort of environment, skeptics have a hard time of it. No one has perfect information, and people—quite rationally—infer a great deal from the actions of others. As a bubble expands, some skeptics begin to disregard their own judgment because they feel that everyone else simply couldn't be wrong. Contrarian voices become softer, which only makes it harder for the remaining skeptics to justify their views. Over time, the quality of information that can be gleaned from the behavior of others becomes worse and worse.[23]

No one is immune from this "boom thinking." All of a sudden, buying a home—once seen as the ultimate responsibility—was available to everyone . . . and their pizza boy.

Renters: A Morality Play

It never hurts to be well acquainted with one's past even if that past happens to include mistakes. At the height of the housing boom, many mistakes were made . . . and made again.

This "play" written in April of 2005, offers some insight into what those who made themselves players in the biggest bubble of all time were thinking.

Cast of Characters:
A.W.: Renter #1
T.D.: Renter #2
K.I.: Renter #3
L.S.: Unwitting Speculator #1
C.D.: Unwitting Speculator #2
M.N.: Real Estate Investor
A.P.: 30-Year Fixed Rate New Homeowner
Chorus: Café patrons and waitresses

TIME and SCENE: Mid-spring 2005 A.D., our great nation is in the throes of a tenacious housing bubble. Whole cities have been tantalized, wooed, and seduced by this Siren song of easy wealth; entire populations rendered giddy by profits . . . on paper. Nearly every conversation heard around the dinner table . . . across the bar . . . in a cab . . . is focused on one subject: the housing market. DISCLAIMER: Any and all events in this dramatic reenactment are purely nonfictional. Any resemblance to real life is intentional, not at all coincidental. Some liberty may have been taken with the facts, but we swear it was in good faith.

Setting the Stage

The scene opens in Café Hon, a locally famous Baltimore eatery in the trendy suburb (sic) of Hampden, where big hair and gaudy make-up are curiously in vogue and admired. Seven colleagues from the Daily Reckoning's HQ are seated around a Formica-topped table.

Lacking an additional 30-year fixed mortgage holder, the table less-than-fairly represents the breakdown of mortgages nationwide: roughly 60 percent fixed rate, 40 percent ARM . . . 25 percent of all new mortgage originations in 2004 were real estate investors.

L.S. (Unwitting Speculator #1) is closing on a house the following day. Mere hours stand between her and the single biggest financial transaction of her young life. Can those stalwart pessimists (Renters #1, #2, and #3) lash her to the mast in time to save her from the Siren's tantalizing tune? We shall see, dear reader . . . below . . .

Act I: A Mortgage Broker's Wet Dream

Renter #1: Hey, L.S . . . I'm going to ask you one question. Your answer will determine how much I speak for the rest of this meal. Is your loan . . . an adjustable-rate mortgage?

Unwitting Speculator #1: Not at all. It's interest only.

[A gasp is heard. Ominous Lon Chaney–style horror music rises from the background.]

Renter #1 (face wincing): Why . . . why?! [Screams of horror coming from the kitchen.]

Unwitting Speculator #1: What?! I was tired of throwing away money on rent every month. I wanted to invest in something real . . . and build equity. Besides, we're going to sell in five years, anyway. So we're cool.

[Somebody snickers.]

Renter #2: That doesn't make sense. You are still throwing away money. The only difference now is you pay a finance company instead of a landlord.

Renter #3: And what if you can't sell in five years . . . doesn't that make you nervous?

Unwitting Speculator #1: [muffled unintelligible remarks . . . something about the location of the house . . . a leafy street . . . children on bikes . . . speed humps . . . shiny happy people . . .]

Renter #3: Answer the question. What if you can't sell?

Unwitting Speculator #1: Well . . . I am a little nervous. [nervous laughter] We're risking a huge amount of money . . . more money than I've ever known. But hey, you only live once!

Unwitting Speculator #2: Oh, come on, don't listen to them. I have an interest-only mortgage, too. [More gasps of horror.] These guys are all gloom and doomers. Remember, they work for the Daily Reckoning.

[Renters' heads snap in unison to glare at Unwitting Speculator #2]

Renter #1: And . . . what about you, *aren't you* nervous?

Unwitting Speculator #2: Nope. I try to take life one day at a time. I don't look that far ahead. I'm doing okay right now . . . and besides, in five years, I hope to be married.

[Unwitting Speculator #2 holds up both hands with her fingers crossed. Smiles.]

All (in unison): Awwww.

Unwitting Speculator #1: Don't you know it's bad luck to cross your fingers with *both* hands?

Act II: Unseemly Profits

Real Estate Investor: What about you Renter #1, why do you rent?

Renter #1: Well, we live down by the water . . . in the neighborhood we want to live in . . . and it's cheaper than a mortgage. And to tell you the truth, I just don't understand the market anymore. Let me give you an example.

When we lived in the same neighborhood before moving to Paris back in 2000, the house across the street went on the market for $97,000. The price was so high, everyone thought the owners were nuts. It was a different time. A friend finally bought the place for $87,000, gutted it, and started renting to college students.

We moved to Paris for four years. Last year, when we were moving back, we looked for a place to buy in Fell's Point . . . low and behold, we saw the same property on the market. Guess how much?

All (in unison): How much . . . tell us!

Renter #1: $357,000. A fourfold increase in just as many years!? Tell me, what market—any market—can sustain that kind of growth?

Real Estate Investor: Hey, a lot of people I know would say that's still cheap. Besides, it sounds like you were a damn fool to move to Paris. You should have held on for the ride. Still, I think you're right. The market is getting frothy . . . that's why I just sold my Baltimore properties.

[Puzzled looks of intrigue.]

Renter #1: Yeah, that's probably a good move. You bought in nice and early, and now you've sold near the top. Then you put the proceeds into a resort property in West Virginia . . . everyone knows that's an undervalued market.

[Fiddle-heavy bluegrass music wafts from the kitchen. More nods of agreement around the table.]

Real Estate Investor: Yup. The price is up already. We only put 10 percent down, but by the time of closing we had accumulated enough equity, the bank said they weren't going to require mortgage insurance. We'd already amassed an additional 10 percent of equity!

30-Year Fixed: Hell yeah! We made over $30,000 on our house before we'd even slept there!

Unwitting Speculator #2: Yeah . . . same here . . . my house is way up already, so I have a good margin of safety. And when I get married . . .

All (in unison): Awwww.

Renter #1: Hey, 30-year fixed, I know you've already made money on your house, but what do you see in the future?

30-Year Fixed: I have a response, but first I'd like to make a comment . . .

There are some neighborhoods that will always hold value. [muffled remarks . . . something about the location of the house . . . a leafy street . . . children on bikes . . . speed humps . . . shiny happy people . . . yada, yada . . .]

Renter #1 (with much enthusiasm): Au contraire! Baltimore is a case study of good neighborhoods gone bad. Look at Druid Hill . . . beautiful row homes. Back in the 1920s F. Scott Fitzgerald and Gertrude Stein held garden parties and entertained European royalty up there. Now look at it. Hell might offer better refuge for a family of four.

On the other hand, in the 1970s respectable folk wouldn't let their children go down to Fell's Point unchaperoned. It was a haven to bikers, ne'er-do-wells, and urchins of the night. Today, they're building spec homes on the water that start at a million plus . . .

Renter #3: Too bad the harbor smells so bad . . .

All (sighing): Yeah . . .

[Pregnant pause. A moment of quiet reflection.]

Chorus: At this point, it's not clear what conclusion, if any, can be drawn from the play.

When will the housing bubble burst?

Is it a bubble at all?

Or . . . will prices keep rising for five years, handing the interest-onlys the last laugh; leaving the renters, humbled once again with egg on their faces . . . and feeling like chumps? Well, dear reader, this is what makes a market.

Still, the renters bumble on . . .

Act III: The Intervention

Unwitting Speculator #1 (jolted with excitement turning to Renter #1): Oh, that reminds me, can I have the day off tomorrow? I'm closing on my house. [Turns to the table.] Should I wear a suit?

30-Year Fixed: Nah . . . you don't have to wear a suit for those yahoos.

[Snickers]

Renter #1: Sure, you can have a day off. But I forbid you to use one of these.

[Renter #1 holds up a pen. Renter #2 and Renter #3 smile at each other.]

Renter #3 (smugly): Ahhh . . . No pens, no signing.
Renter #2 (smug and grinning): Yeah . . . no pens.
30-Year Fixed (gesticulating expansively, raises his voice): Ah, don't listen to *them* . . . (mutters to himself) for crissakes.

[Check arrives. Curtain falls.]

Your Own Personal ATM

As evidenced by the story above, the way our parents and grandparents viewed owning a home was rapidly deteriorating. A home was no longer just a place to live—it was an investment. This pile of bricks and granite countertops was going to make you big money.

It seemed like a sure thing. Home prices were on the rise from 1997 on, nationwide at around 8 percent per year, but in some areas—most notably, Los Angeles County, Las Vegas, and Miami—homes were going up 20 to 30 percent in a single year.

Speculators swooped in, buying up houses just to "flip" them for a profit. In Florida, for instance, buyers were taking up condos that hadn't even been built yet. In Miami, flipping condos came to be a profitable speculation. Speculators would buy a group of 5 or 10 condos even before a single shovelful of dirt had been displaced. The idea was to sell the contracts to other speculators while the place was being built. The second buyer would then sell to yet another buyer when it was completed. Neither the first, nor the second, nor the third buyer had any intention of living in the condo.

The trouble was that the object of their speculation looked rather lonely and forlorn when it was finally put up. Driving by at night, it was noticeable that few of the condos had lights on. Most were empty . . . waiting for their ultimate buyer; the poor sap who would actually live in the place and, presumably, pay for it.

This eventually became such a problem for developers that they tried to squeeze out the speculators, insisting that buyers take up only one of the condos . . . and move in within a specified period of time. In some projects, developers announced special offers . . . which had prospective buyers camping out all weekend in order to get a good place in line to buy when the doors opened on Monday morning.

The special offers and incentives, not to mention the creative financing that was being thrown at them made it impossible for the average homeowner to resist the siren song of the real estate market. They weren't going to sit idly by and watch their home rise in value and not take advantage of it somehow. After all, from 1997 to 2007, total housing values rose from $8.8 trillion to $21.5 trillion.[24]

Your home became your own personal ATM, and the allure of this "free money" was so great that homeowners hopped over to their local banks to get at them, and then whined their way deeper into debt. The financial industry, ever ready to separate a fool from his or her money, rushed to the scene with the offer of home equity lines of credit that could be used "for everyday expenses, like groceries and gas."

Thus did the world's mouth (as the United States has been called) gobble down its own houses one brick at a time. Homeowners, thinking they were getting something for nothing, believed they were merely taking some of their gains off the table—like selling a few shares of appreciated stock. Little did they realize they were selling the table itself . . . along with the kid's bathroom and the family room.

If, for example, the house went from a $100,000 price to a price of $200,000, the homeowner may feel he can "take out" $100,000 of equity and still be living in a $100,000 house. But what he is actually doing is selling half the house to the mortgage lender. Even if the higher prices stick, he still has to live somewhere . . . and now he has to "rent" half his house from the mortgagor.

When a real estate bubble bursts, there are at least two losers—the borrower as well as the lender—and neither walks away easily. The borrower still has to pay his mortgage or he loses his house, and often must pay a mortgage that is higher than the value of the house. Many cannot or will not pay, which bounces the loss back onto the lender.

But such is the cold, cold world we live in that the appeal of rising asset values—whether real or paper—is almost irresistible.

The Trendsetter State

At the height of the boom, the average house in San Jose, California, sold for half a million dollars. How many people in the San Jose area can afford a $500,000 house? We don't know, but we suspect that the number is less than the number of owners.

Americans have became convinced that buying as much house as you can—even more than you can comfortably afford—was a shrewd financial move. But the real bubble action was happening farther south, in Los Angeles County. At the peak of the real estate boom, in 2005, NAHB/Wells Fargo Housing deemed LA County the least affordable metropolis in the nation, where only 14 percent of the population could afford to buy a home.[25]

To plug this gap between affordability and purchase prices, the California boom relied heavily on exotic financing, such as an adjustable-rate mortgage, and because of this reliance, the gap between affordability and purchase prices widened to extreme proportions.

By 2005, almost 40 percent of the state's homeowners—compared to 29 percent nationally—paid at least one-third of their income for housing, according to the Public Policy Institute of California. Even worse than that, one-fifth of all homebuyers paid more than *half* of their incomes for housing.[26]

Recalls Eric Fry, editor of *The Rude Awakening*: "Without easy credit, and lots of it, California real estate could never have achieved its epic valuations. Credit not only enabled first-time buyers to 'stretch' a bit, it also enabled and emboldened speculative builders, second-home buyers, second-home builders and every other variant of housing market participant/speculator.

"But because financing became so exotic, and speculative participation in the market became so great, the simultaneous unwinding of both has been as pleasant as hanging out with your in-laws during a root canal."[27]

The number and variety of nontraditional mortgages flourished from 2001 to 2007 . . . adjustable rate mortgages became common, as did zero-down payment mortgages, mortgages with alluringly low starter rates . . . including interest-only mortgages, flexible payments, and "stated income" applications, in which the borrower is left to use his own imagination in describing his financial circumstances.

These actions and innovations of the lenders, along with the federal government's housing policies were to help Americans buy their own homes, or words to that effect. Easy credit was meant to increase homeownership. Renting a house was seen as a kind of social failure, like dropping out of high school or driving an old Pinto. They had "democratized" the credit market, lenders and government officials alike claimed. Yes, now not only rich speculators could lose their shirts. The common man could lose his, too!

The obvious effect of all these innovations was to turn Americans into a race of housing speculators, not of homeowners. Instead of actually buying and paying for a house, marginal buyers were enticed into these innovative mortgage products, which were more like options to buy a house rather than an actual purchase of one.

As time went on, more and more homeowners became gamblers, betting that property values would rise fast enough so they could refinance again, all of them forgetting one important fact: A house is a house. It provides a service, but it doesn't provide any more service if it is quoted at $500,000 than if it is quoted at $300,000. Same roof. Same air-conditioning. Same everything. Except, when it is said to be worth more, two noxious things result. First, the homeowner can "take out" some of the equity and feel like he is still ahead of the game. He doesn't worry about it when prices are rising, when the loan comes due, he can always take out a little more. Gradually, he gets deeper and deeper into debt. And then, inevitably, his house goes down in price and he gets into trouble.

The other awful consequence is the cost of owning the home goes up. As the house becomes more "valuable," typically the cost of property taxes, insurance, and upkeep mount. Thus, the net value, or net service, an owner gets from his house actually goes down. He has the same roof over his head, but it costs him more.

What the housing mania pointed out, like the tech boom before it, is that a man can make a fool of himself whenever he wants. Generally, he pays the price himself and the rest of the world goes on with its business. But in order to get a real public spectacle going, you need to separate cause from effect. Because it is only when a fellow thinks he can get away with something that he really lets loose.

THE ETERNAL PROMISE OF A NEW ERA

The surfeit of information available to us—through the cable, cell phone, e-mail, IM, Facebook, Twitter—now makes people dumber in another curious way. People become numb to the subtle details and nuances that they actually observe. As processing information takes time and effort, the more of it you have to deal with, the more likely you are to seek shortcuts. Popular interpretations offer a substitute for careful reflection or observation. In other words, instead of actually figuring things out for themselves, people become more susceptible to collective thinking. Public thinking replaces individual thinking—simply because there is too much information to process. Unable to keep up with all the data from Wall Street, for example, people are forced to rely on summaries from CNBC or TheStreet.com.

The pretense of the Information Age was that the introduction of the silicon chip and the World Wide Web had suddenly revealed the value of information. In fact, the amount of information available to people has steadily increased over the past 200 years with new technology and new material: the telegraph, telephone, teletype, radio, television, fax, Minitel, and cheap printing processes. An individual in the twentieth century had vastly more information than an individual in the eighteenth century.

During the tech boom, people were being lured into believing that the stock market would never fail them. During the real estate bubble, otherwise average Americans believed above-average things to be true of their humble homes. Now, in 2009, Americans are once again being lulled to sleep by the soothing words of their president.

It seems that after the past eight years, the U.S. people would be critical, jaded, even, of the next person to take over at 1600 Pennsylvania Avenue. But no . . . it turns out that Dubya disappointed Americans so much that they are willing to lap up every word Barack Obama says—even if it's just the regurgitation of the same mottos and mantras that have been with us since the beginning of time.

"Obama is having the kind of honeymoon that no president-elect has had in at least 30 years," said CNN polling director Keating Holland. "It's no surprise that Americans have a positive view of anything Obama might do—at least until he does something controversial."[28]

As we often say, people believe what they need to believe when they need to believe it. And not unlike the lure of the Information Age of the past 10 years, in the winter of 2009, the American people believed "Yes, We Can!"

Unbeknown to most, they were being ushered into a couple of "new eras." Obama lays out them out in his inauguration speech.

"What is required of us now is a new era of responsibility—a recognition, on the part of every American, that we have duties that we do not grudgingly accept, but rather seize gladly, firm in the knowledge that there is nothing so satisfying to the spirit, so defining to our character, than giving our all to a difficult task."

He also speaks of ringing in a "new era of peace": ". . . we cannot help but believe that the old hatreds shall someday pass, that the lines of tribe shall soon dissolve, that as the world grows smaller, our common humanity shall reveal itself, and that America must play its role in ushering in a new era of peace."[29]

Now, don't get us wrong. We have nothing against peace . . . or responsibility, for that matter. What this shows is that once again, Americans are blindly following the herd, believing whatever is fed to them, just as they did during the "Information Age."

Is it just a coincidence that mass thinking has emerged with mass media . . . or that mass thinking has consequences of its own?

CHAPTER 2

PROGRESS, PERFECTIBILITY, AND THE END OF HISTORY

Mundus vult decipi, ergo decipiatur.
—The world wants to be deceived, so let it be deceived.

—Latin proverb

In the summer of 1989, Francis Fukuyama published a widely discussed essay in the *National Interest,* entitled "The End of History?" The document was remarkable; for rarely did someone manage to get so much so wrong in such a short essay. Fukuyama saw all of history as a march toward democracy and capitalism. He believed the collapse of communism marked the triumph of both . . . and hence, history was dead.

Fukuyama considered the victory of liberal, consumer capitalism to be so complete that he could imagine no serious challenge to it. "What we may be witnessing is not just the end of the Cold War," he wrote, "but the end of history as such: that is, the endpoint of mankind's ideological evolution and the universalization of Western liberal democracy as the final form of human government."

51

Some people must have thought he was joking, but others took him seriously. For the idea that history was a march toward democratic government and Western materialist values seemed incontestable. Democratic consumerism had become so widely accepted that it was scarcely recognizable as an idea. Intellectuals could write about it and argue its finer points, but to most people in the developed world—and many in the undeveloped one—the American model of democratic government with a capitalist economy was no longer an idea, nor an ideal, but just the way things should be. By the end of the twentieth century, it had become as much a fact of life as rising stock prices and never-ending prosperity. Surely we live in the best system possible, people said to themselves, and surely history has brought us here. History must stop now, for haven't we already arrived at its endpoint? Moreover, Western nations and Japan were already beyond history: According to Fukuyama, no further political or economic evolution was possible.

The thinker concluded that the end of history would be "a very sad time." He went on to describe life in the post-historical world: "The struggle for recognition, the willingness to risk one's life for a purely abstract goal, the worldwide ideological struggle that called forth daring, courage, imagination, and idealism, will be replaced by economic calculation, the endless solving of technical problems, environmental concerns and the satisfaction of sophisticated consumer demands. In the post-historical period there will be neither art nor philosophy, just the perpetual care-taking of the museum of human history."

Joking or not, we can barely suppress a laugh. In 1989, the poor man imagined that the world had reached a state of such perfection that there was no point in striving to make things better—they were already as good as they could get! But fewer than a dozen years later, history suddenly revived. The world's two biggest financial bubbles blew up and the United States suffered the worst terrorist attacks in all history.

Fukuyama can cheer up. In markets, as in politics and war, groups of people go a little mad from time to time. History is full of examples—wars, revolutions, booms, busts, bubbles. The very trend he identified with the end of history—greater mass participation—is actually the source of its energy. People do not make history on their own. They make it in crowds. The larger, the more connected the crowds and the more they come to believe that they have reached some state of perfection, the more history they make. Crowds lurch from one popular myth to another. Democratic consumer capitalism was hardly the end of the process, but merely the latest fashion.

In this chapter, we gawk at history like a crowd at a public autopsy. We are curious to see how the man on the table is put together . . . and we wonder what his heirs might do next.

MAKING HISTORY

No history recalls what the 5,000 or so Normans must have felt when they saw the English coastline in 1066, nor what they had for breakfast, or how their wives and daughters missed them at home on that day. Nor does it tell us how the peasants in Toncarville coaxed out a calf whose head was turned the wrong way, or the kind words spoken by a priest to an old woman in the churchyard. Nor does it even record how a merchant noticed that his trade had suddenly diminished when the knights were gone, and how he resolved to make up the difference by moving to Paris and selling fabrics imported from Holland.

Instead, history turns its attention uniquely to the events on English soil, where the small band of warriors debarked to go into battle. Theirs seemed to be a hopeless enterprise. How could such a small army hope to avoid annihilation, let alone conquer a whole nation? But that is history . . . a story of such remarkable campaigns, battles, revolutions, uprisings, popular movements—all presumably marching toward the progress of mankind, all, presumably, "good things." For without them, where would we be? No one knows. What if the Normans had stayed home? What if they had tended their fields, sought better ways to increase crop yields, put up more beautiful buildings, and given another kiss to their wives and children? Would the world be a worse place? We cannot tell.

However, in markets as well as politics, history is not made by the tailor, the baker, or the capitalist going about his work. It is made by mobs of tailors, bakers, and capitalists embarked on some enterprise, which is far beyond what any of them can know or understand, and which is usually absurd and often fatal.

Events in the twentieth century had been kinder to the United States than to their European cousins. Americans had taken part in the major wars, but had suffered far fewer casualties than other combatants. France lost nearly 6 million men in World War I, the United States 116,516. In World War II, the United States had 405,399 casualties, but the Soviet Union had more than 21 million (civilian deaths included). No U.S. cities were leveled.

Nor were there any civilian casualties to speak of. And U.S. industries, instead of being destroyed like those of Germany and Japan, ended the wars in a stronger position than when they had begun them.

It was not, then, reason that had shaped Americans' belief in progress . . . but experience. After such a long spell of apparent progress (interrupted only by a few quarters of negative economic growth in the Great Depression), Americans at the end of the twentieth century had begun to think that progress was the nature of things, and that the level of technological and organizational perfection they had achieved had brought on the blessings of progress at a faster rate than ever before. What's more, many of them thought that the temporary lulls and brief periods of backsliding experienced by the country since the end of World War II had now been eliminated. Thinking Americans attributed this giant leap forward neither to the grace of God nor the beneficence of nature, but to their own genius.

By the time the oldest members of the postwar baby boom generation had reached maturity (late 1990s), progress had begun to look easy, logical, even inevitable. Americans believed themselves to be masters of the business cycle, of technology, of the planet.

MYTHS OF PROGRESS

In what might have been an equivalent of the four-minute mile, Iaroslav Tchij, on a collective farm in the Lvov region of the Soviet Union in 1959, reduced a hog to 100 kilos of meat in just 5.6 hours. This might seem like a leisurely pace, but it took an hour less than for an American to do the job.

The Communist era began after the invention of the telegraph and was still going strong after radio, telephone, and television had become ubiquitous. But as we will see, information provided no defense against exaggeration and myth. Mr. Tchij, for example, was not alone in believing he could increase productivity in such a remarkable way.

In fact, one of the myths of Communism was the idea that productivity would increase without interruption and at spectacular rates. This was not based on any observation. It was derived from theory.

The founding fathers of Communism, like Internet investors, believed that a new era had arrived. It was founded neither on observation nor on hope, but on what they thought were the laws of history. In his funeral oration for Marx, on March 17, 1883, held in Highgate Cemetery, Engels honored Marx as "the Darwin" of economic history. Just as Darwin had discovered the key laws that governed the evolution of natural history, Engels said, Marx had discovered those that governed economic and political history. These laws, such as the concept of "surplus value," which supported Marx's critique of capitalism, were not laws at all, just pretentious *obiter dicta*, as Paul Johnson described them.[1] Yet they formed the basis for the many myths that inhabited the fantasy world of Communist society.

The myth of determinism, for example, meant that everything had already been worked out according to the principles Marx described. The myth of progress, whereby conditions improved year in year out, was a myth disproved by Communism itself. The myth of the Marxist New Era held that the entire world would be re-created, not by God or nature, but by man, following the scientific and rational concepts of historical determinism. Finally, there was the myth of the New Man. This new Marxist man, not having the same hard wiring as other men, would be an entirely new being. He would not need a profit motive, for example. Nor would he wish to accumulate wealth or worry about his own family, as all his material and service-based needs would be supplied by the collective.

As irrational as these notions were, they were nevertheless taken up and endorsed enthusiastically throughout the twentieth century by various despots and crackpots. Not only were they argued over endlessly in the cafés of Paris, but they provided the foundation of an entirely imaginary world.

Soviet policy makers for example (again, like Internet investors) saw no reason why they should be constrained by the growth rates observed in the past. Without private property and private business, they thought that there would no longer be a business cycle to worry about.

Communist growth projections became the measure of reported (though imaginary) growth: The Soviet Union's economy was thought to have multiplied itself 36 times between 1913 and 1959. The economy of the United States, by contrast, only increased by a factor of four. Soviet leaders predicted that the size of their economy would surpass that of the United States in a dozen years.

But even this rate was sluggish to the North Korean dictator, Kim Il Sung. If you could determine economic growth by decree, he reasoned in 1969, why be satisfied with 15 percent? In his text titled *On Some Theoretical Problems of Socialist Economies,* he declared that there was no reason for communist economies ever to slow down, and that growth rates of 30 percent to 40 percent per year could be maintained. Three decades later in his "socialist economy," millions of people were starving.

Kim should have paid attention when his fellow delusionary, Ceaucescu of Romania, addressed the agricultural issue. Ceaucescu decided to put his country in "the forefront of world agriculture." This he accomplished in the most straightforward and expedient fashion: He simply multiplied per acre production figures by four. Marxist myth held that collective farms would be vastly more productive than old-fashioned independent farms. Thus, Ceaucescu merely brought the myth to life, realizing it in the spirit it deserved—mythically.

Even the Communist leaders themselves were myths: Mr. Djugashvili, a rather untalented former seminarian and New Era aficionado, became "man of steel," Josef Stalin. Meanwhile, Kim Il Sung turned himself into a virtual deity, a mythical god, who became an object of worship for his impoverished people.

The astounding thing was how ready people were to believe such myths. American economists calculated that the Soviet economy must be 50 percent or 60 percent the size of the U.S. economy, and gaining ground. For decades, the Soviet Union was listed as the world's second biggest economic power. But it was not true. The Soviet Union and North Korea were not getting richer, but poorer. Their people were not becoming more productive, but less productive.

Progress Marches Backward

In science and technology, knowledge builds up as people make new mistakes: Technology may, like digits in an actuarial table, improve and compound, accumulating gradually over time. But in love, finance, and the rest of life, people make the same old mistakes, over and over again. As soon as the memory of some ancient folly grows moss-covered and forgotten, people trip over it anew. Likewise, man's use of technology—for profits, for war, or even to make improvements in his standard of living—follows the deep cycles of the human heart, rising like the confidence of a dipsomaniac after his first drink and falling into fear and uncertainty when he finally sobers up.

"Progress" is no sure thing. Beyond the cycles of greed and fear, confidence and desperation, are other episodes that surpass human desires and capacity. Following the collapse of the Roman Empire in AD 476, people in Europe did not wish to become poorer. They underwent no genetic change that made them less intelligent or less suited to material comfort or less adept at technological progress. Yet, technological innovation and material progress went into a slump for nearly 1,000 years. According to historians, the order that had allowed trade and prosperity gave way to disorder and poverty. Who wanted such a change? Why would people permit it? Seeing their standard of living threatened, why did they not do something to counteract it? Surely government officials could simply have come up with new policies that would set things right again?

Likewise, in 1914, although lessons had supposedly been learned from the wars of the nineteenth century, the world once again found itself on a road to disaster, with the outbreak of World War I.

From a military point of view, the war had effectively been "won" by France at the first Battle of the Marne in September 1914. France had defeated the German army and forced it back to a line situated not too far from where it had begun. Like many of the other battles fought, the battle of the Marne, with an estimated 512,733 killed, only served to underline the futility of a war. Little was gained at the cost of enormous human sacrifices.

Yet, what came to be known as "The Great War" continued for another four years. By 1916, it had become such a folly of senseless slaughter that the French were on the edge of mutiny. Troops on both sides, seeing no point to the continued bloodshed, often agreed on informal cease-fires. Senior officers repeatedly had to intervene to make sure their soldiers continued to kill each other. Hopelessly bogged down in trench warfare where neither side had a decisive advantage or even a reasonable war aim, sensible men might have decided that enough was enough. Even now, few people can come up with a good explanation for why the nations involved went to war, what they hoped to gain from it, and why they did not stop fighting after it became clear that the war was a losing proposition. It was the costliest war in human history, with an additional 31 million men dead, missing, or wounded.

Moreover, it was no real war in a conventional sense, as neither side had anything to gain, and indeed did not gain anything.

Flights of Fancy

Only two decades earlier, at the beginning of the twentieth century, a spirit of optimism had reigned:

> When the twentieth century opened, humanity was informed that it could make machines that would fly through the air. The whole prospect and outlook of mankind grew immeasurably larger, and the multiplication of ideas also proceeded at an incredible rate.
> —Winston Churchill

It was on December 17, 1903, not long after the turn of the century, that Orville and Wilbur Wright demonstrated that the long-held promise of air transportation was indeed real. On the windswept banks of North Carolina, for the first time in history, an airplane got off the ground and completed a controlled flight.

By 1919, great strides had been made in the design and manufacture of both airplanes and tanks. But was mankind better or worse off than it had been in 1914? Considering the devastation caused in World War I, we can hardly reply affirmatively. The promise of air power had been very real. Airplanes worked . . . but only a few decades later, in World War II, they were used to even more destructive ends, dropping explosives over London, even striking Churchill's wartime bunker.

"We took it almost for granted that science would confer continual boons and blessings upon us," Churchill explained. But it "was not accompanied by any noticeable advance in the stature of man, either in his mental faculties or his moral character. His brain got no better, but it buzzed the more . . . Our codes of honour, morals and manners, the passionate convictions which so many hundreds of millions share together of the principles of freedom and justice, are far more precious to us than anything which scientific discoveries could bestow."

Man had grown too confident for his own good, Churchill concluded: "While he nursed the illusion of growing mastery and exulted in his new trappings, he became the sport and presently the victim of tides and currents, of whirlpools and tornadoes amid which he was far more helpless than he had been for a long time."

At the end of World War I, there were nearly 8 million dead, more than 21 million wounded, and nearly 2 million missing,[2] but that was just the start. The twentieth-century wars were just beginning.

Industrial-Scale Slaughter

Prior to the French Revolution and industrialization, wars were much more limited. Armies would take the field for short periods of time— usually in the summer, when roads were passable and before the harvests. They would do their mischief and then go home. There were few popular wars. Instead, conflicts were between groups of people whose lands and lives were immediately threatened—by an invasion of barbarians from the East, for example. More often, they were localized rivalries—one monarch against another, duking it out with a relatively small number of paid mercenaries. In 1066, William the Conqueror (formerly known as William the Bastard) took all of England with a force of only about 5,000 men.

In the twentieth century, by contrast, wars involved huge numbers of combatants. Even noncombatants were called on to play support roles. In World War II, American women were called out of the home to work in aircraft plants and take up jobs formerly done by men. Whole populations were mobilized and enlisted in the war efforts, which were far more costly in lives and money than any wars in history, despite the fact that these wars often seemed to serve no other domestic purpose than to lead the way to ruin.

Why did such wars occur in the last century and not before? We have two answers. The first is the standard one: Never before was savagery on such a scale possible. It took industrial economies, abetted by ever innovative technology, to produce industrial-scale wars. The second: Never before was it possible for so many people to share so many bad ideas all at once. Thanks to progress in communications, men and women were drawn to group thinking like moths to a flame. Soon, they were talking all sorts of nonsense and making their own lives miserable with wars and upheavals that contributed nothing to their well-being, other than being a distraction from their personal problems.

The Internet was not such a revolution as the New Era dreamers had come to believe. The price of communications had been dropping for the past 200 years—from the telegraph, to telephone and radio, to television, to CB radio. These, coupled with cheap newsprint, increased the availability of information to nearly everyone, but they also made much bigger mobs possible, and bigger bubbles, too. Instead of reducing violence in international politics, cheaper communications increased it. At the beginning of the century, railroads, telegraph, and popular newspapers made possible the biggest, most costly war in all human history—with far more people involved than ever before. By the century's end, the Internet and television made possible the biggest bubble ever—with much greater public participation than at any time in history.

MILLENNIAL OPTIMISTS

"Despite all that's wrong with the world, things are getting better all the time. Somehow, over time, the opportunities overwhelm the difficulties," wrote Porter Stansberry, in the summer 2001 issue of his newsletter.[3] Thus, did he place himself among a large group of millennial optimists, technophiles, and free-market True Believers including George Gilder, Paul O'Neill, James Glassman, Lawrence Kudlow, Michael Murphy, and just about every other right-thinking Republican and Democrat in the Western World. All of them were sure that the forward march of progress was inevitable and irreversible.

"Most people are richer today than they were 100 years ago,"[4] said Stansberry. And they live longer. This seems to prove the case. Surely people will be even richer and longer-lived in the future, won't they? Maybe yes, maybe no. God may have whispered in Stansberry's ear and revealed His plans. Then again, maybe not.

At the end of the nineteenth century, it had also seemed—as it did at the end of the 20th—that progress was inevitable. People expected progress in every aspect of life. The world's economies were booming. The Industrial Revolution was in full throttle and spreading its smoky aroma throughout the world. A person could already hop on a train in

Paris and ride in luxury all the way to Moscow. A man in London could order his spiced tea from the Orient and his carpets from Istanbul. Was there any reason to believe that this bounty—products of new technology, free markets, and enlightened political steward-ship—would not continue?

By the end of the nineteenth century, the overt use of torture had disappeared in the Western world and slavery had been completely abolished in civilized countries. It seemed—at the height of the *Belle Époque*—that manners, art, and personal security were improving. Moreover, as Europe had enjoyed nearly three decades without a major war, there was a widespread belief that war was a thing of the past, not of the future.

Yet, only a few years later, the world began walking backward, and the most costly and barbarous wars in history began. Between 1914 and 1919, France lost 20 percent of her young men of military age—and the century had scarcely begun! With hardly a pause for breath, from 1914 to 1945, people shot, tortured, murdered, blew up, poi-soned, and starved each other on a scale the world had never seen.

The twentieth century turned out to be a period of what Brzezinski called "megadeath," with an estimated 187 million victims. By 1945, all of the world's major economies—save one, that of the United States—were in ruins. Japan, the Soviet Union, and Germany were little more than heaps of ash and twisted metal. France and Britain were mostly intact, but geared up for war, not for peacetime produc-tion. Worse, both were in the hands of socialists and syndicalists, which so inhibited their recovery that they were soon overtaken by their for-mer enemies—Germany and Japan. Progress is never guaranteed, nei-ther material nor moral.

The Rape of Nanking

Like it or not, the world is still ruled largely by the heart: It is full of sin and sorrow, sturm und drang, madness, and the kindness of strangers. It is a world whose history, as Voltaire observed, is "a collection of the crimes, follies and misfortunes" of mankind. On December 13, 1937, the Japanese Imperial Army made history. Previous records in deprav-ity were broken when the devil worked overtime for a six-week period. When it was over, an estimated 377,000 people had been slaughtered.

The victims were not soldiers of the Reich or draftees of the Kremlin. They were men, women, and children of all ages and party affiliations. Democrats. Catholics. Confucians. Bricklayers. . . . They shared one common mistake—they were in the wrong place at the wrong time. These people were not obliterated in an impersonal air raid, such as the 60,000 thought to have been killed at Dresden or the 200,000 killed at Nagasaki and Hiroshima. Nor were they killed methodically and systematically as the Nazis and Bolsheviks usually did with their victims. Instead, they were put to death one by one, or in small groups, after being tortured, degraded, and made to suffer as much as the killers' imagination made possible.

Butchery. Barbarity. Bestiality. It is hard to describe what happened in words that do it justice.

When the Roman legions destroyed Carthage, they took the lives of about 150,000. Timur Lenk killed 100,000 prisoners at Delhi in 1398. He built towers of skulls in Syria in 1400. Yet no cameras recorded the spectacles. Meanwhile, the photos in Iris Chang's book, *The Rape of Nanking*, provide evidence against those who believe in the inevitability of moral progress. The event in question occurred more than 100 years after the Rights of Man had been declared. And nearly two millennia after the birth of the Prince of Peace. The prohibition against murder was well-established in all major religions. Of course, the victims would have welcomed murder—it would have been a comfort, like a stop loss in a bear market.

Japan is one of the world's most law-abiding and polite societies. But storms of evil blow up from time to time. No race or nation is beyond their reach.

Papa Trapp's Tears

Those who believe in the perfectibility of man have a lot of explaining to do. For nothing in all history rivals the imperfections revealed within the lifetimes of many people reading this book. During World War II, victims were dispatched systematically in large-scale operations that required extensive organization and planning by great numbers of people, every one of whom should have known better.

None of this will come as news or a surprise to the reader. What is surprising is that the average person, when the question is put to him, takes for granted that mankind is making moral as well as material progress. Perhaps the average person is right. There are many more humans around today than there were 1,000 years ago. And maybe—like personal hygiene and average height—there might be a slight upward creep in the public's moral stature. But at the least, progress is subject to elemental convulsions that should keep us on our guard.

"The Polish town of Bilgoraj, at dawn on July 13, 1942." Thus, begins Christopher Browning's book, *Ordinary Men,* illustrating the extraordinary things an ordinary man might do. That morning, the men of Germany's 101st battalion of police reserves had a strange job to do. Their commander, a man affectionately known to the troops as "Papa Trapp," was so disturbed by the nature of their assignment that he stood before his men with tears in his eyes. He choked up and could barely control his voice as he explained to the troops that they were supposed to eliminate the entire Jewish population of the city. Able-bodied men were to be shipped off to labor camps. Women, children, and old men—all of them— were to be shot.

The soldiers of the 101st police battalion were not impressionable young fools or Nazi zealots, they were older men, with families of their own. The police battalions were not frontline fighters. They were made up of mature men, who often enlisted in the police brigades so that they might do the work of homeland security and avoid combat far from their homes.

Delivering their orders, Papa Trapp then made his men an incredible proposition: If any of the older ones did not feel that they were capable of taking part in the mission, they could be excused from duty. Trapp then resorted to reason. He reminded himself and his soldiers of the logic of their mission. The Jews represented a threat to German troops. They had pillaged. They supported terrorists!

Hitler had promised to turn his conquests in the East into a "Garden of Eden." He was happy, he explained, that Stalin had begun a terrorist campaign against German forces using partisan fighters to cause trouble behind the lines. "That gives us a reason to exterminate all those who are hostile to us," said the Führer. "Naturally, this vast country must be pacified as soon as possible, which is what we are doing by shooting anyone who dares even to look at us the wrong way."

This was a war against Bolshevism, the Nazis explained. Jews were to be liquidated, not merely because they were Jews, but because they were Bolsheviks. It all must have made sense to the ordinary men who carried out the systematic murders. But not everyone went along. At least one man did refuse to take part. A lieutenant from Hamburg, Heinz Bachmann, said he would have nothing to do with murdering women and children. He was reassigned.

Trapp, himself, did what he considered his duty. But he was shaken by it and avoided the scene of the killing. Witnesses reported seeing him crying like a child. One heard him ask himself why he had been given this dirty assignment. Another heard him comment, "If this isn't avenged on Earth . . . may God have pity on us Germans."

Nothing Fails Like Success

Readers used to economics texts or financial books may find our discussion of military history out of place. Not at all. It is in war that we see most plainly what mischief humans can do. Even the most "rational" men go mad from time to time—in love and war, markets and economics. With luck, they are beaten back before they have an opportunity to do much damage. A real genius, on the other hand, with a mob at his back, can succeed to the point of disaster.

We humans flatter ourselves. Endowed with the power to reason, we believe ourselves superior to the rest of the animal kingdom. But, along the road to Moscow, every dog, horse, rat, and cow that saw Napoleon's grande armée or Hitler's Wehrmacht pass must have had better sense. Even a field mouse might be said to have been better programmed than a field marshal. Scurrying to safety as the troops passed, did these lowly, furry rodents foresee that they would later gnaw at the bones of fallen soldiers, or at the frostbitten fingers of sleeping ones?

The fall of Louis XVI had brought a new era to Europe. France's aristocrats had fled for their lives—agitating Europe's remaining monarchs to intervene in France and restore them to their positions and property. The unrest had reached fever level after the revolutionaries sliced off the heads of Louis and his Austrian wife, Marie Antoinette. All over Europe, aristocrats felt for their own necks and decided to take action.

Eighteenth-century France had some advantages that the modern American reader will appreciate. Gross domestic product (GDP) growth in France was perhaps the strongest in the world. Though France had begun the century trailing England, at the end of the 1700s, it was ahead. What's more, France's population was exploding. Higher production helped feed more little Jean-Lucs and Marie-Hélènes. Soon, the country was crawling with them.

But France had another hidden advantage: It was the first country in Europe to take full advantage of popular democracy. Who would be willing to die for a monarch? How much of your revenue would you have surrendered to a Louis, a Henry, or a Franz Ferdinand?

The armies of Franz II, emperor of Austria (also Marie Antoinette's nephew) were pros. They were kept in the field by money and threats of force. That was the style of the times—until the Revolution. Like the American one that had preceded it, the French Revolution of 1789 turned subjects into citizens and then took advantage of them as never before.

Only a few years after the Revolution, Napoleon Bonaparte, a 26-year-old Corsican artillery commander, took charge of the First Italian campaign in 1796. In a few months of hard fighting, he proved that he had a genius for war and became a popular hero throughout France. There were no approval ratings at the time, but had there been polls, Napoleon would surely have ranked near the top for the next 19 years.

In a series of wars and battles, alliances and misalliances, Napoleon's big battalions gradually brought the rest of Europe to heel. By 1812, all of the Continent, save Russia and Great Britain, was at his feet. France was enjoying a boom. It was Europe's biggest country, boasted the continent's most powerful army, and its new form of government was proving far more efficient at squeezing blood out of its population of turnips. France was Europe's only superpower in the early nineteenth century.

At this point, nothing could stop Napoleon. So, everything did.

He had installed his brother as King of Spain. But the Spanish resisted and began a war of terror against French troops. Then, Napoleon attacked Russia. Only a man with a genius for war could have done such a remarkably imbecilic thing. An ordinary man's ambitions would have been checked long before.

The Baron de Marbot records a remarkable scene in his memoirs of the Napoleonic wars:

[The Emperor] wanted to question several French officers who had spent some time in Russia and knew its topography and resources. Among them, he found Lt. Col. de Ponthon, who had been one of the officers, after the Treaty of Tilsitt, sent by Napoleon, to spend a few years in the service of Alexander [Tsar of Russia]. De Ponthon was both very capable and very modest.

Attached to Napoleon's topographical service, he had not dared, spontaneously, to offer his advice on the difficulties an army would encounter in conducting a war in Russia; but when the Emperor questioned him, de Ponthon, a man of honor, devoted to his country, believed he must tell the full truth to the head of state, so without worrying about displeasing him, he described all the obstacles that lay in Napoleon's path. The major ones were: the unreliability of the Lithuanians [who would provide French forces with their base of operations]; the fanatical resistance of Moscow's defenders; the lack of supplies and forage for the horses; the barren territory French troops would have to cross; roads that became impassable for the artillery after a couple of hours of rain. He emphasized most heavily the rigors of the Russian winter and the physical impossibility of making war after the snows began, often in the first days of October. Finally, at the risk of displeasing the Emperor and compromising his future, the courageous Col. de Ponthon got down on his knees and begged Napoleon, in the name of the well-being of France and his own glory, not to undertake this dangerous campaign, whose calamities he correctly foresaw.

The Emperor, after having listened calmly, excused Col. de Ponthon, without making any response.

A few weeks later, Napoleon began his march on Moscow with more than 300,000 troops, gradually discovering all of the difficulties that de Ponthon had described. A decisive victory by the Russians early in the campaign would have been a blessing for the French. The army might have licked its wounds, swallowed its pride, and recrossed the Neimen River to safety. But the French fought so well they practically exterminated themselves. Arriving in Moscow, Napoleon's troops made an unpleasant discovery: The Russian army had begun a campaign of terror. The city was on fire; there was nowhere to lodge French soldiers for the winter and nothing to feed them.

The Grande Armée of the Republic retreated, harassed at every step by the weather—which turned unseasonably cold unseasonably fast—and by Russian terrorists. Only a few of Napoleon's soldiers made it out of Russia alive.

Soon, France's many enemies were attacking from all sides. Napoleon, the Hero of Italy, was defeated; and France was occupied by foreign troops.

The 1870 War with Germany

France went to war with Germany in August 1870. You can read the history of it and you still won't know why the countries went to war. But the flags came out, the recruiting offices filled, and soon the troops were on the road to the Rhine.

According to Alistair Horne in his account of the war, it would have been hard to find a "more dramatic instance of what the Greeks called peripeteia, or reversal of fortune" in all history.[5]

So confident were the forces under Louis Napoleon that commanders were outfitted with maps of Germany, but none of France. Alas, a bear market in French confidence was about to begin. From epic levels of pride, the French were about to fall to epic levels of despair.

After a couple of minor battles, the French were in retreat and dead soldiers were scattered throughout the countryside. The army was driven back to Sedan and trapped. For the French general MacMahon, the French army was caught in a "chamber pot" and would "soon be in sh**."

Defeated, the Emperor was taken prisoner and Paris besieged. By Christmas, people in the city were starving. "We ate Aunt Reinburg's cat," wrote Berthe Cavaille on December 29. "It's a shame because it was such a pretty animal! . . . I have a piece of dog meat I'm going to marinate and eat like a steak."[6]

Toward the end, one of France's leaders, Leon Gambetta, escaped in a balloon. And finally, the French came to their senses, gave up, and waved a white flag.

Nothing Succeeds Like Failure

Losing the war turned out to be as good as winning it. Following its defeat, France enjoyed the four greatest decades of its history.

The country boomed. People got rich. Property values rose, and people tried to outdo each other by building ever more beautiful and extravagant houses.

Restaurants and bistros overflowed. Artists and performers were drawn to the city like black flies to garbage. Huge sections of Paris were razed and reconstructed, the subway was built, the Eiffel Tower went up, and the *Belle Époque* polished Western civilization to a shine we have not seen since.

But in the years following France's defeat in 1871, its military leaders studied the war and plotted their return to glory. France had lost the war, but its madness had not been entirely exterminated. What had they done wrong, they asked themselves? They came to the conclusion that they had been too cautious, that they should have gone over to the offensive and launched more wild charges. This idea was supported by Colonel de Grandmaison: "In the offensive, imprudence is the best of assurances," *raved de Grandmaison,* "Let us go even to excess and that perhaps will not be far enough . . ." Soon a perfectly good tactic was elevated to a bad strategy.

Forty-four years after Sedan, the French army tried out its new strategy. Once again, no one was quite sure why World War I had begun, or what anyone hoped to gain from it. All of the parties to the war seemed to act sensibly, according to the standards of the day. The flags were flying and the recruiting offices were again full. And the French attacked at the Battle of the Frontiers in August 1914.

With the unthinking enthusiasm of a moonstruck lover, they charged. Within two weeks, France had lost 300,000 men and 1 out of every 10 of its officers. Within the first five months, France lost as many men as all U.S. casualties in World War II. Within the first year, more Frenchmen were lost than U.S. losses in both World War I and World War II. And there were three more years to go. By the end of it, more than 6 million French would be casualties.

And for what? No one knew.

LA DÉBÂCLE DE 1940

Nothing much happens in Bremo Bluff, Virginia. It is little more than a bend in the road; the small town offers little in the way of diversion, which leaves a man plenty of time to think. Thus, with time on his hands, Bevin Alexander, a Bremo Bluff resident and military historian, wondered about World War II and how it might have turned out differently.

At the time, the French had, on paper, the strongest army in Europe. But their tactics were 20 years out of date. It was a new era in warfare and only a handful of military men, mostly in the Wehrmacht, realized it. Had the French not been such blockheads, one could argue, World War II would never have developed as it did. The Germans would have attacked, but they would have met effective resistance and the balance of power in Europe would have been maintained.

But errors are inevitable and seem to come along just when they are needed—to upset the balance of nature and to restore it. It was no more possible for the combatants of World War II to avoid making mistakes than it was for investors in the Great Bubble of 1995 to 2000.

As events happened two generations ago, the Germans attacked where they were not expected . . . and in a manner the French had never seen. Tank commanders such as Heinz Guderian and Erich Rommel cut through the French line and then kept going, not supporting the infantry as the French expected, but operating independently. They moved so fast and showed up in places so far from where they were supposed to be that Rommel's group became known as the "ghost division." Not only were French and British forces unable to respond effectively—they had no idea how to respond. They did not know where the enemy was, what he was doing, or even why he was doing it.

In a few weeks, the French army collapsed. Soldiers threw down their weapons and fled. The French government, in a panic, saw the situation as hopeless and surrendered. The British, along with a few remnants of the French forces, were driven into the sea at Dunkirk.

By February of the following year, the Battle of Britain had already been waged—with an inconclusive result. Churchill had rallied his nation—at the last moment—and, barely, fended off the German assault. Rommel was in North Africa preparing his Deutsche Afrika Korps and a series of breathtaking victories. The German Army was preparing an invasion of Yugoslavia and Greece.

In 1941, the entire world map might have been regarded as a game board—with national forces aligned, arrayed, in motion or *hors de combat* such as the shifting fortunes of the players decreed.

What Goes Around . . .

Life is competitive. People compete alone and in groups—in sports, politics, fashion, sex, business, and economics. In the 1940s, nation-state competition had reached a frenzy—an episodic peak. Germany did this. Russia did that. Greece did such and such. Britain did something else. For a few years, almost everyone and everything in Europe was brought into the game. A person could be conscripted into a labor battalion, sent to the front lines in combat, or herded into a cattle car and shipped to an extermination camp. Politics was a game of force played for mortal stakes.

In just a few months, Hitler had put together an empire that dominated Europe. The Germans occupied half of France. From this line through central France, Germans controlled all the territory of Europe to the center of Poland in the east, and from Norway in the north down to the tip of Greece and the island of Crete in the Mediterranean (and large sections of Africa, too).

But empires that rise up quickly, like bull markets, tend to collapse quickly, too. Napoleon's empire lasted only 16 years. The Thousand Year Reich was destroyed within just four years after Hitler attacked the Soviet Union.

Nature loves symmetry and balance. Draw a line through the center of a leaf, for example, and you will find that it is the same on both sides. And the sea level is the same in San Francisco as it is in Odessa, even though they are on opposite sides of the earth.

Charts of market manias tend to be symmetrical. Sharp upward spikes on the left-hand side are mirrored by sharp downward spikes on the right. Long, gentle inclines on the left are usually followed by long, gentle declines on the right.

This tendency toward balance and symmetry is shadowed in the political world, too. The Roman Empire, which took centuries to build, also took centuries to dismantle. Likewise, the Third Reich, the subject of Bevin Alexander's book, *How Hitler Could Have Won World War II*, was created in just a few years, and it was destroyed in just a few more (see Figure 2.1).

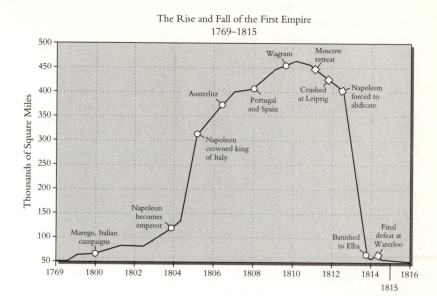

The Rise and Fall of the First Empire
1769–1815

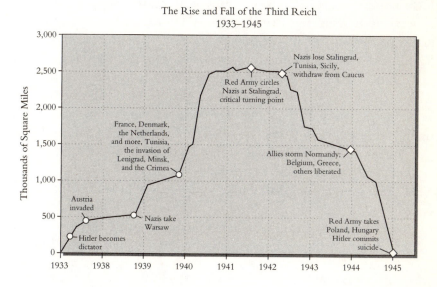

The Rise and Fall of the Third Reich
1933–1945

FIGURE 2.1 Empires, Like Markets, Rise and Fall

They Had It Coming

People get not what they expect from their investments but what they deserve. Quick profits are lost just as quickly. Little gains, accumulated over many years, tend to remain for many years. If it were not so, everyone would always go for the quick gains. And if that were to happen, the gains would disappear like the grass on a lush island that is suddenly overrun by herds of grazing animals.

Hitler's military adventures brought Germany some very quick gains. But ultimately, Germany got something very different from what it expected but very close to what it may have deserved.

Alexander attributes this to human error. First, Hitler failed to destroy the British Expeditionary Force at Dunkirk when he could easily have done so. Then, he failed to destroy the Royal Air Force, which he also could have done. The RAF was near collapse when Hitler switched the air campaign toward bombing Central London. How Hitler made this decision was typical of his amateurish approach to warfare. In attacking British air installations, a couple of Luftwaffe planes had gotten lost and mistakenly dropped their bombs on London. The British retaliated with a raid on Berlin. This so angered the Führer that he decided to bomb London until Britain lost its will to fight. The opposite happened. While the Luftwaffe lost planes damaging London, the RAF was able to rebuild. And the bombs on London merely strengthened British resolve to fight to the end, and gave Londoners a taste for bomb alerts that they have relished ever after.

Then, says Alexander, Hitler failed to attack the British base at Malta, diverting his target to Crete, which was of little military significance. And he failed to give Rommel the minimal support he needed to take the Suez Canal, which would have sealed off the Eastern Mediterranean (and quick passage to the east) to the British fleet.

Annihilate Me

But his most monumental error was his attack on Russia. As historians had noticed, following Napoleon's and, before that, Sweden's attempted invasion: Russia was an easy country to get into, but a hard one to get out of.

Hitler's blunder broke every rule of military strategy. This, combined with his declaration of war on the United States after Pearl

Harbor, put him in the position of fighting the three largest industrial powers on the planet—with his troops spread out over thousands of miles toward every point of the compass. And if that were not bad enough, he then proceeded to carry out the campaign in Russia with such lunatic incompetence that even the Soviet Army was eventually able to destroy him.

But at first, the German army performed so well, and the Soviet Army so badly, that Zhukov seemed unable to accept the invitation. It almost seemed like the ancient rules of warfare no longer applied to this new battle. The Germans attacked over dry ground against an enemy as foolish and incompetent as Hitler himself.

Still, Hitler had gotten himself into a war of attrition that could only end badly. The Soviets produced four tanks to every one Germany produced. The tanks rolled off the assembly line at the Dzershezinsky Tractor Plant in Stalingrad and other places and were in action in a matter of hours. Hitler's tanks could take weeks or months to reach the front line—if they ever reached it.

Finally, the weather changed, and it became clear that the campaign was doomed. Not only that, it became clear, too, that Germany was doomed. The Russians could not be stopped. And Hitler would not make peace. As his generals reported the devastating news from the front, Hitler removed them, labeling them overtly pessimistic and "cowards" who "lacked drive." He even took out Heinz Guderian, the best tank commander in the army.

What these professional soldiers really needed, the Führer believed, was the "glow of National Socialist conviction." But the "glow of National Socialist conviction" would not stop a T-34 tank anymore than faith in a "New Era" would stop a bear market in the Nasdaq.

In the Bath

We play with fire. We play with war. And then, fire and war blow up on us. America, until now, enjoyed the luxury of watching things from a distance. It offered its advice, lavishly . . . its homilies . . . its encouragement to the "little people" of the world. Now, America is "in the bath" along with the rest of the world. Now we will see. We will see if America is really the military, industrial, and social power that it claims to be. We're going to see if "America" really exists. Because it is no longer a matter of preaching, while taking orders and grabbing market share. It's no longer a matter of exhorting others to acts of heroism. Now, America must fight. And send Americans to risk their skins. Things have changed. We're going to see . . .

> —Marcel Deat, writing in the collaborationist French newspaper *L'Oeuvre*, December 9, 1941

Mr. Deat sounded skeptical.

When the Japanese bombed Pearl Harbor, Americans knew the "luxury of watching things from a distance" would no longer be possible. Unlike the patriots of 2001, they prepared for sacrifice, not self-indulgence. They braced themselves for hardships and losses. Rather than buy a new Packard, they were likely to put the old one in the garage and walk to work. Gasoline was rationed. So was almost everything else. Stocks fell to a level never seen before—and changed hands for just six times earnings.

Things had changed; America was in the bath with everyone else. People do stupid things regularly and mad things occasionally. And sometimes, the impulse to self-destruction is so overwhelming that it overtakes an entire nation. It is almost always madness to buy stocks at the peak of a bull market, or to buy a stock at 50 times earnings. Ruin may not come quickly because stocks may rise further. But it comes eventually. The best a person can hope for when he goes mad is that he runs into a brick wall quickly . . . before he has a chance to build up speed. That is why success, in war and investing, is often a greater menace than failure.

U.S. troops at Pearl Harbor were witness to one of the stupidest, maddest acts in all of history. The Japanese had embarked on a campaign of conquest. Rampaging through China and Indochina, they found success easy. Encouraged, they sought to extend Japanese hegemony, by force of arms, throughout Southeast Asia.

What was the point of the military expansion, you may wonder. To secure vital resources—oil, rubber, metals—is the answer. Why did Japan need so many raw materials? To supply its military expansion!

The Japanese had little in the way of raw materials. Of course, they could buy them on the open market. But in the politicized world of the twentieth century, markets seemed unreliable. What if producers decided not to sell? Yet the idea was absurd. Why would producers not sell, when it was in their interest to do so? In fact, the only reason they did not sell was to try to cripple Japanese military expansion! Thus, the Roosevelt Administration, in early 1941, cut off vital supplies—especially oil—to the Japanese war machine.

What were the Japanese to do? For nearly 10 years, they had been "on a roll" of military success. Were they not entitled to believe that their stock would always rise? But attacking Pearl Harbor was a big risk. The Japanese knew what they were up against—a country far larger and with far more resources than their own. Admiral Yamamoto had attended Harvard and spent years in Washington as a naval attaché. Even so, he was no fool—he knew that Japan could not endure a long contest with the United States.

How much better off the Japanese would have been if they had been beaten in China! They could have gone back to their island, renounced the Tripartite Treaty with Germany and Italy, and then could have taken the orders and grabbed market share—selling tanks, planes, and ships to other combatants. Instead, a long string of battlefield successes led to one of the biggest strategic blunders of all time . . . and ultimately to complete ruin for Japan and her economy.

Before the attack on Pearl Harbor, Americans were deeply divided on the war. Most wanted nothing to do with it. A one-year draft law passed Congress by a single vote just months before the attack. Japan could have conquered any Dutch, British, or French colonial territory in the Far East without risking war with the United States. Of all the things Japan might have done, it chose the worst possible course of action. It did the one thing—and probably the only thing—that would bring America into the war as an active, determined combatant.

Admiral Yamamoto recognized his error almost immediately: "We have . . . instilled in [the sleeping giant] a terrible resolve." Churchill meanwhile was ecstatic: "To have the United States at our side was to me the greatest joy. Now at this very moment I knew the United States was in the war, up to the neck and in to the death. So we had won after all! Hitler's fate was sealed. Mussolini's fate was sealed. As for the Japanese, they would be ground to powder."[7]

Twelve days later—on December 11—the German leader proved that he was at least as mad as his Japanese counterpart, by declaring war on the United States. He could have left the Japanese to their folly. Instead, in less than two weeks, the Tripartite Powers had managed to turn the war against themselves in provoking the wrath of the world's largest economy. The United States, protected by two oceans, could turn out jeeps, tanks, planes, and C rations faster than anyone. It could put millions of troops in the field, fully equipped, and bring to bear more bombs against a target than any nation ever.

But in 1941, Axis military power had been in a bull market for nearly a decade. People do not think clearly in a bull market. And their imaginations are dull. They can only see ahead of them what they have just experienced. It was not until the battles of Midway and Stalingrad, both in 1942, that Axis power peaked out. Then, the thinking began, and imaginations began to work again. But by then it was too late.

"All the world is moral" wrote Emerson. Money and markets as well as politics and war. And for every sin is a suitable punishment. In war, the sins are capital and the consequences tragic. Markets are more entertaining: Their sins are comic; their results are often pure farce.

THE SMART MONEY

In August 1998, Bill Krasker, John Meriwether, and two men who had just won the Nobel Prize in Economics, Myron Scholes and Robert Merton, were deeply concerned about swap spreads. Their computer models had told them that the spreads might move about a point or so on an active day. But on that Friday, the spreads were bouncing all over the place.

This was bad news for the Long Term Capital Management (LTCM) hedge fund managers. They had as much as $1 trillion in exposure to various positions. Most of their positions were bets that prices in the future would regress to historic means. Prices that seemed out of kilter with past patterns, reasoned the geniuses at LTCM, would sooner or later come back to more familiar levels (see Figure 2.2).

The LTCM team was making history. They had an edge. They were the smartest people on the planet and everyone knew it. The money they were making—as much as 40 percent per year since the fund began—just proved it. It was hailed as a new "computer age," by *BusinessWeek*, and the professors were its masters.[8] Scholes and Merton were driving fancy new cars. "Merton had dyed his hair red, left his wife and moved into a snazzy pad in Boston," Roger Lowenstein

Long Term Capital Management
1994–1998

FIGURE 2.2   Nothing Fails Like Success
At its peak, Long Term Capital Management's balance sheet was in excess of $100 billion. But the firm was leveraged to the very limit with more than 1.25 trillion in derivative contracts.

reported in his book, *When Genius Failed*. The whole world—and the world's money—seemed to lay at their feet.

The professors' insight was as useful as it was obvious: An investment that is unusually cheap—or unusually expensive—represents a form of potential financial energy. Sooner or later, it will be less unusual.

Their mistake was obvious, too; they thought that the world was more reasonable than it actually is and assumed that "regression to the mean" applied only to markets. Bond prices might regress to the mean, but so would the professors' reputations and their investors' fortunes. Regression to the mean modestly predicts that things usually return to where they usually are. Few things are excluded.

The professors presumed that spreads between, say long bonds and short ones, or between Italian bonds and German ones, were like throws of the dice. Will the spreads widen or narrow? You could look at the historical record, they believed, and compute the odds. If current prices seemed out of line with the odds, they took it as an absurdity and bet that prices would be less absurd in the future.

And maybe they would. But as Keynes once noted, the market can stay irrational longer than an investor or a business can stay solvent.

From Silk Purse to Sow's Ear

Solvency became a big problem at LTCM because the geniuses had borrowed heavily. "If you aren't in debt," writes Lowenstein, "you can't go broke and can't be made to sell, in which case 'liquidity' is irrelevant. But a leveraged firm may be forced to sell, lest fast-accumulating losses put it out of business. Leverage always gives rise to this same brutal dynamic, and its dangers cannot be stressed too often."

On September 23, 1998, William J. McDonough, president of the New York Federal Reserve Bank, brought together the heads of America's biggest banks along with representatives of several large foreign banks. It was an unusual thing to do. In fact, it had never been done before. But the Fed feared the collapse of Long Term Capital Management might expose the banks to a level of "systemic risk" that had never been seen before. LTCM knew that it had to reduce its positions, but it couldn't—not with the market under strain. Despite the ballyhooed growth in derivatives, the credit markets had no liquidity. This is not surprising when everyone wants out at the same time.

"In September, 1998," continues Roger Lowenstein's account of the fall of Long Term Capital Management, "traders were becoming acutely aware of risk. Spreads between 'safe' Treasury bonds and less safe corporate or foreign bonds were spreading. In the crowded theatre of the bond trading, all the players seemed to come to the same conclusion at the same time. Rushing for the exits . . . they posed a danger not only to themselves, but to the entire world financial system."

Lowenstein explains what happens when Mr. Market becomes unreasonable: "When losses mount, leveraged investors such as Long Term are forced to sell, lest their losses overwhelm them. When a firm has to sell in a market without buyers, prices run to the extremes beyond the bell curve. To take just one example, yields on News Corporation bonds, which had recently been trading at 110 points over Treasury's, bizarrely soared to 180 over, even though the company's prospects had not changed one iota. In the long run, such a spread might seem absurd. But long-term thinking is a luxury not always available to the highly leveraged; they may not survive that long."

Lowenstein was describing what statisticians call a "fat tail." A bell curve ought to be perfect—as perfect as the Nobel Prize winners thought the market itself was. In fact, the market is not perfect in a mathematical sense or logical sense. It is only perfect in a moral sense; it gives people more or less what they deserve.

At the extremes, prices no longer follow a logical pattern. Investors become irrationally exuberant when prices reach their peaks at one end of the curve, and they become desperately fearful at the other end. Very few stocks, for example, should ever be extremely expensive or extremely cheap, and normally, very few are either. But at the dark ends of the bell curve, fear and greed haunt the markets, making prices run in unpredictable ways. Investors buy stocks at ludicrous prices at the top and sell them at equally ludicrous prices at the bottom. The tails—on both sides of the bell curve—are fattened by absurdities. But people are free to believe anything they want. And from time to time, they almost all come to believe the same thing. In the mid-1990s, professors were winning Nobel Prizes for showing how markets were perfect and how risk-reward ratios could be quantified as though an investment were a throw of dice or an actuarial table.

When you throw the dice, the odds of any given outcome can be calculated. And they are always the same. Whether you get snake eyes one time or a hundred times, the odds of rolling snake eyes the next time are the same. Dice have no memory. Investors do have memories but not much imagination. They shift the odds constantly, following their most recent experience. The period 1982 to 2000, for example, was marked by such generous stock market returns that investors came to expect them.

Prices are a function of confidence. When investors are confident, prices rise. When they are not, prices fall. But confidence, too, is mean-reverting. It took 18 years of rising stock prices to bring investor confidence to peak levels. It would take several years to beat it back down to the long-term mean. Neither most investors nor most Nobel Prize winners could imagine it, but the odds that the next 20 years would mimic the previous 20 were vanishingly small. When investors are spooked, Lowenstein explains, capital flows from riskier assets to less risky ones, no matter what their underlying value. In a real pinch, no one wants the riskiest investments.

Running Before Walking

Long Term Capital Management had been so sure of its computer models and so eager to squeeze out every possible bit of profit that it found itself in possession of the riskiest bets in the marketplace. But these were not cheap stocks it held. It could not just hunker down and wait for the market to return to its senses. Instead, LTCM held derivative contracts and other investments that neither paid dividends nor had any intrinsic value. What's more, thanks to its stellar reputation, it had been able to purchase its positions on nearly "no money down" terms. At one point, for every $100 in exposure, the fund held only $1 in equity. As little as a 1 percent move in market prices—in the wrong direction—would wipe it out.

In autumn 1998, the market was moving in the wrong direction every day. A fat tail had been reached in credit markets: All the traders seemed to want to get out of the very same positions at the very same time. The professors did not know what to make of it. It was a kind of volatility they did not understand.

The company had been named *Long Term* Capital Management, but just four years after it opened for business, its owners' backs were up against a wall of prices they had said would not be likely in more than a billion years. Their mathematical models, Lowenstein claims, showed the odds of this kind of market were "so freakish as to be unlikely to occur even once over the entire life of the universe and even over numerous repetitions of the Universe."

"The professors hadn't modeled this," Lowenstein wrote. "They had programmed the market for a cold predictability that it never had; they had forgotten the predatory acquisitive, and overwhelmingly protective instincts that govern real-life traders. They had forgotten the human factor."

They were right about regression to the mean. Things that are extremely out-of-whack eventually work their way back into whack. But then they diverge again, and the tails fatten. Sometimes prices diverge from the mean. Sometimes they regress toward it. Give yourself enough leverage and you can go broke in either direction. The geniuses at LTCM lost $4.5 billion—much of it their own money.

The banks lost money, too. They would have lost a lot more had they not come to the aid of LTCM . . . and the central bank not come to the aid of everyone by providing more credit. This new burst of credit was taken up by a new group of geniuses—such as those at Enron. Compared with Enron, LTCM was "like a lemonade stand,"[9] Frank Partnoy told a congressional committee when the subject came up, spectacularly, in spring 2001. Enron earned more in derivatives trading in a single year than LTCM did in its entire existence.

The New York Fed helped save the world from LTCM; but the Fed's effort was such a success that it set investors up for Enron . . . which cost them 16 times as much.

VALE OF TEARS

At a major top, both theory and experience lead investors to think that selling stocks would be a mistake. Not only had stocks been rising for the past two decades, other Nobel Prize–winning economists had recently proven that it never made sense to sell. The efficient market hypothesis, first put forward by Eugene Fama in the 1960s, was another of those fabulous theories worthy of Marx or Freud—profound and totally absurd at the same time.

The profundity lay deep in the details, but the absurdity is right on the surface. The gist of the concept is that markets are the expression of all the information and preferences available. They are, therefore, perfect: They reflect the agglomerated judgment of all market participants. By contrast, any single participant—a lone investor, for example—will have much less to go on. He may think that prices will rise or fall and "vote" with his money accordingly. But his judgment is deficient. He is wrong, and the market is right. The market cannot be wrong just as the will of voters cannot be wrong. Democracy admits to no higher authority than the will of the majority. Similarly, markets always give us the right price. Neither markets nor democracy could be improved upon; for they were both perfect. Again, history seemed to come to a stop.

But when a crowd comes to believe it has been touched by the grace of God, there is no stopping it. The worst that can happen is that its first efforts meet extraordinary success. Then, the bubble grows larger and larger—until it finally finds its pin.

Stability Produces Instability

"Whereas all capitalisms are flawed," wrote economist Hyman Minsky, "not all capitalisms are equally flawed."[10]

The obvious "flaw" in capitalism is that both the capitalists and the proletariat are all human. They are not Digital Men: They do not calmly measure the risk and calculate the return. Instead, they make their most important decisions—such as where to live, what to do, and with whom they will do it—not with their heads, but with their hearts.

A man gets married, for example, not after carefully toting up the pluses and minuses, as a machine might, but as a dumb beast of burden following instincts he will never understand. He lumbers into church as if he were going to war—that is, without a clue. Men do not usually go to the altar or to war after much rational calculation and reflection. Instead, they are swept along by whatever emotional currents come their way, and they risk their lives and their comforts for causes that, in the calm of retrospect, usually seem absurd. Caught up in whatever madness is fashionable, men do the most amazing things. But that is this vale of tears that we live in.

Minsky's *financial instability hypothesis* sets out to show how capitalism is inherently unstable. He might as well have set out to show that beer goes bad if you leave it to sit out too long or that children get cross if they do not get enough sleep. For capitalism, like life and death, is a natural thing; and like all things natural, it is unstable.

But what is interesting in Minsky's oeuvre is a little insight that might have been useful in the late 1990s. Among the delusions suffered by investors at the time was the notion that American capitalism had reached a stage of dynamic equilibrium and was constantly inventing new and more exciting means of making people rich. Booms and busts were thought to be a thing of the past for two reasons: First, because better information made it possible for businesses to avoid inventory buildups; and second, because the science of central bank management had attained a new level of enlightenment. It could now figure out precisely how much credit the economy wanted at any moment and make sure it got what it needed.

In the absence of the normal down phases of the business and credit cycles, the economy seemed more stable than ever before.

But Minsky noted that profit-seeking firms always try to leverage their assets as much as possible. He might have added that consumers do the same thing. Without fear of a recession or credit crunch, *Homo sapiens*, whether in the office or the den, were likely to overdo it. "Stability is destabilizing," Minsky concluded. Nothing fails like success, in other words.

Minsky refers to Keynes's concept of a "veil of money" between real assets and the ultimate owner of the wealth. Assets are often mortgaged, financed, leveraged, or otherwise encumbered. This veil of money gets thicker as financial life becomes more complex and makes it hard to see who is actually getting rich and who is not. When house prices rise, for example, it seems that the homeowner should be the beneficiary. But homeowners now own much less of their homes than they did a few years ago.

Fannie Mae, banks, and other intermediaries have a strong stake in home values. In recent years, Fannie Mae has worn a veil of money as sticky as flypaper. The hapless homeowners hardly had a chance. They got stuck almost immediately. Now, they are hopelessly glued and cannot get away.

Instead of coming up with innovative new ways to make people rich, the United States' financial intermediaries—notably Wall Street and Fannie Mae—came up with ways to make them poor.

"The financial instability hypothesis," Minsky explains, "is a theory of the impact of debt on system behavior and also incorporates the manner in which debt is validated. In contrast to the orthodox Quantity Theory of money, the financial instability hypothesis takes banking seriously as a profit-seeking activity. Banks seek profits by financing activity and bankers, like all entrepreneurs in a capitalist economy, are aware that innovation assures profits. Thus, bankers (using the term generically for all intermediaries in finance), whether they be brokers or dealers, are merchants of debt who strive to innovate in the assets they acquire and the liabilities they market."

The Vicious Circle of Credit

In Minsky's mind, capitalism is naturally unstable and needs government to stabilize it. Roughly, this is also the view of the Democratic Party. In the more orthodox economic view, capitalism is naturally stable and government destabilizes it. Traditionally, this is closer to the Republican Party view. But in the 1990s, even Republicans came to appreciate the stabilizing influence of Alan Greenspan. And by the fall of 2001, under pressure from the voters, both Republicans and Democrats cried out for "new policies" to fight the bear market and rescue the nation from deflation.

In the previous 15 years, public servant Alan Greenspan had exerted a stabilizing influence on world markets. When the markets needed credit, he gave it to them. As we discuss later in the book, this was his response to the Long Term Capital Management blow up. And the Asian economies. And then there was the Russian Default . . . and the Y2K Scare. Finally, there was the collapse of the Nasdaq and the Dow.

Greenspan met each new threat as he met the last one—by offering the market more credit. Each time, his intervention seemed to stabilize the market. And each time, the financial intermediaries found new and innovative ways to pad out the veil of money between assets and their beneficial owners. In the end, Greenspan's efforts were so successful that they led to the biggest economic disaster in world history.

"From time to time," Minsky elaborated in his financial instability hypothesis, "capitalist economies exhibit inflations and debt deflations which seem to have the potential to spin out of control. In such processes the economic system's reactions to a movement of the economy amplify the movement—inflation feeds upon inflation and debt-deflation feeds upon debt-deflation. Government interventions aimed to contain the deterioration seem to have been inept in some historical crises. In particular, over a protracted period of good times, capitalist economies tend to move from a financial structure dominated by hedge [conservative] finance units to a structure in which there is large weight to units engaged in speculative and Ponzi finance."

As we see in the following chapters, in Japan's boom of the 1980s, banks offered the Ponzi finance to their favorite corporate customers. More than a dozen years after the peak, the loans were still going bad, and threatened to bring down the banks themselves. During the United States' boom a decade later, it was consumer lenders—notably Fannie Mae and the credit card companies—who played Ponzi's role.

WHEN GENIUS FAILS . . . AND FAILS . . .
AND FAILS . . .

Over the last 30 years, Americans believed they were on top of the world. Everybody said so. And, logically, they should have been. It was post Reagan Revolution, with the most modern, most capitalistic economy in the world . . . with the latest technology, with the world's best brains, with the top schools, and with Wall Street to "allocate capital" in the best possible way. If workers couldn't get ahead in this economy, they couldn't get ahead anywhere. At least, that was what people believed.

But capitalism is a jungle, not a zoo. It lets animals get fat, but only so they can be eaten by hungrier beasts.

To us, it was fun listening to the conceits and pretensions of the zookeepers. At the end of the 1980s, they announced their triumph over communism, apparently unaware that their biggest potential rivals had just cut themselves loose from a ball and chain. It is not even 20 years later, and both Russia and China are already formidable competitors. China's reserves of foreign currency, for example, are nearly 20 times those of the United States. And now, if the Red Giant decides to dump dollars, America's economy will be hit by a major crisis . . . and possibly paralyzed.

Then, near the end of the 1990s, the dreamers thought they had found some magic formula. The United States no longer needs savings, said the pundits, because now our information technology allows us to create wealth using virtual capital . . . brain capital. "We think, they sweat" said one genius, as if the Chinese and Russians or the Brazilians and Indians . . . couldn't think, too.

After the dot-coms blew up, another hallucination developed. One that sophisticated financial engineering, combined with enlightened macroeconomic management, had made market crashes and recessions obsolete. The geniuses went to work with computers, proving that those fancy derivative contracts (which they were selling) were completely foolproof. They were supposed to run into problems only once in a blue moon. "You're talking about sigma 25 events," they said, as if they had a clue. Scarcely three years later, the moon was blue.

It was all great fun. Watching the show, that is. And it's not over.

Onerous Lines of Flimflam

In our years of reporting on the goings on of the economic world, we can say one thing for certain: People make the same mistakes over and over again, unaware that with each new movement comes a new set of delusions. The principle difference from one age to the next is the line of flimflam each falls for.

We bring with a brief rehearsal of what went wrong: The economy as it was before the spring of 2007 was too wonderful for words; whenever you tried to describe it, it sounded ridiculous. For example: "The richest get richer by borrowing from the poorest."

"We think; they sweat" sums up the relationship between the East and the West. The West was just recycling the East's "savings glut,"[11] added the new Federal Reserve Chairman Ben Bernanke. Meanwhile, derivatives—based on mortgage debt from people who couldn't pay— "helped to make the banking and overall financial system more resilient," said the International Monetary Fund (IMF) in 2006.[12]

Each sentence must have made the gods choke . . . groan . . . and then laugh. But beginning with revelations that all was not well at the investment bank Bear Stearns in early 2007, came a correction. Suddenly, the big spenders saw their houses fall in value. Lenders watched their collateral collapse. Though, at first, the problem was pronounced "largely contained"[13] by then U.S. Treasury Secretary Hank Paulson on April 7, 2007 . . . just three months later, Fed chairman Ben Bernanke admitted the crisis could bring losses "up to $100 billion."[14]

But there was no container large enough to hold the subprime losses. Each time one was set out, it quickly overflowed. Reports in March of 2009 told us the bilge was now 500 times deeper than the Fed had forecast . . . and still rising. And this comes after $11.7 trillion has been committed in the United States alone to pumping it out. Whether the plumbers are plain idiots or clever rogues, we can't say, but it should be obvious after two years of watching them that their pumps don't work.

Mortgage-Backed Temptation

In the waning glory days of the housing boom, we wondered if there was anyone in the United Kingdom or the United States who still lived within his means? Did anyone know where their means are?

Only occasionally did they even bother to find out—like a middle-age man hunting around in closets for an old tuxedo. Then, when he puts on the pants, he realizes he has outgrown them, he spills over the top and nearly splits the seat.

Of course, you couldn't blame people for not living within their means—the whole idea is as quaint as thrift . . . as antique as spats. New credit card offers came every day. And when the offer to buy a house for no-money-down on a teaser-rate ARM was right in front of you, allowing you to afford much more house than you thought you could—as least for a while—who could pass that up?

Most of the time, most people get by, just as most of the time, most people don't get themselves into serious trouble with the law. They know what they can get away with and what they can't. But occasionally, the old standards and guideposts get knocked down. Then, they run into trouble.

Junk bonds, margin buying, program trading, portfolio insurance—each one eventually leads to trouble. People get excited about it . . . they think it is the answer to their prayers . . . they think it is going to make them rich. They do it. And then they overdo it.

In 2007, the same was true for the innovation of easy mortgage credit. Now you can get a mortgage, apparently, over the Internet. Lender and borrower never meet. And then, of course, Wall Street created a whole industry—another new innovation—to take these mortgages and turn them into new and titillating products.

First the mortgages—then the securities derived from them—landed themselves in trouble. What began as a problem for borrowers has turned into a problem for lenders, too.

The slump in the housing market began to make it tough for borrowers to sell or refinance. Or, from another perspective, it made it hard for people to buy houses; homebuilders were so depressed that their wives are hiding their hunting rifles. They have not been in such a funk for 16 years. And the people who finance the homebuilders are not feeling so good either. Countrywide Financial Corporation, one of the nation's biggest mortgage lenders, said conditions "became increasingly challenging"[15] in the second quarter of 2007.

Meanwhile, the homeowners are often stuck—with a nice house, but no way to pay for it. Finally, the long arm of the law stretches out and takes their house away from them. But that is hardly the end of the story. It is only the beginning. Because then the mortgage goes unpaid . . . and the whole bunch of dodgy sausages that were packaged up as "Collateralized Debt Obligations" begins to stink.

"Up until now, hedge funds have been creating a great deal of the miraculous 'liquidity' sloshing around the globe,"[16] offers Dan Amoss, a short-side analyst with Agora Financial (www.agorafinancial.com). "By buying the highly leveraged equity and mezzanine tranches CDOs, they've greatly strengthened the buying power that's been bidding up the prices—and lowering the yields—of risky debt instruments. George Soros' theory of reflexivity was at work during the financing stage of the housing bubble; now it's working in reverse to 'de'-finance the housing bubble."

"Indigestion tends to lower an appetite, and institutional investors' appetite for junk bonds is spoiling just as Wall Street tries to serve them heaps of acidic securities," continues Dan.

"While CDOs have shifted risk away from the banking system by linking borrowers with lenders from around the world, they have not lessened default risk; they've merely transferred it to unsuspecting lenders that are just beginning to push back."

BEAR STEARNS: PRELUDE TO A PANIC

The cracks in the foundation of the housing market began to show in June of 2007, with CDOs and mortgage-backed securities (MBS).

MBSs look very much like bonds. They are created when a company buys a bunch of mortgages from an actual mortgage lender . . . and during the height of the real estate boom, there were plenty of these to go around. The company then uses the monthly mortgage payments as the revenue stream to pay investors who have bought chunks of these securities. An article on Slate.com explained it this way[17]: "They allow lenders to sell the mortgages they make, thus replenishing their coffers and allowing them to lend again. The buyers don't rely on the creditworthiness of individual borrowers, but on the collective creditworthiness of a group of borrowers."

Investing in these securities is fairly safe . . . that is, as long as the housing market is stable and doing well, and interest rates are low. And as long as homeowners stay on top of their mortgage payments, to keep the flow of payments to holders of MBSs nice and steady. But that's a perfect scenario.

And it became increasingly clear that the problem was not "contained" as it had once been promised. In the first quarter of 2007, the Mortgage Bankers Association reported a record amount of delinquencies; 15.5 percent of all subprime adjustable-rate mortgages were 30 days or more delinquent, up from the previous year's fourth quarter's 14.44 percent, which was the highest on record.

To put it simply: the housing fiesta started to nosedive. Interest rates rose and housing started to not look like the "safe bet" it had once been. The defaults on mortgage payments disrupted the flow of payments available to holders of MBSs. And for the firms that had borrowed exorbitant amounts to finance the purchase and trading of these securities . . . well, once the housing values started to fall, serious problems began to occur.

More affected by this was the investment giant Bear Stearns. As subprime lenders began to tumble, Bear Stearns saw much of their revenue fall, since they underwrote the issuance of these securities. And it had all started out so well . . .

The Bear Stearns High-Grade Structured Credit Fund—admittedly a mouthful—was structured in 2004 and posted an impressive (even then) 41-month stretch of positive returns. "But investors were clamoring for even higher yields," commented the *New York Times*, "which would require more aggressive bets on riskier mortgage-related securities and higher levels of borrowed money, or leverage, to bolster returns."[18]

Bear Stearns had the staff and the expertise in underwriting, trading bonds, and mortgage-backed securities. So in 2006, Bear Stearns started the High-Grade Structured Credit Strategies Enhanced Leverage Fund and borrowed $6 billion from various banks to begin investing in packaged securities comprised of subprime mortgage debt.

But in the summer of 2007, Bear Stearns had to pledge up to $3.2 billion of its own cash to bail out this fund, which was buckling under the weight of bad bets on subprime mortgages. After losing 23 percent in the first 10 months of the fund's existence, investors and the banks asked for their money back. But there was no money to give back.

As Moody's, Standard and Poor's, and Fitch all announced downgrades of subprime-linked debt, Bear Stearns told investors in one of its hedge funds that had bought CDOs on a leveraged basis that they would get none of their money back. They were wiped out, said the letter, reported by Bloomberg Bear went on to say that although investors in one of its two endangered funds had been wiped out, investors in the other fund could breathe a sigh of relief—they had only lost 91 percent of their money.

As this news made it up and down the street, the indexes that measure confidence in collateralized debt dropped. "All but one of the 15 ABX indexes fell to a record low," said Bloomberg news. In the words of one trader, offers for CDOs are going "no bid."[19]

These losses, declines, and reverses were "unprecedented," as Bear put it in a letter to investors.[20] But then, they always are.

What happened that summer in the CDO market was the first real crack in what Ludwig von Mises called the "Crack-Up Boom" (more on this in coming chapters). In the first half of 1995, total issuance of securities backed by subprime residential mortgages did not exceed $25 billion. Ten years later, between January and July of 2005, the number was more than half a trillion. What this increase did is now visible to the human eye. Just look at Las Vegas or Central Florida . . . or around any major city. There are split foyers, Spanish colonials, neo-classical . . . you can get wood, you can get brick, you can get stucco—boy, can you get stucco.

Less obvious to the human eye was the extraordinary effect of so much easy, innovative credit on the whole world economy. Borrowers lied about their incomes; nobody cared to check because the lender had no intention of holding onto the loan until it was paid off. No . . . the lender was going to sell it on . . . and on . . . and on . . . until it came to rest in a hedge fund, such as the Bear Stearns Enhanced Leverage Credit Fund.

But then, we began to see—for the first time—what some of these CDO packages might really be worth. And the answer was: "not much."

The Great Unwind Begins

The collapse of the Bear Stearns funds was just the beginning of what many analysts have deemed "The Great Unwind."

After the debacle at Bear, serious speculators and investors were reluctant to take up more debt; they had seen what was happening to the debt they had. Suddenly, buyers wanted to know what those fancy financial sausage derivatives were derived from. They wanted to know what the collateral was really worth . . . and how debtors were going to be able to make their payments. All up and down the capital structure, they were asking questions.

"No Money Down Disappearing as Mortgage Option," reported the *Washington Post*.[21]

When the going was good, you could sell a mortgage or a leveraged buyout (LBO) finance deal—no questions asked. The question marks only appear after something goes wrong. And then, suddenly, there can be a lot of them.

Remember, the present economic system is not capitalism . . . it's a kind of Marxism for rich people . . . in which the elite make the profits while the losses are redistributed, shared throughout the entire population like Mao jackets and influenza. The genius of the present system is that it dupes the masses into thinking they are capitalists, making it possible for the speculators and hustlers to offload their risks onto them.

You can see how it works by looking at the mortgage industry. Lenders make a profit by writing mortgages . . . the mortgages get sold on, repackaged, and bought up by hedge funds, insurance companies, and even pension plans. There are more than a trillion dollars worth of CDOs around and about. No one knows exactly who loses money when they go bust because the downside has been socialized . . . spread to the masses. In the old days, the banker who provided the mortgage loan would have taken the loss when it went bad. Not today. Now, it's likely to be a retired teacher in Anaheim . . . and millions of other make-believe "investors" just like him.

Likewise, the LBO mavens make a fortune in fees. Ultimately, their creations are taken up by the *lumpeninvestoriat*. Again, the dealmakers and speculators take their profits . . . and then the risk of inevitable loss—when the stock goes down—is borne by average investors. And when the speculators get in trouble, the feds rush to their aid with liquidity—more cheap money.

But wait, the problem at the heart of the economic system is not a lack of credit . . . it's that too much easy credit has loaded too many people and too many deals with too much debt. More credit just postpones the inevitable loss . . . which, as we've been saying, will not be suffered by the capitalists who caused it . . . but by the masses.

The Margin Call From Hell

Bear Stearns had gotten the "margin call from Hell."

The Fed and JP Morgan Chase rushed in to give aid and comfort. JP Morgan Chase bought out Bear Stearns for a reported $2 a share.

The geniuses at Bear Stearns had their calculators . . . their Black-Scholes Option Pricing Model . . . their mathematicians . . . their risk figures . . . They had some of the finest minds in the country—or, at least, some of the finest minds money could buy on Wall Street.

And yet, only the year before they had a stock trading for $150. It was down to $2 . . . and the shareholders have been largely wiped out.

"As of last Nov. 30," wrote Gretchen Morgenson in the *New York Times*, "Bear Stearns had on its books approximately $46 billion of mortgages, mortgage-backed and asset-backed securities. Jettisoning such a portfolio onto a mortgage market that is not operative would, it is plain to see, be a disaster. But who knows what those mortgages are really worth? According to Bear Stearns' annual report, $29 billion of them were valued using computer models 'derived from' or 'supported by' some kind of observable market data. The value of the remaining $17 billion is an estimate based on 'internally developed models or methodologies utilizing significant inputs that are generally less readily observable.'

"In other words," she concluded, "your guess is as good as mine."[22]

We can wager our bets on what went wrong at Bear . . . and it has a little something to do with derivatives.

Alan Greenspan said of derivatives in March of 1999, "These instruments enhance the ability to differentiate risk and allocate it to those investors most able and willing to take it."[23]

Another view of derivatives was expressed by someone who actually knew something—Warren E. Buffett, the sage of Omaha. He called them "financial weapons of mass destruction."[24]

Who was right? Ask Bear Stearns' shareholders! That week was "hell week" for the poor people who owned the business. They went skiing or fishing on Friday evening. When they turned on the news Monday morning, they found that they had been wiped out. Bear's bridge-champion chief, Jimmy Cayne, for example, had more than a billion dollars' worth of Bear stock. But when the dust settled it was worth only $30 million.

What went wrong? The firm made a big bet—on derivatives, of course. Not that we feel sorry for Mr. Cayne. He should have known better than anyone what he had. And if he'd been smart, he would have gotten rid of it. Besides, the whole Bear team had it coming. When Long Term Capital Management got into trouble 10 years ago, Bear refused to come to its aid. And it's not as if Cayne is going to be out on the street, begging for quarters. You can still live well with only $30 million.

"We come in every day at 3:30 A.M. and leave at 6 P.M. I'm not used to setting my alarm for 2:45 A.M., but these are extraordinary times," says bond king Bill Gross of PIMCO.

"Bear Stearns has made it obvious that things have gone too far," Gross continues. "The investment community has morphed into something beyond banks and something beyond regulation. We call it the shadow banking system."[25]

"These products [complex derivative instruments, such as collateralized debt obligations and credit default swaps] are virtually hidden from investors, analysts and regulators, even though they have emerged as one of Wall Street's most outsized profit engines. They don't trade openly on public exchanges, and financial services firms disclose few details about them.

"Bear Stearns's vast portfolio of these instruments was among the main reasons for the bank's collapse, but derivatives are buried in the accounts of just about every Wall Street firm, as well as major commercial banks like Citigroup and JP Morgan Chase. What's more, these exotic investments have been exported all over the globe, causing losses in places as distant from Wall Street as a small Norwegian town north of the Arctic Circle."[26]

This new financial network came out of the shadows . . . and started dropping dead in the middle of the street.

THE FALL OF THE DARK TWINS

The months following the collapse of Bear Stearns were a whirlwind of bailouts, failures . . . and the biggest nationalization in history.

Freddie and Fannie were the darlings of Wall Street . . . the leaders of the house price bubble . . . with nearly half the nation's $12 trillion worth of mortgages. A couple of years ago, they could do no wrong. Amando Falcone Jr. found that out the hard way. On February 4, 2003, he resigned from his post as the head of the Office of Federal Housing Enterprise Oversight Office, the committee set up by Congress to police activities at Freddie and Fannie. On the same day, he published a report warning the committee of unusual and risky derivatives exposure on the books at the giant mortgage enablers. The circumstances were suspect. Not only was Mr. Falcone Jr. out of a job, but as then editor of *Strategic Investment*, Dan Denning discovered soon after, the report he'd penned was removed from the committee's Web site.

But that was then, in the heat of the boom. Now, the dark twins can do no right.

But we'll back up for a moment . . .

Franklin Delano Roosevelt, whose family had made a fortune in the opium trade, promised the nation a "New Deal" during the Great Depression of the 1930s. But what he gave it was more like the old false shuffle. The president pulled cards from the bottom of the deck, pretending that government bureaucrats could do a better job of allocating capital than private investors. In 1938, he set up the Federal National Mortgage Association, aka Fannie Mae. Then, as at the time of this writing, the national housing market was in crisis. House prices had been declining for almost a decade. Who wanted to lend money against falling collateral values? Only a fool . . . or a government.

For the next 32 years, the firm resembled a nationwide savings and loan institution—borrowing from large institutions and lending to smaller ones, keeping a piece of the spread for its trouble. But Fannie Mae was an imposter from the get-go. Lenders knew that it had something no free market business ever had—the full faith and credit of the U.S. government behind it. Fannie was able to borrow at below-market rates; lenders knew they had no risk of losing their money in a default or bankruptcy. Fannie, with the aces dealt her by the Roosevelt administration, dominated the business for the next 30 years.

Then, another crisis came along, followed by another bamboozle, this one perpetrated by Lyndon Johnson. Specifically, the feds were spending too much on wars—the War on Poverty at home . . . and one against the Viet Cong across the ocean. Victory eluded Lyndon Johnson on both fronts, but his handling of Fannie Mae should have brought him at least a bronze star. He attempted to balance the government's ledgers (this was in the days when Americans still believed in balanced budgets), so he moved the mortgage business off the federal government's books, privatizing it as a "government sponsored agency." For good measure, he created a competing organization—the Federal Home Mortgage Association, aka Freddie Mac.

Many are the ham-fisted dictators and sticky-fingered kleptocrats who have nationalized industries. Even without a credit crunch for camouflage, Francois Mitterand nationalized 36 leading French banks in 1982. Robert Mugabe grabbed farmland in the Zimbabwe. Evo Morales took the gas industry. And Hugo Chavez seized the Orinoco oil fields in 2007. But Lyndon Johnson rarely gets credit for his great advance in the history of public larceny: he privatized the profits while nationalizing the losses. This formula has been a honey pot for clever *dirigistes* ever since, providing countless opportunities for defeated politicians, hacks, and hustlers—speaking fees, consulting contracts, board memberships, bonuses, stock options (notably, the $170 million spent on lobbyists over the past 10 years . . . mentioned above)—things that wouldn't be possible for a "public" company. In effect, Fannie Mae could pick the taxpayer's pocket twice—once by sticking him with a mortgage he couldn't really afford and a second time by raiding the taxpayers' vault for a bailout.

In the case at hand, by the year 2007, the CEOs of Fannie and Freddie were earning salaries that would have been respectable, even on Wall Street. Fannie's main man, Daniel Mudd, took home $13.4 million in 2007, a year in which the firm lost $2.1 billion. While the Freddie Kruger of mortgage finance, Dick Syron, pocketed $18.3 million for helping Freddie Mac to a $3 billion loss and a 33 percent trim for the shareholders.

In May of 2008, Mr. Mudd told the *New York Times* that he was "seeing the best opportunities since I've been in this business."[27] Two months later, both Fannie and Freddie are "insolvent," said former Fed governor William Poole.

Together, the dark twins of mortgage finance had more than $5 trillion in liabilities. That's more than a third of the U.S. GDP.

The Fed stepped in, opened the discount window a bit wider for the mortgage giants . . . to no avail.

But what did they expect? Fannie and Freddie, along with Wall Street banks, Bear Stearns, and the whole lot made their money by peddling debt to people who already had too much. Did they think they could do it forever?

The headman at the Fed would have done us all a service, in our opinion, if he leveled with the nation.

"Look," he might have said, "the prosperity we have enjoyed for the last few years has been largely an illusion; it was based on debt, leverage, and speculation. We all know you can't get rich by spending more than you earn. And you can create real prosperity by borrowing money and spending it on consumer items. We're now paying the price for those mistakes. Let's just get it over with."

Those words may or may not have been on call for him. He might have doodled something like that on the back of an envelope on the way to Capitol Hill. Maybe they came to him in a dream.

Instead, on September 7, 2008, the U.S. government seized control of the mortgage giants. The *Washington Post* reports:

> Hurricane Hank swept through the nation's capital yesterday with gale-force regulatory winds and a tidal surge of federal cash, upending two of Washington's biggest enterprises and permanently changing the landscape of housing finance in America.
>
> In wresting control of Fannie Mae and Freddie Mac, and in authorizing the Treasury to begin purchases of mortgage-backed securities, Secretary Henry M. Paulson Jr. has taken responsibility for assuring that low-interest loans will continue to flow into the country's hard-hit housing markets. Not since the early days of the Roosevelt administration, at the depth of the Great Depression, has the government taken such a direct role in the workings of the financial system.
>
> Under the deal they could not refuse, Fannie and Freddie directors and top executives will lose their jobs. Shareholders will lose their dividends, voting rights and most of their ownership stake, while agreeing to pay dearly for the government's money and backing. Left unharmed will be holders of trillions of dollars in Fannie and Freddie debt—or securities backed by mortgages that Fannie and Freddie have insured against default—who will get all their money back, with interest.[28]

The story is breathtaking. Staggering. Dumbfounding. But there it is—the biggest nationalization in history. Freddie and Fannie finance three out of four new mortgages. And now, the mortgage industry depends neither on willing buyers and sellers . . . nor on willing lenders and borrowers . . . but on the U.S. government. The Land of the Free has put its housing under the control of the state! Yes, there is still plenty of room for private initiative and private decision making. But, ultimately, millions of Americans now depend on the U.S. government for the roofs over their heads.

We checked the U.S. Constitution for clarification. We were looking for a provision stating that the "U.S. Federal Government shall enter the mortgage finance business and use taxpayers' money to rescue irresponsible lenders and dimwit homeowners from their own mistakes." It wasn't there. But so what? If there is anything the government can't do, we have yet to find it.

Of course, the idea of taxpayers bailing out the mortgage finance industry is ridiculous; taxpayers can't even finance existing federal obligations. Not even close. This year, for example, they'll be a half trillion short. If you figured it properly, the deficit would be trillions more.

The move to bring Fannie and Freddie under direct government control was widely seen as a plus for everyone. Foreign lenders know the game is still rigged—so their money is safe. Homeowners think they'll be able to continue living at someone else's expense. And investors hallucinate that the government has "done something" to put this mess behind us.

The government is in the business of stacking one monumental fraud on top of another . . . trying to give everyone the idea that he or she can live at someone else's expense. Sooner or later, the whole mountain of flimflam falls down.

RICH MAN'S MARXISM

On the heels of the nationalization of Fannie and Freddie were the murmurs coming from the investment bank Lehman Brothers. In September 2008, they reported a quarterly loss of $4 billion—their worst since going public, and second consecutive loss.

Immediately, there was a din on Wall Street. Would Lehman follow in the footsteps of Bear? We didn't have to wonder long . . .

The Federal Reserve invited financial CEOs from far and wide to Wall Street, hoping to entice a buyout or merger to keep Lehman afloat. Bank of America made a bid, but ultimately walked away. Barclays did the same.

On September 15, 2008, after 158 years in business, Lehman Brothers filed the biggest bankruptcy in Wall Street history with $613 billion in debt.[29]

Yes, yet another falls prey to their own devices. Like all hustlers, they weren't smart enough to ignore their own lies. They were the ones who packaged up all that subprime debt—mortgage loans on overpriced property to people who couldn't pay the money back; they knew what was in that "mystery meat." Then, they got the useful stooges at the rating companies to call it Grade A. And then, they bought it themselves! What were they thinking? Not only that, they bought it on leverage—so that if it went bad, the whole company would go belly-up!

And now, mothers no longer want their babies to grow up to be stockbrokers and investment bankers. Now they want them to grow up to be bankruptcy lawyers! That's where the money is!

Governments used to talk of providing "safety nets" for citizens in trouble. That meant offering assistance to people on the margins of society. A man who lost his job would get unemployment compensation. One who was injured would get workman's comp. Poor people were offered food stamps . . . and surplus food from government farm support programs.

Now, the feds offer a safety net for people with money—a kind of rich man's Marxism—in the form of protection against financial losses.

The logic of the safety net—whether used to catch a poor man or a rich one—is that whatever mess you've gotten yourself into, someone else pays for it. You forget to save money . . . you lose your job; bingo . . . someone else provides emergency assistance. During the 1970s and 1980s, Americans began to realize that providing unlimited assistance to the poor had its drawbacks; many people actually seemed to prefer a life of easy poverty to a life of hard work. Many people were "hooked" on public assistance, with several generations of welfare recipients in a single family. We recall, in the early 1980s, asking a young woman in the ghetto of Baltimore what she did for a living.

"I get a check," was her reply.

Poor thing. She never knew the pleasure and pride of a job well done. She never enjoyed the boost to her confidence and self-esteem that minimum wage employment can give.

Later, the Reagan administration reformed the welfare system. We don't know if it did any good or not, but people stopped getting so many checks . . . and stopped talking about it. Now what they are talking about is the safety nets for the rich—and everyone is in favor of them. So far, we've seen the central bank act with remarkable speed to help bankers, speculators, and hedge fund managers. Stockholders have been given a boost, too. And if the housing slump worsens, government will probably rush out some safety nets for homeowners.

Now, capitalists, proles, and the bourgeoisie all get checks. Is that progress . . . or what?

CHAPTER 3

JOHN LAW AND THE ORIGINS OF A BAD IDEA

Everything has been said before, but since nobody listens, we have to keep going back and beginning all over again.

—André Gide

Not more than a hundred paces from the front door of our Paris office begins the rue Quincampoix. If you were to take a leisurely stroll down the rue des Lombards, which abuts it on the south side, you might miss Quincampoix altogether. It is but a simple cobblestoned alleyway, ending unceremoniously no more than five blocks to the north at the rue Boucher. Like many passages in this old part of the city, it is perpetually damp, and frequented by geegaw vendors and various dubious characters. As if to remind us that history hides many secrets, you can walk along the entire length of the rue Quincampoix today, without noticing anything unusual. A historic plaque posted on the corner of rue des Lombards is the only clue that the rue Quincampoix was both the site of one of the most fantastic speculative episodes in economic history and the spiritual birthplace of modern central banking.

It was here, on the rue Quincampoix, that John Law set up the first *Banque Générale* and tested out a "new" theory about how a nation might get rich with the use of paper money. With most of it shrouded in graffiti, the tourist plaque provides precious little information. Brushing over John Law and the Mississippi Scheme, it allots more space to the damning remark made by the Regent of France to his cousin, convicted murderer Count d'Horn, "If I had bad blood, I would pluck it out of me!" In so saying, the Regent effectively refused to grant d'Horn the pardon he needed to avoid the death sentence.

MURDER ON THE RUE QUINCAMPOIX

Count d'Horn's story illustrates the irrational human behavior that occurred in May 1720—the height of the speculative euphoria surrounding the shares of Law's Compagnie des Indes. During the boom's peak, the rue Quincampoix was crowded by day with stock traders, speculators, royalty, and pickpockets furiously trying to cash in on the mania. Soldiers were often brought in at night to clear the streets because the speculators refused to leave. Here, in broad daylight, Count d'Horn and a few accomplices decided they could get rich by mugging a stockbroker. The episode is recounted in Charles Mackay's *Extraordinary Popular Delusions & the Madness of Crowds:*

> The Count d'Horn, a younger brother of the Prince d'Horn, and related to the noble families of d'Aremburg, de Ligne and de Montmorency, was a young man of dissipated character, extravagant to a degree, and as unprincipled as he was extravagant. In connection with two other young men, as reckless as himself, named Mille, a Piedmontese captain, and one Destampes, a Fleming, he formed a design to rob a very rich broker, who was known, unfortunately for himself, to carry great sums about his person. The count pretended a desire to purchase of him a number of shares in the Company of the Indies, and for that purpose appointed to meet him in a cabaret, or low-public house. The unsuspecting broker was punctual to his appointment; so were the Count d'Horn and his two associates. . . .

After a few moments' conversation, the Count d'Horn suddenly sprang upon his victim and stabbed him three times in the breast with a poniard.

The man fell heavily to the ground, and, while the Count was employed in rifling his portfolio of bonds in the Mississippi and Indian schemes to the amount of 100,000 crowns, Mille, the Piedmontese, stabbed the unfortunate broker again and again, to make sure of his death. But the broker did not fall without a struggle . . . and his cries brought the people of the cabaret to his assistance. Destampes, the other assassin, who had been set to keep watch at a staircase, sprang from a window and escaped; but Mille and the Count d'Horn were seized in the very act.

The crime became infamous throughout France, not so much for the horror of the deed as for the noble birth of those who committed it. Viewed from the comfortable distance of history, we might ask, what on earth could the Count, a man of high birth and position, possibly have been thinking? He may, of course, have thought he was acting rationally: The broker had the notes; Horn and his associates wanted them. Why not just take them?

Suffice it to say that the Count got what he deserved, not what he expected. Despite personal attempts at intervention by John Law himself, d'Horn was put to death on "the wheel," a punishment meant only for the lowest of criminals and a stain on the family record. The wheel was a torture instrument popular in France and Germany at the time. The victim was tied and stretched on a heavy wheel, which was then rolled around, thus crushing him until he was on the verge of death. The executioner would then roll up the wheel so that spectators could watch the man die. If the death was so slow that it bored the onlookers, the victim would receive blows to the chest until dead.

But the Count D'Horn is only one example of the characters who color the legend of John Law and his Mississippi scheme—a tale of murderers, schemers, kings, and politicians. We gawk at it today, as though passing a car crash, partly because the Mississippi bubble is a famous example of a recurring pattern of mania in the financial markets, but also because it is recorded in the annals of economic history as the first flirtation with paper money by a "modern" government.

MISSISSIPPI MANIA

Throughout history, many different items have served as money— seashells, cows, beer, salt, copper bracelets, horses, chickens, amber, coral, dried fish, furs, tobacco, grain, sugar, playing cards, nails, rice, slaves . . . even paper. But since ancient times, currency in Western Europe had been based on precious metal: The Greeks used silver as their currency; the Romans began using gold coins after they conquered the Etruscans.

The world's first experiment with paper money—China, AD 910—was abandoned after a few hundred years because it was susceptible to inflation. John Law had brought the idea to Europe and developed it, but neither he nor anyone else ever succeeded in curing its major defect: Central bankers could issue as much paper as they wanted. The story also reveals that the fever for profitless dot-coms in the United States circa 1999 to 2000, ridiculous as it may seem to us now, was not the first time individuals got sucked into irrational behavior en masse, nor is it likely to be the last. "Men it has been well said think in herds," Mackay famously observed, and "it will be seen that they go mad in herds, while they recover their senses slowly, and one by one." Paper money merely fans the flames.

The source of Law's Mississippi mania in the early eighteenth century was the "future earnings" of the Louisiana territory in the heart of the American continent. The trouble was that no one knew what Louisiana was or what future earnings it would have. The territory had only been discovered and claimed for France in 1682—less than 40 years earlier. Investors in Paris who bothered to ask the question were generally satisfied with answer: Louisiana is a large island off the coast of America, which either includes (or is near) the mouth of a river called the Mississippi.

At the height of the bubble, in an attempt to keep up appearances, Law ordered all the beggars, ruffians, and ne'er-do-wells in Paris to be rounded up. He fitted them with shovels and pickaxes, marched them through the streets of Paris, and then all the way to La Rochelle, some 534 kilometers to the West. La Rochelle was the port from which voyagers would embark for New Orleans—the Paris of the New World— which had been established to serve as the headquarters for Law's trading company and to lure prospective workers to the rich fields of Louisiana. The ragtag marchers carried shovels and other mining paraphernalia purportedly for harvesting all the gold they would discover.

But our story starts long before this extraordinary fiasco took place. It begins . . . in the mind of John Law.

GENTLEMAN GAMBLER WITH A PAST

Murder played a role in the fortunes of John Law on more than one occasion. In 1694, 26 years before the Count d'Horn hunted his prey on the rue Quincampoix, John Law committed a murder of his own. In a duel in Bloomsbury Square in London, Law fatally wounded a man named Edward Beau Wilson. Law was caught, convicted, and sentenced to death, but then escaped. He spent the next 20 years on the run in Europe, gambling for a living and making a public nuisance of himself. John Law's life reads like the stuff of legends: murder, sex, political intrigue, wealth, power . . . despair.

In a biography of John Law,[1] Trinity College Dublin professor, Antoin Murphy, has suggested that the legendary Law—the rake, the womanizer, and the escaped convict—may, in fact, have been a calculated image to gain an advantage at the gaming tables of Europe's high society.

According to Murphy, there are several possible versions of the murder. In the earliest "official" version, Law is said to have killed Beau Wilson in a duel defending the honor of a Mrs. Lawrence, a woman whose affections they shared. Law was arrested and sentenced to death, but heroically escaped by jumping over a wall in the prison, breaking his ankle in the process. He was then whisked away to Amsterdam by some friends, which led to the following search warrant being published in the *London Gazette:*

> Captain John Law, a Scotchman, aged twenty-six; a very tall, black, lean man; well shaped, above six feet high, with large pock-holes in his face; big nosed, and speaking broad and loud.

Curiously, this description barely fits Law. A later story, suggests Mrs. Lawrence had simply been introduced as a decoy to hide the identity of the true woman in question, Miss Elizabeth Villiers, who was Edward Beau Wilson's lover, but also mistress to King William III. It is alleged that Law was hired to duel with Wilson in order to rid Elizabeth Villiers of her excessively inquisitive lover. Yet another account of the story researched by Murphy suggests that Beau Wilson was a homosexual and that Law could have been sent to dispatch Wilson to cover up a "relationship" with a "nobleman"—possibly even the king.

Having neither witnessed the crime themselves, nor known the participants, your authors do not pretend to know which version of the story is correct. Murphy asserts that even after having perused the official documentation, the truth is hard to unravel, but there are reasons enough to suspect Law's arrest and "escape" were merely a charade. This would explain, among other things, the inaccurate description of Law in news stories covering his escape. In any case, Law would live the rest of his days branded with the appellation "murderer" and was forbidden to return to England.

After the escape, Law made his way to Amsterdam. Until resurfacing in Edinburgh three years later, he is reported to have spent his mornings studying finance and trade, and nights at the local gaming houses, gambling and entertaining the local aristocracy. During this time, he began laying the intellectual foundations for what could be described as a prototype for modern central banking. He had a natural talent for figures, a willingness to take risks, and a deep interest in the way things work . . . particularly money.

Lowlands Lad Heads Home

Law was born in 1671 to an Edinburgh goldsmith and his wife. At the time, goldsmiths were the bankers of their communities. They made coins, offered loans, provided simple banking services, and took cash on deposit. The notes they gave in return to depositors became the earliest form of paper money in use in the British Isles. Having grown up in a goldsmith's house, Law was well versed in the banking trade, and was reported to have been very gifted with numbers—another trait that would prove useful at the gaming tables.

In 1703, Law took advantage of the fact that English death warrants were not honored north of the Scottish border and returned to his hometown. There, at the age of 32, he became involved in the debate over the establishment of a "land bank."

Scotland at the time was reeling from the failed Darien Venture. This was an attempt to establish a Scottish colony on the Isthmus of Panama that fell through, draining much of the country of available capital. The Darien Venture finds its roots in the historical conflict between England and Scotland. At the time of Law's duel in

Bloomsbury Square, the London East India Company enjoyed a virtual monopoly on trade with the Orient—a remarkable boon to company shareholders, but a nightmare to competitors. In 1695, the Scottish Parliament attempted to break the monopoly by establishing the "Company of Scotland Trading to Africa and the Indies." Although the firm was based in Edinburgh, the board of directors and most of the principal shareholders were English and lived in London. Fearing a loss of their monopoly, directors of the English East India Company campaigned and successfully convinced first the House of Lords, then King William, and later the House of Commons to out-law share ownership in the Scottish trading firm. English capital dried up instantly.

The Scottish East India Company became a national cause . . . and a national disaster. Fueled primarily by a distaste for all things English, fund-raising for the company across Scotland was a success. The new firm raised £400,000—or what was thought to be half the available specie in the nation.

The plan for the campaign was fairly straightforward. Three ships were to be built on the Continent, then used to transport 1,200 set-tlers to establish a colony on what is now the border between Panama and Colombia. There, the settlers would forge an overland trading route to the Pacific. The bay where the settlers landed was known at the time as Darien, so the scheme went down in history as the Darien Venture.

The settlers arrived on November 3, 1698. They quickly made friends and signed treaties with the local Indians, but the Spanish had established nearby colonies and took great exception to the new arriv-als. The English in North America and on the Island of Jamaica were ordered by the king to resist helping or trading with the Scots. In February of the following year, the Spanish defeated a small band of Scottish settlers and seized one of their ships, setting the Darien Venture on a course for failure. Dysentery, fever, internal strife, and outright desertion finished the job.

After eight short, difficult months, the settlers climbed aboard their remaining vessels and headed home. Less than 700 settlers made it back to Scotland. The Scottish East India Company was lost and with it nearly half of Scotland's already meager supply of capital.

Toward a Fiat Currency

Several years later, back in Edinburgh, reacting to what he saw as a dearth of physical specie, John Law began promoting the idea that if Scotland were to recover from the Darien Venture and prosper, it needed paper money.

Having studied banking systems in his travels on the Continent, Law had come to believe that paper money, because of its portability—and availability—would facilitate trade in the country far better than gold and silver, the traditional specie. In *An Essay on a Land Bank,* published in 1704, Law suggested the bank should issue paper notes backed by, and never exceeding, the value of the total state holdings of land—hence the name "land bank." Holders of the notes could redeem their paper for an equal value in land at a time suitable for both parties. "Just how," as John K. Galbraith said of a land bank already established in Holland during the time, "the land would be redeemed by noteholders was uncertain."

In Law's view, the land bank was meant to both relieve the state of having to furnish the gold and silver necessary to keep the economy moving and, perhaps more importantly, give the state the capacity to manage the amount of money in circulation at any one time. Law's proposal for a land bank, while not the only proposal being entertained in Scotland at the time, was brought to the floor of the Scottish Parliament. It was debated, but eventually defeated. Critics panned it as a "sand bank," suggesting, in the popular sailing parlance of the day, that it would run the ship of state aground. The voices of opposition were skeptical that establishing paper credit was a sound policy for the country, given the perilous state in which the Darien Venture had left the economy.

In a second essay, *Money and Trade Considered* (1705), Law had further refined his ideas on the use of paper as money. "What is important about the 'specie,'" he wrote, "is not how much of it one had . . . but how it got used." Presaging what economists today call the "velocity of money," Law believed that to be of any use whatsoever, money must change hands and keep moving. Spending, Law believed, is how a nation gets wealthy.

During the land bank debate, an Englishman named Dr. Chamberlain accused Law of plagiarism. Former personal physician of Charles II, Chamberlain had himself set up a land bank in London eight years prior. Rather than face the challenges of the well-connected Dr. Chamberlain, Law moved on to an idea modern readers will recognize: Instead of backing the paper money with landed holdings of the state, the government should simply back the notes itself. The government, for example, could back its promise to pay the notes with the future tax revenues of the state. Thus, Law's idea—a paper currency backed 100 percent by land—evolved into the fiat currency that serves as the basis for money used by every modern nation today.

Following the refusal to adapt the measures in his proposal and failing to obtain an official pardon for the murder of Beau Wilson from the English courts, Law returned to the Continent and, consequently, to the gaming tables. Over the next 14 years, he is thought to have passed through the gaming houses of Brussels, Geneva, Genoa, and Venice. On two separate occasions, once in Naples and another time in Genoa, he was expelled from those cities as a bad influence on the youth.

While gambling his way through Europe, Law took on a mistress, had two children, and amassed a small personal fortune. A master at calculating odds, Law learned quickly that he could win the most amount of money at the tables by playing a game called "basset" and setting himself up effectively as the "market maker" in the transactions. By assuming this position in each game, Law is thought to have pyramided his wealth to around 1.6 million livres. His studied reputation as a rake, gambler, and womanizer soon earned him renown throughout the capitals of Europe—and won him an audience with Philip II, Duc d'Orleans. It was this meeting—between Law, the gentleman gambler with a past, and the Duc, a rake and gambler in his own right as well as a man of unparalleled political ambition—that would ignite one of the most infamous periods of financial speculation in history.

Although, Philip II was reputedly rather taken with Law and his ideas during their first meeting, he was not in a position to put them in place. In fact, Law's proposals, while promising enough to reach the ears of the Sun King, were famously denied, not because they lacked merit, but because Law was not Catholic.

A SHOT AT THE BIG TIME

Fortune soon smirked in Law's direction. Louis XIV died in 1715, leaving the largest, most powerful nation in Europe to his successor Louis XV—aged seven. Because of the new king's tender age, custom allowed his uncle—Philip II, the Duc d'Orleans—to take control of the royal finances. Philip II became the Regent of France.

The royal finances were a mess. After years of war and the building of extravagant palaces, such as Versailles, the French state was 3,000 million livres in debt. Annual revenues from taxes were only 145 million livres. Annual expenses before interest payments were 142 million livres. If we assume, as does Lars Tvede in his book, *Business Cycles,* that the state had to pay an average of 4 percent per annum in interest on its debt, then this amounted to 120 million livres. The actual surplus available for interest payments was only 145 − 142 = 3 million livres, resulting in a deficit of 117 million livres.

The bag of tricks used by finance ministers of the time included declaring national bankruptcy (not exactly a good option for a new government), raising taxes, "clipping" coins (replacing the coins in existence with new coinage made up of a smaller percentage of precious metals), and selling monopoly trade privileges of the state's colonies or confiscating the possessions of corrupt state employees.

The new regent chose a combination of clipping and confiscation. Through the next year, he managed to scrimp, steal, and inflate his way to 150 million livres more in state revenue: barely 6 percent of the government's outstanding debt. Philip II sent out word that he was looking for an astute financier to assist in saving the French state before it was forced to declare bankruptcy. John Law answered the call. The gentleman gambler with fanciful ideas about a "paper" currency, who was now 44 years of age and quite wealthy, would finally get a shot at playing the game with the highest stakes of all: the creation of money itself.

On May 5, 1716, the Banque Générale was founded with 6 million livres in capital and was assured success from the beginning. The Duc declared all taxes must henceforth be paid with notes issued by Law's bank. For the first time in modern history, paper money was being introduced and officially sanctioned by a government.

The French national debt at the time would, today, have already been seriously downgraded by Moody's. The *billets d'etat*—government bonds issued under Louis XIV to pay for his extravagance—were essentially junk bonds. While they had been issued at 100 livres, the billets d'etat were trading on the open market for 21.50, a rate reflecting investors' fears that the government was about to declare bankruptcy. From the government's point of view, the outstanding billets d'etat were valued at 3,000 million livres at issue, financed at 4 percent, for annual interest payment of 120 million livres. As Tvede shows, from the investor's point of view, the outstanding billets d'etat were worth roughly 645 million livres and paid 18 percent interest, totaling an annual payment of 120 million livres. The high interest rate reflected the billets' junk status.

Saving the Royal Finances

The challenge for Law was to buy back the outstanding government debt at the market rate of 21.50 without driving up the price. If investors discovered the government was reclaiming their billets d'etat and that Philip II could effectively save the royal finances, they would certainly begin asking more than 21.50 per billet. Law solved the problem by offering the bank shares exclusively in exchange for the government bonds. Lars Tvede reports that this "debt-for-equity" swap was very small in proportion to the remaining national debt of 2,850 million livres. The issue of the Banque Générale shares brought back only billets d'etat worth 75 percent of 6 million, totaling 4.5 million livres—nothing compared with the 3,000 million needed.

Edgar Faure, a Law biographer, suggests the Mississippi Scheme had two phases—*le plan sage* (the wise plan) and *le plan fou* (the crazy plan). The wise phase began with three brilliant strokes that illustrated Law's financial acumen. In the first stroke, Law declared his notes were redeemable "at sight" at the bank for the full amount of coins. Importantly, he stipulated that those coins would be of their original value when the notes were issued, lest Philip d'Orleans get the urge to begin "clipping" again. Second, Law declared that any banker printing more notes than he could back up with coins "deserved death."

These declarations effectively set up a prototype for the gold standard organized by Napoleon and the British Empire, and enjoyed by the majority of European currencies during the nineteenth century.

The effect of the regulations was immediate. The paper notes—backed as they were by gold—traded at a premium. Investors had so much confidence in the paper and so little in the clipped coins that they began to pay 101 livres worth of coins for a 100-livre note. As would happen again in the last two decades of the twentieth century, paper outperformed gold! By 1717, just a year later, the price had jumped to 115. The new currency boom spurred trade and commerce. Law was able to expand his operation quickly. He opened branches of his bank in Lyons, La Rochelle, Tours, Amiens, and Orleans. The paper notes of the Banque Générale quickly became a national obsession.

Then Law issued the third part of his plan to recoup all of France's outstanding debt. While it was perhaps the most ingenious of the three moves in "the wise phase" of Law's scheme, it also signaled the beginning of the end. Law convinced Philip II to back a trading company with monopoly trading rights over the Mississippi River and France's land claim in Louisiana. Shares in the new company would be offered to the public, and investors would only be allowed to buy them with the remaining billets d'etat on the market. So begins the famed Mississippi Scheme.

Law's new venture, which would come to be known as the Compagnie des Indes, was granted all the possessions of its competitors—the Senegal Company, the China Company, and the French East India company—giving it exclusive French trading rights for the Mississippi River, Louisiana, China, East India, and South America. Law's enterprise also received the sole right to mint royal coins for nine years; it was allowed to act as the royal tax collector for the same amount of time; and it was granted a monopoly on all tobacco trade under French rule. Again, Lars Tvede helps us out with the investors' point of view on the matter:

A new public issue of 25 million livres was announced—an issue that would raise the total equity to 125 million livres. John Law declared that he expected the shares to be honored by a total dividend of 50 million livres—equal to a 40 percent return on investment. But the offer was really much better than that. The shares were bought neither with coins nor banknotes. You could pay with the Sun King's junk bonds. The calculation was as follows if you wanted to buy 0.5 million livres shares:

Nominal share price:	0.5 million livres
Expected annual dividend:	0.2 million livres
Bought with 0.5 million livres worth of billets d'etat real value 0.2:	0.1 million livres
Real yield on the investment $(0.2 \times 100/0.1)$	= 200 percent!

So you could apparently expect a real return of about 200 percent per annum! 200 percent!

Inflating the Bubble

Immediately after the initial public offering (IPO), applications for shares in the Compagnie des Indes started coming in from all levels of society. So many, in fact, that it took the staff at the bank weeks to sort through all the applications. Traders, merchants, dukes, counts, and marquises crowded into the little rue Quincampoix and waited for hours to find out if their subscriptions had been granted. When the final list of subscribers was announced, Law and his awaiting public learned that the shares had been oversubscribed by a factor of six. The immediate result? Shares in the Compagnie des Indes skyrocketed in value.

The rue Quincampoix was transformed overnight into an open-air trading pit. Rents along the street shot up. Enterprising shopkeepers began renting out their storefronts at exorbitant rates to equally enterprising people who set themselves up as impromptu stockbrokers.

At roughly the same time, the Duc was beginning to notice that the paper banknotes acted like an elixir on the public. Law's theories were no longer an experiment—they were a sensational success. And as he had predicted in his essays 15 years before, the people gained an unimaginable confidence in paper as a means for exchange. This new money began rapidly changing hands; trade and commerce flourished. Using the flawless logic of politicians throughout the ages, Philip II must have thought: People have gained confidence in the paper banknotes; the notes appear to have provided a convenient way for the government to borrow (despite the outstanding debt still on the books); the paper money both traded at a premium and appeared to be reviving France's stalled economy. Why not print more?

The Duc, previously reluctant to involve the government directly in the bank, renamed the bank the *Banque Royale*, bestowed on it the monopoly right to refine gold and silver—and, by the end of 1719, issued 1,000 million new banknotes, effectively increasing the money supply by 16 times its previous amount. Coupled with the rage for shares in the Compagnie des Indes, this new money had the effect of putting firecrackers on the family's hearth fire. The crazy phase began. Shares traded in the free market on the rue Quincampoix shot to 10 times the issue price, and higher.

Speculators swooped in, believing they were going to make a killing on new issues. Law and the Duc were only too willing to oblige them, again, and again. In moves worthy of the Federal Reserve circa 2001, by May 1720, five official proclamations from the Duc's office were issued, allowing the creation of 2,696 million new banknotes. The money supply was soaring!

Like America's baby boomers preparing for retirement in the 1990s, investors in Law's Mississippi Scheme probably should have been concerned. They were buying shares in the new company with junk paper issued by the government. No new capital was being injected nor were any trade proceeds coming out of Louisiana. But the crowd in front of Law's banque had its own ideas, its own logic— and its own imagination.

OUT OF THIN AIR

By all counts, it looked as if the French economy had recovered. In just four short years, the country had cast off despair and was brimming with excitement. Paris, the epicenter of the boom, bustled. Goods, luxury items, and people began pouring in from all over Europe. The population of the capital increased. Prices began to rise. Luxury fabrics—silks, laces, and velvet—came into vogue. Art and furniture were being imported from all over the world and not just by the aristocracy. For the first time in France's history, the middle class was getting in on the act. It looked like a new era: Wages for artisans quadrupled, unemployment fell, and new homes were built at a blistering pace—everyone was going to get rich!

Shares issued in early August 1719 quickly rose to an exchange value of 2,830 livres. But by mid-September, they were fetching twice that figure. After a short correction back to 4,800 in late September, the shares broke through all resistance levels and skyrocketed higher and higher—6,463 on October 26, 7,463 on November 18, and 8,975 just a day later!

Up and up until on January 8, 1720, a single share of the Compagnie des Indes traded at 10,100 livres (see Figure 3.1).

Ordinary folk, buying shares on margin, made unimaginable fortunes: A waiter made 30 million livres, a beggar made 70 million, a shopkeeper made 127 million. A new word was even coined by the aristocracy to describe these people: They were referred to disdainfully as "millionaires." Richard Cantillon, a 23-year-old Irish banker who was working in Paris at the time, made a pile of money estimated at 20 percent of the annual French tax receipts. The stories became legend. The legends fueled the speculative fever even more. One speculator, who had gotten sick, sent a servant of his to unload 250 shares at the market price of 8,000 livres. By the time the servant got to the market, the price had risen to 10,000. He sold, delivered the 4,000,000 to his master as expected, and pocketed a nice bonus of 500,000 livres; then he packed his bags and was gone. In a similar way, John Law's own assistant made a fortune.

Law, himself, became the most celebrated foreigner in France. To the French, he was a hero greater than any king, a financial genius who had restored prosperity to the land. His carriage had to be escorted by royal troops as throngs of admirers fought for a glimpse of him as he passed. The memoirs of Saint-Simeon recall: "Law, besieged by applicants and aspirants, saw his door forced, his windows entered from his garden, while some of them came tumbling from the chimney of his office."

Women from all levels of society plotted to gain his attention. "Law is so run after that he has no rest, night or day," wrote the Duchess d'Orleans. "A duchess kissed his hands before everyone, and if a duchess kissed his hands, what parts of him would ordinary ladies kiss?"

Owing to the "success" of his scheme, by 1720 John Law became the richest man on earth. To get away from the madness and mayhem

Shares in John Law's Mississippi Company
1719–1720

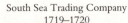

South Sea Trading Company
1719–1720

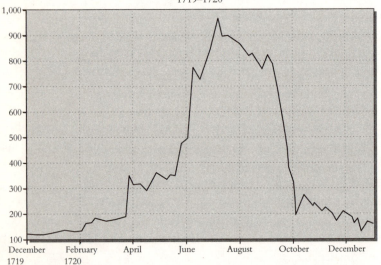

FIGURE 3.1 Spread the Wealth
The "Bubble" Money Finds Its Way into the Economy. Much of the money employed by speculators in John Law's Mississippi Scheme (top) slipped across the border to participate in London's South Sea Bubble (bottom) just 6 months later. It also drove up prices of luxury goods and real estate in France—a pattern repeated three centuries later in Japan and the United States.

stirred up by the trading on rue Quincampoix, Law bought a whole block of buildings on the present-day site of the fashionable Place Vendome. He opened offices in the Hotel Soissons and began to acquire chateaux around the country. By the time he was invited to leave France, he owned more than a dozen of them. At the height of his popularity and wealth, Law's possessions included the French central bank, and the entire Louisiana Territory, which stretched from the Gulf of Mexico to the Great Lakes, from the Appalachians through the Midwest to the Rocky Mountains. His company had a monopoly on French trade with the Americas, India, and the Far East. Law, a Scottish commoner, was granted the title of Duc d'Arkansas—and became the first American duke.

Alas, all things get corrected—even men's reputations.

END OF THE ILLUSION

As Frederic Bastiat noted about a hundred years later, in economics there are things that are seen and things that are unseen. And it is often the unseen that counts. The French in general—Parisians in particular—appeared, for all the world, to be getting rich at a pace never before seen in human history. The Duc d'Orleans was firmly convinced that Law's paper money was the elixir the country needed, so he printed more. "Why shouldn't he?" Tvede asks, "wasn't it evident that the money-printing had made the country prosper? And if so, why not print more? Money was simply like oil to the economic machinery, wasn't it? The more oil, the better the machinery worked!"

Unfortunately, for Law, the fabulous success of his ideas and his popularity incited the envy of more than a few political enemies. Early in 1720, a well-known aristocrat, Prince de Conti, wanted to get in on a new issue of Compagnie des Indes shares, but Law did not permit the sale. De Conti's response? He rounded up all the Banque Royale notes he had previously earned—an amount large enough to fill two carriages—and presented them to the bank. "Voilà, monsieurs!" he is reported to have said. [Here are] "your notes, which are 'payable at sight.' Now, do you see them? Well then, hand over the coins."

The bank complied. When the Duc learned of the Prince's request, he was furious and ordered two thirds of the metal coins to be returned to the bank. But the damage was done. A small fissure in the facade of confidence had opened. Richard Cantillon, well aware that nothing was propping up the notes, sold out his entire portfolio, netting some 20 million livres. Cantillon closed up his banking office and left France, never to return. Two other heavy hitters in the Paris banking scene, Bourdon and La Richardiere, began presenting their notes in small quantities so as not to attract attention. They secretly started to secure silver and jewelry, and had it all—coins included—squirreled away in Amsterdam and England.

Before long, mobs of *lumpeninvestoriat* were trying to break down the doors of the Banque Royale en masse, in an attempt to redeem their plunging banknotes and shares of Law's monopoly holding firm, the Mississippi Company. Average investors of the day began hoarding gold coins, stuffing them under their mattresses or shipping them secretly out of the country. The money supply, which had previously been expanding exponentially, reversed direction.

Believing that he could restore confidence by decree, prevent hoarding, and avoid having money physically removed from the country, the Duc made a series of fatal errors. He declared the notes were 5 percent more valuable than their metal counterparts. That did not work, so he did it again, declaring the notes were 10 percent more valuable. Later, in February 1720, he forbade French citizens from using the gold coins altogether and later informed them that any person found holding coins in excess of 500 livres risked confiscation and penalties.

Finally, the Duc cranked up the printing press. As noted, between February and May of that year, 1,500 million livres worth of banknotes were printed. The total paper money for supply rose to nearly 3,000 million livres. Law then ordered the "malcontents" in Paris to be gathered up and marched through the streets of the city so to make people believe they would be returning with profits from the new world. However, when the same dirty faces began reappearing in the dark alleys from whence they came, confidence continued to ebb, and finally disappeared altogether.

In the end, nothing could save Law's company or the worthless scrip issued by the Banque Royale. The collapse of the Mississippi Company in 1720 ruined thousands of middle-upper class French citizens and destabilized the French currency. Only months before,

France had the outward appearance of the richest, most populated and confident nation in Europe. Now she was bankrupt. From the king's court downward, the citizenry was traumatized by the very idea of stock companies. To this day, the French are reluctant stock market investors. Until recently, they even eschewed the term *banque*, preferring instead names such as *Credit National, Credit Lyonnais,* and *Caisse D'Épargne* for their savings institutions.

Mirror of Folly

Once thought to be greater than the king himself, Law was forced, under protection of the royal guards, to live in the Palais Royale. At one point, when a mob saw his carriage pass, instead of trying to get a glimpse of the man, it attacked the carriage and smashed it to bits. Luckily for Law, he was not inside. Later, Law was given permission by Philip II to leave France altogether—disgraced and in debt to the tune of 6.7 million livres.

By the time of his death in Venice in 1729, Law, the man "of cool calculation and dazzling innovative ideas" would, by outward appearance, be "but a shadow of his former self . . . reduced to an aging trembler with a pronounced tic."[2] But, always the schemer, Law held one more surprise for French and British ambassadors sent to review his estate. An inventory of Law's wealth in 1729 revealed 81 boxes of paintings, sculptures, musical instruments, and furniture. Among the 481 paintings, were originals by some of the great masters. The first page of the inventory, Murphy tells us, lists 22 paintings including a Titian, a Raphael, four Tintorettos, and a Paolo. "Flicking through the inventory, other great names appear," Murphy writes, "including Holbein, Michaelangelo, Poussin, Leonardo da Vinci, and no less than three Rubens!"

Not surprisingly, following the collapse of the Mississippi Scheme, John Law was the target of enough satirical engravings to fill a popular collection—published in 1720 in Holland, under the title, *The Great Mirror of Folly.* One famous engraving—a frontispiece for a short play about the mania—depicts a crowd of share speculators surrounding Law on the rue Quincampoix. The caricature of Law in the scene shows him ingesting gold and silver coins fed to him by the Duc D'Orleans, converting them into paper internally, shall we say, and a frenzied group of investors collecting the bills that fall from his backside.

Montesquieu wrote a satirical allegory based on the Law story lampooning the idea that gold and silver—the pillars of the contemporary monetary system—could be replaced by anything so light and airy as bank credit. And Daniel Defoe made light of Law's scheme with this colorful verse:[3]

> Some in clandestine companies combine;
> Erect new stocks to trade beyond the line;
> With air and empty names beguile the town,
> And raise new credits first, then cry' em down;
> Divide the empty nothing into shares,
> And set the crowd together by the ears.

Economic historians have been, if anything, less kind. Karl Marx suggested John Law had a "pleasant character mixture of swindler and prophet." Alfred Marshal dismisses Law as "that reckless, and unbalanced, but most fascinating genius."

Yet, on the other hand, serious economists in the twentieth century regarded Law's ideas with respect. "John Law, I have always felt is in a class by himself," Joseph Schumpeter wrote in his opus *The History of Economic Analysis.* "He worked out the economics of his projects with a brilliance, and yes, profundity, which places him in the front ranks of monetary theorists of all time." Meanwhile, the writer, J. Shield Nicholson suggested that, despite the catastrophe, John Law may have been an excellent financier; just as Napoleon was a great soldier despite Waterloo.

A Short History of Speculative Manias

There are minor investment manias, and there are major ones. Over the nearly 300 years following the Mississippi mania, the setting for investment manias has repeatedly changed, but the love interest, the dialogue, and the dramatic tension have largely remained the same.

"The saga of the Mississippi scheme [and the South Sea bubble] is historically relevant," writes Marc Faber, "because it contains all the major features of subsequent manias: shady characters, corruption, fraud, dubious practices, the creation of money and the extension of risky loans in order to keep the speculative orgy going, the catalyst, which leads to the initial collapse—usually the revelation of some fraud, the inability of a large speculator to come up with the money to meet a margin call, the revelation that insiders had cashed out, or some adverse economic or political news—and then panic during which greed and euphoria are replaced by fear and the speculators' desire to get out at any price."[4]

Time after time, generation after generation, ordinary people become convinced that they are seeing the dawn of a new era that will bring unimaginable riches and prosperity to all. New era thinking comes in many packages, but is usually inspired by some sort of discovery: gold deposits in California in 1849, for instance, or outside of Sydney and Melbourne in 1851; the application of new inventions, such as canals, railroads, the automobile, radio, PCs, the Internet, and wireless communications; or even the opening up of new territories, such as India, South America, and the Mississippi Territory. Each of these events has given rise to a spell of speculation. As, perhaps, will the opening of China's market in the twenty-first century.

Spells of "irrational exuberance" grip entire populations from time to time, and spread from place to place like an infectious disease. Gaseous fortunes made in the Paris of early 1720 found their way to the speculative halls of London only six months later, where they inflated the South Sea bubble. Richard Cantillon resurfaced there several years later, too, where he wrote one of the first known books on economics. More recently, following the collapse of the Japanese market in 1989 and subsequent central bank rate cuts throughout the 1990s, money flowed from Japan to the U.S. markets. In what had become known as the "yen carry trade," money was borrowed at interest rates approaching zero in Japan and was used to purchase U.S. Treasury coupons yielding 8.16 percent.

Minor manias have occurred with regularity in the past century but have caused little damage. In the United States, stocks in bowling rallied irrationally in 1961, gaming stocks flew off the shelves in 1978, and the first PC companies such as Commodore, Atari, and Coleco (whose original business was above-ground swimming pools) soared in 1983. Likewise, dubious companies such as Presstek, Diana, and Iomega reached nosebleed valuations in 1995. But these minor bubbles are like border wars or revolutions in small countries. They attract little attention and are over before most people become aware of them.

Also recently, there have been larger, but still harmless, speculative manias, confined to individual sectors. Ray Devoe lists at least four: The Great Garbage Market of 1968 involving any stock that appeared to be related to technology, reminiscent of the dot-com frenzy of 1999; manias in uranium, airlines, and color television also occurred—but these did not infect other areas of the market.[5] When these bubbles burst, the participating stocks incurred most of the damage. However, there is always some spillover, as many of the former high-flying stocks are virtually unsellable when a bubble bursts. Liquidity disappears, and large-capitalization stocks with good markets are sold instead.

But major manias, like wars, are another matter. When these major bubbles—1873 and 1929 in the United States, 1989 in Japan, 1997 in the emerging economies—are pricked, the impact on the economy is usually serious and often global. Bubbles usually begin in a low-inflation environment, thus allowing the expanding credit to feed directly into asset prices instead of consumer prices. Consumer price inflation was low in the 1920s, very low in the 1980s in Japan, and low and falling in 1990s America.

Faber explains:

> The bubble model always involves a "displacement," which leads to extraordinary profit opportunities, overtrading, over-borrowings, speculative excesses, swindles and catchpenny schemes, followed by a crisis during which fraud on a massive scale comes to light, then by the closing act during which the outraged public calls for the culprits to be taken to account. In each case, excessive monetary stimulus and the use of credit fuels the flames of irrational speculation and public participation, which involves a larger and larger group of people seeking to become rich without any understanding of the object of speculation.

Investors never squawk when their assets are rising in price, so the money and credit inflation is allowed to continue—and is even encouraged—until it finally reaches such grotesque levels that the smart money cannot help but notice, and begins looking for a way out. Likewise, a major boom is almost always accompanied by some technological or business excitement. In the 1920s, people believed that new machines, radios, and appliances were the source of the apparent boom. In the 1980s, people believed in the quality of Japanese management and Japan's whole enterprise system.

As Hyman Minsky has shown, booms actually play an important economic role—they focus resources on an up-and-coming sector and speed its development. Investors are not crazy to put money into a boom at the beginning; they are crazy to do so at the end, when prices have become absurd.

The bust phase of an investment mania comes about when reality begins to nag, profits are not realized, and confidence turns to trepidation . . . and then fear. A big bust is often accompanied by rapid reductions in the money supply and a contraction of credit, as creditors fear lending to riskier and riskier clientele. Following the deflation of the Mississippi bubble in 1720, despite the aggressive efforts of Philip II to stop it, the money supply in France decreased rapidly. The savviest investors physically removed the gold and silver coins from the country. Having lost confidence in the paper money, spooked merchants and traders engaged in widespread hoarding of the coins, stuffing them in mattresses and burying them in holes in the ground. And bank credit shrank.

Another edict stating that all notes bearing a value between 1,000 and 10,000 livres could only be used to buy government bonds, Compagnie des Indes shares, or be placed in bank accounts further reduced the money supply. One of the central tenets of Law's theory had been proven wrong. Once confidence is shot, a central bank cannot manage the money supply. Still, the idea persists.

John Law died in disgrace, but central banking was as big a hit as income tax. The first modern central bank with any staying power, the Bank of France, was set up less than a century later following another financial disaster: the French Revolution. The rest of Europe soon followed suit.

The strong, centralized governments of the 19th and 20th centuries wanted control over money. Central banks gave it to them. But they had learned their lessons—at least for a while. According to Ferdinand Lips of Lion Capital Group in Zurich, Switzerland, the gold standard of the nineteenth century represented "the highest achievement of the civilized world. The gold standard was neither conceived at a monetary conference, nor was it the brainchild of some genius. It was the result of centuries of experience."[6]

When you enter the Bank of England museum today you are greeted by animatronic seventeenth-century members of Parliament having an argument about money.

"The use of paper money must always be secondary to the precious metals and must flow from credit," says one. "And credit must, of its nature, rise out of the opinion that the paper money was issued in due proportion to the quantity of coins."

"Rubbish," says the other.

Our wigged, latter-day hard money enthusiast is not to be deterred. He concludes, "The value of paper money must always be dependent on the possibility of converting it into silver and gold."

"The Bank of England is famous for the gold (it used to have) in its vaults," writes colleague Dan Denning, "but the Bank itself was capitalized by government debt, not gold. Private creditors pooled their resources in 1694 and made the government a loan of 1.2 million pounds at 8 percent. The loan was secured by customs and excise revenues, which the state commands of course, upon pain of death.

"There were times," Dan says, "when England was not at war, that the Bank notes were convertible for gold. But war and gold standards are mutually exclusive. And so the gold standard was abandoned."[7]

The economic debacle of the 1930s spelled the end of the gold standard for domestic economies. And ever so gradually, the dangers of paper money faded from memory. Little by little, economists, central bankers, and politicians alike came to accept fiat paper currencies, and began to argue about how they could use them to promote greater prosperity than Nature herself allowed—the very same idea once put forward by John Law (see Table 3.1).

TODAY, THE POTOMAC

In the United States, Richard Nixon cut the link between the dollar and gold definitively on August 15, 1971, blaming global speculators for betting against the nation's currency. Since that time, the world has been using a money system that is, to put it in its best light, experimental. As we've seen, the last experiments of this sort—on anything like this scale—were conducted in the eighteenth century. Then, the Bank of England substituted pieces of paper—stock in the South Sea Company—for government debt.

In the U.S. version, circa 2009, the Fed uses pieces of green paper called "dollars" to buy up government debt . . . and toxic tranches of

TABLE 3.1 A Short History of Speculative Excess*

Mania	Era	Country	Object of Desire
Tulip Mania	1636–1637	Dutch Republic	Exotic tulip bulbs, real estate, canals, shares of the Dutch East India Trading Company
Mississippi Scheme	1719–1720	France	Shares of the Mississippi Company, banknotes from the Banque Générale and the Banque Royale
South Sea Bubble	1720	England	Shares of the South Sea Trading Company, government debt
Treasury Bond Bubble	1792	United States	U.S. Bonds (on acceptance of the U.S. Constitution)
Waterloo Speculation	1815–1816	England	Speculation in commodities and trade with the United States
Wildcat Bank Bubble	1837	United States	Cotton, land, silver, banks in the Wild West that printed their own money
Railroad Mania	1847–1857 1873	England, European Continent, United States	Shares in railroad companies, real estate, wheat, building supplies
Precious Metal Mania	1893	Australia, United States	Silver, gold, gold mines, land
Money Panic	1907	France, Italy, United States	Coffee, railroads, bank lending
Postwar Boom and Bust	1920–1921	England, United States	Stocks, commodities, ships
The Great Crash	1929	United States	Stocks bought on margin
Collapse of Bretton Woods	1974–1975	United States, worldwide	Stocks, REITs, office buildings, tankers, Boeing 747s
Black Monday Collapse	1987	United States, worldwide	Stocks, luxury real estate, office buildings, the dollar
Japan Inc.	1990	Japan	Nikkei shares, real estate
The Great Tech Wreck	1996–2000	United States, worldwide	Stocks, especially Internet and telecom companies
The World Wide Crack Up Boom	2007–20??	United States, worldwide	Stocks, Bonds, Commodities, Real Estate, Fine Art . . . you name it

*In the 1990s, investors in U.S. equities markets had come to believe that booms and busts were no longer a part of the investment landscape. Au contraire, the 1996–2000 bubble attracted—and consumed—a larger amount of capital than any other speculative bubble in history. Speculative manias often accompany the opening of a new territory, the introduction of a new technology, or the end of a war.

mortgage-backed securities. Thus the long-running spectacle continues. Today, for the benefit of those who haven't been paying attention,
we clarify the plot.

The dramatis personae are many. But they fit into two camps. In
one is a whole line of Promethean protagonists—prominent economists and politicians, beginning with Fed chairman Arthur
Burns . . . followed by the epic hero Alan Greenspan. Currently, the
lead is being played by Ben Bernanke, supported by Barack Obama in
the White house and Timothy Geithner at the Treasury Department.
In the other camp are, well, the gods.

It's an antique story, but the current action began in 1971, when
Richard Milhous Nixon snuck in and stole the gods' golden fire. Not
surprisingly, the gods were cheesed off. They had put the metal in the
ground themselves. And gold's record for maintaining steady prices
was second to none. An ounce of gold would buy about as much in
1950 as it would have in 1800 . . . or 1700, when Isaac Newton was
Master of the Mint. But modern political economists turned their
backs on the Periodic Table's number 79.

They wanted a different kind of price stability . . . a stability they
could mess with. Henceforth, the Nixon team announced, the world
financial system would dispense with gold entirely. They would control the value of money themselves. They no longer needed gold
backing them up.

As to this proposition, David Ricardo spoke for the gods:

> Experience shows that neither a State nor a Bank ever had the unre-
> stricted power of issuing paper money, without abusing that power: in
> all States, therefore, the issue of paper money ought to be under some
> check and control, none seems so proper for that purpose, as that of
> subjecting the issues of paper money to the obligation of paying their
> notes, either in gold coin or bullion.[8]

And thus were the lines drawn. Who would prevail? The gods or
the Man? It would be a first for mankind. But in the 190 years since
Ricardo wrote, had man evolved into a more perfect being? Given a
once-in-a-lifetime opportunity to stiff foreign creditors by printing
up dollars at will, would a nation of angels be able to resist?

You may guess the answer. But what is extraordinary about this tale is that the telling has taken so long. And then, when it inevitably goes the way it always goes, people are astonished by it!

It looked as though the question would be settled quickly when prices ran wild in the 1970s. Inflation in July of 1971 was almost the same as it is today—about 4.4 percent. But then, Richard Nixon judged it such a threat to the nation that he imposed price controls. Still, without gold anchoring the dollar, prices rose. Ten years later, CPI was running over 10 percent . . . and gold had soared over $800. The gods were having their fun.

But then, into the Fed stepped a colossus of a man; "Tall Paul" Volcker moved quickly to rescue man's paper money. He tightened lending and pushed up 30-year Treasury yields over 15 percent. The dollar advanced and the gods retreated. Man was proud again. The drama seemed to be over. The fellows with their feet on the ground had triumphed.

For the next 20 years, crises came and crises went. Each one was dealt with by softening up man's money with more cash and credit. And each one seemed like such a success; man's confidence grew. Consumer price inflation remained low and gold fell. By 1999, gold coins were practically the only thing you left on the seats of your car in Baltimore . . . confident that no one would bother stealing them.

And as recently as November of 2007, William Poole, President of the Federal Reserve Bank of St. Louis, speaking for the whole race and sounding like Scipio after the destruction of Carthage, announced:

> Macroeconomists today do not believe that policies to stabilize the price level and aggregate economic activity create a hazard. Investors and entrepreneurs have as much incentive as they ever had to manage risk appropriately. What they do not have to deal with is macroeconomic risk of the magnitude experienced all too often in the past.[9]

But today, the macroeconomic risk seems as great as ever before. What has gone wrong? The gods had set a trap. Between the Nixon and the Bush II administrations, low rates of consumer price inflation caused our heroes to err. With the quality of their money in no apparent danger, they allowed themselves to print more and more of it.

Money was available to anyone who asked for it. For 25 years, the cost of credit fell . . . leading Americans to borrow and spend . . . until they had borrowed and spent too much. And after the limp recession of 2001–2002, the quantity of paper money increased even faster—three or four times faster than GDP. Fancy new instruments—ARMs, SIVs, CDOs, Swaps, and MBSs—gave people even more rope. And then, the gods roared with laughter.

And now Mr. Bernanke has panicked. He offers even more money and credit to a world that already has too much. Where do the dollars come from? Oh, silly reader, they come from the same place that shares in the South Sea Company . . . or shares in the Mississippi Company (the French version) came from—they just printed them up!

And now, they don't even have to print them up. When the Fed buys U.S. debt, it merely makes an electronic notation . . . like an IOU that disappears as soon as the power goes out.

Neither the Mississippi Bubble nor the South Sea Bubble would have happened had not John Law invented the first central bank—the Banque Generale—in 1716. Americans wouldn't have been so bumptious in 1929 had it not been for Fed chairman Benjamin Strong's little "coup de whiskey" intended to help out his friend Montagu Norman at the Bank of England. The Japanese wouldn't have goosed their stock market up to 39,000 (currently near 12,000) had it not been for the exceptionally low interest rates following the Plaza Accords in September 1985; rates were cut four times the following year, sending Japanese property and equities soaring. And Americans never would have gone on a residential property binge had the prime rate not been kept exceptionally low for an exceptionally long period under the leadership of Alan Greenspan.

Centrally planned prices send the wrong signals and cause people to miscalculate. And no price causes as many miscalculations as the price of credit—controlled at the short end by central bankers. Of course, anyone can make a mistake. But to make the kind of mess we're seeing in the capital markets now, you need a theory. Of course, central bankers had one.

The foundation for modern central banking theory was laid down in the year Alan Greenspan was born—1926. That was when one of the first "neoclassical" economists, Professor Irving Fisher, published "A Statistical Relationship between Unemployment and Price Changes,"[10] arguing that a little inflation was a good thing, since it seemed to stimulate employment.

Then, "in the 1970s," writes Nobel Prize winner Edmund Phelps in the *Wall Street Journal*, "a new school of neo-neoclassical economists proposed that the market economy, though noisy, was basically predictable. All the risks in the economy, it was claimed, are driven by purely random shocks—like coin throws—subject to known probabilities."[11]

By 2001, the Fed opened a new museum in Chicago. Visitors were invited to look at the economy as though it were a science project. They were confronted with a problem and asked what would be the appropriate response—lower rates or raise them? Then, they were given the correct answer.

Today, America's central bank applies a "rule-based monetary policy"—supposedly founded on the "scientific" discoveries of Irving Fisher and his heirs. What's the rule? Balance out inflation against unemployment. When inflation threatens, raise rates. When the economy is menaced by unemployment, cut them. And always, like a dishonest butcher, make sure your thumb lingers on the inflation side.

Professor Fisher lived long enough to see the gods laughing at him. Just days before the stock market crash of 1929 he famously said, "stock prices have reached what look like a permanently high plateau."[12] Then, when the crash came he suggested that the "market was only shaking out the lunatic fringe,"[13] and claimed that prices would soon go much higher. A few months later, Fisher had lost his fortune and his reputation, but still told investors that recovery was just around the corner.

So far, as Alan Greenspan has only gotten a few chuckles, as he attempted to explain in the *Financial Times* in 2008, where he was and what he was doing when the world's biggest bubble took shape. But the more he explains, the more people understand: that the "science" of central banking is nothing more than claptrap, and Mr. Greenspan is a scalawag. More on the Maestro in a moment.

HELL TO PAY

There are good booms . . . and then there are bad booms.

A good boom is like the one following World War II. Real money was invested. Production increased. Real savings were spent. Wages increased.

Profits increased. At the end of the boom, people were wealthier than they were at the beginning of it.

A bad boom is based on bad money. When the Fed (by way of the Treasury) prints up an extra dollar bill, the gesture lacks sincerity; like a duelist who first smiles and shakes your hand, then walks back 20 paces and pulls a trigger; you know he didn't really mean it. Instead of being built on real savings, the faux boom is built on monetary inflation and credit. And when it comes to an end, people are no better off. Their money is worth less than it used to be. And the average fellow has dug himself deeper into debt in order to enjoy the boom years.

"But many people really have gotten much richer during this boom, haven't they?" you might ask.

Yes, a Crack-Up Boom is fundamentally a financial boom. Money comes into the system—a lot of it. People don't know it's phony money; they can't tell the difference. This money hangs around the financial industry and everyone there has a good time. But society, as a whole, is not any richer because Monet paintings are more expensive . . . or because stocks are more expensive . . . or because a hedge fund manager makes a billion dollars. Society is richer when people generally earn higher wages, stash away more savings, and pay down debt. That is not what is happening.

"Well, okay, maybe in the end, a lot of people regret it . . . in the meantime, why not join the fun?" Be our guest. Buy a Warhol. Put some money into China. Get a parking space in New York for $225,000. Better yet, start a hedge fund. That's the best way . . . make "2 and 20" on other people's money. Take big risks . . . the bigger the better. Heck, the bigger the risk, the more you'll make . . . right up until the end. Then, of course, the hedge fund will get wiped out. But what do you care? The investors will take the loss.

Which, of course, raises a key question: "When will this boom end?"

The Great American Housing Bust

By mid-2007, in the waning days of the housing bubble, the whole world economy was enjoying a spell of catastrophic prosperity. That is to say, things were going far too well . . . for far too many people.

And here, dear reader, we let you in on one of the deepest secrets of human life: Things do not work in a straightforward, simpleminded way.

If they did, then perhaps bureaucrats, Bolsheviks, and world-improvers really could make things better. But there is good . . . and there is evil. The race goeth not always to the swift, nor the battle to the strong. And bubbles don't always blow up when you want them to.

We say that just to set the stage. What follows is a brief theatrical discourse on the nature of life in the universe in general . . . and life in this great worldwide super-bubble of 2007 in particular.

Things were going remarkably well—especially for people who count; that is, the people who make the headlines and write them. Paris Hilton was out of jail. Stephen Schwarzman had successfully off-loaded his private equity business. The glitterati glittered more than ever. The investorati were as happy as pigs in merde, too . . . for their portfolios, almost no matter where they are or what is in them, were getting fatter by the day. Restaurants were full in London, New York, Shanghai—wherever the great money machine was switched on and humming. And the speculator, who depends on a fulsome supply of greater fools to buy him out of his bets, is in heaven, too. In the United States, there's one born every minute, just as Mr. Barnum said. But in Asia, heck, they can't even count them.

At art auctions, hedge fund impresarios turned up—wads of cash in their pockets, consultants by their sides—and bid the most remarkable prices for the most unremarkable works of "art." But thus does the great machine churn money—from one hand to the next . . . from dimwit to genius . . . from greedy SOB to saintly do-gooder . . . from fool to knave. It was breathtaking to watch.

But behold! There is more to it.

There are rules, lesson, patterns . . . and hell to pay.

When things go so well, for so long, it seems as if all the cuss words had been struck from a dictionary . . . as if negative numbers had been removed from the number scheme. It is as if bad seeds had been removed from nature . . . and bad genes from humanity. It is as if we finally had God without the devil . . . and Heaven without Hell.

No chance of going to Hell? Well, hell . . . then let's have some fun! No negative numbers? Well . . . what are we waiting for? Let's reach for higher rates of yield; to hell with the risk.

Unfortunate acts of Nature happen as Nature will have them. Hurricanes, cyclones, droughts—nature will have her way with us.

But unfortunately, acts of market tend to happen when men reach for yield.

The markets, which are fairly benign most of the time, are occasionally wicked. But that is just the way the world works. God reigns—most of the time. But the devil sneaks in on occasion, and causes mayhem. Mankind's history is one of progress, usually . . . but not always. There are also long periods of ferocious backsliding. Inflation, too, is common, at least since the invention of paper currencies. But woe to the poor sod who thinks it's automatic, guaranteed, and immutable.

"God and the Devil are about as four to three," writes Samuel Butler. "There is enough preponderance of God to make it far safer to be on his side than on the Devil's, but the excess is not so great as his professional claqueurs pretend it is. It is like gambling at Monte Carlo; if you play long enough you are sure to lose, but now and again you may win a great deal of excellent money if you will only cease playing the moment you have won it."[14]

Usually, taking the broad sweep of human history, man gets richer one year to the next. It's a bit like a street brawl in South London. The stronger, faster, bigger man is the better bet—usually. But, the runt can land a lucky blow from time to time. And let the big man forget the risk . . . let him become too confident . . . too drunk, too fat, too sure of himself . . . and the little guy will knock him down every time.

Let a boom run long enough, dear reader, and it will turn into a bust. Already at bubble stage in many places and many markets—when the devil finally gets his due, it is likely to come as very unpleasant to many people. In the long run, of course, it is God's world. But even He likes to see us get a good kick in the seat of the pants from time to time.

The Worldwide Crack-Up Boom

A kiss is still a kiss . . . and a bubble is still a bubble. When a kiss is over, it's over. When a bubble pops . . . well . . . that's all she wrote! All kisses end—even the wettest "French" kisses. And so do all bubbles—even sloppy mega-bubbles of liquidity.

"This one will be no exception," we remember thinking before the carnage got underway. But, of course, it's not the certainties that make life interesting, it's the uncertainties—the known unknowns and the unknown unknowns, as Mr. Rumsfeld said. We are all born of woman and end up where all men born of women end up—dead. But that doesn't mean we can't have some fun between baptism and last rites.

The worldwide financial bubble we faced was both worldlier, and more financial than any in history.

And, in the summer of 2007, it was still very much alive. So much alive that the media could hardly keep up with it. *Forbes* magazine, for example, tried to estimate the wealth of the world's richest people. But the rich don't typically give out their balance sheets, telephone numbers, and home addresses. So, there's a fair amount of guesswork in the calculations.

When it came to guesstimating the net worth of Stephen Schwarzman, founder of Blackstone, the Forbes crew wandered off into fiction. They put his wealth at about $2 billion. Recent filings in connection with the new Blackstone IPO show he earned that much in a single year!

In that phase of the bubble, it is as if your neighbors were throwing a wild party and you weren't invited. You detest them . . . envy them . . . and want to join them, all at once. A very small part of the population is having a ball; everyone else is getting restless and wondering when the noise will stop.

Meanwhile, the experts, commentators, kibitzers, and analysts were saying that there is a whole new phase of the giant bubble about to unfold; things could get a whole lot crazier. Even many of our respected colleagues were pointing to a text by the great Austrian economist, Ludwig von Mises, for a clue. What we have here, they say, is what Mises described as a "Crack-Up Boom."[15]

Before we go on, readers should be aware that the "Austrian school" of economics is probably the best theory about the way the world works. Like our newsletter, *The Daily Reckoning*, it is suspicious of efforts to control the natural workings of an economy, in general . . . and suspicious of central banking, in particular. The fact that it was a one-time "Austrian," Alan Greenspan, who became the most celebrated central banker in history, only increases our suspicions. He was able to master central banking, we imagine, because he understood what it really is—a swindle.

What Is a "Crack-Up Boom?"
Von Mises:

> This first stage of the inflationary process may last for many years. While it lasts, the prices of many goods and services are not yet adjusted to the altered money relation. There are still people in the country who have not yet become aware of the fact that they are confronted with a price revolution which will finally result in a considerable rise of all prices, although the extent of this rise will not be the same in the various commodities and services. These people still believe that prices one day will drop. Waiting for this day, they restrict their purchases and concomitantly increase their cash holdings. As long as such ideas are still held by public opinion, it is not yet too late for the government to abandon its inflationary policy.

> But then, finally, the masses wake up. They become suddenly aware of the fact that inflation is a deliberate policy and will go on endlessly. A breakdown occurs. The crack-up boom appears. Everybody is anxious to swap his money against "real" goods, no matter whether he needs them or not, no matter how much money he has to pay for them. Within a very short time, within a few weeks or even days, the things which were used as money are no longer used as media of exchange. They become scrap paper. Nobody wants to give away anything against them.

> It was this that happened with the Continental currency in America in 1781, with the French mandats territoriaux in 1796, and with the German mark in 1923. It will happen again whenever the same conditions appear. If a thing has to be used as a medium of exchange, public opinion must not believe that the quantity of this thing will increase beyond all bounds. Inflation is a policy that cannot last.[16]

Mises is describing the lunatic phases of a classic inflationary cycle.

At first, no one can tell the difference between a real dollar—one that is earned, saved, invested, or spent—and one that just came off the printing presses. They figure that the new dollar is as good as the old one. And then, prices rise . . . and people don't know what to make of it. Later, they begin to catch on . . . and all Hell breaks loose.

You see, if you could really get rich by printing more currency, Zimbabweans would all be as rich as Midas, since the Mugabe government runs the presses night and day.

Von Mises died in 1973—long before this boom really got going—let alone cracked up. He may have never heard of a hedge fund . . . or even a derivative, for that matter. A world money system without gold? He probably couldn't have imagined it. People spending millions of dollars for a Warhol? Twenty million for a house in Mayfair? Chinese stocks at 40 times earnings? He would have chuckled in disbelief. He understood how national currency bubbles expand and how they pop, but he probably never would have imagined how insane things could get when you have a whole world monetary system in bubble mode.

He'd have recognized the beginning of this bubble . . . and he'd have recognized the end, but the middle . . . or the beginning of the end—that would have dumbfounded him. During his lifetime he saw a Crack-Up Boom in Germany in the 1920s . . . and a few more here . . . but he never saw a worldwide Crack-Up Boom.

No, dear reader, no one, anywhere, has ever seen a worldwide Crack-Up Boom. (See Figure 3.2.) We're the first, ever. Pretty exciting, huh?

FIGURE 3.2 The Worldwide Crack-Up Boom
Along with the housing bubble in the United States and much of the Western World in 2003–2008, many of the world's globalized markets boomed . . . and busted, too. The BRIC economies—Brazil, Russia, India, and China—all crashed in 2008, as did U.S. equities markets. Commodities, as indicated here by the CRB Index, gold, oil, and copper, had their worst year since the Great Depression.

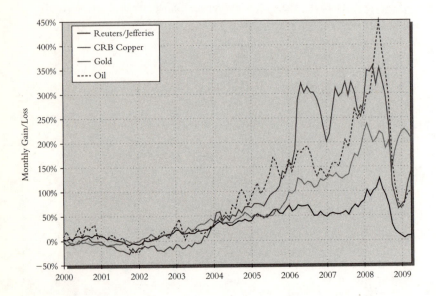

FIGURE 3.2 (Continued)

FIN DE BUBBLE EPOQUE

When Ronald Reagan moved into the White House, total U.S. debt equaled 168 percent of GDP. The next 27 years took the total to 370 percent; it was heralded as a triumph of the Anglo-Saxon free enterprise system, but it left people with an additional $27 trillion of debt. And now, the economic system that created so many heavy balls and such long chains is in the recovery room, looked after by quacks and prayed for by most of the world.

You can explain the model in a few simple sentences: Encourage people to spend. When they run out of money, encourage them to borrow. When they tire of borrowing and spending, lend them more at lower rates.

As a way for people to build wealth, this economic model of the Bubble Period was as ineffective as a bad banker. It was a "have your cake and eat it, too" school of financial success with an obvious flaw. People noticed it when the correction began. They went to their cupboards and found there was nothing there. Homeowners—who had borrowed heavily against their houses—found their equity had disappeared. Capitalists found they had no capital. Workers lost their work.

And this year, governments' tax receipts are collapsing, too. In the United States, they're down 14 percent in the first half of this fiscal year. Expenses, on the other hand, are exploding. This leads to a question: Governments must borrow on a Herculean scale—but from whom? The United States is expected to float a record $2 trillion in IOUs for 2009—about 15 percent of GDP. If the downturn persists, as it has in Japan, we could see the U.S. national debt rise to Japanese levels—close to 200 percent of GDP.

In London, the numbers are smaller, but the math is similar. The government has projected $175 billion deficits over the next two years. But this might be just the beginning. If deficits continue at this rate, Britain, too, could find itself back in the 1950s—after two world wars, with public debt at two times GDP.

What justifies such sacrifices? In time of war, citizens collect scrap iron . . . sell their jewelry . . . and buy bonds—anything to help pay for bullets and keep the Huns East of the Rhine. But what now? People clamp even bigger balls and longer chains on themselves . . . and for what? Taking flowers to the recovery room, they look in on the bubble model as though on a weary friend. "He supported us all," says an anxious relative . . . "We must do all we can to save him."

"Pull the plug," is our advice.

Of course, when he was in his prime the bubble was fun—laughing, singing, spending . . . a grasshopper on stilts! And there were all those friendly ants in Asia ready to lend him money. At the peak, the United States had net borrowing of some $2 billion per day (trade deficit/365).

But now, take the United States' anticipated budget deficit and divide it by 365. You get a figure of nearly $6 billion per day. Even at his peak, the old bug didn't bring in that kind of money. And now, the foreigners are in recession, too. They've got their own aches and pains to cure. So, how will the United States finance the biggest deficit of all time? How has Japan done it?

Japan's economy has been locked up for 19 long years. It financed its confinement itself, drawing on the savings of a remarkably long-suffering population. Stimulus packages came and went. On average, they cost about 3 percent of GDP per year. The biggest came in 1998, with a price of 6 percent of GDP. Financing this house arrest was easy—Japan began the period with a savings rate of 14 percent of GDP.

The United States, on the other hand, began with a savings rate of zero. More recently, the savings rate has been reported as high as 5 percent as middle-aged squirrels desperately hide a few nuts for a long winter retirement. But the gods can add it up. Even if every dollar of U.S. savings is tossed down the public hole, it will still be two-thirds empty.

Anticipating the problem, the Fed has already leapt into the hole itself. It offers to buy the government's bonds itself. Of course, the Fed has no real money. It must create money to make the purchase. It's the latest miracle treatment, say the quacks in charge. If the Fed creates enough new money, it will offset the losses caused by the downturn. Then, happy days will be here again. The whole world seems to believe it. Stocks are rising. Ben Bernanke said in a rare *60 Minutes* interview in May of 2009, that the U.S. economy would recover before Christmas.[17] The convalescence may be long, he continued, with his vision apparently restored; but it will be steady.

How the gods must howl! "In the Bubble Epoque people tried to get something for nothing . . . Imagine, they thought they could get rich by borrowing money and spending it. Have you ever heard of something so ridiculous? Ha ha! Now, they think they can get rich by spending money that doesn't even exist."

"But that's not the half of it," one of them is sure to notice. "They're digging themselves deeper into debt—trying to revive the very oaf who pushed them down in the hole in the first place."

COME WHAT MAY

At the Daily Reckoning, the warnings of the gods don't fall on deaf ears. "A hard rain's gonna fall," we keep saying . . . and saying . . . and saying . . .

But there is a very important difference between the weather and the markets. In nature, you get occasional catastrophes. But, despite the climate change theorists, these episodes of wind and water, heat and cold are not the fault of the human race. At least, not since the Flood. It was not man who caused Vesuvius to erupt, or who swamped Galveston, or caused the creeping freeze of the "Little Ice Age" in Europe, at the end of the middle ages. No, man is innocent. Nature herself is the culprit.

But who caused the Crash of 1929? What made the tech bubble blow up in 2000? Who's behind the huge run-up in prices in Shanghai in 2007?

Ah, there's the difference. Nature acts more or less independently of mankind. She may be cruel, but she is not perverse. She does not conspire to bring down a shower only when most people have left their umbrellas at home. Nor does she collude to cause temperatures to drop just when people have forgotten to cut firewood. No, she can be tough, but she is not malicious.

Markets, on the other hand, have a malevolent streak. They get together and cause storms precisely when they will do the most damage—just take a look at the housing market.

The crash of the Nasdaq, for example, was caused by the people who bid up prices in the years preceding. In the five years ahead of the

2000 crash, prices rose six times. Had buyers not been so bullish, sellers would not have had so much to sell. In the event, prices fell in half . . . and then in half again.

The crash did not just happen; it happened because of the bubble in tech shares. A bubble is a natural market phenomenon. But bubbles are created by man; all bubbles are destroyed by men, too. And then, investors are underwater.

Sic transit gloria bubbli.

CHAPTER 4

THE ERA OF CROWDS

Half the population no longer reads the newspapers; plainly, they are the more clever half.

—Gore Vidal

One evening, in the heat of the tech frenzy, we overheard a conversation in car number 8 of the Eurostar. We were traveling en route from London to Paris, reading Alan Abelson in *Barron's*, when two men entered the car and sat down nearby. They were casually dressed. Mid-40s. Americans. The sort of men you might find managing an electronics store or enjoying the Super Bowl with friends. One took out a Swiss Army knife the size of a chain saw and opened a package. Out of this, he drew a new watch and put it on—a monstrous thing, it looked like a flying saucer had landed on his wrist. Soon they were joined by a third man whose belt was too tight.

"Whoa," said one, looking at the stock pages of *USA Today*, "look at this . . . I bought this company at 30 two days ago. It's up to 47."

"I got a friend who knows someone at the company. They're going to announce a merger or something. The stock is supposed to go to between 70 and 75."

"What's the name of the company?" asked the one whose belt was too tight.

"It's called e-Plus, I think. Yeah, I think there's a hyphen in there. E-Plus. The stock symbol is PLUS."

"What's it do?"

"I don't know . . . computers or something high tech. But I've already made $1,700 on this stock."

"Why didn't you tell me about it? I don't like to miss a move like that. What d'you say was the symbol?"

"P-L-U-S."

A moment later (and we are not making this up), he had his cell phone out.

"Lenny? Hi, I'm calling you from France." [Note: We were still in England.] "Yeah, I'm on the train. Can you hear me okay? Look, I want you to check out a stock for me. It's called e-Plus . . . No, I don't know what it does . . . technology or something." Then, turning to his friend, "He says he's never heard of it!" Then, back to Lenny on the phone, "Okay . . . look, my buddy says they're going to make an announcement or something. Buy me 20 shares. The price should be about $47. It's going to $75. Okay . . . No, I'm in France . . . so I can't send you a check until next week. Just 20 shares, okay?"

Oscar Wilde complained of people who knew "the price of everything and the value of nothing." In this age of information, these guys were ignorant of everything except the price. The company's numbers, its business plan, its position in the industry, its management, its record of the past and hopes for the future—all were as unknown as the contents of a sausage or the voter registration rules of a distant galaxy.

These fellows were not investing. They were having a lark. They were like baboons at a Buckingham Palace dinner party. Throwing the food around. Laughing. Playing. Getting rich. They had no idea of the rules. No concept of the history. No clue about the risks. Investing was a game to them. And thanks to their ignorance, they were winning.

Did e-Plus have earnings? Did it really have a solid business? Do not bother to check the fundamentals. Most likely, there were none. If you had to ask, it was not for you. The more you knew, the less likely you were to want to buy it. And if you didn't buy it, it couldn't make you rich.

This kind of stock play was not one you should approach with information . . . and certainly not with knowledge, or with its distilled derivative—wisdom. It was the kind of speculation that needed to be made in near-complete ignorance. With reckless abandon, even.

The prevailing formula of the New Era was that Information = Wealth. Information was thought to be the capital of the age. The reciprocal of this algebra was that Ignorance = Poverty. But the investment markets of the late 1990s seemed to show that the exact contrary was also true: At least a certain kind of ignorance was producing spectacular stock market profits. Ignorance = Wealth . . . and at the same time Information = Wealth . . . ergo, we had the proof of what we had guessed: Information = Ignorance.

Swamped with facts, blinded by details, overwhelmed by an infinity of data, and paralyzed by endless analysis—information was making us all dumber.

And maybe poorer, too. The inflation of the information supply rendered it as worthless as Weimar Deutschmarks. Like any inflation, we were impoverished by it. And, like currency during inflation, the information, knowledge, wisdom, and judgment that had been saved up for so many years and used to guide our investment decisions was devalued.

WHEN A CROWD TURNS INTO A MOB

Everything happens at the margin. The marginal person is neither consistently good nor bad, smart nor dumb, bullish nor bearish . . . but is subject to influence. Buy him a drink on election day, and he may vote whatever way you want. Stir him up with the right sort of demagoguery, put him in a crowd, and he could lynch Mother Teresa.

The twentieth century would be the era of crowds, Gustave Le Bon predicted in his 1896 book, *The Crowd*. Crowds had taken over almost all Western governments. There were still monarchs and emperors in their palaces, but popular assemblies were gaining ground everywhere. Modern communications provided the means. Cheap newspapers, trains, and the telegraph made it possible for an entire nation to think almost the same thing at almost the same time. Mobs, which had formerly been limited to fairly small groups in urban areas, became national, even international. Soon, the vast crowds would be interested in politics . . . and in getting rich.

Crowds tend to amplify whatever emotion an individual may feel. People who are normally sensible, who drive on the right-hand side of the road, who can figure out how to use the electronic controls of their home sound system, who have no trouble picking out the lowest price at the supermarket—put them in a crowd and they become raving maniacs. In markets, greed and fear are loosed. Prices are bid up to levels that no sane man would pay if you put it to him on his own, or they are driven down to levels that no sane man could resist. But what does it matter? Sanity has gone out the window. During the last stages of a bull market, like the opening stages of a war, the crowd gets very brave. In the final stages of a war or a bear market, on the other hand, people give up all hope; they become desperate and flee to safety. Reason does not merely sleep . . . it drops on the floor unconscious.

THE MADNESS OF CROWDS

Professor Joseph Lawrence of Princeton University earnestly declared: "The consensus of the millions of people whose judgments decide the price levels in the stock market tells us that these stocks are not overpriced."

"Who then are these men," he continued, "with such a universal wisdom that it gives them the right to veto the judgment of this intelligent multitude?"[1]

There is little doubt what the intelligent multitude thought. They had priced stocks at 20 . . . 30 . . . 40 times earnings. Who could question the judgment of so many?

In large groups of people, complex and even elegant ideas get mashed down to a fermenting syrup of empty jingles, slogans, and campaign folderol. From time to time, Mr. John Q. Public takes up the brew and quaffs it like an alcoholic with an empty stomach. In practically no time at all, it has gone to his head. Professor Lawrence gave us his opinion. Writing in the summer of 1929, his timing was unfortunate: He was right about what the multitudes thought at the time; but a few months later, the multitudes had changed their minds.

"That enormous profits should have turned into still more colossal losses," wrote Graham and Dodd in their review of the 1929 crash and the aftermath, "that new theories have been developed and later discredited, that unlimited optimism should have been succeeded by the deepest despair are all in strict accord with age-old tradition."[2]

Traditions are not created in the course of a single generation. What makes them valuable is that they develop little by little, wrought by heat and cold, beaten into a serviceable shape by countless pounding over many generations, through many complete cycles.

After the Enlightenment, people came to believe that traditions did not matter. If they just had enough information and enough time to think it through, they believed they could reason their way toward anything and everything they wanted. But there's the rub. Knowledge costs time and effort. Like the difference between real profits and virtual ones, the transformation of data, or information, into knowledge requires time and effort. The more important the knowledge acquired, the more time and effort it takes to get it. Wisdom can take decades. Rules and principles—such as "love thy neighbor" or "buy low, sell high"—can take centuries to evolve.

WISDOM AND TRADITION

In the early 1920s, age-old tradition had told investors to watch out for stocks—they were dangerous. In 1921, the great mass of investors judged a dollar's worth of corporate earnings to be worth only $5 of stock price. But something happened in the late 1920s that changed the stock-buying public's view. There was a "new era" in the 1920s, complete with a number of important new innovations such as the automobile, electrical appliances, radio broadcasting, and so on. By 1929, lightheaded investors were willing to pay $33 for every dollar of earnings—and they still considered it a fair trade. Then, of course, came the crash.

By the end of the year, investors asked themselves: "Whatever made me think General Electric was worth so much?" Mr. John Q. Public never had a clue—then or now.

Groups of people neither think nor act as individuals do. As mad as individuals can be, groups of individuals can be even madder. Not only do they act differently, they think differently, too—usually in a manner that is simpleminded, and often moronic or delusional.

Gustave Le Bon wrote:

A crowd thinks in images, and the image itself immediately calls up a series of other images, having no logical connection with the first. Our reasoning shows us the incoherence there is in these images, but a crowd is almost blind to this truth, and confuses with the real event what the deforming action of its imagination has superimposed thereon.

Before St. George appeared on the walls of Jerusalem to all the Crusaders, he was certainly perceived in the first instance by one of those present. By dint of suggestion and contagion the miracle signalized by a single person was immediately accepted by all.

Such is always the mechanism of the collective hallucinations so frequent in history—hallucinations which seem to have all the recognized characteristics of authenticity, since they are phenomena observed by thousands of persons . . .

In the freewheeling play of mobs—whether conducting a battle, watching CNBC, or listening to a campaign speech—the frontier between fact and fiction comes unstuck. Crowds cannot tell the difference. If a man says to the crowd that Martians are about to attack a planet or that they are being victimized by the International Monetary Fund (IMF), each member of the crowd has no personal experience or knowledge to contradict him. In fact, a crowd cannot be certain about anything; its knowledge is of an entirely different kind than that of an individual. A group takes up events or facts only in the crudest and most elemental way. The individual experiences of group members—infinitely varied and nuanced—count for almost nothing.

A generation that has lived through the Great Depression, for example, or the Great War, is likely to remember the event itself, but to *understand* it only as anecdotal evidence of the public knowledge. A man could have lived happily through the 1930s with no idea that he was part of a great anything. But once informed that he had experienced the Great Depression, his particular experiences take on new meaning and are reinterpreted to support the collective sentiment.

MASS COMMUNICATIONS

As technology progressed, modern communications enabled more and more people to feel and act as though they were physically together. Ideas were quickly spread—instantaneously, in fact—so that a man watching CNN in Dubuque was in direct and immediate contact with events that happened all over the world. Television, radio, newspapers, magazines—all helped shape the masses' thoughts, and ensure that all were thinking more or less the same thing at more or less the same moment.

The rise in TV coverage of Wall Street during the 1990s, for example, greatly amplified and exaggerated popular awareness and involvement in stock markets. Without leaving his office or bedroom, an investor could get caught up in the current excitement just as though he were on the trading floor.

The great achievement of the Internet was that it allowed people to get stirred up with mob sentiments . . . and to do something about them immediately. In the mid-1990s, thousands of people became convinced that they could get rich by day-trading stocks via their home or office computers. The 24-hour-a-day online chatter available on the Internet also allowed people to take part in rabble-rousing demagoguery—no matter where they were. They could get riled up about the Monica Lewinsky affair, about Enron, or about any number of things . . . and feel as though they were right there in the Tuileries garden during the French Revolution. They could join the mob without leaving home!

It was widely said that the Internet would make people smarter by giving them access to much more information. What it really did was make people more in tune with mob thinking—for now their own thoughts were crowded out by the constant noise of the World Wide Web.

A man on his own may have had his own experience, good or bad, with the Internet. But once connected, he was likely to have an opinion of the new medium formed not by his own experience but by the collective rattle of sentiment over the e-waves. Once caught up in groupthink, the judgment of the group, even when absurd, is hard to resist.

BEYOND NIETZSCHE

Nietzsche identified two different kinds of knowledge. There are the things you know from personal experience and observation, which he called *erfahrung*, and we will call "private knowledge." There are also the abstractions you think you know—the kind of thing that is reported in the paper and discussed on the editorial pages—which he called *wissen*, and we will call "public knowledge."

What Nietzsche missed was that, not only are there two forms of knowledge, there are also two entirely different ways of reasoning.

The first is the type of reasoning you do with things you know about. If you see someone climb too far out on the limb of a tree, for example, and see the limb break, you might reasonably conclude by analogy that the same thing could happen to you in similar circumstances. Continuing the Nietzschean tradition, we'll call this kind of thinking *schwer uberlegen*. It involves reasonable inferences from firsthand experience or observation.

But if you turn your thoughts to the War against Terror or the next election, you are using a different thinking process altogether. Instead of thinking about things you know, you are thinking about things you cannot know and cannot explain. We call this type of thinking *lumpen denken*. For example, open any newspaper to the editorial page and you are likely to find something similar to the following "Op Ed" in the *International Herald Tribune* by Zbigniew Brzezinski, entitled "Time for America to Intervene." Immediately, we are in a different world.

Your authors disagree with Brzezinski. America cannot intervene, because the nation exists only as an abstraction. A U.S. soldier can shoot someone, a U.S. plane can drop a bomb, but the United States itself is much too big. Whatever "America" does will only be done by a tiny percentage of the whole thing . . . most Americans will play no role, some will be opposed . . . and more than a few will be completely unaware of what is going on.[3]

What were all the interests involved? How could anyone know what they were? It was not remotely possible. But that did not stop Brzezinski.

"Ultimately, the 4.8 million Jewish Israelis cannot permanently sustain the subjugation of 4.5 million Palestinians (1.2 million of whom are second-class Israeli citizens)," he raved, "while Israel's own democracy and sense of moral self-respect would be jeopardized by continuing to do so. . . .

"In these circumstances, America cannot ignore world public opinion. . . ."[4]

The authors have no opinion on the situation in the Mideast. We are Americans, but we have no more interest in what happens between Israel and Palestine than we have about what happens between Zimbabwe and South Africa. We choose Brzezinski's views at random as an example of *lumpen denken* from a man who has made a career of it. Reading carefully, we cannot say whether the former National Security Advisor is right or wrong, for there are no firm footings on which to leverage an opinion. There is hardly a single word in the entire document that is not subject to interpretation, argumentation, and subornation. There are no facts that do not give rise to anti-facts and no conclusions that cannot be contradicted by the very same facts and circumstances. Cicero described the whole experience of public knowledge and *lumpen denken* as "carrying an unlit torch into a dark room."

Brzezinski presents his feelings as if they were logical . . . as if they were the result of some reasoning process. But there was no iron logic behind them. Not even the logic of papier-mâché. His "logic" is just words . . . and hollow public sentiment. Yet, newspaper editorial pages, Internet chat rooms, campaign speeches, TV, and talk radio—even conversations you overhear at a café—are full of just this kind of empty reasoning.

GROSS LUMPEN DENKEN

"The world economy is in trouble," explained Yale professor Jeffrey E. Garten, another editorialist in the *International Herald Tribune* in January 2003. "Corporate investment and trade are slowing, factories are producing more than they can sell, and deflation is threatening many regions. Germany and Japan are stagnating. Big emerging markets, from Indonesia to Brazil, are in deep trouble. Washington must bring together its economic partners—the Group of Seven nations made up of Canada and Japan and four in the European Union—to get the global economy moving again."[5]

What a marvelous world *lumpen denken* creates! Got a problem? Just get a group of policy hacks together. Garten thought they could decide—among themselves—to alter the entire world economy.

The United States was already doing all that it could, he said. Interest rates had been lowered. The nation was "already running huge budget deficits," he noted with approval. But what about those Europeans? We've got to encourage them to lower rates, too, and spend more, too, he thought. And, oh yes, we can also "push Japan to restructure its growth-strangling bank debts."

Hey, that ought to do it. But wait, if you're going to fix the globe's economic problems, why stop there?

Remember, we would have to reconstruct Iraq, he says. That could cost $1.2 trillion, an amount "that does not include the costs of the administration's vision of spreading democratic and free market institutions in the Gulf region." For $1.2 trillion we would expect reconstruction worthy of a Hollywood celebrity surgeon. That was an amount equal to $49,896 per person in Iraq—or 19 times the average annual income. Where would the money come from? Here again, Garten is helpful: "The Bush administration needs to be working with Congress to incorporate the requirement [for the $$$] in planning—something which Mitchell E. Daniels Jr., director of the Office of Management and Budget, has been reluctant to do." We never met Daniels, but we were glad to discover that he is not as insane as Garten.

"We are entering a decade of political and military tension," the latter continued as if he could predict the future, "and nation-building is going to be a major part of America's response." Why not? After fixing the world economy, the hacks ought to be able to build a nation or two without breaking a sweat.

The trouble is people take this kind of *lumpen denken* seriously. They think they can understand big issues as well as small ones and manipulate world events as though they were fixing a lawn mower.

ABSTRACTIONS AS PUBLIC KNOWLEDGE

Crowds of people can "know" things. But it is abstract public knowledge, not direct personal experience, which determines how crowds understand events. Public knowledge has its own peculiar character, for it must be dumbed down to a level that can be absorbed by a mob.

A learned and thoughtful man may speak before a crowd and get no positive reaction whatsoever. A real demagogue, on the other hand, will distill his thoughts into a few simpleminded expressions and soon have enough admirers to run for public office. Readers who have wondered why it is that politicians all seem to be such simpletons now have their answer: It is a requirement for the job. For, en masse, mankind can neither understand complex or ambiguous thoughts nor remember them.

That is why crowds can only remember history in its most intellectually vulgar form. Like everything else, history must be reduced to its lowest common denominator for mass consumption, usually ending up as pure myth. Take this simple matter "of fact": France and the rest of the Allies were victorious in World War I; Germany was the loser. As every schoolchild knows, it is true. It is *wissen*, as Nietzsche termed it; or public knowledge. No one has ever actually seen or experienced it—because it is purely an abstraction—but it is nevertheless considered true.

And yet, if you were to tell a French woman—whose two sons were killed in the war and whose husband was blinded by a grenade—that she should celebrate the victory, she would take you for a fool. A third of France's capital had been used up. Millions were dead. An important part of the country was in ruins. What kind of victory is that?

Ah . . . but France recovered its territories of Alsace and Lorraine! For whom was this an advantage? Did the surviving men in Lorraine find their petite new *femmes* more beautiful than their hefty old *fraus*? Was their *choucroute* tastier than their *sauerkraut* had been? Could they drink more of their local hooch, now that it was called *vin blanc* and not *weiss wein*? Not likely. Instead, they toiled the soil as they had before the war . . . . And for years afterward, they would occasionally discover unexploded bombs from World War I—which often blew up when scraped by a plow.

And in the years following, were the victors of World War I better off than the vanquished? Alas, no. By the 1930s, France, Britain, and America were still in a slump—while Germany boomed. Whereas the Allies seemed tired, worn-out, and aimless—Germany entered a period of remarkable grit, pride, and energy.

Was France more secure, now that it had control over the west bank of the Rhine? Not at all. Germany quickly rearmed, and as subsequent events were to show, became a far bigger threat in 1934 than it had been 20 years earlier.

If France was the winner, what had she won? You might just as well say the French had lost the war as won it.

A FACT IS A FACT, AND YET . . .

What kind of strange knowledge is this, dear reader? The process of *lumpen denken* tells you a "fact" is true, and yet, the exact opposite is also true. And what kind of thought process makes sense of it . . . what kind of reasoning can bring you to two conclusions at the same time, each one separated from the other as day is from night?

This is how the thinking process of a mob differs from an individual. The mob can come to believe almost anything, because the knowledge it builds on is as unsound as its conclusions. An individual's knowledge is much more direct and immediate. A man knows what will happen if he holds a burning match too long or insults his wife; he is rarely mistaken.

Yet, even for an individual, reason is less sure than most people think. We humans flatter ourselves. We believe we are reasonable people, and we almost are. So successful are we at applying reason to the things close at hand that we cannot resist applying the same process to things far afield, about which we haven't a clue. We try to make sense of the events around us by describing the "reasons" they happen . . . and then we extrapolate, looking logically forward to what those reasons will produce next.

Unlike the tsetse fly or the wallaby, a human can put 2 and 2 together. A man working up close, with things that make sense to him, comes up with 4 more often than not. But, when he applies these same reasoning abilities to other people's business—such as how to achieve peace in the Mideast or profit from a boom on Wall Street—the facts turn to mush and the whole equation soon degrades into complete nonsense.

Reason, as it turns out, is our greatest strength. Alas, it is also our greatest conceit. Simple statements of fact, such as "I am a liar," confound us all. If this statement is true, it disproves itself. If it is untrue, well. . . .

Even in mathematics, the most rational of all pursuits, reason is not as clean as it looks. Bertrand Russell's *Principia Mathematica* tried to establish the logical foundations of all mathematics. Kurt Godel, a brilliant mathematician, pointed out the inescapable contradiction in Russell's work in 1931. Years later, Russell, who had moved from one dubious proposition to another over the years, recalled, "I realized, of course, that Godel's work is of fundamental importance, but I was puzzled by it. It made me glad that I was no longer working at mathematical logic."[6]

Godel, one of the world's most gifted mathematicians, died in 1978. He starved himself to death, crouched in a fetal position, refusing to allow nurses to enter his room because he feared that they were trying to poison him.

Poor Kurt. All he had left were his powers of reason. The Cartesian logic that made his career sparkle tarnished his death: He thought people were trying to poison him; therefore they were.

EVEN THE PROS GUESS WRONG

The problem with this silly old ball we live on, as we have tried to elaborate in this book, is that life is infinitely complex. The closer you look, the more you see. What seems simple from a distance—say, the disciplining of a teenager or the politics of South Africa—becomes alarmingly complicated up close. The whole truth, being infinite, is unknowable. And for every tiny piece of it, there is a revolver in some poor fool's mouth . . . and a special corner of Hell waiting for him.

"Nobody knows anything," they say in Hollywood, recognizing the complexity of the film business. A studio might spend $100 million on a blockbuster movie, and the thing might be a complete dud. Or, a young guy with $20,000 might produce a big hit. The old-timers know that even a lifetime of experience is still no guarantee. Even the pros often guess wrong about which films will be box-office hits.

But walk up to a man on the street, and he is likely to have an opinion. He may have even bought stock in an entertainment company after hearing about the blockbuster films planned for the summer.

He has not read the scripts, met the actors, or ever earned a dime in the cinema business—nor even worked as an usher. Yet, he has an opinion based on what he has read in the paper or heard on TV.

People have opinions on everything—especially things they know nothing about. Voters in Baltimore during the 1980s could hardly figure out how to get their own municipal government to pick up the trash or fill in potholes. Yet, though very few had ever been to South Africa—and almost none spoke the languages or could identify the major ethnic groups of the country—they nevertheless had strong opinions about how to reorganize its government.

The more people knew about the situation in South Africa, the harder it was for them to have a simple opinion. A knowledgeable man, asked to comment on the situation, prefaced his thoughts with "I don't know . . . "

Thanks to Information Age communications, people grow more ignorant every day. Tall weeds of groupthink and common knowledge crowd out the few pullulating shoots of real wisdom and truth. Collective dumbness spreads like kudzu. Soon there will be nothing else alive; we will know nothing at all.

CROWD CONTROL

"Love afar is spite at home," wrote Emerson. A man neglects his wife, but takes a keen interest in the plight of women in the Sudan. Or perhaps he worries about public sanitation in New Delhi, but forgets to take out the trash.

Groupthink is popular because it is easier than private thinking and the stakes are lower. A man's public attitudes are buttressed by others, held up by the media, and reinforced by constant repetition. His private thoughts, on the other hand, are fragile, lonely, and often desolate. He cannot even get his own children to clean up their rooms or his wife to agree to his family budget; who can blame him for wanting to tell others what to do?

Masses of people do not go to war because it will make their private lives richer, longer, or better . . . but for abstract principles that few can explain or justify. Lebensraum . . . Preserving the Union . . . Driving the Infidel from the Holy Land . . . Making the World Safe for

Democracy . . . the Domino Theory . . . the jingo hardly matters. But it must be simple if the masses are to understand it, and bright enough to lure them to their own destruction.

Before the development of the modern state following the American and French Revolutions, wars engaged relatively few people. They tended to be small-scale, seasonal affairs . . . though combatants were often very nasty to each other and anyone who got in their path.

But in 1793, after the French monarchy had been pushed aside by the Convention, France was menaced on all sides. At every border was a foreign army, many of them bulging with aristocratic French émigrés, eager to invade to topple the popular new government and restore the monarchy. Thus, threatened, the Convention began the first *levée en masse* of conscripts to fight for *la patrie*. Many of the officers (Lafayette, the great hero of the American Revolution, was one of them), had gone over to France's enemies, which left the way clear for talented young officers from modest backgrounds to rise quickly. Thus, it was that Napoleon Bonaparte assumed command of French forces in Italy and promptly rose to become the nation's greatest hero.

That Bonaparte was a military genius, few would dispute. But what made his campaigns so historically puissant was as much a product of demography and collective involvement as it was of the man's talents for war. As we see in the next chapter, France had enjoyed a baby boom in the eighteenth century. These young and restless citizens pushed the monarchy out of the way of history. They made it possible for Napoleon to bring his many "big battalions" to bear in wars thousands of miles apart—and to replace his fallen soldiers when he put them in harm's way.

LONG SLOW MARCH OF HISTORY

It was in 1806 that Wilhelm Friedrich Hegel first proclaimed history to be at an end. He saw in Napoleon's defeat of Prussia at the battle of Jena the same victory Fukuyama thought he saw in the summer of 1989—the triumph of the ideals of the French Revolution. Mass participation in government, both Hegel and Fukuyama believed, brought permanent peace and prosperity. History must be over.

But history did not end in 1806 . . . (nor in 1989). Instead, in 1806, "history" in the sense that we know it today, had barely begun. Never before were so many people caught up in the collective exercises that fascinate historians. As the nineteenth century developed, more and more people—by fits and starts—became involved in politics through the growth of democratic assemblies and parliaments. This democratization of the Western world threw no obstacle in history's path. To the contrary, it cleared the way and paved the road for the most historical century in mankind's experience. It was in the twentieth century that the world became saturated with politics, democracy, and not coincidentally, war.

For the first time, armies of citizen soldiers were available to almost all European powers . . . along with the full resources of thoroughly collectivized societies. Thanks to modern communications—railroads, telegraphs, telephone, newspaper, television—the mobs, which had heretofore been limited by the range of voice and rumor, spanned time zones. As we have already seen, whole nations became engaged in mob sentiments and took up adventures that even the lowest village idiot might have previously regarded as hopeless.

Fukuyama was as wrong about economics and democracy as he was about history. The popular view—which he took up—was that the demise of communism signaled the total defeat of Marx's ideas.

"The century that began full of self-confidence in the ultimate triumph of Western liberal democracy seems at its close to be returning full circle to where it started," he wrote, "not to an 'end of ideology,' or a convergence between capitalism and socialism, as earlier predicted, but to an unabashed victory of economic and political liberalism." National socialism was destroyed in World War II, he pointed out. The Union of Soviet Socialist Republics fell apart in the late 1980s.

"CAPITALISM" SUFFOCATED

The fall of communism hardly marked the end of this trend. Communism was as forlorn an enterprise as any, but it was only a part of the collectivizing trend of the past two centuries. Democracy itself was part of the trend; it was merely a different form of collectivized decision making.

In a communist system, the means of production are said to be in the hands of the people to begin with, the fruits of which are then distributed through the political process. In modern democracy, property is held by individuals, but according to the whim of the democratic assemblies, the usufructs are shared out to favored groups. Even though title to property is in private hands, owners have limited control over their own facilities. Property owners are told whom they must hire, under what conditions, and how much they must be paid, . . . and so forth. They are told how to treat the fauna and flora on their premises, and regularly must stand in line to comply with zoning and building code regulations.

Owners, themselves, increasingly democratized through the capital markets, are also pressed into service collecting taxes from their workers as well as providing other social, health, and police functions, such as policing the speech of employees and forbidding smoking on company property.

There was a time, of course, when American democracy emphasized the rights and freedoms of individuals against the state. But by the late twentieth century, those days were far in the past. American democracy—at the time the Berlin Wall fell—had come to correspond more to the European conception of the term, in which the will of the individual was subordinated to the interests of the group as determined by elections. Majorities had come to take on the mantle of king, with even more sacred rights. The king at least owed his post to God—and usually feared his master. But whom did majorities fear? Majorities could do no wrong, for there was no higher authority. They owed their positions to no one—except the crowd.

Was there really such a clear line between the United States' wonder system of 1989, 1999, or 2009 . . . and all that preceded it?

THE MYTH OF DEMOCRACY

Mobs can only hold simple ideas in their minds . . . ideas so belittled by the dumbing down process that they are little more than myths. That is as true of democracy as it was of communism.

The important point is that democracy allowed for increased participation in politics and its spoils, just as did communism and fascism.

Kings and emperors might make decisions based on their own individual judgment and consciences. They would be more or less successful at enforcing or applying those decisions, depending on the circumstances. But mass participation changed the nature of politics and government, making them more tyrannical than ever before, and, curiously, more resistant to change.

It is an odd tyranny Americans suffer. We have no words to describe the squishy dictatorship of the majority, or the satin chains we wrap around ourselves. Alexis de Tocqueville saw it coming 200 years ago. "I think," he wrote, "that the species of oppression by which democratic nations are menaced is unlike anything the world has ever seen."[7]

In empires and kingdoms, Tocqueville noted, the power of the authorities was absolute, often capricious, and dangerous. But the king's armies could not be everywhere. And his agents tended to be thin on the ground. Most people living under these forms of government had very limited contact with the authorities. Taxes were low. Regulations were few. And the regulators themselves often lived in fear of being strung up by a mob. The king's grip may have been awful, but his reach was short.

Democracy is different. It invites people into the governing class and thus turns them into unpaid agents of the government, and ultimately their own oppressors.

Tocqueville predicted:

After having thus successively taken each member of the community in its powerful grasp and fashioned him at will, the supreme power [of democracy] then extends its arm over the whole community. It covers the surface of society with a network of small complicated rules, minute and uniform, through which the most original minds and the most energetic characters cannot penetrate, to rise above the crowd. The will of man is not shattered, but softened, bent and guided . . . men are seldom forced to act, but they are constantly restrained from acting. . . . Such a power does not destroy, but it prevents existence; it does not tyrannize, but it compresses, enervates, extinguishes, and stupefies a people . . .

Thus, their spirit is gradually broken . . . gradually losing the faculties of thinking, feeling, and acting for themselves. [People then console themselves at the loss of their liberties] by the reflection that they have chosen their own guardians.

Every two or four years, Americans celebrate their democratic freedom by shuffling off to the voting booth. Then, they go back to doing as they are told.

"LIBERTY" REGULATED

In medieval society, a man's role in life was thought to be determined by God. Kings were kings because God wanted it that way, and a peasant's lot in life was God's doing, too. He could make the most of it . . . or the least of it, but his duties and privileges were fairly clearly defined and not of his making.

The promise of modern society in general, and democracy in particular, was that man could decide for himself what role he would play. God no longer wrote the laws; man would write them, in his assemblies, by citizen representatives elected by popular vote.

This new system caught up larger and larger numbers as the voting franchise was extended throughout the nineteenth and twentieth centuries. Theorists imagined a system where the advantages and disadvantages of any proposed law could be argued out in public; and then after sober reflection, each voter got to cast his ballot. In practice, the various forms of democracy function with all the features, for better or worse, of collective rule making, tempered by the habits and characteristics of the group on which it has been imposed.

But the liberty to write whatever laws was an open invitation to mischief. As Herbert Spencer realized, increases in apparent liberty soon turned into decreases in real liberty.

Here, he reports on the English Parliament in the nineteenth century:

> Legislation . . . has followed the course I pointed out. Rapidly multiplying dictatorial measures have continually tended to restrict individual liberties, and this in two ways. Regulations have been established every year in greater number, imposing a constraint on the citizen in matters in which his acts were formerly completely free, and forcing him to accomplish acts which he was formerly at liberty to accomplish or not to accomplish at will. At the same time heavier and heavier public, and especially local, burdens have still further restricted his liberty by diminishing the portion of his profits he can spend as he

chooses, and by augmenting the portion which is taken from him to be spent according to the good pleasure of the public authorities.[8]

As it was in England in the nineteenth century, so was it in the United States in the twentieth century. More and more laws—enacted by a democratic legislature—had the effect of restricting liberty. But as they did so, they brought more and more people together—giving them a stake in each other's pocket and in the economy and stock market in general.

Democracy has a lie at its very core—that you can cheat, murder, and steal as long as you can get 51 percent of registered voters to go along with you. People are perfectly happy to vote their way into other people's bank accounts—and feel morally superior doing so. For they always do so in the name of some high-minded chutzpah, whether it is concern for the environment or the poor—or making the world free!

"No one's liberty or property is safe as long as the legislature is in session," is the common dictum. Gradually, legislatures insinuated their way into nearly every aspect of commerce. Despite Fukuyama's assertion, in the United States as in the other developed nations, by the end of the twentieth century, roughly a third to one half of the entire gross domestic product (GDP) of Western nations was being redistributed through the political process.

HIGH-MINDED CHUTZPAH

The major trend of the entire Western world since the French Revolution has been toward more voting and less liberty. "Give me liberty or give me death," said Patrick Henry, at a time when government regulations were almost nonexistent and the total tax intake was less than 3 percent. What could he have been thinking?

Perhaps he was referring to the liberty of a people to decide who gets to boss them around. Mussolini described the concept better than Henry. "Fascism," he explained, "is for liberty. And for the only liberty which can be a real thing, the liberty of the State and of the individual within the State. Therefore, for the Fascist, everything is in the State, and nothing human or spiritual exists, much less has value, outside the

State. Fascism . . . the synthesis and unity of all values, interprets, develops and gives strength to the whole life of the people."

People exercise this collective liberty by voting. That is what democracy is all about. At first, in the United States and elsewhere, only a few people voted—white male landowners. New Zealand was the first country to allow women to vote—in 1898. Since then, more and more people have received the liberty to cast ballots.

Early in the twentieth century, it was thought that voting was the key to peace, prosperity, and freedom. Even today, most people believe this—after a century of evidence to the contrary. In World War I, the major combatants had already instituted universal manhood suffrage. Fat lot of good it did them. After the war, it was almost universally believed that the spread of democracy would prevent future wars. Hardly a decade after the Armistice, people in Germany voted Hitler into office, while Italian voters gave Mussolini their highest post.

Readers expecting financial advice may find this critique of democracy misplaced. But our purpose is to show how the world works. Humans are gregarious animals, not solitary ones. They do their thinking, and make history, in groups, not alone. Democracy amplifies group thinking in politics just as stock markets provide a focus for collective thinking in the financial world. Neither necessarily makes the world a better place, but each makes it a different place. And, together, they may make it a more dangerous one.

Democracy does not make people richer. One of the greatest economic success stories of the postwar era was Hong Kong—whose residents never had the right to vote for anybody. What's more, as voters increased in the Western democracies, economic growth rates went down, not up.

Are people who live in democracies more free? Are they more peaceful? Does democracy make people richer? Happier? Not on the evidence.

"Whole libraries have been written on the subject [of what a democracy is]," writes Lucien Boia in "The Myth of Democracy." "The fact is, democracy refuses to be bound in a simple, unequivocal formula. It's a moving target, with multiple and contradictory personalities. It is not a 'thing,' nor even an 'idea'; it is a mythology."

Louis XVI of France was no democrat, Boia points out. He was an "absolute monarch." He was considered almost divine, with power, so it was said, unrestrained by the popular will. It was a system of one man/one vote. Louis was that man; he had the vote. And yet, what could Louis do? He could make war. But he would have to find a way to raise money to pay for it. He could ask bankers to finance it. He could try to levy taxes, but good luck.

Louis could do none of these things without the support of a great many people in many different positions. In fact, he was hemmed in tighter than a Baptist deacon . . . restrained in every direction. His agents might oppose him, or the church, or his moneylenders, or the bourgeoisie. Even a negative comment from his mistress might cause him to lose heart.

Louis could proclaim a law. But who would enforce it? He could announce a war, but whom could he get to fight?

It was said that Louis was all-powerful. If Louis had all the power, ordinary citizens must have none. But compared with today's elected George and Jacques, Louis was barely more powerful than an American voter. And in the end like Tsar Nicholas II, not only was Louis unable to prevent a revolution—he lacked even the power to save his own life.

When the revolutionaries broke down the doors of the Bastille—considered the symbol of Louis' repressive regime—they discovered a small bit of the truth. The Bastille was almost empty. Louis could repress almost no one. Absolute monarchs disappeared from the planet not because they had too much power, but because they had too little.

THE LAND OF THE FREE

Today, thanks to the blessings of democracy, citizens of the Land of the Free and other Western democracies pay taxes 5 to 10 times higher than those under the absolute monarchs and submit to rules and regulations that Louis could never have imagined.

Today, United States' prisons are overflowing, and the president can make war on just about anyone he chooses. Yet, neither Fukuyama nor the popular mind can understand what has happened nor imagine any improvement.

The general promise of modern democratic consumerism—though never stated explicitly—is that citizens will get happiness on earth through public health and safety measures, and through modern capitalism's ability to help its citizens produce and distribute wealth. Humans—being rational decision makers—have chosen the Western democratic-capitalist system, according to Fukuyama, as if it were a liquor store that made home deliveries!

But whether it is called communism or liberal democracy, the important promise is the same—participants imagine that they will get something from the system that they could not have gotten through their own private efforts. The power of majorities being much greater than that of kings, citizens expected much more from them than subjects had expected from their monarchs. Nor could they imagine any reason that the promise might not be fulfilled.

"A crowd is not merely impulsive and mobile," Gustave Le Bon explained. "Like a savage, it is not prepared to admit that anything can come between its desire and the realization of its desire. It is less capable of understanding such an intervention, in consequence of the feeling of irresistible power given it by its numerical strength. The notion of impossibility disappears for the individual in a crowd."[9]

A TIME FOR EVERY PURPOSE

War, like romance, needs a little madness. Leading a wild cavalry charge, the last thing you would want would be a group of intellectual kibitzers by your side. Instead, you would want real men . . . whose thoughts are as uncomplicated and blunt as a mace.

With such men behind you, you might have a chance of success—of crashing into the enemy line and breaking it up. But any hesitation or doubts, and you would be finished.

Neither the god of war, nor the god of love, favors half measures. "Audacity," said Danton to France's generals in 1792. "We need audacity, more audacity and always audacity."

The soldier, the politician, the football fan—all are particularly susceptible to crowd thinking. Just observe fans at a football game; they stand and wildly cheer their teams as though the outcome of the game actually mattered to them. The idea of being on the winning team is itself a primitive form of groupthink. It is not thinking at all, of course, but merely a brute sentiment that overtakes an entire group and causes

its members to surrender their individual will to the will of the majority. Emboldened by the bodies pressed around them, people do the
most amazing things.

A football game engages the crowd's sentiments for a short time,
and the fans are aware that it is only a game. They become much more
fully engaged when the enterprise involves deeper, more abstract
ambitions, such as making them all rich or masters—not just of the
football field—but of the entire world. It is important to realize that it
is not rational thought that motivates them, but a primitive, simpleminded sentiment, often an inchoate desire that can barely be expressed
in words. Nor can it be subject to rational challenge.

Le Bon writes:

> Notwithstanding all its progress, philosophy has been unable as yet to
> offer the masses any ideal that can charm them; but as they must have
> their illusions at all cost, they turn instinctively, as the insect seeks the
> light, to the rhetoricians who accord them what they want. Not truth,
> but error has always been the chief factor in the evolution of nations,
> and the reason why socialism is so powerful today is that it constitutes
> the last illusion that is still vital. In spite of all scientific demonstrations
> it continues on the increase. Its principal strength lies in the fact that it
> is championed by minds sufficiently ignorant of things as they are in
> reality to venture boldly to promise mankind happiness. The social
> illusion reigns today upon all the heaped up ruins of the past, and to
> it belongs the future. The masses have never thirsted after truth. They
> turn aside from evidence that is not to their taste, preferring to deify
> error, if error seduce them. Whoever can supply them with illusions
> is easily their master; whoever attempts to destroy their illusions is
> always their victim.

And here we offer a nuance. The crowd spirit that unifies an army
or a football team is beneficial to its purpose. Without it, the cavalry
disperses and cannot hope to accomplish its mission. Perhaps that is
why nature has bred it into the human condition; like patriotism, perhaps it has its purpose.

While the mob thinking may be essential to certain kinds of competitive activities, it is worse than superfluous to others. "When everyone is thinking the same thing, no one is really thinking," they say on
Wall Street. Markets are unlike battlefields in that groupthink rarely

pays off. When people all expect to get rich by buying the same stock, it is the sellers who will get rich, not the buyers. The stock will quickly rise in price far beyond what a reasonable buyer should pay. Soon, those holding the stock will have paid too much for it. And to whom will they sell? All the buyers have already bought.

HEADING FOR THE EXITS

In economics, the problem is known as the *Fallacy of Composition*. In short, what may work for a single person may not work for a group. Looking back at the cavalry charge, an individual soldier could rein in his horse as he approached the enemy . . . letting his comrades make the initial contact with bayonets and musket balls. The cavalryman may increase his own chance of survival. But if all the horsemen did the same, they would almost certainly fail and probably be shot to bits as they hesitated before the enemy lines.

The paradox arises over and over again in economics and else-where. The owner of a business may be better off firing employees, cutting expenses, and improving the profit margin. But if all business owners suddenly fired workers, consumer spending would fall. Soon, businesses would notice falling sales and profits.

Charles Kindleberger mentions the phenomenon of spectators standing up at sporting events. When a few stand up, they get a better view. But when all stand up, the advantage disappears. A man may sell an overpriced stock and reap a tidy profit. But if other stock-holders all attempt to do the same thing at the same time, the price will plummet. Instead of making a profit, they may all end up with a loss.

The great mass of citizens in a participatory system believe things so degraded by the crowd that they are mostly untrue. They may believe that the king has a "divine right" to tell them what to do, for example . . . or that the majority of their elected representatives does. Or, that they are racially superior, have a "manifest destiny," or are in danger of being knocked down by a falling domino. In politics, lies, nonsense, and foolishness run their own course—often sordid, some-times pathetic and occasionally entertaining. But in markets, the out-come is always the same: maddened by a lie, participants run right into the Fallacy of Composition like a panicked mob into a theater exit. They may believe that they can all get rich by buying stocks, but getting rich is relative. Only a few can do it. Compared with most people in history, almost all U.S. investors are rich already. But it is only the comparison to other living investors—their friends and neighbors— that matters to them. Can they all be richer than their friends and neighbors? It is no more possible than that all their children will have above-average intelligence.

At the end of 2002, for example, America's baby boomers believed they could retire by selling their houses at appreciated prices. But to whom? The first to sell may do well, but what would happen to real estate prices if all 78 million boomers decided to sell at the same time?

As mass participation in markets increases, it brings in more and more capital and more and more people who do not know what they are doing. Prices rise, which confuses even many of the old-timers who should know better. Thus, the stage is set for the final, disappointing act. Ultimately, the common myth of the masses fails them for it is fanciful or physically impossible.

LE BON'S "GENERAL BELIEF"

Essential to any society is what Le Bon calls a "General Belief"—a very large myth—that holds it together. Marxist Leninism—or at least lip service to it—held the Soviet Union together for seven decades, for example. Even in the 1960s, when people began to realize that the creed was a loser, they stuck with it for another three decades for they had nothing to put in its place.

When a general belief is at its peak, participants do not recognize it as a belief at all. It seems self-evident and beyond question. After the fall of the Roman Empire, Europe lived under the general belief that God had organized things the way they were and intended for them to stay that way. And perhaps he did. But with the French Revolution, suddenly, the general belief changed.

The general belief in mass democratic consumerism was not fully formed at the end of the eighteenth century. People still saw it as an idea that they could dispose of if it did not suit the times. Between 1790 and 1820, as Gustave Le Bon tells us, the general belief in France switched three times: First it moved from its monarchist God-ordered vision to a revolutionary credo; then the revolutionaries extinguished themselves or fell under the spell of Napoleon's Empire; and then, after the victorious Allies packed off Napoleon to St. Helena, it returned to a decrepit monarchy.

It would take another full century for the general belief in democratic consumerism to reach adulthood.

THE AMERICAN CENTURY

Sydney Smith, in the mid-Victorian era, asked if anyone would really care to see an American play or listen to an American tune. It was he who called the whole nation an "experiment in vulgarity." Perhaps it was. Perhaps it still is. But that did not stop Americans from making money. Indeed, it seemed to encourage it.

The *Figaro* newspaper has been around in Paris for a long time. It reprinted a copy of its front page from 1900—as part of its first edition of the year 2000—which included an article about Senator Andrews Clark. The *Figaro*'s Washington correspondent said Clark was the richest man in the U.S. Senate, richer than the next eight richest senators put together. He made his money, the article tells us, starting with nothing but a team of oxen. He drove them out to a copper mine, the Verde Mine, where he made his fortune. By the turn of the century, he had banks, railways, rubber plantations, you name it.

Was he vulgar? As vulgar as a bus station, no doubt. But, in New York, he also had a collection of masterpieces from the "modern French school," that probably adorn the walls of some public museum today. The *Figaro* wondered wistfully whether it might be possible to get "this prodigious businessman" to Paris, where "our artists and poor would have no reason to object."

While America's intellectuals fawned over their English and European cousins, America's dynamic businessmen built McDonald's fast-food restaurants. And made films that are shipped all over the world. And marketed music that people now hear (and often cannot escape) in even the most remote and desolate outposts of humanity.

DEMOCRATIC CONSUMER CAPITALISM

Joseph Conrad, in his novel *Nostromo* described this quality of American business when his character, Holroyd, says, "We shall run the world's business whether it likes it or not."[10] Indeed, that is what happened in the twentieth century. It turned out to be an American Century, just as Henry Luce had suggested.

"We must never forget the meaning of the twentieth century, or . . . the triumph of freedom," announced President Clinton. It was freedom that the United States had in abundance in 1900—and which set people like Senator Clark and Holroyd on their paths to commercial glory. Freedom allowed them to be prosperous and vulgar at the same time. The more prosperous they were, the more vulgarity they could afford.

A century more, and American consumer capitalism stood unchallenged. There were McDonald's golden arches and Gap stores all over the world—but the general belief had become as invisible as the feudal order in the Middle Ages. East, West, South, and North—wherever you looked at the close of the twentieth century, you could see neither it nor anything else, for there was nothing to contrast against it. Fukuyama's "The End of History" appeared to have arrived. "The triumph of the West, of the Western idea, is evident first of all in the total exhaustion of viable systematic alternatives to Western liberalism," wrote Fukuyama in his famous essay.

By the twentieth century's end, everyone expected America to dominate the next century, too, with its culture, its businesses, and its stock market. Nearly every editorial page made some reference to "American Triumphal-ism." Nearly every editorial writer was appalled by McDonald's and contemptuous of the great *hoi polloi* of middle-class America, but proud to sit with them on top of the world. Consumers, investors, and politicians still believed that the United States had a competitive edge in the twenty-first century. They claimed that the U.S. economy was free, and more flexible and innovative than those of other nations.

Fortunately, foreigners believed it, too. They continued to accept dollars as the currency of choice, although the dollar—America's most successful export—became less valuable, intrinsically, with each one in use. Even Cuba, a country that still clings to politics like the Pope clings to the cross, had accepted the dollar as legal tender. But the American dollar was overbought. Nobody said so, for the myth had become invincible. There was no alternative opinion. No one seemed to notice that America had long ago shifted from a high-investment, high-growth economy—where people were free to get rich or go bust on their own merits—to a high-spending, highly regulated economy, where people expected something for nothing . . . and were willing to vote to get it.

COME THE REVOLUTION

Recently sitting at a café in the heart of the Latin Quarter in Paris, and listening to the conversations at neighboring tables, not once did your authors hear anyone mention the credos of Marx, Lenin, Freud, Foucault, or Sartre. They might as well all be dead.

Thirty years ago, this street corner was so smitten by politics that the revolutionaries of the era pried up the paving stones and built barricades. "Come the revolution," they would say to each other, "things will be different." Cafés and restaurants were crowded then, too, but not with tourists. Instead, they were full of ideologues—greasy-haired youths who smoked, drank, and squabbled about the fine points of Marxism until the wee-hours. Che was not on their T-shirts, but on their lips and in their brains, such as they were.

Probably the scene was not much different 219 years ago. The French Revolution was "the source of all the present communist, anarchist, and socialist conceptions,"[11] wrote Prince Peter Kropotkin.

At the end of the eighteenth century, France enjoyed an exaltation not too different from that of the United States at the end of the twentieth century. It was the biggest country, with the biggest economy and Europe's dominant military power. (It was French intervention that had allowed the American colonies to escape British rule a decade earlier.) France could even lecture other countries on the benefits of free enterprise!

But success is self-correcting. Turgot and the Physiocrats had been applying their "laissez-faire" principles to the French economy, to great effect. In doing so, they disturbed powerful interests close to the monarchy who were concerned with protecting their privileges and their markets—much like the West Virginia steel mills and Kansas farmers of the Bush years. In 1776, the same year in which the American War for Independence began and Adam Smith published his *Wealth of Nations*, Turgot was ousted.

"The dismissal of this great man," wrote Voltaire, "crushed me . . . Since that fatal day, I have not followed anything . . . and am waiting patiently for someone to cut our throats."[12]

Someone came along with a knife just a few years later. On July 14, 1789, a Paris mob attacked the old fortress at the Bastille. There, they liberated "two fools, four forgers, and a debaucher,"[13] wrote an observer at the time. The prison guards were promised safe conduct in return for surrender, but once they laid down their arms, the mob cut them to pieces and was soon marching through the streets of Paris with their heads, torsos, and other body parts on the ends of pikes.

For the next 25 years, France rocked and reeled from one collective madness to another. The Marquis de Sade was released from prison, while thousands of decent people took his place. Paper money replaced gold and silver. Identity cards were required of every citizen, called "Certificates of Good Citizenship." Permits were required for nearly everything. And travel was strictly controlled.

ASSAULT ON TRADITION

Every revolution is an assault against tradition—whether it is a New Era on Wall Street or a new era in Paris. The church was plundered. Local languages, schools, and legal jurisdictions were dismantled. Even the old forms of address were tossed out—henceforth, everyone would be called "citizen."

Finally, the French could stand no more. Napoleon Bonaparte brought order to Paris with "a whiff of grapeshot" at a critical moment.

But today, the only revolutions one talks about in the Latin Quarter are in technology and fashion. There are lesbians on every street corner, but you can search an entire city and find only a few moth-eaten communists who lost their minds 30 years ago. There are Che T-shirts, but who cares what Che said, except a few tenured relics of the 1960s? There are no Republicans either. For how was Bush's agenda different from Clinton's, Chirac's, Blair's, or Louis XVI's?

They all do the same things—tax, spend, and regulate as much as they can get away with.

What is this strange intersection that we have come to? All major governments seem to have come together in some unholy socialism, but where are the socialists? Few politicians will even admit to the creed they all share. And what voter really cares?

"We lived through the Reagan revolution . . . mainly rhetorical . . ." wrote economist Gary North. "After Reagan, we lived through the Bush–Clinton counter-revolution. Now we are getting more of the same under the present administration: more controls on our lives, more government spending, larger federal deficits."[14]

"The Reagan victory did not shrink the State," North continued. "We are not going to see lower taxes, reduced government regulation of business, a lower federal budget, the repayment of the national debt, better schools, safer cities, and smaller welfare rolls. . . ."

The revolution, begun in Paris more than 200 years ago, continues; but in the mid-1900s the crowd turned its attention from tragedy to farce—that is, from politics to economics, from war to commercial competition, and from ideology to consumerism.

THE LONG, SLOW, SOFT DEPRESSIONS OF THE MODERN AGE

Offering an explanation for the strange events of the new century, economist Paul Krugman suggested the following, "The world became vulnerable to its current travails, not because economic policies had not been reformed, but because they had. That is, around the world, countries responded to the very real flaws in the policy regimes that had evolved in response to the Depression by moving back toward a regime with many of the virtues of pre-Depression, free-market capitalism. However, in bringing back the virtues of old-fashioned capitalism we also brought back some of its vices, most notably a vulnerability both to instability and to sustained economic slumps."

Krugman imagined a kind of social contract after the Great Depression in which voters agreed to tolerate capitalism, but only with safety nets and regulations to make sure no one got hurt. In his mind only, these restraints produced a stable prosperity in which the benefits were shared out among the population during the 1950s, 1960s, and 1970s.

"The America I grew up in—the America of the 1950s and 1960s," he said, "was middle class. . . . Yes, of course, there were still some rich people," he admits, "but [thank God!] there weren't that many of them. The days when plutocrats were a force to be reckoning with in American society, economically or politically, seemed long past."

Krugman was writing to an appreciative audience in the *New York Times* magazine in October 2002. Typically, he let himself get distracted by envy, worrying that the rich might be making a comeback. The compensation for the nation's top 100 CEOs rose from just $1.3 million in 1970 (in 1998 dollars) to $37.5 million in 2000. There are not enough of these super-rich Americans to fill a zoning department in a mid-size town, yet Krugman was so indignant about it that he missed the important point altogether: The triumph of American laissez-faire capitalism, which conservatives celebrate and Krugman rues, was a sham. By the close of the twentieth century, true capitalists had almost disappeared from the face of the earth. *Capitalism* is a pejorative invented by Marx to describe a system in which the rich owned the means of production and exploited the masses. The system Marx described never really existed the way Marx imagined, though a casual observer with a chip on his shoulder may have been tempted to see it that way.

Marx's economics were as fanciful as his history. But at least one of his predictions proved correct . . . though not at all in the way he thought. As the champagne glasses were hoisted and the new millennium was rung in, the Marxist vision had triumphed at least as much as the laissez-faire vision of Smith and Turgot; the means of production were owned by the workers. (Curiously, the most laissez-faire economy in the world in 2002 was in Hong Kong—a city under the direct control of still-communist China. And the world's fastest-growing—and in many ways freest—economy was on the Chinese mainland.)

COLLECTIVIZED RISKS

Both in the United States and Japan, the freewheeling laissez-faire capitalism of the nineteenth century gave way to a consensual, collectivized capitalism of the twentieth century, with massive state involvement and mass participation by people who would not know a balance sheet from a bed pan. The very rich CEOs that galled Krugman were only hired guns—not genuine capitalists. Their extravagant pay levels were testimony not to the victory of raw capitalism, but to its defeat. Real capitalists would never allow so much of their money to get into the hands of managers.

If there were any real capitalists around, they must have been sleeping. For they had let their managers practically steal away their businesses and ruin their investments. Corporate debt rose 382 percent in the 1990s, more than 30 percent faster than GDP growth. Nor were the borrowings used for capital improvements that might make the capitalists more money. Instead, much of the borrowed money was frittered away on mergers, acquisitions, and stock buy backs. These maneuvers were not designed to enrich real capitalists, but merely to drive up the share price by impressing the new class of citizen-shareholder, the *lumpeninvestoriat*.

Likewise, what capitalist would stand still for such generous stock options—given away to employees in the heyday of the boom years as if they were turkeys at Thanksgiving?

Modern corporations are owned by small shareholders, not big ones—often through collectivized holdings in pension funds, mutual funds, and so forth. These small holders have neither the gumption nor the power or incentive to resist absurdly high executive salaries. In the late 1990s, even CEOs of companies whose earnings were falling or approaching bankruptcy were paid as if they were star quarterbacks in the Super Bowl. Maybe they were especially talented, and maybe they were not. But the mere fact that they were paid so much and appeared on magazine covers seemed to awe small shareholders and impress analysts. The great mob of investors took up the stock of these celebrity managers with no serious thought about them and too little interest to justify a serious investigation.

Stock market investors had come to act like voters!

Mass capitalism produced mass delusions—and a new shareholder arithmetic. It might have made sense for Warren Buffett to object to stock options and look carefully at executive compensation: As a substantial shareholder, much of the money that went to overcompensate key employees would have otherwise gone to him. But the two or three cents a small stockholder might have had at stake made serious investigation not worth the trouble.

THE GREAT BARGAIN

Krugman believed that a grand bargain was struck following the Great Depression of the 1930s. Capitalism would remain the economic system of the West, but it would submit to the control of government to avoid future debacles. In a sense, this was true. Capitalism in the United States was not the same after the Roosevelt Administration finished with it. But this was merely part of the bigger trend toward a mass capitalism directed by government for its own purposes. Share ownership became increasingly widespread. By the end of the century, enough Americans owned shares to elect a president. Share ownership rose from just 5 percent of the population at the beginning of the twentieth century to fully 56 percent of its households at its end.

Like any large group of people removed from the facts or from direct experience, shareholders were as subject to mass emotions as a group of voters or a lynch mob. With only public knowledge to go by, they could be readily whipped up by the financial media and were ready to amplify any fad to the point of absurdity.

The first large movement of mass capitalism took place in the United States in the 1920s. Share ownership was uncommon in 1900. There were only about 4,000 stockbrokers in the whole country. Thirty years later, the number of brokers had increased more than 500 percent. Stocks became such a popular subject that even shoeshine boys had an opinion on them.

The Dow shot up from 120 on the first day of business in 1925 to 381 at the peak in 1929.

Then, after the bubble burst, the United States experienced its first bout of mass depression. Unlike previous busts, the 1930s brought suffering to the entire nation, not just a handful of rich capitalists. A quarter of the workforce became unemployed. In 1931 and 1932, more than 5,000 banks failed. The bear market on Wall Street dragged on and on, with the Dow not returning to its 1929 high until 1954.

For the first time, too, voters demanded that their government "do something." The Roosevelt Administration did something. It arrived on the scene with a program of monetary and fiscal stimulus, following the most recent fads in macroeconomics. Never before had a government attempted such forceful intervention. And never before was an economy so unimpressed. Instead of bouncing back as it had following the Panic of 1873 or the Bust of 1907, the nation lay down in a gutter of recession, bankruptcy, and sluggish growth. And it stayed there for the next decade. Even then, it seemed to take the biggest war in world history to pry the poor fellow up again.

"Too little, too late," was the professional opinion of the leading economists. Government had made a good attempt, but not massive enough or fast enough.

SHAREHOLDER NATION: FOR BETTER . . . OR WORSE

Another interpretation, out of step with the fashions of the day, was that the government's own efforts to help the economy out of its funk had actually made the situation worse—by stretching out the painful readjustments that needed to be made over a long period of time and at much greater cost.

Either way, it was a New Era in capitalism. For now, government—often acting through its bureaucrats at the Federal Reserve—promised to soften capitalism's rough edges. It would put into place safety nets to protect people from serious injury, on or off the job; and it would manage the nation's monetary and fiscal policies so as to ease the pain of the downward slope of the business cycle. Henceforth, budget deficits would become an economic tool and not merely a convenience for pusillanimous politicians, unwilling to raise taxes to pay for their programs. And henceforth, the market would not determine interest rates based on the supply of savings and the demand for it. Instead, interest rates—at least at the short end of the interest-rate curve—would be set by the central bank for the good of the economy.

But Krugman believed that in the 1980s a neoconservative push for deregulation reinstated the rough-and-tumble capitalism of the pre-Roosevelt era. And that a return to pre-Depression policies inevitably led to Depression-era economies that explained Japan in the 1990s and the United States in the early 2000s.

If anyone can figure out how the shallow deregulations in the United States in the 1980s produced the long malaise in Japan in the 1990s or the current slump in States, he is not working on this book. The Japanese adopted capitalism following the war. But Japan's capitalism never bore much resemblance to the raw capitalism of Krugman's imagination. The essential feature—the disposition of capital—was never in the hands of freewheeling capitalists. Instead, groups of bankers, large corporate combines, and government made major capital decisions.

And even in the United States, the Reagan-era reforms hardly changed the nature of late-twenty-first-century capitalism. Barely a single thread in the massive public safety net was unraveled. Government spending went up by every measure—as a percentage of personal income, in nominal dollars, and in real ones. The fundamental trend toward mass consumer capitalism accelerated. While only 23 percent of households owned shares in 1989, by the end of the century fully half of all U.S. households were little pseudo-capitalists. And of them, nearly half counted the majority of their wealth in the form of shares in public companies!

The United States had become the Shareholder Nation—every bit as obsessed with stock prices as Japan had been 10 years earlier. Risk had been collectivized—so that hardly anyone felt immune from a slump.

Scarcely noticed by economists of any persuasion was the way in which government became a partner in the managed, risk-averse capitalist systems of the late twentieth century. Governments throughout the developed world had increased their share of gross domestic product (GDP) during the entire century. In the United States, from an estimated 8.2 percent of GDP in 1900, by the century's end the government spent about 30 percent of GDP. Taxes soared, too. At the dawn of the twentieth century, there were still no federal income taxes in the United States. They would not arrive until more than a decade later. And even then, the first federal income taxes applied only to the richest citizens. Conservative politicians argued against the imposition of the tax, warning that the rate could eventually rise as high as 10 percent. But the threat seemed so preposterous that the constitutional amendment was passed over their objections.

By the end of the century in the United States, the average federal income tax rate had reached 13.2 percent with a top marginal rate of

39.6 percent (2001 figures). Meanwhile, as taxes of all kinds multiplied and rose, the total tax burden on the average American was much higher—between 30 percent and 40 percent. Taken together, across the spectrum of developed Organisation for Economic Co-operation and Development (OECD) nations, the top personal income tax rates averaged about 47 percent and the top corporate income tax rates 34 percent by the year 2000, with total government spending among the leading developed nations consuming an average of 38.8 percent of GDP (OECD figures for 2000).

This left politicians and central bankers even more keenly concerned about the economy and its markets. Not only were voters demanding that the government "do something" to promote prosperity, the government's own revenues depended on it. To its citizens, government was no longer an incidental expense—but a major one, their largest single expense item. For the economy, government was no longer a minor parasite—but, likewise, the biggest one.

Reagan Administration economists had realized that parasites depend on the health of their hosts. The stronger the host economy, they reasoned, the larger the parasite could become. The genius of supply-side economist, Art Laffer's Curve (said to have been drawn out on a napkin at lunch), was that reducing marginal tax rates would actually increase gross revenues to the state. Reagan, in his first term, took advantage of this insight, cutting the top marginal rate from 70 percent to just 50 percent. The result was the same as with the Kennedy cuts of 20 years before—government revenues increased along with economic activity.

In short, democratic government was no longer a spectator, or even a disinterested referee. It had become the biggest participant in the supposedly free markets of the Western world. It was the biggest spender in consumer economies. It was the biggest borrower. It controlled money and credit. It was the watchdog on the capital markets, its chief observer, and its chief beneficiary. Is it any wonder George W. Bush rushed to "do something" to protect its revenues? Is it any wonder that Barack Obama—the man who would be FDR—has superseded him in every way and now promises to rout and stifle bubbles wherever they may be detected?

CHAPTER 5

TURNING JAPANESE

I'm turning Japanese, I think I'm turning Japanese, I really think so.
— The Vapors, 1980

One of the initial inspirations for this book was the striking parallel between the United States and Japan—the world's two largest economies—in the early 2000s:

Between 1971 and 1985, the Japanese stock market went up about 500 percent.

In the United States, the bull market began 10 years later, in 1981. From 1981 until 1995, U.S. stocks also went up 500 percent.

In 1985, the Japanese market really took off—tripling in the next 5 years.

In 1995, the U.S. market really took off—tripling in the next 5 years.

In 1990, the Japanese market peaked out and began to decline. Eighteen months later, it was down some 30 percent.

By 2000, the U.S. stock market peaked out and began to decline. Eighteen months later, it was down about 30 percent (see Figure 5.1).

Eerie isn't it? But the parallels do not stop there.

FIGURE 5.1   Bubble Echo—10 Years After
In 1985, the Japanese stock market took off, tripling in the next five years. The same thing happened in the U.S. markets 10 years later.

In 1992, then–Prime Minister Miyazawa wanted to help the banking system with public funds (read: a bailout), but public sentiment was strongly against it.

U.S. officials, 16 years later, found themselves facing a credit crunch of epic proportions—and responded with the largest injection of liquidity the U.S. markets have ever seen.

And the parallels continue. Take savings rates. As stocks went up in Japan in the 1970s and 1980s, savings rates fell by about 10 percentage points. In the United States, the same thing happened—just 10 years later. Unfortunately for the Americans, they started with a savings rate much closer to zero than the Japanese did. But it is not what happened, but the moral of the story, that matters.

A few years back, we were told the story of an amateur pyrotechnician. Convinced that diesel fuel would not ignite and wanting to show off to coworkers, he passed a cigarette lighter over a stream of fuel spilling out of a tank, without effect. Then, just to prove his point, he repeated the trick, perhaps coming in closer contact with the fuel. He is presently recovering from burns over most of his body.

This book is written in the spirit of one of the inquisitive onlookers in that story: amazed that anyone could be so foolish, fascinated by the spectacle of it all, and happy to let someone else conduct the experiments.

The economic engineers in Washington, D.C., too, might be just a little curious. Since they are so ready to open the jets of both monetary and fiscal stimulus, they may at least wonder what it really takes to set an economy on fire. We suggest a visit to Japan.

There was no other example of a major economy in the postwar era that had run into such trouble—only Japan. "Japan is different." Perhaps it was true; everybody said so. But how?

THE JAPANESE ARE DIFFERENT

The Japanese had undergone a startling transformation in the space of less than a decade: They were considered the world's smartest and most dynamic people in the 1980s, yet many observers in the 1990s perceived them as incompetents who were incapable of learning how to change or of carrying out the restructuring that their economy so badly needed.

The cause of their economic woes, according to the popular view, was their propensity to save money and their prudent attitude to spending. Even though they lived well, traveled abroad, and bought luxury goods, the Japanese saved an average of 13 percent of their earnings, compared with less than 2 percent for Americans. With little consumer spending, there seemed to be no kindling with which to ignite a good fire; the whole economy thus remained damp and cold.

The recurring nightmare of Fed governors was that Americans would suddenly start to act like the Japanese. Instead of spending more than they could afford, they might begin to spend less, which would douse the U.S. economic blaze in a matter of weeks. The United States' economy and stock market depended on two habits of recklessness: the way Americans spent their money and the way foreigners invested it. Any movement toward prudence, no matter how slight, would likely cause a collapse of sales, earnings, stock prices, employment, and so on. In short, if Americans started to behave like the Japanese, the American economy would begin to resemble Japan's.

An island nation, Japan abounds with as many eccentricities as a circus. The Japanese have a word to describe it: *Nihonjinron*, which means "the idea of being Japanese." They have always considered themselves exceptional and, not surprisingly, superior. Immigration into the country is strictly limited. The Japanese tend to mistrust outsiders and occasionally even go so far as to despise them. This does not prevent them from traveling, but when they do so, they tend to venture abroad in groups—to gawk at the *gaigin*.[1]

Being Japanese means not only considering oneself superior, but also proving it from time to time by direct competition with foreigners. Early in the 20th century, competition took a disastrous form. The Japanese tried to achieve military domination of the entire Pacific Rim. The campaign worked all too well. Encouraged by success, the Imperial forces persisted until they finally found something that could stop them, the United States. Humbled, the Japanese retreated to their islands and plotted their next campaign.

Central to the Japanese idea of themselves is what the French call *solidarité* and what the Japanese call *wa*. It is the idea that all citizens must stick together and work in harmony toward the same national goals. But while the French are outspokenly critical of their institutions and the goals they set, the Japanese tend to remain silent.

If any group were particularly susceptible to mass thinking, it would be the Japanese. Solidly behind the Imperial Japanese Army during the 1930s and 1940s, the Japanese people trudged just as mulishly behind the large industrial combines of the 1970s and 1980s. Even today, when a fad catches on in Japan it seems to become obligatory. Consider a typical bunch of Japanese school kids entering the Louvre, for example; nearly every one will have dyed his or her hair orange.

The Japanese even think differently, it is said. The "dry" logic that leads to critical analysis in the West is said to be "wet" in Japan— leading to greater social cohesion. And the personal sense of right and wrong, guilt and shame, encouraged by Judeo-Christian religions in the West, finds a completely different expression in Japan. People are ashamed if they let down the group, or fail in their responsibilities to the group. But, if the group goes astray, so, too, does the individual.

Japan's economic behavior in the 1990s made it seem very different from the United States, too. While the U.S. economy boomed,

Japan's Main Streets were as silent as a dead battery. Whereas the United States ran a frightening current account deficit, the largest ever recorded, the Japanese ran a persistent financial surplus of stunning size, equivalent to almost 10 percent of GDP. While everything went well for America, everything seemed to go badly for Japan.

JAPAN INC.

By 2001, the Japanese market had been in the doldrums for more than a decade, with declining, weak, and often negative economic growth. So moved was former Treasury Secretary O'Neill by the Japanese plight that he entertained the issue from a humanitarian, rather than a central banker's, point of view: The question, he said, was "How do we help the people of Japan achieve a higher standard of living?" The problem with such generous sentiments is that they ignored the reality of the situation. "Japan is the largest net creditor in the world," retorted the chief economist at Mitsubishi Research, as reported in the *Washington Post,* "and is thus the richest country in the world."[2]

How could this be? How could people suffer an entire decade of stagnation, with the stock market losing 65 percent of its value, and still be in the lead? How was it possible?

Even 10 years after its peak, Japan was actually in better economic condition in many ways than the United States. The Japanese worked fewer hours. They paid less in taxes. They got more in social services for the taxes they paid. They were in better health and lived longer. At the end of the twentieth century, the average employee in manufacturing in Japan, for example, worked five fewer hours per week than a similar worker in the United States. On average, an American put in two more full weeks of work than a Japanese employee. On average, the government received 12 percent of the average worker's earnings. In the United States, this number was 16 percent. Compared with U.S. workers, the average Japanese employee took more overseas vacations, and he bought more luxury goods. Two-thirds of the world's high-end products were bought by the Japanese.

Furthermore, Japan was and still is a marvel of well-functioning social services. Health care is practically free. Public transportation is ubiquitous and efficient. Trains pull into the station, on average, 18 seconds before the scheduled arrival time. As a partner at Accenture (formerly Andersen Consulting) in Japan remarked: "The average standard of living and the satisfaction level are higher here than in the U.S."[3] Indeed, Japanese women live longer than any other group in the world, and Japanese men have life expectancies second only to Swedes.

Yet, despite these advantages, the hard fact remained: At the beginning of the 21st century, it was as if Japan, which had boasted the world's second largest economy in the 1980s, no longer existed. U.S. economists, and Americans generally, believed that the Japanese must have done something incredibly wrong; after all, they had disappeared off the face of economic Earth. Economists in the United States had repeatedly urged the Japanese to increase their money supply. Inflating the currency, according to U.S. economists was the key. If the yen were destroyed, little by little, Japanese consumers would be more willing to spend, rather than save.

But both monetary and fiscal policy had failed to work. Now, said the U.S. economists, generously offering yet more unsolicited advice, the Japanese needed to reform their economy. They needed the guts to tackle the tough problems, to mark the bad loans and bad business to a ruthless market, to restructure whole industries if necessary, and to introduce dynamic U.S.-style capitalism to the island.

U.S.-style capitalism was the last thing that the Japanese wanted. After World War II, they had created a completely different style of capitalism. It was far removed from the free-wheeling capitalism described by Marx. The means of production were not really owned by rich, independent capitalists, but by big commercial groups, who borrowed their money from the big banks. These in turn obtained their money from the savings of the ordinary Japanese people. It was a society in which the risks and rewards of capitalism had been collectivized, in a uniquely Japanese way.

THE INVISIBLE HAND

The original idea of U.S. capitalism rested on a notion introduced by Adam Smith in the 18th century; that individuals pursuing their own self-interest were guided by an "invisible hand" toward outcomes that were beneficial for everyone. In Smith's mind, the invisible hand was the hand of God. Markets, and economies for that matter, were naturally occurring phenomena, like forests or beehives. They were ruled by laws that God had prescribed for them. Smith is often described as the world's first major economist. In fact, he thought of himself as a "moral philosopher," in that his efforts were directed toward discovering the laws by which God's universe was run.

This was a very different view from that of contemporary economists, Japanese economists included. Instead of trying to figure out what makes the world work, modern economists preferred to assume God's role—trying to make it work their way. Not content with mere observation, U.S. and Japanese economists got involved, pulling the levers and pressing the buttons that make the great machine whir and hum.

Japan's contribution to the history of capitalism may result from the singular circumstances in which it arose. In post–World War II Japan, capitalism was imposed on a near-feudal industrial system. But by the middle of the 1990s, Japan's economists, business leaders, and governmental interferers still could not even imagine an invisible hand. Their religion lacked a central god, and their economy had only recently emerged from feudalism. Their society functioned not as a hodgepodge of individuals, each lusting after his own objectives, but more like an ant colony in which each little worker knew precisely his place and busied himself for the good of the ensemble. It was a form of cooperative, consensual, centralized, post-feudal capitalism.

Just as slaves arriving at American plantations in the 17th century often took the last names of their masters, Japanese workers were known by the name of the company for which they worked. Workers slaved away for long hours (a typical employee might work from 8 A.M. to 9 P.M. during the boom years) for relatively little money. He would sing the company song when called upon, or when drunk. Companies treated their employees not as cost centers, to be shed quickly when sales headed down, but as serfs or retainers. Workers were practically guaranteed jobs for life. "Rice sticks together" say the Japanese—even when it gets burnt.

The big enterprises, too, were considered permanent. The Japanese system emphasized large companies, joined together by cross-held shares and networks of cooperating projects. Rarely did a small, upstart challenge them. Rarely, then, did the big companies face fundamental competition from within the country. New technologies and new products were created or brought into the big company system, refined by tireless workers, and then put into service—producing goods that could then be exported, often to the United States.

It was a strange form of capitalism—the big companies did not even care about producing profits! Like the dot-coms of America's bubble years, they regarded the lust for profits as short-sighted, "short-term" thinking. What they wanted was market share and growth. After all, they were out to dominate the world!

EXPECTING A MIRACLE . . .

In April 1949, Ambassador Joseph Dodge fixed the price of the yen at 360 to the dollar. The yen was cheap . . . cheap enough to give the Japanese an economic opening. They would become a manufacturing nation, making goods more cheaply than their competitors. Thus, began the 40-year boom that would turn Japan into the world's second largest economy and, briefly, give it the world's largest stock market and the world's most expensive real estate.

The Japanese were disciplined workers, indefatigable imitators, and meticulous businessmen. Applying their united energies to the task of economic growth, they produced spectacular results. Japanese cars, for example, triumphed against long odds. The Big Three U.S. automakers had previously enjoyed a near-monopoly position in an extremely competitive, capital-intensive industry. The odds of being able to mount a major challenge to Detroit seemed so remote that Japan's central planners at MITI actively discouraged Honda and Nissan from attempting it.

But the automakers pushed ahead. They entered the U.S. market with small cars that seemed to pose no threat to the Big Three. Gradually, while Detroit remained complacent and inattentive, the Japanese improved on their car production skills and sales techniques. Almost before Americans had noticed, a major part of the U.S. auto market was in Japanese hands.

U.S. business school students had to learn a whole new set of buzz words in the late 1980s. *Kaitzen,* the concept of ongoing improvement, was introduced to them as though the idea itself were an innovation. They soon learned about *zaitech, tokkin funds, keiretsu, baburu,* and all the rest of it; they scattered the Japanese words in their conversation as if they were sprinkling soy sauce on tempura. They also learned how to eat raw fish without getting sick.

The U.S. admiration for Japan was adulterated with fear, loathing, and jealousy. By the mid-1980s, it was beginning to look as though Japan might take not only U.S. autoworkers' jobs, but America's place as the world's most important economy. Japanese banks were becoming the biggest in the world. Japanese industrial companies dominated several other industries already, and looked as though they could triumph in any industry they targeted.

What's more, the Japanese were beginning to spend money as well as make it. They were buying up trophy properties all over the world—including Hollywood studios in California, and the Exxon building and Rockefeller Center in New York. In France, Japanese buyers purchased a Renaissance chapel, complete with stained glass windows, intending to dismantle it stone by stone and ship it to Japan, thus provoking the French to pass a law prohibiting the export of national treasures!

Japanese buyers also took front seats at major auctions in London, Paris, and New York, where they bought famous works of art for phenomenal prices. Just as American tycoons would do 10 years later, the Japanese began buying art as if they actually liked it. Crime boss, Susumu Ishii, for example, moved into stocks in 1985. Between 1986 and 1987, his portfolio—greatly aided by powerful friends in politics and finance—rose 5,000 percent. He applied $7.5 million of his fortune to buying works of art by Renoir, Chagall, Monet, and others. Meanwhile, the Yasuda Fire and Marine insurance company paid nearly $40 million for van Gogh's *Sunflowers*. Ryoei Saito spent $82.5 million on another of van Gogh's paintings, *Portrait of Dr. Gachet,* and a further $78 million for Renoir's *Au Moulin de la Gallette.*

Yaumichi Morishita, however, outdid them all, spending $300 million on late 19th-century French paintings. Asked why he liked the French Impressionists, his reply was worthy of American art collector Dennis Kozlowski a decade later: "Impressionist paintings go better with modern décor."

. . . AND GETTING ONE

In the 1980s, a bestseller entitled *Japan as Number One*[4] was an expression of a popular prediction. For as Japan edged upward, America seemed to sink down. The future looked obvious: Japan's organized, focused capitalism seemed unstoppable. At least the Japanese thought so. Prime Minister Yasuhiro Nakasone urged his countrymen on as if they were marching on Singapore. "[S]hed all sense of ignominy and move forward seeking glory," he told them.

Faced with the yellow menace, the chattering classes in the United States called for reform. "Economic Pearl Harbor," cried the politicians. The United States needed central planning like the Japanese, said critics. Americans needed to learn Japanese management techniques, claimed the consultants. U.S. businesses needed to be more long-term oriented, declared the analysts. The United States needed to impose import restrictions, added the protectionists.

What was bothering Americans so much was that, not only were they losing market share to Japan, but they were beginning to feel like losers in other ways, too. While the Japanese seemed to do everything right, Americans seemed to do most things wrong.

In the 1980s, the Japanese economy was a marvel—the most successful, most dynamic, most self-confident economy the world had ever seen. U.S. businessmen cringed and quaked before the threat of Japanese competitors.

It was against this background that the world's most important finance ministers met at the Plaza Hotel in September 1985. Threatening various trade sanctions and barriers, the U.S. Treasury Secretary squeezed out an agreement: They would work together to drive the dollar down, mainly against the yen. For the money, Japanese goods were better than U.S. goods, the ministers seemed to believe, but a higher yen would at least make them more expensive.

If the Japanese assault on U.S. economic interests was a "Pearl Harbor," the Plaza Accord came near to being a Battle of Midway. Japan's aspirations were dealt a setback. Japanese products were suddenly harder to sell on world markets. Within a few months after the ministers had returned home, the yen had risen by a full 40 percent—making Japanese exports nearly twice as expensive as they had been in the summer. By early the following year, GDP growth had been cut in half. The Bank of Japan had to react. What could it do?

Keynesian and Monetarism were well known in Japan. The central banker's trade was simple enough; when an economy slowed down, the bank made access to money cheaper and easier. Indeed, the Bank of Japan did just that: It cut rates. The official discount rate was cut four times in 1986—down to 3 percent. At the time, corporate profits were already in decline, just as they would be 10 years later in the United States. But investors were still bullish on Japan, Inc. Money still flowed, and spurred by the rate cuts, stocks suddenly became the object of obsession at every sushi bar in town.

Early in 1987, two interesting events occurred. The national telephone company, Nippon Telephone and Telegraph (NTT), went public, and the industrial world's finance ministers held another meeting, this time at the Louvre in Paris.

Of the NTT offering, all that needs to be said is that it had the stretch marks of a bubble. Economists only had to read the paper or look out the window: So great was the demand that citizens had to stand in line to fill out applications to buy the shares, which were to be allocated by lottery. In a scene that recalled the events on rue Quincampoix nearly three centuries before, the shares were quickly oversubscribed. Some 10 million people applied for them during a two-month period; not one of them knew the price. Individual investors believed that since the government made the public offering, they were safe. Investors felt as if they were buying a piece of Japan itself. The government, they believed, would never allow the company—or the market—to inflict losses on the people. So they bought NTT without trepidation.

The Japanese stock market was believed to have the same kind of protection that Alan Greenspan would later offer U.S. investors. In the United States, it was called the "Greenspan Put," described in greater detail later in this book. The Fed chairman had the option of reviving stock prices whenever he wanted, people thought, simply by lowering short-term interest rates. In Japan, the public had perhaps an even greater level of confidence. They believed in the system; they thought that Japan and its collective capitalism were permanently successful.

Japanese share prices, already absurdly high, became even more absurd after the results of the Louvre meeting were announced. In the interval between the Plaza Accord and the new Louvre Accord, the dollar had indeed been driven down. From a high of 259 to the dollar at the time of the Plaza meeting in 1985, the yen had risen to 122 to the dollar at year-end 1987. This time, the danger to the United States was not that the dollar was too high, but that it was becoming too low. The finance ministers agreed to take action again, this time to run down their own currencies in order to boost the dollar up. The Japanese cut rates again—down to a postwar low of 2.5 percent.

Investors loved it. A lower yen would make Japanese companies even more competitive, they reasoned, pushing up Japanese stocks even further. Nippon Telephone and Telegraph jumped to a market capitalization greater than Y50 trillion, or about $376 billion. It alone was worth more than the entire value of West German and Hong Kong stock markets combined.

Japan Air Lines shares traded hands at more than 400 times annual earnings. Fishery and forestry firms were priced at 319 times earnings. Shipping industry shares had a multiple of 176. How could you justify such prices? Western investors, less caught up in the madness, could not. They began selling. But, just as they would do in the United States 10 years later, in Japan, investors, analysts, and economists put their imaginations to work to try to figure out a rationale for such outrageous prices.

"Japan is different . . . more long-term oriented," they would say.
"Japan is the Land of Technology," they would point out.
"Western fixation on 'dry' P/E numbers doesn't work in Japan," they would explain.
"Japan is the world's leading economy . . . the most innovative . . . most efficient . . . most dynamic . . . most productive society on earth . . ." they would continue, "of course stocks are going to be priced differently. If you added in all the hidden assets [mostly overpriced real estate] and figured out the real profitability of Japanese companies, the figures would look much different." (Yes—worse.)
"The Japanese have no alternative but to invest in stocks . . ."
"It's a New Era . . ."

Almost every gas that was later to be pumped into the bubble on Wall Street, 1998 to 2000, had already been field-tested by the Japanese.

Almost any explanation would do—or none at all. Even an earth-quake in Tokyo, in mid-1989, seemed to provoke bullish investors to buy more.

Whatever wet logic the Japanese used to justify buying expensive stocks and real estate, it had gotten completely waterlogged by the end of the decade. People seemed ready to buy practically anything at nearly any price—no matter how absurd.

THE NEW RACE

Throughout Japan, in the second half of the 1980s and the early 1990s, property values had been shooting up so fast that ordinary household-ers could not keep up with them. The price index for commercial land in Japan's six major metropolitan areas tripled between March 1986 and March 1990. In 1987, land values rose so steeply that the total increase exceeded Japan's aggregate output for the year. A typical family found that its earnings from increased stock and real estate val-ues were greater than its salary income. Families took out 100-year, multigenerational mortgages in order to be able to afford tiny, nonde-script houses in the Tokyo area. It seemed almost reasonable, given the Japanese penchant for thinking long-term and the sloppy logic of the time. At the peak of the bubble, Japanese property was priced as though it were worth four times the value of all the property in the United States. The Imperial Palace and surrounding park were said to be worth more than the whole of Canada.

Where did all this apparent wealth come from? As in the United States 10 years later, the Japanese had become confident to a fault. In the late 1980s, they could look back on nearly half a century of growth and prosperity. Was it an accident? Hardly, they told themselves: It was the result of their own hard work, their own self-discipline, their own gift for commerce, industry, and investment. As in the United States 10 years later, four decades of success had turned the Japanese into a race of geniuses!

Markets make opinions. And no opinion is so tenaciously held as a man's good opinion of himself. As in the United States the following decade, the Japanese came to think not only that they were superior businessmen and superior investors (for hadn't they alone been able to see the true value of Japanese shares?) but that they had evolved to a higher level of species. *Shinjinrui*, or "the new people," was the name they coined for themselves. What made them new was that they seemed to have an understanding of the way the world worked that had been denied to the generations before them.

Unlike their parents and grandparents, who had never dared, the *Shinjinrui* were keen to spend and borrow as if there was no tomorrow. They would pay $300 for a shot of whiskey in a nightclub, or $1,000 for a Louis Vuitton handbag. They prized expensive designer labels as a way of advertising their membership in the new race: Japan thus became the world's top market for luxury goods, with Hermes, Gianfranco Ferre, Yves Saint Laurent, and dozens of other expensive retailers lining the streets of the Ginza shopping district. Indeed, the *Shinjinrui* loved consumption, engaging in the process so conspicuously that they made public spectacles of themselves. But where did the money come from? Business earnings were already headed down by 1987. Salaries had risen only modestly. What had happened?

A WORLD-CLASS, CREDIT-GOOSED SPENDING BINGE

Of course, owners of stocks and real estate enjoyed the benefits of the "wealth effect." They had no greater incomes, but when they studied their net assets, they were pleased to see that they had gone up. Tax cuts, too, encouraged extra spending.

But the biggest boost to Japan's consumer economy came from debt. The Japanese are world-class savers, but little noticed by economists at the time, they had also become champion borrowers during the boom years, with debts rising to 130 percent of income. Just as people caught in the euphoria of investment bubbles have always done, the Japanese went on a credit-financed spending binge. The number of credit cards in circulation tripled. The Japanese, normally thrifty people, soon had debt levels equal to those in the United States. Total bank lending increased, too—rising by $724 billion from 1985 to 1990. Consumer credit companies, or "nonbanks," also increased lending by some 700 percent during the same period.

For every debt, there is a credit—as accountants will tell you. "For every boom, there is a bust," we add. And for every day of absurdity, there is a day of reckoning. During its bubble, Japanese savers funded the country's capital spending binge, with 95 percent of the nation's debt domestically owned. The country remained a net creditor to the rest of the world during the entire period, with its net foreign asset position holding roughly steady at around 10 percent of its GDP.

All this new money and credit was bound to have an effect. At a macro level, nothing gives an economy such a sense of well-being as a jolt of money it did not have to earn. Typically, businesses pay their employees, and then the money comes back to them, minus savings, when the employees buy the products and services they produce. Sales revenues are thus offset by employment expenses. But when the employees spend their savings or credit, the cash comes into corporate coffers as if from heaven. Since the companies paid out no extra salaries to receive the money, a higher percentage of it—speaking from a macro perspective—falls to the bottom line as profit. All of a sudden, businesses see higher sales and higher profits, and believe the increased demand is a signal that they should expand production. So, they build new factories, offer new products, and hire new employees. But the new demand generated by credit cannot last. People may borrow, but they must also pay back—sooner or later, one way or another.

For example, if a man borrows a million dollars, he can buy many things. It will seem as if his standard of living has gone up immediately. His extra spending may help persuade merchants and manufacturers that they need to offer more items for sale. They, too, may borrow money to take advantage of the perceived opportunity that has come their way. Sooner or later, the man will not be able to borrow another million dollars. In fact, he will be asked to repay the first million that he borrowed. When that happens, the whole shebang begins to collapse. Not only can the man no longer afford to spend in the manner to which he was hoping to become accustomed, he is actually obliged to reduce his expenses below their original level to be able to pay back the borrowed money. The merchants and manufacturers, who had also taken out credit to meet the new demand, now find that their sales not only fail to live up to expectations, but that they are less than they were before they began expanding. It can take decades, but there can be no other outcome.

DISSAVERS, DEBTORS, AND OTHER MALCONTENTS

The same effect is produced by taking money out of savings and spending it. On a macroeconomic level, "dissaving" seems to come out of nowhere and produces an astonishingly pleasant effect. But the problem with dissaving is that you cannot do it for long. Pretty soon, you have no more savings to dis. Then, you have to start saving again, whether you like it or not. The virtue of spending more than you can afford becomes the vice of thrift: Businesses still have the cost of paying out wages, but the money does not come back in sales.

The decisive moment comes, and not necessarily for any particular reason, when dissavers and debtors decide that they cannot continue. The confidence that they felt when they borrowed and spent so freely begins to ebb away. First they begin to wonder whether their expectations will be realized. Maybe stocks will not continue to rise as they had forecast, they say to themselves. Maybe property values will stabilize or even fall, they begin to worry. They hesitate: "Maybe I should wait before I buy another car . . . or a bigger apartment," they may think to themselves. Hesitation produces a drop in sales, which produces unease and disorder throughout the system. Companies hire fewer workers. Overtime pay is reduced. New expansion projects are set aside and then discarded. Profits fall. Investors back off. As sales and asset prices fall, investors begin unloading their stocks and real estate at lower and lower prices. A new spirit settles over the group. Unlimited confidence turns into a mood of resignation, despair, and even panic. The day of reckoning has come.

In the trough of the cycle, the contraction of credit has an effect every bit as alarming as the expansion phase had been agreeable. Instead of adding money, which was not offset by payroll expense, money is now withdrawn with no compensating savings to the companies. Normally, in a recession, corporations cut back on their payrolls. Consumers, who are also employees, have less to spend. Sales go down, but at least corporate costs have been cut—protecting profit margins. But when consumers increase savings or begin to pay back loans instead of taking out new ones, sales and profit margins are hit hard. On the same income (or payroll expense, from the employers' point of view), consumers spend less money. The results are disastrous and can only worsen when—to protect profits—companies react to falling sales by cutting back on employees' salaries. Then, consumers really do have less money to spend and reduce their buying even further.

Newton's Third Law applies to economies as well as to physics. Actions produce equal and opposite reactions. A bubble produced by borrowing and spending collapses into an antibubble of exaggerated thrift, bankruptcy, and debt cancellation. This is, of course, what happened to Japan following the collapse of its bubble, beginning in January 1990.

COLLAPSE OF THE MIRACLE ECONOMY

Worried by rising prices in the real estate sector, the Bank of Japan decided to take action. For the first time in nine years, it raised the official discount rate from 2.5 percent to 3.25 percent at the end of May 1989. Short-term interest rates increased by a full percentage point between January and June of that year, perhaps also indicating tighter policies in the bank's open market operations.

On October 11, 1989, another increase in the discount rate took it to 3.75 percent and short-term rates continued to climb, ending the year at 6.25 percent—within a mere 25 basis points of where short-term rates stood in the United States, when its bear market began 10 years later.

On December 29, 1989, the Nikkei Dow reached its peak of 38,915. In the following 21 months it dropped 38.5 percent. But during this time, real estate prices, as measured by the Japanese Real Estate Institute, continued to rise. It was not until two years later, in 1991, that property prices finally peaked out—about 15 percent higher than they had been at the end of 1989. In some areas, however, price increases were much greater: in the prefecture of Chiba, for example, property prices rose more than 90 percent.

By way of comparison, the U.S. stock market peaked out almost exactly 10 years later—on December 31, 1999. Over the next 33 months, the S&P 500 lost 45 percent of its value—an initial decline worse than in Japan. During the same period, U.S. home prices rose—just as they had in Japan. According to Fannie Mae's index, the amount of the increase was—surprise—15 percent.

By all accounts, Japan's economic and financial news for 1989, on the brink of the Nikkei's decline, was very positive. There were few signs of inflation; with consumer prices rising less than 3 percent per year (as they would in the United States 10 years later). Unemployment remained near record lows. By most outward appearances, things had never been better: Japan had managed to achieve what most economists thought almost impossible—full employment with low inflation, high growth, massive increases in asset values, and a large trade surplus, too. Could there be any doubt that the Japanese were especially blessed? Or especially smart?

RATES RISE, STOCKS FALL, AND LOANS GO BAD

Late in January, 1990, the Nikkei 225 fell 5 percent in 3 days. Investors dismissed it. Then, in February, the index dropped another 4.3 percent in 3 days. The financial media, again, paid little attention. Stocks were falling, it was reported, "for no apparent reason."

Meanwhile, interest rates were rising. Long-term government bonds fell to yield 7.3 percent. Commercial banks raised prime lending rates to 6.25 percent. The Bank of Japan, still trying to let air out of the bubble, increased the discount rate on March 20, 1990, to 5 percent. Stocks continued to fall.

The invasion of Kuwait by Iraq on August 2, 1990, caused much anxiety in markets worldwide. Concerned about rising oil prices, the Nikkei 225 lost 11 percent in a single day. Again, the Bank of Japan raised the discount rate—to 6 percent. Stocks continued to fall.

Land prices were beginning to soften, too. Though overall real estate rose until about mid-1991, prices were already beginning to collapse in the most expensive urban areas by the middle of 1990. In 1990, the value of real estate in Japan's six major cities had equaled the nation's entire GDP. By the end of 1993, prices had been cut in half—a loss equal to half of GDP. Bank lending, which had multiplied during the boom and bubble phase, was backed by rising real estate values.

The next phase was obvious and inevitable—the loans, worth trillions of yen, were going bad.

THE LOST DECADE

Over the next 10 years, growth was slow or negative. No Promethean light shone on Japanese eyes. Computers and the Internet—the twin innovations that, according to Paul O'Neill, Secretary of the Treasury, had boosted U.S. productivity and offered a new "golden age of prosperity to America," provided none of their blessings to the Japanese.

Just as Japan's economy was shrinking, so, too, was its population, literally. Furthermore, the population was aging: Japan has more people over the age of 65, proportionally, than any other major country. One of the reasons for this was that the reproductivity of the average Japanese woman had fallen well below the 2.08 level needed to sustain population levels. Instead, Japanese women have an average of only 1.34 children. Thus, Japan had one of the oldest populations in the world, with one in five people over the age of 65.

But in midsummer 1992, 30 months after the beginning of Japan's slump, hardly anyone believed that the Japanese miracle economy was in serious trouble.

The *Economist* ran a special report in its July 11, 1992, issue entitled: "How Japan Will Survive Its Fall." Focusing primarily on a rise in consumer spending by 3.3 percent in the first quarter of that year, the article suggested, "The economic slowdown in Japan should not be confused with a Western-style recession. Which is why Japan will come bouncing back" (see Figure 5.2).

"Most of the victims of the economic slowdown are so far confined to the financial and property sectors. High employment is helping to support consumer confidence," the *Economist* explained. "Much is made of the fact that business investment . . . is falling. But consumer spending, which is almost three times as big, grew by 3.3 percent in the year to the first quarter . . . . The main reason that Japan should be able to dodge a deep recession is that it starts off with the soundest fiscal and monetary policies of any industrial economy. This gives the government more ammunition with which to fend off a recession."

FIGURE 5.2 The Lost Decade
Rather than a quick and spectacular collapse as in previous crashes, the Japanese
economy continued to wrestle with increasing levels of loan write-offs (top) and bad debt
(bottom) throughout the 1990s.

"OUR WEALTH IS SLIPPING AWAY"

The *Economist* was wrong about practically everything. Japan's economy did not come bouncing back. High employment did not support consumer confidence for long: Consumer spending fell. And the fiscal and monetary policies, which were supposed to be so sound, proved completely inadequate to the task.

On July 1, 1991, the Bank of Japan did what central banks do in a slump—it loosened monetary policy. The discount rate was cut from 6 percent to 5.5 percent. Thus began a series of cuts, not unlike those that would begin in January 2001 in the United States. By September 1993, the discount rate stood at 1.75 percent, the lowest rate in the bank's history. Yet, the recession continued until the end of 1993, and that was not the end of the interest rate cuts: In April 1995, Japan cut the rate another full point—bringing it, in the *Financial Times*'s words, to "effectively zero."

Moreover, nominal growth rates, which had been around 7 percent throughout the bubble period, remained near zero during the early 1990s. Manufacturing profits fell nearly 25 percent in 1991 and another 32 percent in 1992. Bankruptcies rose, especially among companies engaged in real estate or fund management.

Banks, so eager to lend when real estate values were rising, all of a sudden found few opportunities. Bank ratings fell. Loan loss reserves mounted. In 1993, Japanese banks wrote off 4.3 trillion yen in non-performing loans. In 1994, the total rose to 5.7 trillion yen. Still, the banks were a long way from clearing their balance sheets of the bad debt. And the greatest blow to Japanese banking still lay nearly a decade in the future. On January 22, 2003, the largest Japanese bank, Mizuho Holdings, announced losses of 1,950 billion yen and bad loans amounting to 2,000 billion yen.

Until 1994, consumer prices had been rising in Japan. It was widely argued that continued consumer spending, along with government fiscal and monetary stimulus, would save the day. But in mid-1994—a full four and a half years after the beginning of Japan's slump—consumer prices began to fall. For the first time since the Great Depression, a major economy experienced consumer price deflation.

Once prices began to fall, Japan entered a rare and disquieting phase in her financial history. In the world's post–World War II experience, there was no precedent for it . . . and no cure. "Our wealth is slipping away,"[5] Eisuke Sakakibara, a former Vice Minister of Finance, told *Time* magazine in autumn 2002—a decade after the pain had begun. Why did prices fall? Because consumers were not buying, economists explained. Why were they not buying? Because prices were falling.

Across the archipelago, consumers were cutting down on spending (if they were spending at all), banks were reluctant to make loans to businesses, and employers were reducing salaries and laying off workers. Japanese consumers began shopping at secondhand stores. Residents in upper-class districts were reported to be combing through their neighbors' trash for used furniture. The banking system was so swamped with bad debts that it had neither the will nor the money to help new business ideas get off the ground.

The Japanese central bank and the government both tried to cure the problem in the conventional way; by making more money and credit available. Not only did the central bank lower the discount rate to near zero and bring down interest rates, the government began a program of public works that was the dream of concrete vendors the world over.

Alex Kerr laments the destruction in his book, *Dogs and Demons: The Rise and Fall of Modern Japan*:

> Japan has arguably become the world's ugliest country. To readers who know Japan from tourist brochures that feature Kyoto's temples and Mount Fuji, that may seem a surprising, even preposterous assertion. But those who live or travel here see the reality: the native forest cover has been clear-cut and replaced by industrial cedar, rivers are dammed and the seashore lined with cement, hills have been leveled to provide gravel fill for bays and harbors, mountains are honeycombed with destructive and useless roads, and rural villages have been submerged in a sea of industrial waste.[6]

Across the nation, men and women are at work reshaping the landscape. Work crews transform tiny streams just a meter across into deep chutes slicing through slabs of concrete 10 meters wide and more.

Builders of small mountain roads dynamite entire hillsides. Civil engineers channel rivers into U-shaped concrete casings that do away not only with the rivers' banks but with their beds. The River Bureau has dammed or diverted all but three of Japan's 113 major rivers. Meanwhile, Japan's Construction Ministry plans to add 500 new dams to the more than 2,800 that have already been built.

Japan's government did just what Keynes recommended—it spent money. Fiscally conservative during the boom and bubble years, the government went on a spree of what Alan Booth calls "state sponsored vandalism"[7] in the 1990s, taking the budget deficit to a remarkable 5 percent of GDP in 2002. The construction process begun in the 1990s of roads to nowhere, concrete shorelines, bridges and dams, meant that Japan, per square mile of available territory, covered 30 times as much surface in concrete as in America. Indeed, the Japanese obsession with concrete went to absurd extremes: In 1996, the Shumizu Corporation announced its plans to build a hotel on the moon using specially developed techniques for making cement on the lunar surface!

Above all, these useless make-work projects fattened the national debt from 60 percent of GDP to 150 percent. By the end of the 1990s, Japan's government debt equaled 15 times its tax base, or almost twice the closest historical record—Britain in the interwar period.

THE ONOUE AFFAIR

If the "lost decade" of the 1990s brought a bear market to Tokyo's stock exchange and to the nation's property market, it also produced a bull market in financial scandal, involving many banks and brokerage houses throughout the islands. Reputations were ruined; fortunes were lost; a few people committed suicide . . . business as usual following a major bubble. One such scandal was the Nui Onoue case. It was a bizarre affair. After exploring several accounts, typical Western readers know less than when they began. Was the protagonist's name Madam Nui Onoue or Onoue Nui? The reporters could not seem to make up their minds. Rumors circulated about links with the *burakumin*,[8] the underworld, and the animal kingdom. A pet ceramic toad, in particular, attracted attention. At a time when the Japanese stock market was as big or bigger than the New York Stock Exchange, Madam Nui was the largest single player on the Tokyo exchange. The Industrial Bank of Japan and its affiliates had lent the 61-year-old spinster as much as 240 billion yen. She was the International Bank of Japan's biggest shareholder, with 3.1 million shares. Moreover, she owned 8 million shares of Dai-Ichi Kangyo Bank, 2 million shares in Sumitomo Bank, 6 million shares of Tokyo Electric Power, 3 million in Fuji Heavy Industries, and 3 million of Toshiba.

Although no one seemed to be sure as to the source of her fabulous wealth, the woman became a kind of cult leader. Businessmen in blue suits would show up at her two restaurants in a seedy district of Osaka and stay until the wee hours. What could they have been doing? According to reports, they would witness Madam Nui seeking help from the divinities in bizarre midnight rituals. The "Dark Lady of Osaka" was thought to be connected not only to the burakumin but also to the mikkyo—an exotic Buddhist cult.

In August 1991, the woman was arrested and charged with obtaining loans under false pretenses. It was then revealed that she faced bankruptcy as well as prison, with debts totaling more than 400 billion yen. Day by day, the odd little story grew bigger, until the scandal touched some of the biggest banks in the country, and rumors went flying that various underworld crime figures were involved. Later in the year, on October 22, the chairman of the Industrial Bank of Japan, Kaneo Nakamura, resigned.

The absurdities that had been fashioned in the 1980s were coming apart at the seams in the 1990s. Remarkably, Japan's central bankers, finance ministers and other economic garment workers were unable to mend them. At first, few people could believe it—the fabric had seemed so durable. But in January 1990, the weaknesses were apparent. Over the next dozen years, the Japanese economy deflated. GDP grew less than 1 percent per year from 1992 through 1995.

By the end of the decade, Japan had erased 17 years of stock market gains. In summer 2001, the Nikkei dropped to 10,977—its first time below the 11,000 mark since 1984. Over a period of 11 years, investors had lost 75 percent of their money as the Nikkei Dow fell from a high of nearly 40,000. Tokyo's unemployment rate—once almost a nonexistent number—has risen to 5 percent, almost exactly the same as America's level. Even Japan's GDP growth and that of the United States had converged: Both were running below 1 percent—an eight-year low for the United States, and very nearly an eight-year average for Japan.

If only Alan Greenspan had been able to work some of his reputed magic on the other side of the world, it might have prevented some personal tragedies: By the end of the century, the Japanese were throwing themselves onto train tracks in such high numbers that the railways had put up mirrors in stations to force the jumpers to "reflect" before killing themselves.

OBVIOUS PARALLELS

In the two years following December 1989, Japan's stock market fell by 40 percent. But the Japanese economy held up well during those two years. In fact, GDP growth did not turn negative until 1992. Capital spending slowed sharply, but consumer spending continued to boom. Property prices continued to boom for two years after the stock market tumbled. The parallels in the United States a decade later were so obvious that we can still recall the story through the headlines it produced: "America's economy looks awfully like Japan's after its bubble burst," said a subhead from the *Economist* in June 2002. "America's economy over the past 2 years has in many ways mirrored the performance of Japan's immediately after its bubble burst," continued the magazine.[9]

In the United States, as in Japan before it, the coming of the slump was both unexpected . . . and largely unnoticed. Even as the nation's economy entered a recession in March 2001, according to the National Bureau of Economic Research, leading economists denied it. "The overall signal remains one of moderation in the pace of economic activity," said the chief economist for the Conference Board, on February 22, 2001, "with no recession looming on the horizon."[10] The recession officially began just seven days later. But then, it was the Fed's turn to not notice.

"Fed's Parry says U.S. isn't in recession," reported *Bloomberg News* in April 5, 2001, referring to statements made by Robert Parry, President, Federal Reserve Bank of San Francisco. "U.S not in recession, Fed must be vigilant," added Michael Moskow, President, Federal Reserve Bank of Chicago on April 4.

"Fed's McTeer says the U.S. economy not in recession," agreed the president of the Federal Reserve Bank of Dallas on the same day. Nothing is confirmed until it has been thrice denied.

"I don't think it's apt to make a comparison," said U.S. Treasury Secretary Paul O'Neill, in November 2002, referring to Japan. "They're not an open economy," he continued. "One of the things that has really been beneficial to our economy is this openness and the challenge that we have permitted to come in here, from foreign suppliers from all over the world. . . ."

"Economists say America is unlikely to follow into Japanese-style deflation," said a *Wall Street Journal* article of November 2001, "because U.S. leaders reacted to their slowing economy much more quickly than Japanese leaders did."

The subject bored most Americans, but it haunted a few economists like an unsolved crime. The U.S. economy seemed to us to be following a script written in Japan. With only an occasional improvisation and a broad allowance for cultural differences, the essential dialogue in America 1995 to 2001 was very much that of Japan 1985 to 1991.

PLUS ÇA CHANGE, PLUS C'EST LA MÊME CHOSE

The plot was much the same ("the more things change, the more they remain the same")—hotshot new era meets cold realities of marketplace. The love interest was identical—investors fell head over heels for financial assets, abandoned all sense of reason or dignity, and made fools of themselves. The first couple of acts were similar, with rising action in the investment markets and a climactic sell-off.

But now, the curtain had gone up on Act III . . . and the U.S. audience expected a twist. Unlike the dumbstruck Japanese, U.S. investors and consumers believed that the prompt action of the hero, Alan Greenspan, would save them. Greenspan, wielding his rate-cutting sword, chopped off 450 basis points in 10 months, while it took the Japanese central bank more than four years to do so. Bullish economists thought his speed would prove decisive.

Most economists had no idea when the Japanese market would turn up, because they had no idea why it turned down in the first place. But they continued to believe that lower rates would save the United States. In April 1992, when the Nikkei appeared to be hitting a low at 17,000 (from a high of 39,000 a year and a half earlier), a consensus of a dozen top forecasters still predicted Japanese economic growth and rising stock prices. But 10 years later, the Nikkei was hovering around 10,000, and the Japanese economy was suffering from its fourth recession of the past decade. Short-term rates for the Japanese had been "effectively zero" for more than five years.

In the United States, enlightened officials acted promptly. In Japan, they dithered. The Fed cut 4.5 percent from key rates in the first 10 months of 2001, while the Japanese central bank took four and a half years to do the same work. Congress rushed out a plan to spend $100 billion to stimulate the economy, whereas the Japanese Diet took longer. Would the speed of U.S. official response prove decisive? Could credit-fueled overcapacity really be corrected faster by offering *more* credit, more cheaply, more quickly?

Investors waited in vain for the turnaround in Japan to begin. The "reform and restructuring" story, wherein Japanese corporations undertook to adopt the U.S. program for providing shareholder value— mergers, acquisitions, cost-cutting—drew investors into Japanese stocks on several occasions over the decade from 1990 to 2000. Wall Street firms loved restructuring. They had made money in the 1980s helping U.S. companies adopt the practices of Japan, Inc. Now they hoped to make money helping Japanese companies adopt the U.S. model.

LACK OF IMAGINATION

Year after year, Japanese companies announced new restructuring plans. And the Japanese government announced further reform measures including more fiscally stimulating budgets. So stimulating were these budgets that $1,130 billion of new government debt was added, bringing the ratio of government debt to GDP up from 60 percent in 1992 to more than 100 percent in 1999.

Perversely, more and more stimulus produced less and less real growth. From 1996 to 2000, deficits rose from 4.3 percent of GDP to 7.2 percent, while real growth fell from 5.1 percent to 1.2 percent. Still, Japanese consumers were unwilling to spend their money: They saved it and paid off debts. They accumulated financial assets, instead of beach houses.

Whatever the Japanese had done wrong (nobody was quite sure what), Americans were convinced that they would not make the same mistake. After all, Americans were not fanatical savers. They had no large financial surplus. They cooked their sushi. And they had "Easy Al" Greenspan at the head of the Fed, not some uptight banker who would jump in front of a train if things went badly.

The Japanese experience was so unprecedented that economists at the end of the 1990s, just like the media mentioned earlier, could still scarcely believe it and were utterly unable to imagine that it might continue. But it did continue. While the United States enjoyed the biggest boom (and then bubble) in its history, the Japanese economy and stock market were as lifeless and clammy as a cigar butt.

"Japanese government warns of low growth and pain," reported a headline in the *Financial Times*. The news from Japan had scarcely changed since George Bush, senior, threw up on Prime Minister Miyazawa in 1991. It has been nothing but bad since.

Columnists, analysts, and economists who, just a short time before, had been busy trying to explain first why the Japanese would dominate the world economy for a long time, and then why the slowdown was not too serious, were now explaining why Japan would not recover anytime soon. With an alarming lack of imagination, they turned to the familiar reasons, merely giving them a spin in the opposite direction. The Japanese government was out-of-date, managers were incompetent, and Japanese workers, after all, would never learn that the secret of a healthy economy is borrowing and spending. Rarely was the financial press so unanimous as it was in the late 1990s on the subject of Japan. Every headline evoked a nation in the throes of economic despair: "Stocks Plunge to a New Low," "Japan's Jobless Rate Surges" (to its highest level since World War II), and "Japan's Industrial Production Falls for 5th Month," were typical.

Of course, no comparison is ever perfect. Every situation is different. Each day is new. But the novelty of a situation is often less instructive than its familiarity—the things that are not new about it. In the mid-1980s, Japan was enthusiastic about memory chips and automobiles. In the mid- and late-1990s, it was the Internet and the telecosm that set U.S. imaginations on fire.

In North America, telecom companies spent billions of dollars to lay millions of miles of fiber-optic cable.

"Build it and they will come" was the motto of the time. But once it was built, less than 3 percent of it was actually used. Excess capacity, whether in North America or Nippon, tends to reduce prices and profits.

Another distinction without a difference between Japan and the United States was the concentration of bad debt in the Japanese banking sector, for which no parallel was said to exist in the United States. While Japan's banks held bad business debt, the United States' innovative lenders held bad mortgage and consumer debt as well as business debt.

Corporate debt may never have reached the magnitude in the United States that it attained in Japan (at its peak, Japan's corporate sector owed an amount equal to 225 percent of GDP, whereas in America, the figure rose to 55 percent, according to 2002 Federal Reserve Board figures), but that does not mean that there were not just as many—or more—exaggerations ready to be normalized by a slump. The large amount of consumer debt in the United States, for example, could rival the bad loans dragging down Japanese banks. Unlike Japan, where the personal savings rate never fell below 12 percent, the United States' savings rate was never spectacular, declining from a prebubble level of 6.5 percent in late 1994, and nearly disappearing in the late 1990s.

COLLECTIVE HALLUCINATIONS

While American businesses were in relatively better shape than Japanese businesses at the close of the bubble period, U.S. consumers were in worse shape. What would happen when they could no longer pay their bills? Would U.S. capitalism be any less accommodating to zombie voters than Japanese consensus capitalism had been to zombie industries? We do not know the answer, but we think we will find out soon.

The illusion of wealth in Japan was gunned by massive increases in the prices of real estate. In the United States, housing prices rose modestly, except in a few places such as Manhattan and Silicon Valley, where the increases were extravagant. But, in the United States, the same illusion arrived daily in the stock price quotations. More people in the United States owned stocks than in Japan. In fact, at the century's end, stocks constituted 30 percent of total household financial assets. In Japan, that percentage peaked at 16.5 percent in 1990.

The parallels were there for anyone to see.

Yet, when the going was good in the United States—in the late 1990s—Americans hardly noticed the resemblance. While the U.S. economy benefited, or so it seemed, from every favorable omen and every serendipitous advantage, from the Info Tech revolution to the Peace Dividend, Japan's economy lay as inert and friendless as a retired tax collector. Within a few years, Japan had gone from being the idol of the entire world to being an object of open contempt. In 1989, U.S. businessmen were practically straightening their hair and dying it black in fawning imitation of their Japanese role models. A few years later, they were offering the Japanese advice and seemed almost indignant when the Japanese refused to take it.

But the most important similarity between the U.S. economy and the Japanese was both completely obvious and utterly ignored: Never before had so many people had such a keen interest in the stock market and the economy. Never before were crowd dynamics so crucial to understanding how markets work. At the height of the bubbles in both the United States and Japan, people came to believe that there was something so special about their economies that the normal rules and limitations no longer applied.

Unrestrained, people thought they were doing a reasonable thing when they bought stock at preposterous prices—because they believed prices would be even more preposterous in the months ahead. Likewise, they saw no reason to curtail borrowing and spending—not when things could only get better: During the boom and bubble years in Japan, capital spending nearly doubled and banks lent extravagantly to large industries. Meanwhile in the United States during the 1992 to 2000 period, per capita fixed investment increased 73 percent. "In both cases," commented Harvard economist Jeffrey A. Frankel, "people had decided that the structure of the economy had changed fundamentally. People thought they found the secret to eternal youth."[11]

JAPANESE INVENT MANDATORY BORROWING

The problem was that business profits actually shrank during the later years of the bubble economy, leaving businesses unable to pay their debts. When the assets (in the form of stocks and real estate) backing the loans weakened, the whole economy suffered. Capital spending, employment, and consumer spending all went down together.

Admittedly, in the United States, bank lending was less pronounced than the 60 percent share in corporate debt held by bank loans in Japan. Instead, most corporate borrowing in the United States came directly from the capital markets, and this, optimists argued, would be marked to market much more quickly. (The liquidation of the Big Five alone—Enron, WorldCom, Quest, Tyco, and Computer Associates—wiped out nearly half a trillion worth of corporate debt.)

In Japan, pressure to keep the dream alive was almost irresistible. Thanks to easy credit, companies that should have gone out of business were still alive.[12] "Zombie" companies still use resources—and still make payroll—with borrowed money. Matsushita Electrical Industrial Company, for example, lost more than $2 billion in 2001. Yet, it refused to cull even one of its 130,000 employees. Business survival was not so hard in Japan; lower rates and liberal credit policies made it soft and easy.

Not only was it *easy* for businesses to borrow in Japan, it was almost *mandatory*. Government, bankers, and businesses all supported each other even when it seemed contrary to their own interests. Government—through the Bank of Japan—made plenty of money available at negligible rates. Bankers even made the money available to their insolvent clients. In a revealing incident, Shinsei Bank, owned by Ripplewood Holdings of New York, was told by regulators that it had to lend to customers who would otherwise fail. Whether they needed it or not, businesses tended to borrow money just to be good partners. These lending conditions encouraged the vampire companies to stay in business. In trying to end a recession quickly, by making money readily available, Japanese authorities made it almost eternal.

In the United States meanwhile, experts denied the existence of the zombie economy phenomenon. "We simply don't have time for zombies," one explained. In the U.S. version of capitalist legend, the marketplace drives a quick stake through the heart of a dying company and saves the shareholding townspeople from the terror of confronting these ghouls in the dark.

Yet, according to Michael E. Lewitt of Harch Capital the myth is a far cry from reality. "The U.S. economy is being stalked by vampire companies," Lewitt suggests in the October 15, 2002, edition of the *HCM Market Letter* "that are effectively dead to their creditors but frighteningly alive to their competitors." Lewitt pointed out that WorldCom, William Communications, and Global Crossing, despite having filed for bankruptcy, were "still feeding upon the bodies of their still solvent competitors."

In fact, the U.S. airline industry has been haunted for decades. "Eastern, Pan Am, Continental, Braniff, and others," writes Lewitt, "were able to emerge from bankruptcy (sometimes more than once) and feast on the flesh of American, UAL, U.S. Air, and Northwest. Allowed to walk the earth, drained of life but still living, these vampire companies are emerging from bankruptcy to create more of their kind as they disrupt the cost structures and competitive balances of their industries."

FAILURE OF CENTRAL BANKING

What was the matter with Japan? Had it no central bank? If anything, the Bank of Japan was even more central to the Japanese economy than the Federal Reserve System. Then, what was the matter with their central banker? Why couldn't Mr. Hayami or Mr. Mieno accomplish the feats of economic management that were credited to their counterpart in the United States, Mr. Greenspan?

There were many explanations. Any competent editorial page editor would tell you that the Japanese had "failed to restructure" their economy. Perhaps the editor had some definite idea what he meant by that, but it was unlikely. Typically, restructuring only arose as a solution when the conventional methods—monetary and fiscal policy—had failed.

And they certainly had failed in Japan. The Japanese authorities cut interest rates until they were giving away money and spent it until they were practically insolvent. Despite these efforts, the cooperative energy and collectivized rigging that had made the Japanese economy so successful now made it difficult to set things right. Lower interest rates had achieved nothing for Mieno, Matsushita, or Hayami.[13] In fact, they probably only postponed the day of reckoning, turning a crash into what Paul Krugman called "a long, slow-motion depression."[14]

Krugman continues: "I wish I could say with confidence that Japan's dismal experience is of no relevance to the U.S. And certainly our nations are very different in many ways. But there is a distinct resemblance between what happened to Japan a decade ago and what was happening to the United States economy just a few weeks ago. Indeed, Japan's story reads all too much like a morality play designed for our edification."

Wouldn't it be just like Nature to put on a morality play for U.S. investors and policy makers? Didn't she warn Caesar of the ides of March and put shoe-shine boys on the streets of New York to offer stock tips? And wasn't it Nature who put first-hand accounts of Napoleon's disastrous campaign against Russia in the hands of Hitler's generals as they crossed the Berezina? Didn't she put Bezos' mug on the cover of *Time* when AMZN was nearly $100 a share . . . and ring the bell at the very top of the United States' bubble with deliciously absurd statements from people who should have known better?

But these little glimpses into the future must be ignored. Or else, history would be as drab and meaningless as a joint session of Congress. Humpty-Dumpty never eases himself down off the wall gracefully—he falls!

Indeed, the U.S. slump could even be worse than Japan's: Unlike the Japanese, whose domestic savings financed the boom, U.S. savers did not fund their nation's consumer spending binge. Instead, it was financed by borrowing heavily from foreigners. In other words, it was the kindness of strangers—willing to invest their surplus dollars back into the U.S. economy—that made U.S. consumer spending possible.

FED GETS WORRIED

There are thousands of economists at the Fed. They prepare research papers with titles such as "Finding Numerical Results to Large Scale Economic Models Using Path-Following Algorithms: A Vintage Example." These papers may never be read by anyone (not even by their authors), but one that came out in spring 2002 was, relatively speaking, a best-seller.

"Preventing Deflation: Lessons from Japan's Experience in the 1990s" rolled off the Fed's presses in June 2002. Had it been published earlier—say, two and a half years earlier—it would almost certainly have been as ignored as other Fed publications. For, at the time, hardly anyone believed that the Japanese experience could provide any lessons worthy of learning. The Japanese on the other side of the planet seemed hopelessly out of it and unable to do anything right. The United States, on the other hand, could do no wrong. But that is one of the great charms of this old ball we live on—it turns.

While the United States enjoyed such a bright sunny boom that it misled an entire generation, Japan had suffered its dark 12-year-long night of bear market, recessions, bankruptcies, and deflation. It seemed impossible that Japan's somber comedy might someday come to North America. But then . . . as the Dow dropped below 8,000, WorldCom went belly-up, and unemployment rose . . . all of a sudden, in the words of a Credit Suisse First Boston bond market strategist, "Everyone's talking about the Fed's deflation paper. You're starting to see a lot of people talk about Japan and comparing it to here."[15]

Alan Greenspan was still a hero in the fall of 2002. By contrast, Ya-sushi Mieno[16] had become not a villain, but worse, a nonentity. Now he was just another central banker, one who had been unlucky enough to plant his own little derriere in the first chair at the Bank of Japan and find himself presiding over the world's second largest economy during its largest ever decline. Greenspan was still regarded as one of the men who "saved the world" after the crisis of 1998. Mieno was widely viewed as one who nearly destroyed it; at least, that was the implication of the Fed's research paper and the widely held view of U.S. economists.

The Fed was spooked. Falling prices had become a persistent problem in Japan; the island had experienced consumer price deflation ever since 1996. In nominal terms, the Japanese economy was no bigger in 2002 than it had been in 1995. So, in the fall of 2002, the Fed launched a public relations initiative to convince the world that it had nothing to fear from deflation in the United States; the Fed would destroy the currency before it permitted stable prices.

Deflation in the United States was "unlikely" said Fed governor Moskow. The risk was "extremely small," added then Fed governor Benjamin Bernanke. "Extraordinarily remote," were the odds given by Alan Greenspan.

Then Bernanke seemed to threaten the entire world monetary system, saying "We have a technology called a printing press." But, despite his assurances that deflation was no problem, Greenspan's sleep must have been disturbed in the fall of 2002 by thoughts of "turning Japanese." The mainstream press had taken up the idea and his staff economists were offering solutions. What became of Mieno, Greenspan must have asked himself? For instead of being "extraordinarily remote," the risk of deflation was, in fact, extraordinarily close at hand. Prices had not been rising so slowly for 60 years, and manufactured good prices were in outright deflation. Only services and energy prices were still rising. Fed governors were neither unaware of this nor indifferent to it: On the contrary, they were running scared.

By the fall of 2002, the news from Japan seemed to get worse and worse. Indeed all the economic data would seem to corroborate this statement: Even after a 12-year slump, Japan's nominal GDP collapsed at a 10 percent annual pace in the second quarter of 2001, and this despite a key lending rate of 0.001 percent.

WE SMELL SUSHI

No country has ever tried as much fiscal stimulus as Japan. After cutting rates down to "effectively zero," the Japanese embarked on the biggest program of unnecessary government spending in history.

With no military to waste money, it had to turn to public works. New highways to nowhere . . . new bridges . . . new rail lines, by the late 1990s, the little island of Japan was pouring more concrete than all the 50 states. It was very stimulating to cement sellers. But as to the economy . . . it did nothing. Here we are, 18 years later . . . and the Nikkei index is still down by two thirds.

"Japan's rural areas have been paved over and filled in with roads, dams, and other big infrastructure projects, the legacy of trillions of dollars spent to lift the economy from a severe downturn caused by the bursting of a real estate bubble in the late 1980s," wrote the *New York Times*.[17]

Public spending was so aggressive, it boosted Japan's government debt to 180 percent of GDP—more than two times the current U.S. level. But did all that cement buy Japan out of its slump?

You be the judge. Housing prices in Japan are now back down to where they were in 1975—nearly 90 percent below the late-'80s peak. And stocks? The Nikkei index is back down to where it was a quarter century ago. Stocks sell for half their book value—and they're still considered too expensive for beaten-down, hyper-fearful Japanese investors. The downturn began in 1990. Over the following 19 years, it did more property damage than the Great Tokyo Fire of 1923 and the Enola Gay combined, wiping out wealth equal to three times the country's GDP. This was despite interest rates at zero . . . and a heroic effort at Keynesian stimulation.

If the United States were to follow Japan's example, it would have to leave its interest rates near zero for the next decade . . . and add about $10 *trillion* to its public debt. And if it got the same results, you'll be able to sell your house in 2026 for the same price you paid in 1992.

But the simpletons have no other idea. "In a nutshell," bragged the *New York Times* report, "Japan's experience suggests that infrastructure spending, while a blunt instrument, can help revive a developed economy, say many economists."[18]

Are these, perhaps, the same economists who thought U.S. super-consumption, eternal-debt economy would never fail? The same economists who thought the bankers were providing a public service, by offering so many people so much credit . . . and then planting their debt bombs all over the planet? The same economists who forecast rising stock prices in 2008?

Probably.

Invasion of the Zombies

Back in the 1990s, when Americans still believed in capitalism, they sent a steady stream of advisors and kibitzers to Japan. The world's second largest economy was in a stall and seemed in no hurry to get out of it. Its largest banks were "zombies," said the Americans; they were propped up by the Japanese government in order to avoid losses and embarrassment. If the Japanese wanted to get things moving again they should let those banks fail . . . let the free market do its work . . . let the chips fall where they may. Then, capitalists, entrepreneurs, and scrappy businessmen could pick them up and build with them.

The Japanese didn't take the advice. To this day, 19 years after the beginning of Japan's long, soft, on-again, off-again depression, the economy is still in a slump . . . and expecting negative growth again this year. Altogether, Japanese investors are said to have lost a sum equal to 300 percent of the nation's annual GDP . . . the equivalent to a loss of about $45 trillion in the United States.

Years ago, we predicted that when the crisis came in the United States, Americans wouldn't take their own advice. Alas, we were right. Instead, they are keeping the zombies alive, just like the Japanese did. And the zombies are sucking the blood out of the economy.

Of course, Japan tried to fight it, too, and that effort didn't work. Just look at the evidence: the Japanese tried fiscal stimulus (government spending) and monetary stimulus (central bank policies). They ran deficits of 6 percent of GDP—equivalent to about a trillion-dollar deficit in the United States. And they took interest rates down to near zero and left them there for years. What else could they do?

Still, in the spring of 2009, Japanese investors were about $15 trillion poorer than they had been 19 years before. This is why we "say" these efforts didn't work. Maybe the damage might have been a lot worse if the Japanese had not done what they did.

Whatever the case, Obama is following the lead of Hata, Obuchi, Mori, and Murayama. And Ben Bernanke, too, will follow the lead of the Japanese. He will cut rates . . . just like the Bank of Japan did.

But there are two crucial differences between Japan and the United States. First, Japan had a healthier economy, with a positive trade balance, and huge savings. Second, the United States has the world's reserve currency.

Japan could easily spend 6 percent of its GDP trying to replace private spending with government spending. The Japanese saved 19 percent of GDP. The government could simply borrow from its own people—like the United States did to finance World War II. But America can't finance huge deficits internally; it doesn't have the money. Its people don't save. They have no savings to lend their government. Any money the government gets from Americans will have to come out of current private spending or out of other investments. Obviously, this is not going to do much good, since there is no net increase in spending or investing. Nor can the U.S. government expect to bring in unlimited financing from foreign sources. The foreigners save, but they need their money to rescue their own economies.

What's worse, the more the U.S. government has to compete for funds with other borrowers, the more interest rates will go up—worsening the picture for the economy as a whole.

The other point is vitally important, too. Not only did Japan have a cushion of cash to comfortably sit out the correction, it had no reason to do otherwise. With money in the bank, the Japanese were never threatened by an economic breakdown. And what money they owed, they owed to themselves.

America has neither of those two comforts. Millions live paycheck to paycheck, depending on credit cards to fill in the gaps. When unemployment rises above 10 percent . . . maybe above 15 percent . . . they will howl so loud the government will be forced to take desperate measures, which could send the deficit to $2 trillion. Then, crushed under the weight of so much debt, it won't be long before the feds realize that we don't "owe it to ourselves."

Instead, we owe trillions to foreigners. Foreign central banks alone hold about $2.4 trillion worth of U.S. government debt. About $10 trillion is said to be the total of all U.S.-based securities in foreign hands. That is a burden that could be easily lightened . . . if, for example, the dollar weren't worth quite so much . . .

What will happen when the feds really go to work on the dollar? Ben Bernanke has pledged to drop money from helicopters, if that is what it takes to head off a Japan-like slump.

Mr. Market wants a correction. The feds want to stop it. And never before have the feds had so many ways and means to try—all of which depend on reducing the value of the dollar in order to encourage the illusion of prosperity.

Here, we sense a pause—for clarification—is in order. When the feds speak of "stimulating" the economy with lower rates and rebates, they are merely speaking the humbug language of modern economics. The only thing that really stimulates a consumer economy is more consumer spending. And consumers can only do their consuming if they have money. So, the only thing the feds can do is to give them more money to spend. But the feds don't have any real money. All they have is the machinery of credit and inflation—they can make borrowing less expensive, in nominal terms . . . and they can "print up" more pieces of green paper and distribute them to the public. That is to say, the only thing they can do is to inflate, lowering the value of each bit of currency in circulation.

The greenback floats on air; theoretically, the financial authorities can create a gust of wind and push it in any direction they want. A few years ago, a Paul Volcker might have resisted; he might have urged the Fed to protect the currency and curb inflation. But Tall Paul is now in the private sector . . . warning his clients to take cover. Some years ago, too, a few die-hard Republicans might have opposed a fiscal stimulus package as just more reckless spending from the Democrats. Not anymore. Nothing stands in the way of destroying the dollar . . . except Mr. Market himself.

It is shaping up to be a grand show. Mr. Market on one side. The market manipulators on the other. We don't know how it will turn out . . . but we are pretty sure there will be blood on the mat when it is over.

DR. GONO OR: HOW I LEARNED TO STOP WORRYING AND LOVE INFLATION

When pressed for an answer to the question "what will 'turning Japanese' look like?" what can we do but turn to the master? Forget Keynes. Forget Friedman. The economist that everyone should be paying attention to is Gideon Gono.

Inflation is coming back in style. And Gideon Gono is its star. While other central bankers flounder, he's proven that you can have inflation . . . and have it more abundantly than you want.

Gono, if you haven't heard of him, was Robert Mugabe's right-hand man. And Robert Mugabe is the number one man in Zimbabwe, an African country with a real "riches to rags" story. It was one of the wealthiest and safest countries in Africa when it was run by Ian Smith in the 1970s. But the meddlers and world-improvers couldn't leave well enough alone. They helped put Mugabe in power. Since then, the place has gone to Hell.

Gideon Gono, 47 years old, lives in a 47-bedroom mansion in Harare. He says he doesn't drink, only sleeps four hours a night, and runs regularly. He is known as "Mr. Inflation" for his Olympian efforts to increase the country's money supply. He does this the old-fashioned way—by printing pieces of paper with lots of zeros on them. *Newsweek* magazine seems to have found him in a talkative mood:

Asked what he thought of the worldwide credit crash, he replied:

> I sit back and see the world today crying over the recent credit crunch, becoming hysterical about something which has not even lasted for a year, and I have been living with it for 10 years. My country has had to go for the past decade without credit . . . Out of the necessity to exist, to ensure my people survive, I had to find myself printing money. I found myself doing extraordinary things that aren't in the textbooks. Then the IMF asked the US to please print money. I began to see the whole world now in a mode of practicing what they have been saying I should not.[19]

The Trouble With Zeros

In spring of 2009, Zimbabwe took a couple of bold steps. First, it announced that henceforth citizens would be allowed to use currency other than the stuff produced by its own central bank. This came as a great relief to the people of the nation, who were already using U.S. dollars to replace the Zimbabwean brand. With 230 million percent inflation, the Zimbabwe dollar has not been so much a store of value but an incinerator of it.

Second, Gono announced that he was taking 12 zeros off the Zimbabwean currency.[20] Twelve seems like a lot. And it seems like only yesterday that Gono introduced the first note with 12 zeros on it—the 1 trillion Zim dollar note.

But that's the problem with zeros. They've got holes in them. You add nothin' to nothin' and you still got nothin'. Easy come. Easy go. You can as easily add zeros as take them off. At the end of the day, the extra zero gets you zilch.

Zero is a perfidious number. Nobody likes it. Nobody wants to be "a zero." Nobody wants to get a zero on a test . . . or zero returns on his investments.

It is a line that leads nowhere . . . with no substance in the middle of it. You can add a zero . . . or multiply by zeros; it gets you nowhere. And what is a zero? Is it something? Or nothing? No one knows.

Within the space of 76 hours, Zimbabwe led the world in two opposite directions. On Monday, with prices rising at 231 million percent per year, Zimbabwe was the world's hyperinflation record holder. On Wednesday, it led the world in deflation . . . with prices falling 99.999999999 percent overnight.[21]

Once again, we are profoundly grateful to the nation of Zimbabwe and to its central banker. The latter has turned the former into a marvelous laboratory for bizarre monetary experiments.

The pile-up on the global financial highway has yielded its toe tags and broken mirrors. More than $30 trillion has been lost. Of course, the world's monetary cops have been on the scene for about a year and a half, trying to get the traffic moving again. But just read the paper. Instead of a recovery . . . every day brings more skid marks and fresh collisions.

Tokyo or Harare?

A little bit of the old juice from the central bank will cure a typical recession. It is nothing more than a pause in the inventory cycle, allowing businesses to clear their shelves before they are restocked. But this is not an inventory-driven recession; this is a balance-sheet depression. The problem is not really an absence of credit, but an excess of debt. Steve Keen, on his Web site DebtWatch, chronicled the ongoing debt crisis in this way on November 29, 2008:

> When its Bubble Economy burst at the end of 1990, aggregate Japanese debt was equivalent to 162% of GDP—consisting of a 108% private debt to GDP ratio and a 54% government ratio. In 2008, aggregate debt was 259% of GDP—made up of a slightly smaller private ratio of 94% and a much larger government ratio of 165%.

> On this empirical record, the portents to the USA to be able to get out of this crisis by debt-financed government spending and direct financial sector bailouts—which effectively swap private debt for government debt—are not good. The latest Flow of Funds data records the aggregate US Debt to GDP ratio as 381% of GDP (with the private sector's share of that being 290%). This is more than twice the level that the Japanese economy started with when it entered its Lost (Two?) Decade(s).[22]

It is not just the debt itself that must be eliminated. There are too many factories producing too many goods for too many people who can't pay for them. You can see excess capacity in the unemployment lines, too. Suddenly, the world seems not to need so many sales clerks, or welders, or financial engineers. The United States alone may have $1 trillion of excess output capacity and 10 million people too many in the workforce.

Debt and excess capacity can be liquidated quickly—as they were in the panics of the 19th century—through bankruptcies and defaults. But, today, liquidation would have to take place over the dead body of U.S. Fed chief, Ben Bernanke. While that would be our preferred method, alas, it's not going to happen.

Another way to eliminate debt and excess capacity is to work your way out of them. Unfortunately, that process takes a long time—especially with the feds keeping zombie firms alive and fighting the correction every step of the way. Japan has been working off its excess capacity for the last 19 years. Property prices in major Japanese cities began going down in 1991. They fell for the next 13 years, bottoming out in 2004, 87 percent below their peak.

Few policy makers will want to follow the Japanese example— certainly not those of the United States. Americans lack several things the Japanese had . . . such as patience, a favorable trade balance, and a thick cushion of domestic savings. On the other hand they have one thing the Japanese did not have; the United States can pay its debts in a currency it alone controls. If it chooses, it can resort to a third way to get the traffic moving; it can inflate away the debt.

"We conclude that, under a paper-money system, a determined government can always generate higher spending and hence positive inflation," said Bernanke.[23] But with $7 trillion in excess in debt and spare capacity, neither business nor labor has any pricing power. Normally, it would take a long time before inflation returns.

Mr. Gono's experiment, however, proves that if a government is determined enough . . . it can always destroy its own currency. In January of 2009, Zimbabwe produced a monetary freak— the world's first one trillion dollar note. Then, it had a value of about 26 euros. Now, you can use it to buy a cup of coffee in Harare—provided you also have $3 US. In February, banks were supposed to begin distributing the new currency—in which all 12 zeros on the trillion-dollar note have been lopped off.

Mr. Gono added so many zeros to the national currency, he practically gave inflation a bad name. But now it is inflation that people want—desperately. And day by day, the world glances over Mr. Gono's shoulder. First curious . . . then appalled . . . and finally, admiringly.*

"I am confident that we will meet whatever challenges the future may bring."[24] said the Fed Chairman Benjamin Bernanke when he was sworn in.

Here come the zeros.

THE LONG, SOFT, SLOW SLUMP . . .

"It's dead out there," said a London taxi driver early in May of 2009. "I don't know why I bother to come to work. Everybody's afraid to take a taxi. They're afraid it might bankrupt them. It's silly really. They could save a lot of money by getting rid of their cars and just taking cabs. But I would say that, wouldn't I?"

The taxi driver was talking his book. But he was talking sense, too.

"People consider taking a cab a luxury. And it's easy to cut out. You can see them on the street. They raise their arms to hail a cab and then they think again. They put their arms down and go look for a tube [subway] stop. They probably don't really save much money, but it's psychological. Suddenly, everybody thinks he has to save money. I can't remember anything like it."

---

*The greatest central banker of our time . . . is going . . . going . . . Gono! In February of 2009 Gideon Gono was replaced in a "power sharing" move by a fellow named Tendai Biti.

Poor Mr. Biti still has his work cut out for him. His predecessor made a mess of Zimbabwe's economy. But Mr. Biti looks like just the man to correct it. He apparently has no training in economics. That's a definite plus. The paper describes him as a "44-year-old lawyer [who] was a student leader active on human rights issues." Good luck.

(From a BBCNews.com article, "Profile: Zimbabwe's Tendai Biti," February 10, 2009.)

But one man's expense is another man's income. The man who saves a pound by not taking a London cab, denies a taxi driver a pound of revenue . . . who then buys a pound less of gasoline . . . or a pound less of clothing . . . or a pound less of something. Cutting back on spending is clearly good for the individual, but it does to an economy roughly what a visit from a sniffling grandson does to a bedridden great-grandmother. Pretty soon, the old lady is dead.

"Losses happen," Marcus Aurelius might say. "Get over it."

Instead of getting over it, the feds are going to fight it every step of the way.

*   *   *

Christopher Wood previewed the similarities between Japan and the United States in his 1992 book, *The Bubble Economy*, but at the time the analogy seemed to apply in reverse:

> Like America, Japan has its own sort of moral hazard problem. The vast majority of people active in Japanese finance or commerce, including most foreigners, still subscribe to the notion that Japan Inc. will never let financial institutions go bust, that all credits are good, and that all deposits are safe. [As in federally insured America, this reassuring belief in the system's underwriting of all sorts of credit risk amplified the speculative bubble.] It also raised the danger of great disappointment or worse should this widely shared conviction ever be challenged. For in a consensus society, the longer the suspension of reality, the greater the potential for panic when everyone suddenly changes their minds. This extreme outcome cannot be dismissed out of hand, since the level of speculation witnessed in Japan in recent years was itself extreme and therefore does not lend itself to mild corrections.

Wood was both right and wrong. The deposits were not safe. Financial institutions were finally allowed to go bust. Not all credits proved good. But still, the Japanese did not panic. In their system of collectivized capitalism, everyone seemed to have such a stake in things as they were that no one was prepared to let the forces of creative destruction run their course. The banks, the government, the workers, the media—all the people who had worked so tirelessly to build Japan, Inc., now rallied to prevent it from correcting its mistakes quickly. Thanks to their efforts, Japan has endured a long, slow, slump beginning in January 1990 and continuing today.

"There is a crack in everything God has made," explained Emerson in his essay "Compensation." "It would seem there is always this vindictive circumstance stealing in at unawares, even into the wild poesy in which the human fancy attempted to make bold holiday, and to shake itself free of the old laws—this back-stroke, this kick of the gun, certifying that the law is fatal; that in nature nothing can be given, all things are sold."

There is always a day of reckoning; it can last 24 hours or 24 years. "Great bear markets take their time," said Jeremy Grantham, speaking of the U.S. market. "In 1929, we started a 17-year bear market, succeeded by a 20-year bull market, followed in 1965 by a 17-year bear market, then an 18-year bull. Now we are going to have a one-year bear market? It doesn't sound very symmetrical. It is going to take years."

Japanese stocks returned to their 1984 trend line—17 years later. [And again several years after that.]

The U.S. bubble market began in 1995. If the United States were to repeat the Japanese experience, stocks could be expected to return to their 1995 trend line, with the Dow below 4,000, in the year 2012, at almost the very moment when America's baby boomers will most need the money.

Nature in her wisdom, and God in his grace, always make sure people get what they've got coming, not what they expect. Welcome to Hiroshima, mon amour.

CHAPTER 6

THE FABULOUS DESTINY OF ALAN GREENSPAN

We know that the gold the devil gives his paramours turns into excrement after his departure.

—Sigmund Freud

On July 7, 2001, the Federal Reserve System (the Fed) opened a museum in Chicago. Press reports describe an exhibit that presented visitors with an economic problem and invited them to guess what the Fed should do. Should it raise rates, lower them, or do nothing? The exhibit then explained what Alan Greenspan did in the same real-world situation. In the popular mind, central banking had become a science. There was a right and a wrong answer. And the chairman of the Fed, Alan Greenspan, could be counted on to give the right one. In a cynical age, he was one of the few people about whom people had few doubts or misgivings. He was the steward of the most successful managed currency in history, the most prominent central banker since John Law, and the best-known public servant since Pontius Pilate.

Alan Greenspan was born on March 6, 1926, at a time when central banking was already firmly established in the United States. But the

Federal Reserve System, as it was called, was hardly the majestic tower it was to become by the end of the century. The nation's central bank was still a callow institution, awkward as a teenager and just as unsure of itself. Fed chairmen were not yet celebrities.

The Federal Reserve System was set up, almost surreptitiously, to function as the United States' central bank. It was not called a "central bank," for that would be telling too much. The United States was a freer country back then, with states that still made an effort to guard what independence they had left. A central bank would have been a bit too much for the Congress of 1913. So, the politicians—hardly realizing what they were doing—voted for the Federal Reserve and got a central bank as part of the bargain.

GOLD'S GOOD-BYE

At the time of the Fed's creation, the United States was part of a monetary system that had been in place since 1880: the "pure form" international gold standard, in which national currencies were freely exchangeable for gold. But the Federal Reserve Act explicitly called for the new Fed "to furnish an elastic currency." The full title of the act read as follows: "An Act to provide for the establishment of Federal Reserve banks, to furnish an elastic currency, to afford means of rediscounting commercial paper, to establish a more effective supervision of banking in the United States, and for other purposes." It was probably the "other purposes" that most interested lawmakers: A little easy money before an election wouldn't hurt.

The pure form gold standard died, along with manners and architecture, in the trenches of World War I. Under the strain of war financing, Britain cracked and the system fell. "The act was no sooner passed than the conditions taken for granted ceased to hold," wrote Milton Friedman and Anna Schwartz in their *A Monetary History of the United States*. "Before the System began operations, World War I had begun. Very soon, the belligerents effectively left the gold standard and a flood of gold started coming to the United States to pay for purchases by the Allies."

Friedman and Schwartz went on to describe the system that Alan Greenspan would find when he arrived on the job 72 years later: "The discretionary judgment of a group of men was inevitably substituted for the quasi-automatic discipline of the gold standard."

The establishment of the Fed represented a major break with the previous century, in which gold was always present. The men of the nineteenth century had coasted through their time on the lessons of the eighteenth: the experiences of John Law's Mississippi Scheme, the South Sea Bubble, the East India Company Bubble, the French Revolution's assignats, and various real estate and canal bubbles in Britain. They distrusted paper money, insisted on gold-backed currencies, and enjoyed a century of relative financial stability.

Gold was not entirely out of the picture after World War I. What emerged in the interwar years was a system of gold exchanges, with currencies still linked to the price of gold. But the links were loose and slipped from time to time. This interwar standard lasted until the end of World War II, when it was replaced by the Bretton Woods system, in which governments, but not individual citizens, could still trade currencies for gold. They had merely to go up to the "gold window" at the central bank and demand gold in exchange for their paper currencies.

The Bretton Woods agreement was nullified on August 15, 1971, when Richard Nixon noticed that the line at the gold window was growing longer and longer. Foreigners had lost confidence in the dollar and wanted gold. Little by little, America's gold reserves were leaving the country. Closing the gold window, and thus effectively ending the Bretton Woods monetary era, seemed the quickest way to solve the problem.

Of course, it was not nearly that simple. Unable to redeem their holdings of U.S. paper dollars with gold, foreigners sold their dollars in the open market, which drove down the price. Cheaper dollars made imports more expensive. Consumer price inflation rates soared in the United States as dollar holders, foreign and domestic, rushed to dispose of the quickly depreciating currency. Anyone who had saved dollars, or had fixed, dollar-based streams of incomes, took a loss.

It was robbery, but who noticed? Most people did not bother to think and did not think to bother. Monetary issues had not attracted a crowd in the United States since William Jennings Bryan gave his famous "Cross of Gold" speech in July 1896. Bryan's complaint had been that "hard money" (or currency backed by gold) offered farmers and working men no easy way to discharge their debts. Instead, the poor fellows had to repay them!

Bryan would have loved the money system that followed the collapse of Bretton Woods, for it held no trace of gold. From 1971 until the end of the century and beyond, governments were free to inflate their currencies by as much as they could get away with. It was a worldwide system of managed currencies, in which the explicit backing of currencies by gold was not only unnecessary, but actively discouraged by the International Monetary Fund, on the grounds that it reduced a nation's flexibility to deal with whatever economic problem threatened it.

Yet, throughout history, gold had proven to be a reliable foundation for money systems: A gold Byzantine coin, for example, had been used for eight centuries—holding its value even as kings and empires came and went. Gold worked for obvious reasons: It was rare; it was portable; and it was malleable. While planet earth yields her gold grudgingly and coddles every ounce, paper rolls out of the factories by the truckload and starts a fire as easily as a fortune. Every ounce of gold that was ever mined, even from the time of Croesus, had retained its value and its usefulness up to the time Alan Greenspan was born.

By contrast, paper money had never lasted very long. Collectors would line their walls with examples of unbacked paper money that had gone bad. Sooner or later, it all went bad. History provided no counterexamples. But gold was still very much a part of the monetary system when Alan Greenspan was born. On that day, an ounce of gold could be purchased for $20.63. The same ounce of gold might have been purchased 12 years earlier for just under $19—where the price of gold had remained virtually fixed for almost 200 years. Gold had anchored the dollar for so long that it hardly seemed necessary to ask its price. By decree, it never strayed far from where it had been the day before. And in 1926, 13 years after the creation of Federal Reserve System—whose stated goal was to protect the value of the dollar—was there any doubt that the dollar would remain strong?

LINCOLN'S GREENBACK

Central banking had its first rehearsal in America in the 1860s. Until the War Between the States, people could decide for themselves whose banknotes they would accept. The coins of Britain and other sovereign nations circulated freely in the Americas and could be used by anyone who chose to do so.

There was no nationally chartered central bank at the time. The only legally recognized money was specie, that is, gold or silver coins. The economy's currency consisted solely of banknotes redeemable in specie on demand. Private competition thus regulated the circulation of paper money.

But by 1862, Lincoln's government was toting up the cost of killing Southerners—and it was more than the Northern bankers were willing to lend. Already straining under the financial burden, Lincoln sought relief in the familiar way. A Legal Tender Act was passed in early 1862, permitting the federal government to issue paper money. Lincoln's greenback was not backed by anything except government promises. The new greenbacks were issued directly by the government and were legal tender for all payments except tariff duties and interest on the Treasury's debt.

In opposition to the Act, Senator Charles Sumner pondered whether it was really necessary "to suffer the stain upon our national faith [of inconvertible paper money]—to bear the stigma of a seeming repudiation . . . ? It is hard—very hard—to think that such a country, so powerful, so rich, and so beloved, should be compelled to adopt a policy of even questionable propriety."[1]

Mr. Lincoln's greenback is still with us. Both the currency and its managers are regarded with suspicion by only a few economists, conspiracy buffs, and crank commentators. Otherwise, they enjoy the kind of reputation that is usually reserved for live war heroes and dead rock stars. But things that need to be managed will soon be mismanaged . . . at least, that is our hypothesis.

It is hard for us to imagine, but there was once a time when the nation's money had no central managers. Economic historians—believers in the unrelenting forward march of progress—describe the antebellum banking period as one marked by frequent crises, instability, and bank failures. Thus, Lincoln's new centralized monetary authority, and even his unbacked paper money, looked to many like an improvement.

But the prior era—the Jacksonian era—is thought by some historians to have been the most stable monetary system the United States has ever had. "The alleged excesses of the fraudulent, insolvent or highly speculative 'wildcat' banks were highly exaggerated," writes Jeffrey Rogers Hummel in his history of the period, *Emancipating Slaves, Enslaving Free Men*. "Total losses that bank note holders suffered throughout the entire antebellum period in all states that enacted free-banking laws would not equal the losses for one year from today's rate of inflation (2 percent) if superimposed onto the economy of 1860."[2]

It did not take the currency managers of 1863 long to get into bad habits. They had printing presses back then, too. The Union's money supply quickly doubled. And by the next year, the greenback had already fallen to 35 cents worth of gold. People tried to protect themselves by dumping greenbacks and hoarding gold and silver coins. Soon, private minting of coins was made illegal. And Congress attempted to "shut down trading in contracts promising future delivery of gold." In those days, however, the greenback did not enjoy the universal confidence that it does today. Lincoln's government was forced to backtrack: Foreign governments still required gold-backed money.

Much of Lincoln's central banking apparatus was dismantled in the late nineteenth century. But you cannot keep a bad idea down for long. The Federal Reserve System was put in place in 1913, after the Panic of 1907 convinced bankers that they could dress up their cartel in the cloak of philanthropy and sneak through Congress.

At the outset, the Fed was primarily a decentralized backup system with 12 districts across the United States. But the U.S. entry into World War I changed all that. The Fed was a key player in financing the war and became a significant holder of short-term government debt. Reluctant to give up its starring role at the end of the war, the Fed went on to inflate the currency and was also a pivotal player in the short, deep recession of 1920 and 1921. During the 1920s, led by Benjamin Strong, then head of the New York Federal Reserve Bank, the Fed really "turned on the crank" (to borrow an expression from William Anderson) in a coordinated effort to prop up the British pound.

"Turning on the crank" is indeed what the Fed tends to do.

FROM DECADENCE TO DEPRESSION

In the same year that Alan Greenspan was born, Irving Fisher published his well-known article "A Statistical Relationship between

Unemployment and Price Changes." The article described what later came to be known as the Phillips Curve, a function purporting to show that mild inflation was not so bad; in fact, it seemed to stimulate employment. By then, the governors of the Fed had already figured out the key formula of central banking in the twentieth century: lower rates to heat up the economy, raise them to cool it down. As long as inflation did not get out of hand, everyone believed, lower rates would stimulate a healthy boom.

In the year after Greenspan's birth, a remarkable episode in Fed history came to pass—one that would set the tone for the next three quarters of a century.

In July 1927, Ogden Mills, the U.S. Secretary of the Treasury, organized a meeting at his home on Long Island. He invited the most powerful moneymen of his era—the central bankers of England, France, the United States, and Germany. Present were Benjamin Strong of the Fed, Montagu Norman of the Bank of England, and Hjalmar Horace Greeley Schacht of the Reichsbank. Emile Moreau, head of Bank of France, hated travel almost as much as he hated England's central banker. So, he sent a subordinate, Charles Rist, to represent him.

The problem before them was gold. More to the point, the problem was the run on England's gold, due to the mispricing of the pound sterling by Norman. The Bank of England had set the price of the pound too high after World War I, precipitating an economic crisis in Britain. The proposed solution was that they all increase credit together. Strong was a close personal friend of Norman; Schacht and Norman were friendly, too. It was the French who were causing problems, just as they would 44 years later. France threatened to redeem its credits with the Bank of England by drawing down England's stock of gold.

Strong decided to help take the pressure off the pound by lowering U.S. interest rates and making U.S. gold available to the French. Indeed, as he blithely told Rist, he was going to administer a "little coup de whiskey to the stock market."[3] Adolph Miller of the Federal Reserve Board (FRB) subsequently testified to the Senate Banking Committee in 1931 that this episode constituted "the greatest and boldest operation ever undertaken by the Federal Reserve System and, in my judgment, resulted in one of the most costly errors committed by it or any other banking system in the last 75 years." An economist at J.P. Morgan remarked shortly after the Long Island meeting: "Monty and Ben sowed the wind. I expect we shall have to reap the whirl-wind . . . We are going to have a world credit crisis."

A credit crisis did develop—but only after two years of ballooning debt. The stock market had already nearly doubled since the end of 1924. Then, following the Long Island conference, Wall Street shot up another 50 percent in the second half of 1928. In the three months leading up to August 1929, it ran up another 25 percent.

New credit instruments were developed, such as installment pur-chase plans, so that more and more people could participate in the prosperity. John J. Raskob, director of General Motors and chairman of the Democratic Party, wrote "Everybody Ought to Be Rich."[4] In 1929, as in 1999, people widely believed that new technology—radio, telephone, automobiles, electrical appliances—was making possible a whole new era of wealth.

Having lowered rates to help the English, the Fed became nervous about what it saw as excessive borrowing and "irrational exuberance" in the stock market. In 1925, the discount rate charged to commercial banks for Fed funds was only 3 percent. In a series of increases, it rose to 5 percent in 1928. But the mania continued. Finally, in August 1929, the Fed hiked the rate to 6 percent and the bubble was pricked.

These rate increases took the blame for the bust that followed. But the real rate of return on borrowed funds was so high that it is doubt-ful that the increases had much effect. If you could earn 25 percent on your money in three months in the second quarter of 1929, on Wall Street, a 1 percent increase in the cost of money would not be a seri-ous deterrent. Money from Europe rushed into the United States to take advantage of rising stock prices. An extra point of interest expense did little to tilt the balance away from U.S. investments.

Still, the balance tilted enough that investment slid from the posi-tive to the negative side of the scales in a trice. Stocks crashed. Businesses failed. Prices fell. By 1931, wholesale prices were 24 per-cent below those of 1929 and would soon drop another 10 percent. By 1931, 15 percent of the labor force was thrown out of work; two years later, it would reach 25 percent. More than 10,000 banks failed.

Banks back then were like mutual funds, or stock portfolios, today. There was no deposit insurance. Losses were real. Final. Wealth simply disappeared.

Fearful of banks and wary of stocks, people turned to gold to protect themselves. Bank deposits fell. People preferred to keep their cash—or gold—in hand. This was a problem, as the financial system depended on the health of the banks and their willingness to lend. When people withdrew their money, the banks failed and depositors became even more fearful of the banking system.

Failing banks became such a problem that President Hoover tried persuasion to convince people to leave their money in the banks. He sent straight-talking Col. Frank Knox around the country on a campaign to discourage hoarding of currency or gold.[5]

As banks failed, the supply of money declined. Thus, the value of money increased (prices fell). The United States was still on the gold standard, so the value of gold increased accordingly. But soon, forward-thinking economists, led by Britain's John Maynard Keynes, saw the need for more money, and more credit, to get the economy moving again. Gold seemed to bar the way.

Frightened that America might devalue the dollar (in terms of gold), investors began to move their capital abroad, or into gold itself. In February 1933, there was a run on U.S. gold—$160 million left the Treasury. Another $160 million was called away in the first four days of March. The commercial banks were losing gold, too: Investors withdrew over $80 million in the last 10 days of February and a further $200 million in the first four days of March.

One such investor was Arthur Dewing, a professor at Harvard Business School. He was so alarmed that he went into the Harvard Trust Company on Harvard Square and took out his entire balance in the form of gold coins. "When the crowds inside the bank reported Dewing's action to the people on the street," says Peter Bernstein recounting the story in his book *The Power of Gold*, "a mob gathered on the Square, fighting to get into the bank to follow the example set by the distinguished professor." Dewing was subsequently criticized for "unpatriotic behavior" and left the faculty soon afterward.

Into this rush to obtain gold wheeled America's new president, Franklin Roosevelt. On March 8, Roosevelt held his first press conference, assuring the nation that the gold standard would remain. On March 9, he pushed the Emergency Banking Act through Congress, giving him the power to regulate or prohibit gold ownership. Less than a month later, he replaced Hoover's persuasion with outright force—the leader of the free world made it illegal to hold gold. Two months later, Roosevelt abrogated all contracts in which payment was stipulated in terms of gold, including obligations of the U.S. government.

Anything so popular that the government declares it illegal is bound to be a good investment. Market demand, confirmed by government edict, caused gold to rise in value by 69 percent between Roosevelt's inauguration in March 1933 and January 1934. In terms of purchasing power, gold had risen almost 100 percent during following the greatest financial crises in America's history.

"This is the end of Western civilization," declared Lewis Douglas, Director of the Budget. And, in a sense, it was.[6]

The bust had claimed Alan Greenspan's father as one of its victims. Reduced to financial ruin and divorced from Alan's mother, he almost disappeared from family life; but by the time Alan was eight years old, his father had bounced back. He gave his son a copy of a book he had written, optimistically entitled, *Recovery Ahead*. Neither Herbert Greenspan's writing nor his economic forecasts proved very good. Alan would go much further, as the history of the twentieth century records. But not necessarily by being much better at either writing or forecasting. As he grew up, the boy Alan revealed two talents very similar to those of John Law himself: He was good with numbers and good at schmoozing people in high places.

THE MOST RATIONAL WOMAN IN THE WORLD

"I think, therefore I am," said René Descartes. And since all I have to go on is my own thinking, Ayn Rand might have added, "I'll decide for myself what makes sense for me, based on my own 'rational self-interest.'" Ayn Rand made a special place for herself in the history of philosophy. In the late 1950s, 1960s, and even into the 1970s, thousands of intelligent, nerdy young people trudged through her books *The Fountainhead* and *Atlas Shrugged* thinking that they had found a profound truth. According to Rand, instead of listening to parents, priests, politicians, police officers, neighbors, lovers, friends, teachers, they should use their powers of "reason" to decipher their very own ethical code.

Rand's "Objectivism" exalted the rational faculties above everything else. There was little room for instinct and none for revealed truth, custom, or experience. Thus, it was perfect for the sharp, jagged steel of adolescent minds, as yet unworn by actual experience. It was an exhilarating doctrine for young people who did not know any better. All of a sudden, they believed they were free to do what they wanted to do and go wherever they wanted to go, limited only by the horsepower of their own minds.

Around Rand in her New York apartment, "The Collective" gathered, alive with intellectual chatter. For a group of people who believed in freedom above all else, the members followed a curious code of behavior; anyone who disagreed with Rand was booted out. Economist Murray Rothbard, for example, was proclaimed persona non grata after he disagreed with Rand on the role of the state. Rothbard, an anarchist, saw no role whatever for government. Rand believed government should limit itself to providing defense, courts, and policing. Later, Edith Efron was banished after Rand overheard her making a critical remark.

With the heretics and nonbelievers disposed of, not surprisingly, the remaining freethinkers of The Collective all came to think the same thing. And why not? They believed that they were in the company of "the most rational woman who ever lived." These proto-libertarians practiced pure reason above all else; at least, that was their conceit. How could they defy their reason-drenched goddess?

Such was the heady world of Randian libertarianism when Alan Greenspan joined The Collective in the 1950s. He soon rose to become Rand's "special pet,"[7] as Efron put it. Alan and Ayn seemed to have found a special bond, said observers. In the little group of liberty lovers, Alan was allowed more liberty than most.

Free from the shackles of convention and tradition, members of The Collective were liable to think anything they wanted—no matter how absurd. Rand herself hated facial hair and distrusted people who did not smoke. A short Russian Jew, she admired tall blond men as heroic figures; they were men as they "could be and ought to be." She married one of them, Frank O'Connor, after meeting him at a studio the week after she arrived in Hollywood. Another, Nathaniel Branden, 25 years younger than she, would become her lover with Frank's knowledge and consent. In a world of rational self-interest, people could convince themselves of nearly anything, even that adultery and cuckoldry were acceptable. But the strain of having to think so hard nearly broke many of them, including O'Connor . . . and Branden's wife, too.

Why shouldn't Branden sleep with the woman he admired so much? Rand had already written an apologia—"Virtue of Selfishness."

"Man is the rational animal," she said. That is, he has the capacity to reason, unlike a rabbit or a goat. A rational man is capable of figuring out what will bring him happiness and subordinate his whims to his reason, Rand believed; making many readers wonder if she had ever met one.

But reason is no defense against absurdity. Even the smartest humans are easily impressed and readily misled. In pursuit of their own happiness, they are as likely to buy tech stocks at 200 times earnings as they are to take up some woebegone campaign to make the world a better place.

Followers of Rand's "rational self-interest" were capable of almost any mischief they chose to get into, without the least trace of moral arrière-pensée.

In the 1970s, Alan Greenspan had found something he wanted. He had given up his career as a jazz musician with the Henry Jerome band years ago and gone over to his father's calling—economic forecasting. However good his forecasts were, his ability to court people in positions of power was probably better. On September 4, 1974, the atheist Greenspan placed his hand on the Talmud. Then, the libertarian Greenspan swore to do his duty to the U.S. government as chairman of the President's Council of Economic Advisors. Ayn Rand looked on, along with Rose Greenspan, Alan's mother. Both were proud.

Had Alan Greenspan gone over to the enemy, a reporter asked Rand? "Alan is my disciple,"[8] she explained. "He's my man in Washington." Would her man bring Washington into line with her free-market convictions, someone wanted to know? The most rational woman who ever lived conceded that the task could take time.

Greenspan had not dissembled during his confirmation hearings. He had told the inquisitors what he believed. As a libertarian, he thought government should be reduced to its essentials. As a conservative economist, he also believed that government's deficit spending was to blame for 80 percent to 90 percent of the inflation at the time.

He also expressed his opinions on gold.

GOLD AND ECONOMIC FREEDOM

"An almost hysterical antagonism toward the gold standard is one issue which unites statists of all persuasions," Greenspan had written. Expressing himself in the *Objectivist,* a publication founded by Rand, the future most celebrated central banker of all time continued: "They seem to sense—perhaps more clearly and subtly than many consistent defenders of laissez-faire—that gold and economic freedom are inseparable, that the gold standard is an instrument of laissez-faire and that each implies and requires the other."[9]

"Gold and Economic Freedom" was Greenspan's favorite topic back in the 1960s:

> Money is the common denominator of all economic transactions. It is that commodity which serves as a medium of exchange, is universally acceptable to all participants in an exchange economy as payment for their goods or services, and can, therefore, be used as a standard of market value and as a store of value, that is, as a means of saving.
>
> The existence of such a commodity is a precondition of a division of labor economy. If men did not have some commodity of objective value which was generally acceptable as money, they would have to resort to primitive barter or be forced to live on self-sufficient farms and forgo the inestimable advantages of specialization. If men had no means to store value, that is, to save, neither long-range planning nor exchange would be possible.[10]

Then, after a long discussion of how money works, Greenspan gave the objectivists the conclusion they wanted to hear:

> In the absence of the gold standard, there is no way to protect savings from confiscation through inflation. There is no safe store of value. If there were, the government would have to make its holding illegal, as was done in the case of gold. If everyone decided, for example, to convert all his bank deposits to silver or copper or any other good, and thereafter declined to accept checks as payment for goods, bank deposits would lose their purchasing power and government-created bank credit would be worthless as a claim on goods. The financial policy of the welfare state requires that there be no way for the owners of wealth to protect themselves.[11]

This is the shabby secret of the welfare statists' tirades against gold . . . . Deficit spending is simply a scheme for the confiscation of wealth. Gold stands in the way of this insidious process. It stands as a protector of property rights. If one grasps this, one has no difficulty in understanding the statists' antagonism toward the gold standard.

The hard-money man before them at the confirmation hearings had worried several of the politicians conducting the interview. "To get along, you go along," was the Washington expression. They were concerned that Greenspan might be an inflexible ideologue, whose mind had been inalterably stocked with Rand's black or white furnishings.

"I have great, great difficulty with the fact that you are a free enterprise man who does not believe in antitrust, does not believe in consumer protection, does not believe in progressive income tax," Senator Proxmire expressed his views. "The latter may be consistent with a laissez-faire position, but you seem to be opposed to many of the social programs that we have been able to achieve."

Proxmire need not have worried. Alan Greenspan was about to redecorate.

THE TEMPTATION OF ALAN

It was a dark moment in U.S. economic history. Alan Greenspan took up his post approximately 60 days after Gerald Ford took the oath of office, at the end of the Watergate scandal, and at one of the lowest points in stock prices since the Great Depression. The Dow was at 770; by early October, it was below 600. The October 7, 1974, issue of *Barron's* included a selection of profitable U.S. companies changing hands at less than three times earnings. "The average price of these stocks works out to be about $15," the paper explained, "against average 1974 estimated earnings of nearly $6.60 a share—for an average P/E of 2.3."

Investors wanted nothing to do with stocks when Greenspan arrived in Washington. Twenty-five years later, they could not bear to be separated from them. Over that quarter of a century—and readers may have observed this themselves—the U.S. government did not exactly fall in line with Ayn Rand's thinking. Instead, Greenspan changed his look. The scruffy libertarian became the dignified head of the world's most powerful central bank. The gold bug of 1966 remade himself into the celebrated custodian of the world's most-managed currency.

The price of gold stood at $154 on the day Greenspan was sworn in as chairman of the President's Council of Economic Advisors. It would rise sharply over the next half-dozen years—to a high of $850 an ounce in January 1980.

The Federal Reserve System is merely a cartel of member banks that make their money by controlling money and credit to their own advantage. They do not have much interest in rigidly protecting the value of the dollar, but neither do they benefit from its quick destruction. Instead, they generally prefer to let the dollar drift to ruin gently. At 3 percent inflation, for example, the dollar loses half its value in just 14 years. But 3 percent is widely considered not only acceptable, but advisable; modest inflation is widely thought to be good for an economy. That is the lesson of the Phillips Curve.

But inflation in the U.S. economy in the late 1970s was nearly hitting double digits (CPI-based inflation was 9 percent in 1978). The Fed had raised the discount rate a full percentage point on November 1, 1978, the biggest increase in 45 years, but still inflation refused to be dampened. Voters squawked. Politicians fulminated. Economists railed. When Paul Volcker took over the Fed in 1979, he knew he had to do something: He sent the discount rate up another full percentage point—to 12 percent. In addition, the Fed shifted its attention to the reserves, imposing reserve requirements on managed liabilities.

Then, on February 15, 1980, the Fed hiked rates another full percentage point—to 13 percent. And on March 14, it again tightened up reserve requirements and extended these requirements to nonmember banks. Finally, it announced a voluntary credit restraint program, urging banks to curtail lending, especially for speculative purposes.

All this tightening of credit had the desired effect: Inflation rates began going down and would continue to do so for the next 22 years.

So great was the pain of Volcker's cold-turkey monetary policy that stocks plummeted. Jobs were lost. Speculators were ruined. Yields on long bonds rose to 15 percent. And a mob gathered on the Capitol steps and burned Volcker in effigy.

But Volcker's program was successful. Coming from such high levels, interest rates fell along with inflation rates, more or less steadily for the next two decades. So did gold: From its high of $850 on January 19, 1980, it came down to a cyclical low of nearly $253 in July 1999. At its peak in the late 1970s, a single ounce of gold was worth about the same as the entire 30 Dow stocks. This is one of the reasons why comedienne, Bette Midler, expressed her preference to be paid in South African gold coins instead of U.S. dollars![12]

In January 1980—on the first two business days of the year—gold reacted in a major way: It rose $110 an ounce to $634. The rise was so sharp that central bankers began to wonder if gold should be returned to its role as the foundation of the world financial system. U.S. Treasury Secretary G. William Miller announced that the United States would hold no more auctions of its gold. "At the moment," he told the press, "it doesn't seem an appropriate time."[13] Thirty minutes later, the price of gold had risen $30 to $715 an ounce. The day after, it rose to $760. And finally, on January 21, gold hit its record high of $850 per ounce.

In the 12 years leading up to January 1980, gold had risen at an average annual rate of 30 percent per year. The inflation rate was only an average of 7.5 percent during that period. The 12-year return on gold exceeded the return on stocks in any 12-year period in history. And at the end of it, more money was invested in gold than in the entire U.S. stock market. By 1980, many investors were convinced that gold was the only true money and that it would go up forever. "Gold is indestructible," they would say. "Gold is forever," they chorused. "Remember the golden rule," they chided: "He who has the gold, rules!"

And so, they bought gold . . . and regretted it for the next 20 years.

Over the next two decades, gold and the Dow parted company dramatically. By the end of the century, they were barely on speaking terms—with the Dow ending the century on December 31, 2000, at 10,787 and an ounce of gold at just under $273.

On the day Alan Greenspan arrived in Washington in 1974, the Dow stood at only 785. Hardly had he discovered the door to the washroom when the stock market began an epic march to glory. On December 9, 1974, stocks hit a cyclical low, with the Dow at 570 and the average P/E of the S&P at 7.3.

THE MAESTRO

Ayn Rand died of lung cancer in 1982, on Alan Greenspan's birthday. (At least the gods have a sense of irony!) By then, Greenspan had already moved far beyond her. She despised central planning, but her disciple was on his way toward becoming the most successful central planner in history. Only four years after Rand's death, Greenspan was appointed head of the Federal Reserve System. But by then, the former gold bug had become a managed currency bug. He was getting along magnificently.

"Alan, you're it," Bob Woodward, author of *Maestro: Greenspan's Fed and the American Boom,*[14] quotes E. Gerald Corrigan on October 20, 1987. Greenspan had been at the helm of the Fed just 11 weeks, and the Dow had just crashed 508 points.

"Goddamit, it's up to you. This whole thing is on your shoulders," Corrigan continued.

In his book, Woodward observes the scene like a ground squirrel watching a bank robbery. He notices every movement, but seems to have no idea what was going on. Greenspan, however, knew exactly what he was doing: A true Randian, Greenspan never put the interests of others ahead of his own. He was just going along.

"The Federal Reserve, consistent with its responsibilities as the nation's central bank, affirmed today its readiness to serve as a source of liquidity to support the economic and financial system," said Greenspan's press release. Forget the gold standard, the Fed chief seemed to say; we'll make sure there is plenty of paper money and electronic credit for everyone. And so there was.

And in every subsequent crisis that came along—the Gulf War and recession of 1993, the Asian Currency Crisis, the Russian Crisis, the collapse of LTCM, the threat of the Y2K computer bug, and finally, the Great Bear Market of 2000 onward, the Greenspan Fed reacted in the same way: by providing the market with more money and more credit. The figures are breathtaking. Since assuming control of the nation's currency, Chairman Greenspan has added $4.5 trillion to the money supply (as measured by M3)—doubling the total amount printed by all the Fed chairmen before him (see Figure 6.1).

"He helps breathe life into the vision of America as strong, the best, invincible," gushed Woodward. But it was the hot breath of

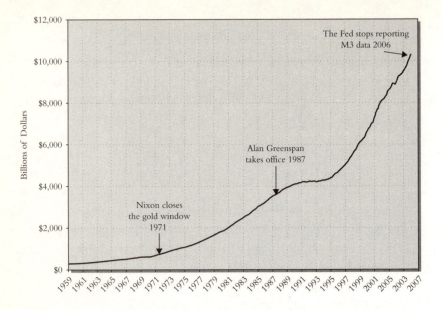

FIGURE 6.1 Fast Cash from the Greenspan Fed
Sixteen years after Nixon closed the gold window, Randian acolyte and onetime goldbug, Alan Greenspan began authorizing more paper money than all previous Federal Reserve chairmen combined.
Source: Federal Reserve.

nearly unlimited credit that caused the United States to get a little light-headed.

The effect of all this money and credit was to spur the biggest boom in financial assets in world history. Volcker had broken inflation's back; now the Fed could ease almost at will. When stocks and real estate prices rose, as they had in the United States in the late 1920s or Japan in the 1980s, no one complained. It was only inflation in consumer prices that brought howls of discontent and rumors of a personnel change at the nation's central bank. Asset prices could rise to the point of absurdity; no effigies of the Fed chief would be burned. No search would be begun for his replacement

IRRATIONAL EXUBERANCE

"How do we know when irrational exuberance has unduly escalated asset values, which then become subject to unexpected and prolonged contractions, as they have in Japan over the past decade?" asked the Fed chairman, when he was still mortal. The occasion was a black-tie dinner at the American Enterprise Institute in December 1996.

"We as central bankers," Greenspan continued, "need not be concerned if a collapsing financial asset bubble does not threaten to impair the real economy, its production, jobs, and price stability. But we should not underestimate or become complacent about the complexity of the interactions of the asset markets and the economy. Thus, evaluating shifts in balance sheets generally, and in asset prices particularly, must be an integral part of the development of monetary policy."

In 1996, the bear market of 1973 to 1974 and the crash of 1987 were still functioning as caution signs. Greenspan spoke on the evening of December 5. On the morning of the 6th, markets reacted. Investors in Tokyo panicked, giving the Nikkei Dow a 3 percent loss for the day, its biggest drop of the year. Hong Kong fell almost 3 percent. Frankfurt 4 percent. London 2 percent. But by the time the sun rose in New York, where the Fed chairman was better known, investors had decided not to care. After a steep drop in the first half-hour, as overnight sell orders were executed, the market began a rebound and never looked back. By the spring of the year 2000, the Dow had almost doubled from the level that had so concerned the Fed chairman.

Whereas the Maestro was alarmed at Dow 6,437, he was serene at Dow 11,722. In 1996, he had been pressured by politicians of both parties to go along with the gag. Stocks were rising and everyone was happy. The last thing they wanted was a sourpuss at the Fed upsetting things. Conveniently, Alan Greenspan came to believe—or said he did—in the New Era and all that came with it—even his own power to guide the economy.

Wall Street has an expression for fund managers whose conversation seems intended to support their current market holdings. "They are talking their book," say the old-timers. A fund manager with a huge short position says he is sure the market is going to fall; another whose beat is natural resources says he expects a bull market in his sector immediately; and one who specializes in technology is almost certain to tell you that tech stocks are the only way to make money on Wall Street.

All of a sudden, after his irrational exuberance comment, Greenspan seemed to wake up and realize what business he was in. Whatever else he might be doing, he was the lead PR man for U.S. consumer capitalism, the U.S. economy, the dollar, and the capital markets.

Stocks were already expensive in 1996. But they were getting even more expensive and no one—not the politicians, the brokers, or the investors—wanted to see the process come to an end. The Fed chief had momentarily forgotten that what benefited Alan Greenspan was not objective commentary on the level of stock prices, but helping stock prices go even further. The higher stocks rose, the more convinced people became that the top man at the central bank knew what he was doing. Greenspan's "book" was long stocks, not short.

Appearing before Congress a few weeks later, the Fed chief saw his mistake clearly.

Jim Bunning, a Republican senator from Kentucky, must have thought he had a direct link to the market gods. Somehow, he knew that the stock market was not overpriced. Greenspan's position was "misguided," he said, adding that it might "become more of a threat to our economy than inflation ever will be."

Phil Gramm, a Republican from Texas, was more modest. Still, he did have an opinion, and it was at odds with the Fed chairman's. "I would guess," he ventured, "that equity values are not only not overvalued, but may still be undervalued."

Bunning then put it to him straight: "If we get prime interest rates at double digits, we are going to stop this economy in its tracks. I don't want to see that happen on your watch, and I surely don't want to see it happen on mine."[15]

Greenspan got the message. "I have the same view," he replied.

The chairman had learned his lesson quickly. Once skeptical of the New Economy, he began talking his book: "This is the best economy I've ever seen in 50 years of studying it every day,"[16] he told Bill Clinton in May 1998.

"What we may be observing in the current environment," he said in December of that year, "is a number of key technologies, some even mature, finally interacting to create significant new opportunities for value creations. New technology has radically reduced the costs of borrowing and lending across traditional national borders,"[17] he added.

Even in mid-2001, after trillions had been lost in the capital markets and a recession had begun in the United States, the chairman still sounded like the Wall Street analyst Abby Joseph Cohen: "There is still, in my judgment, ample evidence that we are experiencing only a pause in the investment in a broad set of innovations that has elevated the underlying growth in productivity . . . The mildness and brevity of the downturn are a testament to the notable improvement in the resilience and the flexibility of the economy," he added, once it seemed the recession was over.

In Greenspan We Trust(ed)

Late in 2000, investors still had high hopes for stocks. That was not to deny that there had been losses—substantial losses. Almost $1 trillion had already been lost on the Nasdaq. Companies such Theglobe.com, Career Builder, Webvan, and Audible, Inc. were already nearly out of business. Investors were still exuberant, but thought they had become much more rational than they were the year before.

It was one thing for the loopy dot-coms to go belly-up. The Dow was quite another matter. "There is no way," investors would say, "Alan Greenspan will allow a serious bear market or a serious recession." Wasn't that the real bargain that had been struck with the central bank, after all? Americans would allow the bankers their profits, their limousines and boardrooms . . . they would permit a gradual ruin of the nation's currency, too. But in exchange, the Fed would manage the economy so that people did not have to worry about a serious decline. That was why savings rates were low in the United States. People did not have to save for a rainy day—because it never rained.

"In effect," wrote Paul Krugman in *Upside,* "capitalism and its economists made a deal with the public; it will be okay to have free markets from now on, because we know enough to prevent any more Great Depressions."[18]

And so it was that the entire world turned its weary eyes to Alan Greenspan. The *capo di tutti capi* (boss of bosses) of central bankers was meant to save not merely U.S. investors, but the entire world. Everyone knew that, worldwide, the United States was the "engine of growth," and that Americans were the best consumers—always ready to buy what they did not need with money they did not have. And, despite the damage done to the Nasdaq, it was widely known that Greenspan had what it took to keep the U.S. wealth machine delivering the goods.

Investors bought the Dow in the year 2000, confident that Greenspan would not allow prices to fall. He would not want prices to fall because falling stock prices would make people feel poorer; and poorer people would buy less—threatening the entire world economy.

The Greenspan Put

That he had the will to prevent stocks from falling was beyond question. Almost everyone agreed that he had the means, too—the so-called "Greenspan put."

A put option allows its holder to sell at a predetermined price, that is to "put it to" the person on the other side of the trade. In a falling market, a put option is a way to make profits by forcing the other fellow to buy at an above-market price.

Greenspan's put option was his control of short-term interest rates. Lowering rates, so nearly everyone thought (including central bankers), was the way to stimulate demand for money, which, in turn, would increase consumer spending and business investment, and practically force investors to buy stocks. "In Greenspan We Trust,"[19] proclaimed a *Fortune* cover in late 2000. Before the rate cuts began, the knowledge that the Fed would begin to cut seemed to be enough.

Like a cross-dresser, Greenspan had everything he needed to do the job, except the essentials. The nine telecom giants had borrowed approximately $25.6 billion by the end of 2000 and the Fed chief had no way to make telecom debt worth what people paid for the stock. He could not replenish consumers' savings accounts. He could not make Enron a healthy business, erase excess capacity, or make investment losses disappear.

In addition to the bad theory at the top of the bubble, Greenspan had bad information. The Information Age brought more information to more people—including to central bankers—but the more information people had, the more opportunity they had to choose the misinformation that suited their purposes.

THE MYTH OF PRODUCTIVITY

The third and final quarters of 1999 produced some very healthy numbers for labor productivity. The Bureau of Labor Statistics recorded the rate of increase at 5 percent in the third quarter and 6.4 percent in the fourth. It was partly on the basis of these numbers that the historic shift of money from the Old Economy to the New one was justified and explained. The Old Economy was said to be growing sluggishly, while the new one seemed to be propelled forward at ever-faster speeds by the incredible productivity gains made possible by information technology. "Incredible" was the operative word. When the productivity numbers were deconstructed, they looked less than credible, if not outright fraudulent.

To put this number in perspective, labor productivity increased in the United States from 1945 to 1962 at an annual rate of about 3.1 percent. Then it declined. Between 1965 and 1972, labor productivity increased at only a 2 percent to 2.5 percent rate. It then collapsed to as low as 0.3 percent . . . and remained around 1 percent until 1995.

As Kurt Richebächer put it, "After three years of near-stagnation between 1992 and 1995, productivity growth all of a sudden began to spurt in [the last quarter of 1995]. What caused that?"[20]

What caused it was that the Bureau of Labor Statistics changed the way it calculated productivity. It began to look at what it called a "hedonic" price index that took into account not just the price of computer equipment, but its computational power. On the surface, this makes some sense. If a dollar buys twice as much computational power one year as the next, it is as if the price of computing power had fallen in half.

The third quarter of 1995 was the first time this change took effect. It miraculously transformed $2.4 billion in computer spending into $14 billion of output, instantly boosting GDP by 20 percent, lowering inflation and increasing productivity (output per hour).

As more and more money was spent on information technology, and computational power continued to follow Moore's law—doubling every 18 months—GDP and productivity numbers began to look like someone with too many facelifts—grotesque and unrecognizable. But it was not until the last quarter of 1999 that this hedonic measure really put the productivity numbers in their most flattering light. Info tech spending went wild in the last half of 1999—urged to excess by the Y2K threat. This activity was amplified by the Bureau of Labor Statistics to such an extent that its message could be heard all over the world: 6 percent productivity was a triumph—the New Era was paying off!

The number for the fourth quarter, to repeat, was spectacular. Incredible. It was revised later to an even more incredible 6.9 percent.

The only trouble was that it was not real. It was, like the New Era that supposedly made it possible, a fraud. More computational power is not the same as economic growth. And being able to turn out more computational power for each hour of labor input is not the same as an increase in labor productivity. Like the millions of lines of code and the millions of miles of fiber-optic cable, computational power is only as valuable as the money that people are willing to spend to get it. And that is measured, not by hedonic numbers, but by real dollars and cents.

What was true for the nation's financial performance was also true for that of individual companies. Companies engineered their financial reports to give investors the information they wanted to hear. What they were often doing was exactly what Alan Greenspan worried about—impairing balance sheets in order to produce growth and earnings numbers that delighted Wall Street. Curiously, during what was supposed to be the greatest economic boom in history, the financial condition of many major companies actually deteriorated.

FOR THE WRONG REASONS

Tut by 2000, Alan Greenspan no longer noticed; he had become irrationally exuberant himself. Markets make opinions, as they say on Wall Street. The Fed chairman's opinion had caught up with the bull market in equities. As Benjamin Graham wrote of the 1949 to 1966 bull market: "It created a natural satisfaction on Wall Street with such fine achievements and a quite illogical and dangerous conviction that equally marvelous results could be expected for common stocks in the future."

Stocks rise, as Buffett put it, first for the right reasons and then for the wrong ones. Stocks were cheap in 1982; the Dow rose 550 percent over the next 14 years. Then, by the time Greenspan warned of irrational exuberance, stocks were no longer cheap. But by then no one cared. Benjamin Graham's giant "voting machine" of Wall Street cast its ballots for stocks with go-go technology and can-do management. Stocks rose further; and people became increasingly sure that they would continue to rise.

"Greenspan will never allow the economy to fall into recession," said analysts. "The Fed will always step in to avoid a really bad bear market," said investors. Over the long term, there was no longer any risk from owning shares, they said. Even Alan Greenspan seemed to believe it. If the Fed chairman believed it, who could doubt it was true? The more true it seemed, the more exuberant people became.

"What happened in the 1990s," according to Robert Shiller, author of the book *Irrational Exuberance,* "is that people really believed that we were going into a new era and were willing to take risks rational people would not take . . . people did not feel they had to save. They spent heavily because they thought the future was riskless."[21]

But like value, risk has a way of showing up where it is unexpected. The more infallible Alan Greenspan appeared, the more "unduly escalated" asset values became. Having warned of a modest irrational exuberance, the maestro created a greater one.

"Greenspan Arrests Wall Street Collapse," said a headline in the French financial journal, *La Tribune,* in early December 2000. Greenspan had apparently done it. He had saved the day.

But Greenspan had done nothing yet. And what could he do? Lower short-term rates? Would it work? Why would people, and businesses, who were already deeply in debt, want to borrow even more?

Perhaps lowering the price of credit would do no more to alleviate credit problems than lowering the price of Jim Beam whiskey would help cure dipsomania. In both cases, the problem was not the price of the elixir, but the use to which it has been put.

JUNK BONDS AND BAD BETS

In the late 1990s, every silly idea that came along could belly up to the credit bar and imbibe almost as much as it wanted. Trillions of dollars worth of capital were raised, spent, and then disappeared. What was left were IOUs, stocks, bank loans, and bonds. The quality of these debt instruments was falling rapidly.

By 2000, the junk bond market was suffering through its worst funk since at least 1990. The average junk bond mutual fund lost 11 percent that year, its worst performance since 1990. So-called TMT companies (telecommunications, media, and technology) were the worst creditors in the junk bond market. They borrowed huge sums to build out promising new communications networks. ICG Communications Inc., for example, had borrowed $2 billion by the time it filed for Chapter 11 bankruptcy protection in November 2000.

Falling prices for junk bonds meant rising costs of credit for the borrowers—and not just TMT borrowers. J.C. Penney's bonds yielded 18 percent, Tenneco Automotive's bonds yielded 21.3 percent, and the gold producer Ashanti's bonds could be bought to yield 27 percent. These were all troubled companies. But that is what you get after a credit binge: companies with problems because they have taken up too much capital and spent it too freely. You also get consumers with problems, for the same reasons.

When credit is too cheap, people treat it cheaply. The result is trouble. But was it not the sort of trouble that can be cured by even cheaper credit? In 2000, the U.S. economy was near the end of one of the biggest credit binges in history. The headaches and regrets could not be dodged or ignored. The zeitgeist of the market was changing. Instead of dreams, there would be nightmares. Venture funds were being replaced by vulture funds. And hard-nosed, bitter-end investors and workout specialists were taking the place of naïve amateurs. The focus of these serious investors was no longer on cleaning up in the market, but on merely cleaning up. Moreover, investors, who used to believe everything was possible and who accepted every fairy-tale business plan, chapter and verse, were beginning to believe nothing and accepted only Chapters 11 and 7.

Among the sad stories making their way around the World Wide Web at the time was one from Philadelphia concerning Warren "Pete" Musser—one of Wall Street's most aggressive promoters during the Internet mania.

Musser was no fool. The 73-year-old investor built one of the most successful new-tech incubation companies in the nation—with huge stakes in the well-known stars of the Internet world—such as ICG, VerticalNet, and U.S. Interactive. He did not get to this position overnight. Instead, he began the firm decades ago and knew his business well. "Of all the guys who should have known better," commented Howard Butcher IV, an investor, who had been a longtime Internet skeptic, "he's a consummate stock promoter. You'd think he would have unloaded it and had his big nest egg of cash instead of being in debt."[22]

But Musser apparently succumbed to the risk that all stock promoters take (and maybe even Alan Greenspan): He came to believe his own hype. And to his own disadvantage. He was forced to sell 80 percent of his shares to cover an old-fashioned margin call. The shares, worth $738 million a few months before, brought in less than $100 million. It was too late for Musser, but the financial press worldwide continued to report that Greenspan was on his way with help.

Shareholders, too, believed that Greenspan still held the big put option that would save them from losses. But did he? Could a change in policy by the Fed save the Mr. Mussers of this world? Or were their investments so suicidal, so hopeless that they could not avoid self-destruction? In finance, there is smart money, dumb money, and money so imbecilic that it practically cries out for euthanasia.

Pets.com spent $179 to acquire each dog food customer. After the company had gone belly-up, what was left? How could a change in interest rate policy bring back the millions that had been spent? Likewise, TheStreet.com lost $37 million in the first nine months of 2000—or nearly $400 for every one of its paying customers. TheStreet .com announced the closing of its U.K. office and a 20 percent cut in employees. Maybe someday it would find a business model that worked. But how would a lower Fed funds rate help investors recover the $37 million? And, how would lower rates bring back the $100 billion that AOL/Time Warner lost in 2002?

A cut in the Fed funds rate does not suddenly make borrowers more creditworthy. No one was going to jump at the chance to lend money to TheStreet.com or Amazon or other CWI (companies with issues) borrowers just because the Fed cut rates. For if a man borrows more than he can afford, and spends the money on high living instead of on productive investments, lower interest rates do not make you want to lend him more. He needs to put his financial affairs in order first—and he cannot do that by borrowing more money.

The way to make money, according to George Soros, is to find the trend whose premise is false and bet against it. The premise of 2001 prices on Wall Street was that Alan Greenspan, public servant, would be able to do what no one has ever been able to do before—prevent stock prices from regressing to the mean.

Many reasons were offered for his likely success: The "productivity miracle" was popular, until most figures showed productivity growth regressing to the mean. "Higher GDP growth rates" was also a winner, until GDP growth also slowed. "Information technology" had a ring to it, but it needed the objective correlative of higher productivity and economic growth to give it substance. How about "higher corporate profits?" Alas, that fell into the gutters of Wall Street as corporate profits slipped up along with everything else, including the myths of the "endless expansion" and the "perfect inventory control systems." Only one thin reed remained standing—the idea that Alan Greenspan was in control of the U.S. dollar and its economy.

Yet, little in the history of the Fed justified the confidence people seemed to have in it. The bank's primary duty was to protect the dollar and the banking system. Since its creation in 1913, however, more banks had gone bust than ever before—10,000 in the Great Depression alone. And, over an 87-year period, it had turned the dollar from a hard currency into something with the consistency of custard pudding.

THE VIRTUE OF INSCRUTABILITY

Still in the autumn of 1999, Greenspan provided testimony on the Fed's ability to see around corners: "The fact that our econometric models at the Fed, the best in the world, have been wrong for 14 straight quarters does not mean that they will not be right in the 15th quarter."[23]

The record shows that he neither smiled nor chuckled to himself when delivering this sentence. Yet, if the Fed could not see the oncoming economic traffic, how could it avoid a collision? The odds were that it could not.

Still the Greenspan put seemed to offer investors a no-lose wager. If things ever really got bad, hydrologist Greenspan would open the sluices—as he did when Long Term Capital Management nearly dried up, and when the Asian currency crisis threatened world markets. The Fed's control of the irrigation gear, in the parlance of Wall Street, "kept things green."

By the end of the year 2000, the Nasdaq had been cut in half. Surely it was time to exercise the option, open the floodgates, and delight the vegetables? However, it was important not to move too fast. The main hazard was a moral one. If investors saw no risk of loss, they would make ever more reckless bets. Greenspan also understood the virtue of inscrutability. If his responses were known in advance, the market would discount them. He was trapped: As long as the public believed in the Greenspan put, people would continue to buy stocks at more and more ridiculous prices. Why shouldn't they? After all, the put option implied that they could not lose money. But if the Fed chairman renounced his put option, stocks would collapse, causing all the unpleasantries he had wanted to avoid.

The Fed claimed it had never "targeted the stock market" when it set interest rate policies. That is probably both true and insufficient. When the stock market went up, people thought themselves wealthier and spent more freely. The stock market created wealth (stock options and portfolio values) that competed with the offerings of the Bureau of Printing and Engraving for the goods and services of the world economy. The Fed could not ignore it. And now that the stock market was destroying wealth, Greenspan could not afford to ignore it, either. Eventually, he would move to lower interest rates . . . and everybody knew it.

AMID THE BUBBLES

The press reported that Alan Greenspan made a habit of soaking in a hot bath for at least an hour every morning. Lounging amid his suds, the great man must have reflected on many different subjects—not the least of which, his own curious career. There, 200 years after the creation of modern central banking, the maestro must have contemplated his achievements, appropriately . . . amid his bubbles.

The U.S. currency had become the world's most prized paper money thanks largely to him. Or so he believed. It was he who had kept inflation under check for so many years. And it was he who had guided the U.S. economy so well that U.S. dollar assets became the envy of the entire world.

But Greenspan's success was even greater than most mortals could imagine. Was he not the first man in history to preside over a two-decade period in which fiat paper money gained value against gold? In 1980, it took as many as 850 dollars to buy an ounce of gold.

Twenty-two years later, that very same ounce changed hands at only $280. Greenspan, former gold bug, now a paper bug, must have smiled to himself.

At a gathering of numismatics in New York in 2001, Greenspan recalled the recent success central bankers had had in controlling inflation. This offered hope for the future of managed currencies (as opposed to those backed by gold or other real assets), he suggested. He spoke modestly.

The coin collectors would appreciate the magnitude of his achievement more than anyone. Like John Law had done ever so briefly in the fall of 1719, Alan Greenspan, the Maestro, had made paper money rise in value against real money.

He had hailed money as "one of the great inventions of mankind." But it was fiat money—paper issued by governments with no precious metal backing—that was the real breakthrough. Paper money, like pro forma earnings, could be anything the government said it was. A valuable tool in self-delusion and deceit, paper money could also suddenly become worthless.

Of that, Greenspan was also well aware. But that is what makes his achievements so . . . well, almost unbelievable. Any fool could make real money—such as gold coins—worth something. But it took real talent to make paper more valuable than gold.

Greenspan made a joke of it: If paper money ever failed, he mused, we would have to go back to exchanging seashells or oxen.

"In that unlikely event, I trust," he said, "the discount window of the Federal Reserve Bank of New York will have an adequate inventory of oxen: Heh, heh . . . "[24]

As January 2001 began, economists must have been on the edge of their chairs. Would the Fed, which had debased the currency it was supposed to protect, now turn out to be the savior of the whole economy? Nowhere in the Federal Reserve–enabling legislation is there any mention of a "chicken in every pot." Nor is there any discussion of "protecting Wall Street's commissions"; nor of "bailing out underwater businesses"; nor of "stimulating consumers to buy"; nor of "helping Americans go further into debt"; nor of "reinflating leaky bubbles." Yet, those were the things the Fed now aimed to do.

GREENSPAN'S PUT IS SHOT

Before Keynes and Friedman, economists believed in a Newtonian economic world. A boom could be expected to produce a nearly equal and opposite reaction. The more people got carried away in the up part of the cycle—that is, the more they borrowed and spent unwisely—the more they would suffer in the ensuing downswing. Economics and moral philosophy were in harmony, both of them elements of the most human science—the study of what people actually did. The Great Depression was seen as an inevitable repercussion of the 1920s boom, made worse by governmental interference with the market's corrective mechanisms.

But with the publication of their book, *A Monetary History of the United States* (1963), Milton Friedman and Anna Jacobson Schwartz reinterpreted the Great Depression. They offered policy makers and investors the hope of resurrection without crucifixion, Easter without Lent, gluttony without fat, boom without bust.

"The U.S. economy's collapse from 1929 to 1933 was by no means an inevitable consequence of what had gone before during the boom," wrote Friedman and Schwartz. "It was a result of the policies following those years. Alternative policies that could have halted the monetary debacle were available throughout those years. Though the Reserve System proclaimed that it was following an easy-money policy, in fact, it followed an exceedingly tight policy."

"The monetary authorities could have prevented the decline in the stock of money," they continued, "indeed, could have produced almost any desired increase in the money stock."

Greenspan was determined not to repeat this mistake. He would follow Friedman's advice and gun the monetary stimulus until the muffler melted. But what if Friedman were wrong? What if policy could not produce any outcome the policy makers wished? What if the crash and depression were not merely monetary phenomena, but market and economic (and human!) events? What if it was not the banking crisis that caused the losses in the markets, but the other way around?

A lower Fed funds rate—the rate that the Fed charges member banks to borrow money—allows the banks to lend at lower rates, too. But in a deflationary bust, people lose jobs, the values of stocks and other investments fall; sales and profits decline, while there are still big debts to pay. Lowering the price of money might have some effect, but not necessarily the desired one.

If only Alan Greenspan were really at the controls of some vast machine! He might twist a knob . . . or push a lever . . . and the machine would do as he wanted. Instead, Greenspan's lever sent the machine going in an unexpected direction.

Great markets work like best-selling novels—with a plot that involves an ironic twist or two. We cannot imagine a blockbuster novel in which the dramatis personae get exactly what they expect. (Suppose Scarlett had married Ashley Wilkes and lived happily ever after? Margaret Mitchell would have sold a few copies to her friends and relatives and that would have been the end of it.) Nor would we want to live in such a world; it would be as dull and earnest as a poem by Maya Angelou.

MAXIMUS GREENSPAN

"The mildness and brevity of the downturn are a testament to the notable improvement in the resilience and the flexibility of the economy," said Alan Greenspan to a congressional committee during hearings in July 2002.

"The fundamentals are in place," he continued (as the stock market rose) "for a return to sustained healthy growth: imbalances in inventories and capital goods appear largely to have been worked off; inflation is quite low and is expected to remain so; and productivity growth has been remarkably strong, implying considerable underlying support to household and business spending as well as potential relief from cost and price pressures."

Again, Greenspan spoke with no smile on his face. Nor, as far as we know, were his fingers crossed. He said what he said as though he meant it . . . as though he believed it himself. Certainly, his listeners seemed to believe it. The politicians looked grave when the cameras turned in their direction. They posed silly questions prepared for them by eager staffers. And laughed at their own dull jokes. None seemed to have the slightest idea of how ridiculous and pathetic the whole show really was.

The spectacle seemed designed for prime time; to reassure the Shareholder Nation that it faced nothing more troubling than a temporary "failure of confidence" on the part of skittish investors . . . and that as soon as a few miscreants were behind bars, the whole nasty episode would soon be forgotten. Noone was rude enough to point out that it was the star witness, Alan Greenspan himself, who bore much of the blame for the bubble and its aftermath. Nor did anyone seem to wonder how the nation's central banker could correct his mistake.

After the crash of 1929, similar hearings were held by similar groups of Washington hacks. That was before the days of air-conditioning. Few matters were important enough to sweat through a summer in the nation's capital. But when the weather softened, the politicians turned up the heat for the benefit of the rubes and patsies in the home districts. Albert Wiggins, head of Chase National Bank, was discovered to have shorted his own shares and made millions. Sam Insull presided over the WorldCom of the 1920s—Commonwealth Edison—a $3 billion utility company whose books were audited by Arthur Andersen. He fled the country when the cops came looking for him. And poor Richard Whitney, who had once headed the New York Stock Exchange, went to prison for embezzling as much as $30 million from the NYSE pension fund.

Seventy years on, Greenspan, by contrast, was still greeted as a hero in congressional hearing rooms. The politicians—and the *lumpeninvestoriat*—were still counting on him to save the world as we know it.

People expected so much—perhaps too much—of Alan Greenspan. They expected his aim to be perfect. But in his first 11 tries, he failed to set interest rates at the precise level needed to revive the stock market.

In every respect, Greenspan's rate cuts were doomed. They caused qualified borrowers to hesitate . . . while inviting unqualified ones to go more deeply into debt. And they produced a new round of inflation in an unintended sector: real property.

A recession is supposed to lower consumer spending and increase savings levels. But, the recession of 2001 had not. Instead, consumers borrowed and spent more than ever before, confident of clear skies tomorrow. Instead of being alarmed, Greenspan told Congress that this reckless behavior was "an important stabilizing force for the overall economy."[25] No one was heard to guffaw. But by mid-2002, consumers were nearly as helpless and desperate as the central bank. Paul Kasriel, an economist at Northern Trust, pointed out that for the first time since World War II, the average net worth of Americans was going down. It rose by about $3,700 per year in the last few years of the 1990s. But in the first two years of the new century, it had fallen by about $1,000. The stock market had wiped out between $5 trillion and $7 trillion. Only real estate prices seemed to defy the general deflationary trend.[26]

THE LAST MAN STANDING

The consumer was the last man standing in the U.S. economy. Greenspan was compelled to do all he could to hold him upright— even if he was already dead. No longer was the Fed chairman merely luring rich investors into blowing themselves up. By knocking 475 basis points off short-term rates, he enticed millions of innocent consumers deeper into debt—urging them to buy new SUVs and refinance their homes as if the fate of the nation depended on it. Consumers did themselves no favor by taking on bigger mortgages and auto loans, and a few were beginning to realize it. Greenspan, meanwhile, was beginning to look less like the world's savior and more like the ambitious rascal he actually was.

The lenders were flush, but the borrowers were up to their necks and having a hard time keeping their footing in the swirling water. By the close of 2002, foreclosure rates were at 30-year highs, bankruptcies were at a new record, and business profits were still falling.

And Alan Greenspan? From comedy to tragedy . . . from poetry to pure doggerel . . . Greenspan's oeuvre seemed to find its most farcical moment on August 30, 2002, when the Fed chairman addressed a Fed symposium in Jackson Hole, Wyoming.

Six years earlier, he had described stock market investors as "irrationally exuberant." Now he claimed he could see nothing untoward, even with the Dow 100 percent higher. He would not know a bubble if it blew up in his face, he seemed to say; he would have to wait and check in the mirror for bruise marks.

And even if he had been able to spot the bubble expanding, the Fed chairman continued, he would not have been able to find a pin. The hundreds of economists at the Fed were powerless, "confronted with forces that none of us had personally experienced . . . aside from the recent experience of Japan, only history books and musty archives gave us clues to the appropriate stance for policy."

Greenspan—the only member of *Time*'s "Committee to Save the World" triumvirate still in office, the Caesar of central banking—could not last much longer.

The pundits were edging his way, golden daggers in their hands. From Paul Krugman in the *New York Times* to Abelson in *Barron's,* they were escalating their attacks—from criticism to open contempt.

The Maestro had given the nation exactly what it had asked for; he had struck up the band and puffed up the biggest bubble in world history.

On November 14, 2000, Bob Woodward's hagiography of Greenspan, *Maestro,* went on sale. Greenspan's reputation was never greater than on that day. On that same day, an ounce of gold—the reciprocal of Greenspan's reputation—could be bought for just $264. Who knew that gold was about to begin a major bull market? After an initial drop, to below $260 in February and again in April of 2001, it rose sharply.

While gold had entered a bullish phase, Greenspan's reputation was in decline. Not only did he help inflate the bubble and fail to prick it, he rushed to supply additional air pressure whenever it began deflating on its own.

Only days after his Wyoming speech in 2002, the price of gold rose to $320. By the end of the year, it hit the $330 mark.

A photo in the summer press showed the titan of central banking looking a little tired. Even an hour soaking in his bubbles did not seem to be enough. Absurdity takes energy. In his pictures, the Fed chairman rested his chin against his arm, as if he were running low.

The minutes of past meetings of the Fed's Open Market committee reveal a surprisingly more confident and energetic chairman. In September 1996, for example, Greenspan told his fellow central bankers: "I recognize there is a stock market bubble at this point." Then, referring to a suggestion that margin requirements be raised to dampen speculation: "I guarantee that if you want to get rid of the bubble, whatever it is, that will do it."

What became of these insights? What became of the Alan Greenspan of that era? He was no Volcker; the former Fed chief was made of sturdier stuff and was willing to go against the mob. Greenspan bent.

The Fed chief already had reinvented himself to suit his ambitions. Had not the gold-buggish Ayn Rand devotee remade himself into the greatest paper-money monger the world had ever seen? Had not the man who once wrote that gold was the only honest money already betrayed his own beliefs as well as the nation's currency?

Who knows what Greenspan really thought. Maybe it was among the fluffy suds of his bathwater that he came to believe the nation's capital markets had been transformed by a "productivity miracle."

And maybe, while searching for the soap in the warm, slippery embrace of his own tub, he allowed himself to believe that there was no need to raise margin requirements, or to warn investors about the dangers of a bubble market, or to try to prick it himself.

GREENSPAN'S OPUS

How will history judge Alan Greenspan? Does anyone care? Collectively, even with the benefit of hindsight, men are apt to turn a pig into a ballerina. They might make a hero of the former Fed chief or a scoundrel of him.

"There's no doubt, in my opinion, that Greenspan has the best record of any Fed chairman in history,"[27] said Nobel Prize–winning economist Milton Friedman late in 2002. Not entirely coincidentally, it was Friedman who had laid the intellectual foundation for Greenspan's easy credit policies.

There were, of course, competing views. "History will treat Mr. Greenspan unkindly as the bartender in chief for the New Age economy, which begat the New Age bubble,"[28] opined Paul McCulley, fund manager with Pacific Investment Management Company. Greenspan kept serving drinks long after consumers and investors had passed their legal limit, said his detractors. Shouldn't he bear some of the blame for the resulting crash?

Having no opportunity to peek at tomorrow's news, we know neither what will happen in the economy or the stock market, nor what the chattering classes will make of it. We have recounted Greenspan's fabulous career, not to condemn the man, but merely to show how humans are. They are perfectly capable of holding rational ideas and arguing, rationally, any point that suits them. One day, their reason leads them to positions that seem irrefutable; the next, the opposite opinion may seem just as irresistible, or even more so.

What is even more remarkable is that they can hold an idea, and even cherish it, while doing something that is completely at odds with it. The only Libertarian member of the Congress, Representative Ron Paul of Texas, once caught up with Greenspan and called him to account. Handing him a copy of "Gold and Economic Freedom," an essay Greenspan had written for Rand's *Objectivist* in 1966, the gist of which was that money not backed by gold was a sort of fraud on the public, Paul posed the question:

"Would you like to add a disclaimer?"

"No," said the man who had created more unbacked paper money than any man in history, "I reread this article recently—and I wouldn't change a single word."

THE MESS THE MAESTRO MADE

Murray Rothbard had Alan Greenspan's number a long time ago.

"I knew Alan thirty years ago," Rothbard wrote in 1987, when Greenspan was first appointed to head the Fed. "and have followed his career with great interest since . . . Greenspan's real qualification is that he can be trusted never to rock the establishment's boat . . . at no time in his twenty-year career in politics has he ever advocated anything that even remotely smacks of laissez-faire, or even any approach toward it . . . Alan is a long-time member of the famed Trilateral Commission, the Rockefeller-dominated pinnacle of the financial-political power elite in this country. And as he assumes his post as head of the Fed, he leaves his honored place on the board of directors of J.P. Morgan & Co. and Morgan Guaranty Trust."[29]

We are annoyed at Alan Greenspan, not because he set the U.S. middle class on the path to destruction but because his book, *The Age of Turbulence*, got so much more attention than the book we wrote with Lila Rajiva, *Mobs, Messiahs, and Markets*. Mr. Greenspan's empty tome came out right after ours . . . and promptly knocked ours out of its brief moment in the limelight.

But now others are getting annoyed at Mr. Greenspan, too—for more serious reasons. Says Nobel Prize winning economist Joseph Stiglitz:

> Alan Greenspan really made a mess of all this. He pushed out too much liquidity at the wrong time. He supported the tax cut in 2001, which is the beginning of these problems [deficits didn't matter to him, either] . . . He encouraged people to take out variable rate mortgages.[30]

The critique we leveled against the Greenspan Fed three years ago is now widely accepted; the feds saw the little recession of '01 . . . and panicked. They put out too much money and too much credit for much too long, causing bubbles all over the world. So free and easy were U.S. banks and credit institutions during this period that bank robbers stopped wearing ski masks and carrying guns; all they had to do was to ask for the money like everyone else.

The free-floating loot produced a holiday atmosphere that looked to most people like real prosperity. "See," they said to each other, "the free market works."

"Greed is good," said Gordon Gekko. Financial incentives were thought to be the key to everything—higher productivity, higher profits, growth . . . everything. You want an executive to perform? Give him stock options! You want an investment manager to make you money? Give him a piece of the action. You want to win over the poor and minorities? Let them get in on this great money-making machine. Columnist Thomas L. Friedman keeps telling us that the terrorists would come over to our side if they just had more financial incentives . . . if they had jobs . . . if they had university degrees . . . if they had credit cards and mortgages. But it emerged in England that of the terrorist suspects nabbed so far, the average one was a doctor working for the National Health Service!

Money isn't everything. Especially the kind of money that the Fed creates.

Wildness Lies in Wait

We found amusing that once the cracks in the subprime market, and the housing market as a whole began to show, the press finally began to give credit where it was due. Two articles—one in *Forbes* and the other in the *Wall Street Journal*—single out our own dearly beloved former Fed chairman, Alan Greenspan.

"Our present misery dates back to Alan Greenspan's easy money policy of a few years ago," wrote Martin T. Sosnoff in *Forbes* in 2007. "When the risk-free rate was pegged at 1%, financial market players, starved for higher yields, moved out on the quality spectrum for long maturity goods. Insurance underwriters, brokers, banks and some hedge funds that play the carry trade game have taken hits to their net asset value, but not enough to cripple them permanently."

"The housing debacle already has cut 1% out of GDP," he continued. "Fortunately, we are heading to the first anniversary of the decline in new construction, but there's more coming and no likely recovery before 2009. Existing home prices have peaked until the country absorbs new home inventory and coming defaults on mortgages outstanding."[31]

The Wall Street Journal added this:

When the Fed cut interest rates to the lowest level in a generation to avoid a severe downturn, then-Chairman Alan Greenspan anticipated that making short-term credit so cheap would have unintended consequences. "I don't know what it is, but we're doing some damage because this is not the way credit markets should operate," he and a colleague recall him saying at the time.

Now the consequences of moves the Fed and others made are becoming clearer.

Low interest rates engineered by central banks and reinforced by a tidal wave of overseas savings fueled home prices and leveraged buyouts. Pension funds and endowments, unhappy with skimpy returns, shoved cash at hedge funds and private-equity firms, which borrowed heavily to make big bets. The investments of choice were opaque financial instruments that shifted default risk from lenders to global investors. The question now: When the dust settles, will the world be better off?[32]

And the question marks began to appear everywhere. But even so, without a hint of irony, the citizens of the United States turned to the instigators of the credit and housing meltdown—the central banks—to bail them out.

Creative Booms and Busts

Of course, what the majority of people don't realize, this is the way real capitalism works. It goes from crisis to crisis . . . from creative boom to creative destruction. From fully functioning, liquid markets to markets as frozen solid as the polar ice cap in the days before global warming. From boom to bust . . . from profit to loss . . . from wealth to poverty . . .

But now, in step the central banks. The boom is fine, they say but we'll put a stop to those nasty busts. How? By providing more credit! By buying up the securities that free-market players didn't want—including subprime-backed mortgages. By injecting billions of dollars into the system.

Here, readers may already be suspicious.

"Now wait a minute," they may be saying to themselves. "Wasn't this whole problem caused by too much liquidity in the first place? Isn't more liquidity going to make the situation worse?"

Bingo!

What a joy it is to watch central bankers at work! They are charged with keeping this great modern, capitalist economy going. In practice, that means keeping the bubble in speculative finance from deflating too fast. Of course, the bubble is largely the central bankers own making—a direct consequence of the liquidity they injected after 9/11 . . . and the subsequent EZ credit conditions throughout the world economy.

But even so, Ben Bernanke and the whole company of central bankers from Tokyo to London to New York got to work making sure that the bubble gets enough hot air.

"Bernanke's First Big Mistake"

When the injection of money into the markets didn't seem to work—in fact, the markets seemed to just shrug it off, the Feds responded by cutting the discount rate on August 17, 2007.

The discount rate is what the Fed charges for banks that need to borrow funds from the Fed. They call this "having to go to the discount window." Now . . . normally, if you need to borrow from the discount window, the Fed doesn't take kindly to this. But if you need to go two times, then the Fed is looking into your books!

Well, this time, the Fed said, "Come on, borrow. And do it at a cheaper rate. We understand." Some financial commentators, including our old friend Marc Faber, were beginning to see the Fed's emergency rate cut as "Bernanke's first big mistake." He panicked, they said, and took the Fed in a direction it shouldn't go. Instead of holding the line against inflation, the Fed is now bailing out Wall Street financiers and speculators.

Where the Fed was headed is the direction Wall Street wanted it to go. Cutting rates suddenly, the Fed has come to the aid of speculators and the financial industry. Doing so, the Fed signaled that it offers what used to be called the "Greenspan Put" to investors—the assurance that it will always provide money on easy terms, when it is needed.

When do speculators need a helping hand from the Fed? When they are losing money, of course. And when do they lose money? When their bets turn out to be not as good as they thought they were. Why would the Fed want to protect speculators from their own mistakes?

Ah, dear reader, you must be either naïve . . . or a true capitalist. Otherwise, you wouldn't ask such a question.

There was a time when the business of the United States was business. Americans made things and sold them at home and on the world market. General Motors was our most important industry. So, what was good for GM was good for America.

Now the business of the United States is debt. Americans buy things they don't need with money they don't have. Financing debt—corporate, hedge fund, subprime, prime, mortgage, LBO, government—is our most important industry. So what is good for Wall Street, the reasoning goes, is good for America.

And things were just as bad on the other side of the pond. Poor Mervyn King. The man is the head of the Bank of England. He was just trying to do the right thing. When the credit crisis began that summer he, alone among central bankers, stood firm. No bailouts, said he. If we rescue reckless lenders and imprudent speculators, he opined, it could "sow the seeds of a future financial crisis."[33]

But integrity in a central banker is like honesty in a politician or chastity in a prostitute—the quality is completely at odds with his profession. Economists talk about the "moral hazard" of allowing investors to do the wrong thing and get away with it. But the hazard is greatest for central bankers themselves. Not since Paul Volcker has any central banker been able to stand up straight. Instead, they bow to pressure—from politicians, the public, the media, and the squirrelly economics profession itself. This has led to what some economists refer to as an "asymetrical response" from the financial authorities. When the going is good . . . they are reluctant to tighten up on credit. But when the going is not so good . . . they ease up quickly.

Mr. King resisted pressure for a few weeks. Then, in September, when the tabloids began running photos of depositors lining up to get their money back from troubled mortgage lender Northern Rock, he buckled. He turned to the cameras and offered to help out. "You need money . . . " he almost said. "Just come see me."

Little did he know, this would become the war cry in the battle of the coming months. Inflation versus Deflation; Markets versus Market Manipulators.

BE CAREFUL WHO YOU STIMULATE

The Fed cut rates . . . central banks all over the world "injected liquidity" into the system. But no matter what action was taken, stocks and houses continued falling . . . and so did employment. In the beginning of 2008, the bull was bleeding to death.

So, in an effort to stop, or at least slow, the bleeding, on February 13, 2008, President Bust signed a $168 billion economic rescue program, calling it a "booster shot for our economy."[34]

This stimulus package meant $300 to $1,200 in tax rebates for many Americans . . . and most happily took that check.

But what actually happens to the money? It ends up overseas. The feds can stimulate . . . but what they are really stimulating is Asian factories . . . the gold market . . . and global speculators, not the U.S. economy. Problems in the United States are too deep to be cured by a little more spending money. Besides, as we keep saying, the real problem in the United States is that people have borrowed and spent too much. Offering them more credit is not a solution; it's a temptation . . . like wearing a short skirt while counseling a sex addict . . . or turning your back on a kleptomaniac and then wondering what is missing.

Now, back to the rebate package . . . at $146 billion it was almost exactly the same amount as Frederic Mishkin figures the U.S. economy lost in 2007 in consumer spending due to the bear market in housing. Fed governor Mishkin says that families cut back spending by seven cents for every dollar their houses go down in price (with a lag, we presume). That comes out to about $150 billion of reduced spending. Assuming consumers spend their rebate checks, the economy should have come out even.

But the drop in consumer spending caused by housing is just a small part of the deflation that was hitting the U.S. economy. In the first few months of 2008, stocks were down 15 percent from their peak . . . and finance and housing industry leaders were reporting huge losses . . . with more to come.

What's more, the collapse in consumer purchasing power comes not just from a fall in their house prices, but also from the fact that they aren't rising. At the peak of the bubble, homeowners were taking out as much as $250 billion per quarter in refinancing, home-equity lines, and other housing-related credit. Now, that source is drying up.

The feds can try to replace that money, but they are not likely to succeed.

The feds can try to play out more lines of credit to strapped families, but what they are really doing is giving them more rope with which to hang themselves. The real problem is that U.S. wages have not kept pace with inflation . . . which means, the average American is not as rich as he used to be. He can only pretend to be rich . . . by exchanging more of his leisure time for dollars . . . and by borrowing. Both of those "coping mechanisms," as Robert Reich called them, are now exhausted. Now, he's going to swing.

WILL THE FEDS SUCCEED?

"We're in the helicopter phase now," said Howard Simons, a strategist at Bianco Research in Chicago. He's referring to Ben Bernanke's famous remark . . . that he would drop money from helicopters, if necessary, in order to avoid a deflationary meltdown. On March 11, 2008, Bernanke's helicopters dropped $200 billion. In the two days following, the hedge funds were still failing. What's worse, there were rumors that a big bank may be in big trouble.

We take a moment to explain how it works. The banks lent a lot of money to hedge funds. The funds didn't hedge . . . they gambled. As a result, many got themselves into trouble; they can't repay the money.

The banks sent out margin calls—asking for more cash from the hedge funds, but the funds don't have it. For example, in beginning of March, the Carlyle Fund got the "Margin Call from Hell" from its bankers. The banks wanted $97.5 million. That didn't seem like much a few months ago, but now money was hard to come by. Carlyle bet $31 for every single dollar it had in capital. With that kind of leverage, the managers stood to score a fortune if the markets went their way. But if prices went in the wrong direction, and the bets went bad, it didn't take much bad news before the fund went broke.

So, Carlyle went belly-up. It couldn't make its margin call. And all over town, other fund managers were biting their nails . . . and refusing to pick up the phone. The bankers paced the room, too. You know the old saying: when you owe the bank $100,000 . . . you can't sleep at night. But when you owe the bank $1,000,000, it's the banker who can't sleep. Well, a lot of bankers lost sleep in Manhattan and London . . . wondering which of their clients would be able to repay . . . and which wouldn't. And the last thing the Fed wants is for some large bank to make the headlines with news that it is broke. That's what the Fed is for, after all. It's a banking cartel . . . designed to protect the banks from their own stupid mistakes.

Of course, the big mistake the banks made was lending money to people who lent money to people who lent money to people who couldn't pay it back. The subprime mortgage lenders didn't worry, because they sold their loans on to packagers who sold them on again—often ending up in the portfolios of highly leveraged hedge funds, to which the banks had lent money. S&P now projected that the losses from subprime would rise to $285 billion, up about $20 billion from their last estimate. Our estimate is that the losses will top $1 trillion . . . and if you throw in the collateral damage, lower house prices, the bill will rise to more than $6 trillion.

Houses in Southern California lost 17.9 percent from March 2007 to March 2008. The median price sank to $408,000. In the summer, the median price was more than $500,000.

As expected, by us, retail sales were slumping . . . unemployment reached a two and a half-year high. And America's CFOs believed the country to already be in recession.

But the question on everyone's mind was: will the feds succeed?

First, there is the practical issue of how lending to impaired banks in the middle of a credit crunch actually stimulates the real economy. The presumption is that there are worthy projects—new factories, business expansions, new technological developments, new employees to be hired—just waiting for credit from the banks. Now, with their balance sheets restored (they laid their subprime-infected credits off on the Fed in return for Treasury bonds) . . . they'll be able to lend again; that's the theory.

But what new factories? Who's hiring? What businesses are expanding? The country is in a recession, for Pete's sake. Besides, in the late stages of a credit bubble, few people borrow to actually expand the economy. The borrowers, instead, are hedge funds and speculators—just the people the banks are now afraid of. That's just the way a credit cycle works. At first, the borrowers are solid . . . with sensible plans for the money. Each dollar they borrow results in, say, another 75 cents to the nation's GDP. But as the cycle goes on, the borrowers become more and more reckless. Asset prices tend to move up quickly, so the borrowers figure they can't lose . . . and the lenders figure they have nothing to worry about because the collateral is becoming more and more valuable. As credit quality declines, each additional dollar borrowed adds less and less to the real economy. By the end, it may take an extra $10 worth of credit to produce a single extra dollar of GDP.

We take it as a given, at this stage, that more lending from the Fed cannot actually improve the real economy. In fact, it makes it worse—propping up failing companies, increasing speculation, misallocating resources, and adding to debts that will have to be paid, one way or another, by somebody or another, eventually. A better question is: How much damage will the feds do to the real economy?

THE SAVINGS GLUT

Greenspan's real legacy was that he finally made central banking work. Ben Bernanke has pledged not to mess it up. By targeting inflation, he says, he will be able to make the financial world even more stable and predictable. And if the party ever starts to wind down, he has told fellow economists that he will drop money out of helicopters, if necessary, to keep it going.

But of all the twisted concepts that came out during the end of the housing era, the explanation of the world's international financial system offered by Bernanke is perhaps the most elegantly preposterous. Americans are not spending too much, said Bernanke. The problem is that Asians are spending too little. As a result, they have a "savings glut" that Americans helpfully recycle into granite countertops and home entertainment systems.

Bernanke managed to condense a whole universe of lies, misapprehensions, and conceits into two short words. Yet as compact as they were, they covered up a grotesque system of global finance so out of whack that even congresspeople are appalled: One nation buys things it doesn't need with money it doesn't have. Another sells on credit to people who already cannot pay—and builds more factories to increase output.

This idea of the savings glut encouraged the fantasy that Americans were doing the savers a big favor by taking their money. He made it seem like such a benign and salutary exchange. They do the saving . . . we'll do the spending. They do the producing . . . we'll do the consuming. "They sweat," said one financial pundit; "we think."

The conceit of it had about the same effect upon U.S. investors and consumers as finding an overturned liquor truck in the street. Soon, they were helping themselves to armloads of bottles—and the party was on!

"We are so clever, we no longer have to do the hard work," they told themselves. "We are such geniuses; we no longer have to save. We are so 'inventive' . . . we are so 'creative' . . . we have the most 'dynamic economy' and the most 'flexible' markets. Hey, let's face it—we're just smarter than everyone else."

But now, the cops are on the scene and people are throwing up in the bushes. "The party is over," declares the financial media. U.S. subprime borrowers (and lenders) no longer look like geniuses. Instead, they look like the yahoos they always were. Suddenly, many of the biggest players on Wall Street and in Greenwich don't look so smart. And the Europeans pat themselves on the back—"See . . . Americans are morons," they tell each other. "Just like we thought."

THE BURDEN OF LOSSES

It would be much simpler for us if the world were set up in a more orderly and predictable way. But then, it wouldn't be nearly as much fun. Even the feds could control a simpleton's world. What a dreary place that would be!

Still, ships' compasses don't intentionally lead us onto the rocks. More money = more inflation, that's the rule. Besides, it's not just a matter of money. The feds are clearly sowing the wind with their quantitative easing. They deserve to reap the whirlwind.

But wait . . . it's inflation they *want*. Nature, in her wisdom, rarely gives a rascal what he wants. Instead, she gives him what he deserves. What then, do the feds deserve? We know their crime . . . what will be their punishment?

Ah ha! Maybe they deserve the doldrums . . . locked in irons, with no wind at all!

They want to lower the debt burden by instigating inflation. They want to increase the velocity of money—by lightening it up a little so people are eager to get rid of it. They want to get lenders lending, and consumers consuming—all eager to turn over their dollars as fast as possible. They want to shift the burden of losses from the people who made them to the people who didn't. Well, what if the dollar doesn't cooperate? What if it grows heavier? What if it seems more solid? And what if dollar-denominated debts stick like tar to the people who incurred it?

Seems impossible, doesn't it? And yet, that is what happened in the Land of Rising Sun.

Our hypothesis seemed so sure . . . so airtight. The feds have no alternative but to try to inflate the currency. Because it will reduce the debt load on consumers . . . and, not coincidentally, on the government, too. It will also induce people to spend money, rather than save it. This will increase the velocity of money, which will have a further inspiring effect on animal spirits.

If at first they don't succeed, the feds will try, try again. And sooner or later, they'll get the inflation they desire—first in moderation, then in exaggeration.

But what if it doesn't happen that way? What if the feds—and the entire debtor class—were tortured before they were finally killed? And what if we—those who think we know what is going on . . . and who are stacking up gold coins in our home safes in anticipation—are driven mad by deep corrections in the gold market? What if gold sinks to $600 . . . and stays there for years?

What if the markets stay irrational for longer than any of us can stay solvent . . . first wiping out the bulls in a major new break in the stock market . . . then wiping out the bears with a major new break in the gold market?

And then, when we have all given up hope . . . and sold all our stocks . . . and all our gold . . . and are curled up in a corner, whimpering, clutching a handful of crumpled dollar bills, maybe then Mr. Market will feel sorry for us. Maybe he'll finally come over and put us out of our misery . . . delivering the coup de grace of blow out inflation . . . à la Weimar or Harare?

Anything is possible.

QUANTITATIVE EASING

Greenspan's EZ credit terms created a worldwide boom. Now, in the spring of 2009, we pay for it with a worldwide bust.

Isn't that the way it always works? For every action there is an equal and opposite reaction. For every bubble there's a pin. And for every politician there's an envelope with $100 bills in it.

But Greenspan's successor wants to get his picture on the cover of *Time* just as much as his former boss did. He's determined to beat the bust. If he can do it, *Time* will probably give him the Man of the Year award. If he can't, he'll probably get the "Schmuck of the Year" award from us.

He's tried cutting rates. In fact, he cut them more than Greenspan, who stopped at a nominal rate of 1 percent. Bernanke didn't stop. Once he had his chainsaw in gear, he just kept cutting . . . down to zero.

Greenspan didn't put in jeopardy the Fed's own balance sheet either. When he was running things, the Fed held only a bare minimum of Wall Street's junk assets. Now, they've got trillions' worth of them.

Nor did Greenspan resort so nakedly to printing money. And now, the Bernanke Fed found a new superdrug, "quantitative easing." What is quantitative easing, you may want to know? It describes the Fed's latest ploy, in which it buys toxic assets from banks. The banks thus increase their reserves. If they were to maintain the same loan-to-reserve ratio, they would have to lend out more money. But when the Fed buys assets from the banks, it does not borrow the money; it creates it out of thin air. In other words, between quantitative easing and printing money there is not enough space to wedge a subway ticket.

So far, this new treatment has produced no signs of recovery. But don't worry; the quacks won't give up. They'll give larger and larger doses—until the patient dies.

Soon, they will embark on "inflation targeting," too. No kidding. That's what it says in the paper. Bernanke is going to set a target for inflation . . . say 3 percent . . . and keep the printing presses running hot until prices are rising by at least that much.

Inflation is now only a problem because there isn't any. In the United States, the consumer price index crested at nearly 6 percent last year. Now, it appears to be headed down to zero . . . and perhaps below. That is what the feds are desperate to avoid. When consumer prices fall, consumers become obsessively frugal. They know that if they just wait, they'll be able to get what they want at a lower price. And then, why not wait a little longer . . . and get the item even cheaper still? This "propensity to save," as economists call it, becomes self-reinforcing. As consumers stop spending, lower demand causes prices to fall further . . . which incites consumers to dilly dally even more . . . which causes prices to sink again.

That is the Japanese-style deflationary cycle that gives Ben Bernanke a nightmare. But, there's not much he can do about it—at least nothing honest. Rupert Murdoch says the financial crisis has caused $50 trillion in wealth to vanish. The feds have put back only $3 trillion (arguably) so far. Just looking at the numbers, it doesn't seem as though prices will be rising anytime soon. For every dollar the feds put into the system, $17 disappears.

What's a fellow to do? The only way out, as near as we can see, is the road taken by Gideon Gono. "Monetizing the debt" . . . "quantitative easing" . . . "printing press money"—it will no doubt go by a number of different euphemisms and code words. It's what happens when the Fed buys U.S. Treasury debt directly. For this purpose, it simply creates a ledger transaction . . . effectively adding to the money supply.

But even printing money does not automatically and immediately cause consumer price inflation. According to classical economic theory, the shelves must be cleared and the excess capacity must be reabsorbed before prices will rise. That could take a long time. But we're not sure it works like that. If money were suddenly dropped from helicopters, merchants probably wouldn't wait for their inventory to disappear before raising prices. They'd be concerned that they were giving away something that was valuable in exchange for something that was not.

When this kind of inflation happens—perhaps worthy of the adjectival modifier "hyper"—it can happen suddenly, and violently

We never thought central bank management was a science. It certainly isn't. The theories that guide it are unproven in practice . . . and unbelievable in theory. Instead, it's all guesswork, bunkum, and dead reckoning. Which is to say, the Fed will hit its target or we reckon the economy will be dead.

Maybe Ben Bernanke is a champion marksman . . . and maybe he isn't. We don't know, but if we were you, dear reader, we wouldn't stand too close to the target . . . if you know what we mean.

CHAPTER 7

RECKONING DAY: THE DELEVERAGING OF AMERICA

No man ever had a point of pride that wasn't injurious to him.

—Ralph Waldo Emerson

By the end of the twentieth century, America was riding so high, it could only come down. But how? Let us take a moment to review: We have seen that man is rational, but not always and never completely. In fact, he makes his most important decisions with little resort to reason. That is, he chooses his mate, his career, and his lifestyle on the basis of what appeals to him, using his heart not his head.

And no matter how reasonable he thinks he is, he still gets carried away by emotion from time to time. In markets as in politics, he is a fool as often as not—driven by whatever emotion that has taken hold at that moment—fear, greed, wanton confidence, disgust, the desire for revenge, bonhomie. . . . But markets and politics are even more subject to delirium because they involve large groups of people. And one of the major achievements of modern technology was that it made the mobs larger than ever before.

The madness of crowds has two important features. First, crowds can only know things in their crudest, most dumbed-down form. Since the truth is infinitely complex, it follows that what a crowd thinks is almost always reduced to a point where it is more lie than truth. Second, though the same emotions beset individuals as well as crowds, a man on his own rarely causes much trouble. He is restrained by family, friends, and the physical circumstances. A crowd, on the other hand, so magnifies his emotions and so corrupts his ideas that soon the whole society is on its way to hell.

The particular road to hell on which Americans were embarked at the debut of the twenty-first century was a feature of their own unique situation. A half century of economic progress and a 25-year bull market had led them to believe things that were not true and to expect things that they were not likely to get. Never in the history of man had any people been able to get rich by spending money . . . nor had investment markets ever made the average buy-and-hold investor rich . . . nor had paper money, unbacked by gold, ever retained its value for very long.

In the late 1990s, however, all these things seemed not only possible, but inevitable. Everything seemed to be going in Americans' favor. Then, suddenly, at the beginning of this new century, everything seemed to be going against them. The federal surpluses had turned into the biggest deficits the nation had ever seen, estimated to exceed $3 trillion by the year 2013.

The U.S. trade deficit had been a source of pride during the boom years; it had resulted in billions of dollars in foreigners' hands, which were reinvested in U.S. capital assets. But by 2003, the trade deficit had become a source of embarrassment, for the dollar was falling and foreigners seemed less and less willing to accept it. U.S. consumers had driven the entire world economy in the late 1990s, but by the early 2000s they were so heavily burdened by debt that they could barely stagger forward themselves. Even the United States' significant lead in military capabilities had turned into a hugely expensive cost center that the nation's taxpayers could scarcely afford.

These problems might have been surmountable by a young and vigorous nation . . . but Americans were getting older, and their institutions were beginning to look decrepit, too. A structural change was necessary, but the structure of America's democratized markets and its degenerate collectivized government made change difficult. The majority could not be wrong, they believed. And the majority thought it was entitled to a retirement it had not earned, government programs it did not want to pay for, and a lifestyle it could not afford. The United States' majority expected its leaders to "do something" to make sure they got what they expected, instead of what they had coming.

Americans cannot turn back from the promise of something for nothing. It would be too reasonable . . . too sensible . . . too humble. Yes, the administration could cut expenses. It could renounce its worldwide gendarme role, for example, and return to defending the nation. Large spending cuts would enable the government to balance the budget and still give citizens a tax cut. And yes, people could cut their own expenses and begin saving 10 percent of their earnings, as they did in the 1950s and 1960s. The trade deficit would be eliminated and debts could be paid off. And yes, the dollar could probably be saved, too. Maybe it would be marked down a bit, but a stern "strong dollar" policy (perhaps bringing Paul Volcker out of retirement to give it credibility) might arrest its decline.

After a difficult recession—in which stocks have been marked down and living standards reduced—the U.S. economy might recover and rest on a firmer foundation of domestic savings.

But no, none of these things are very likely. To do so would contradict every theory Americans have come to love and force them to admit that they had been wrong. When an economy enters a slump, the government is supposed to increase spending, Keynes had taught them. The authorities could have avoided the Great Depression, Friedman added, by printing more dollars. If consumers cut back on their spending, it would be disastrous, said economists from Seattle to Boca Raton.

People do not give up their general belief easily, especially one as attractive as something for nothing. How could U.S. consumer capitalism, which had been phenomenally successful for so long, fail them now? It can't, they will say to themselves. Why should they have to accept a decline in their standards of living, when everybody knew that they were getting richer and richer? It cannot be.

Americans can no more retreat from the dream than Napoleon could have brought his troops back from Germany, Italy, and Spain and renounced his empire . . . or the average investor could have sold his stocks at the end of 1999. Things do not work that way. "A bear market must continue until the end," say the old-timers on Wall Street. People must carry on with a trend until they are ruined by it, say your authors.

Besides, said Americans to themselves in early 2003, if there were problems, they must be the fault of others: terrorists, greedy CEOs, or policy errors at the Fed. There was nothing wrong with the system, they assured themselves.

As we will see, that is why Americans' borrowing actually went up after the first recession began in 2001; as joblessness increased, Americans mortgaged more and more of their houses and bought new cars at a record rate. And it is why the U.S. federal government actually increased its spending . . . and its deficits (enormously) . . . after its tax revenues began to collapse early in the new century. And it is why the trade deficit grew larger and larger—even as the dollar fell. By the beginning of 2003, the entire nation—its stocks, its currency, its military, and its consumers—seemed hell-bent.

IN THE MOOD

Most economists will tell you that the economic system is controlled by mood changes at the Fed. But sometimes things happen even when U.S. central bankers are not particularly in the mood for them.

When the Fed governors feel the need for a little more bustling about in the nation's shops and factories, they administer a little "coup de whiskey," as Fed chief Norman Strong once put it. When they are in the mood for calm, by contrast, they take away the whiskey bottle, and the party soon dies down. Since World War II, the Fed's mood swings have seemed to correspond well with the ups and downs in the economy. An associate of Alan Greenspan, John Taylor, had codified the observation in what was called the Taylor Rule. As the economy, and inflation, heated up, the Fed's overnight lending rates also rose. As the economy, and inflation, cooled, the Fed's shortest rates came down, too. But sometimes things happen even if U.S. central bankers are not particularly in the mood for them.

Despite a flood of money and credit creation, as well as widespread predictions of recovery, in the first years of the twenty-first century the markets refused to cooperate. Whatever was ailing the U.S. economy, it did not seem to yield to a shot or two of whiskey. For the first time in the postwar period, monetary easing—even the most aggressive easing in the Fed's history—proved a flop.

Throughout 2001, the Greenspan Fed did what it had to do, and the only thing it could have done: It cut rates. Month after month, sometimes 25 basis points were cut, sometimes 50 basis points. At first, nearly every economist and every investor expected a "second half recovery." But a genuine recovery never came. Unemployment went up; profits went down.

Consumers took the bait offered to them by the Fed: lower interest rates. Debt continued to rise. By mid-2001, private-sector debt equaled 280 percent of gross domestic product—the largest debt pile in economic history. Then, in the first quarter of 2002, consumers borrowed at an annual rate of $695 billion—breaking all previous records. Their incomes, on the other hand, rose at an annual rate of only $110 billion. And for the 12 months ending in April 2002, $5.9 of debt was added for every $1 of growth in GDP. By the end of 2002, private sector debt had hit 300 percent of GDP.

"LET'S ALL JOIN HANDS AND BUY AN SUV!"

Dallas Fed governor, Robert McTeer told the Richardson, Texas, Chamber of Commerce in February 2001, if we all go join hands and go buy an SUV, everything will be all right . . . preferably a Navigator."

After the terrorist attacks, the calls for consumer spending began to sound as much like patriotic jingos as economic analysis. Thrift came to be seen as an enemy of the state, almost as diabolical as Osama bin Laden.

"On Long Island," the *Los Angeles Times*[1] tattled on a man 3,961 kilometers away, "bakery worker Carlos Gaviria said the market collapse has caused him to rein in his personal spending. 'If enough people do the same,' he said, 'it could add up to something big.'"

"What's going on on Wall Street . . . tells me that whatever money I have, I have to hold on to, because it isn't predictable what's going to happen tomorrow," Gaviria told the *Times*. "By holding my money, maybe I am affecting the economy itself."

Even Robert McTeer recognized it. Later in the year, he explained: "With industry already in a slump, the only thing that has kept the nation out of recession has been the willingness of consumers to dig into their pockets and buy. That spending has been fueled by an ever increasing use of credit."[2]

"They [Americans] have been doing something that's probably irrational from the point of view of the individual consumer," said McTeer, speaking of the trend he and other Fed governors had helped put in motion, "because they all need to be saving more: saving for retirement, saving for college and all that. But we'd be in bad trouble if they started doing that rational thing all of a sudden. We're happy they're spending. We wish that they didn't run up a lot of debt to do it."[3]

CONFIDENT TO A FAULT

In the fall of 2001, instead of falling, U.S. consumer confidence took its biggest jump in more than 10 years. Nearly every price and every statistic revealed a startling lack of worry.

Even the War Against Terror was conducted with remarkable confidence. U.S. troops had no qualms. One of the most striking things about this unusual "war," was the lack of doubt among U.S. troops as to why they were in it. This was probably the first U.S. military deployment since World War II during which almost no one questioned the reason for it. Of course, the war produced very few U.S. casualties. Even battle fatigue was almost nonexistent. "The two-week Shah-e-Koh battle," reported the *Washington Post*, "produced only one minor case of battle fatigue, far fewer than is statistically likely,"[4] according to a combat specialist.

Likewise, in the economy, the absence of qualms or question marks was unsettling. Consumers increased personal consumption at a 6 percent rate in the fourth quarter of 2001—the same quarter in which the economy was supposed to be reeling from the recession and the terrorist attacks of September 11. "Never before have consumers spent with such abandon during a recession," commented Stephen Roach, chief economist at Morgan Stanley.

Consumers go more deeply into debt only when they are pretty sure the extra debt will be no problem for them. In 2000 alone, they borrowed another $198 billion against their own homes. The total in 2002 was $1.2 trillion. Even following a recession, they were sure jobs would be plentiful. Nor did they fear that interest rates would rise. Not that rates couldn't rise—they just didn't seem to think about it.

Nor were investors greatly worried that stocks were too expensive. They were more concerned about how they would feel if stocks rose and they missed out on the bull market. They bid up stocks to price levels the world had never seen . . . and was unlikely to see again in their lifetimes. At the end of 2001, the S&P traded at 44 times earnings. And the P/E ratio of the median Value Line stock reached 20.3 (as figured by Ned Davis Research)—a new record high.

The confidence of U.S. consumers and investors was taken as good news throughout the world. People thought it meant good things to come. A contrary view was that it was merely a sign of good things that had already come and gone. Confidence is a trailing indicator. The more there is of it, the greater the boom left behind, and the greater the trouble that lies ahead.

Why were consumers and investors so confident? Looking backward, they had plenty of good reasons for optimism. The Dow had seemed to go nowhere but up for the previous two decades (with a little leveling off in the most recent two years). Inflation and interest rates had been going down for about the same length of time. The Soviet Union had capitulated. The United States was in a class of its own militarily—not merely the world's only superpower—but the world's only real power of any sort. Never before had there been such an imbalance between U.S. military spending and that of the rest of the world. Challenges to the United States' military and economic might had been feeble; both the battle against recession and the War Against Terror had been waged with a few casualties. Was it any wonder that Americans looked back with pride and the warm glow of confidence?

But looking forward was another matter. In a bull market, "stocks climb a wall of worry," say the old-timers, but on this polished stone of self-satisfaction, stocks found few footholds. Not that there wasn't plenty to worry about. There was the current account deficit, for example, and the dollar. Sooner or later, the rest of the world would begin to ask questions, even if Americans did not. Then, the dollar would fall . . . and so would U.S. financial assets.

And, of course, there were stocks themselves, esteemed so highly by ordinary investors that there was almost no chance that they would be able to live up to the expectations that had been set for them. Sooner or later, it was reasonable to think, disappointment would lead to disinvestment. Jeremy Grantham told *Barron's* that every bubble episode was eventually fully corrected. He challenged readers to think of a single counterexample. None came forward. But these things did not seem to worry Americans. They drove ahead confidently. Hands on the wheel . . . foot on the throttle pedal . . . and their eyes fixed on the road behind them!

In the fall of 2001, encouraging consumer confidence was easy work. Consumers were ready for it. For 20 years, they could not help but notice that interest rates had been coming down—lowering the burden of debt. Inflation, little by little, reduced the weight of it. Except for a slight recession in the early 1990s, consumers had known nothing but economic expansion and nearly full employment since 1982.

Who could doubt that there would always be work available for anyone who wanted to do it? Who imagined that Alan Greenspan's aggressive cutting of interest rates would not quickly put the economy on the road to recovery? Who would have thought that lower interest rates would not be a godsend for consumers—enabling them to continue spending?

The problem with consumers was not that they lacked confidence, but that they had too much. Their apparent financial success combined with the success of the Fed, had made them confident to the point of recklessness. Thus, they were ready meat for the innovators in the financial industry. Never lacking ingenuity, innovators came up with new and better ways to turn consumers' confidence into consumer debt—just as Minsky had predicted. Soon auto manufacturers were offering zero percent financing. And mortgage mongers were allowing customers to borrow up to 100 percent (2002 figures) of the appraised value, pay interest only for up to 15 years, and even skip payments from time to time.

Almost unnoticed, homebuilders had even found a way to by-pass the typical mortgage requirement that a prospective borrower must at least be able to pony up the down payment himself.

A borrower with none of his own money at stake seemed a poor credit risk. But a loophole in the Fannie Mae rules allowed a nonprofit group to put up the down payment in order to encourage home ownership among disadvantaged groups. Homebuilders soon realized that they could fund down payment assistance (DPA) groups themselves and sell more houses to more marginal home buyers. By the end of 2002, DPA plans were involved in 20 percent of new mortgages.

And where stocks were concerned, even after nine months of recession, instead of sinking to recession levels, during which you can buy a dollar's worth of earnings for 8 to 12 bucks, a dollar's worth of earnings would have cost you about $40. Stocks were so high that earnings could double in 2001—as most analysts were predicting—and P/E ratios would still be at the top of the bull market range even if stock prices went nowhere.

What kind of recession was this? Perhaps it was the perfect one—as phony as the boom that preceded it. We remind readers that the boom was built on a lie: that thanks to a cluster of New Era stars, the earth would never again sleep in darkness. Things would get better and better, forever and ever, amen. So brightly did these stars sparkle that investors went mad looking at them—sure that they were going to get rich without working! And so, they bid up stock prices and thought they saw their wealth go up. And thus the promises of the stars seemed to be coming true.

A DANGEROUS DOLLAR

One of the startling features of U.S. consumers' super confidence was that it was matched by an even greater confidence abroad: Foreigners seemed to admire the U.S. economy even more than did the Americans themselves. With no gun to their heads, Europeans and Asians willingly sent valuable goods to America taking pieces of green paper, called dollars, in return. No paper currency has ever lasted forever and few have held their value for more than a few years, but foreigners took dollars readily. Of all the remarkable success stories of financial history, none equaled the U.S. dollar.

Between 1997 and 2001, foreign holdings of U.S. assets jumped nearly 50 percent, from $6.2 trillion in 1997 to roughly $9.2 trillion. Meanwhile, U.S. assets abroad totaled $6.8 trillion in 2001. Of the total paper dollars in circulation, a surprising 80 percent (approximately) were held overseas by the beginning of the twenty-first century.

But what could the foreigners do with all these greenbacks? If trade volumes were balanced, they would typically surrender their dollars back to Americans as payment for goods coming from the United States. But as the years went by, Americans made less and less that the foreigners wanted to buy. The trade deficit of the United States went from $29.5 billion in 1991 to $43.5 billion by the end of the first quarter in 2003.

Unable to buy enough goods from the United States to balance the books, foreigners were left with hundreds of billions of dollars on their hands. One might expect that they would sell their dollars on the open market. If so, the price of the dollar would have fallen. This is the usual mechanism for keeping the account balances in line. A lower dollar would make foreign goods more expensive to Americans and U.S. goods less expensive to foreigners. The likely result: higher exports from the United States/lower imports from abroad.

But, by the spring of 2003, that had not happened. Instead, the foreigners had taken their dollars and invested them in U.S. assets. They had used their surplus dollars to buy stocks, bonds, real estate, and private businesses in the United States.

This was an act of surpassing faith. For the foreigners were doubly at risk. Not only might the prices of U.S. assets fall—stocks, for example, were more expensive on Wall Street than on most foreign markets, with the average price/earnings ratio on the S&P in October 2001 at about 27—but the dollar might fall, too.

Perhaps they did not know it. Perhaps they did not believe it. Whether from ignorance or blind faith, foreign investors in U.S. assets were holding a hand grenade—one with a loose pin. But so great was their confidence that they were unafraid. Instead of dumping U.S. dollar investments, they bought more. (They would later come to regret it: In the 12 months ending January 31, 2003, European investors in U.S. S&P stocks lost 38 percent of their money in euro terms.)

Still, in the autumn months of 2002, the foreigners schlepped and sweated and gratefully took U.S. dollars in payment—about $1.5 billion per day. To the argument that the dollar should fall, dollar bulls replied: The dollar was no typical currency; it had become an imperial currency, the leading brand of the world's only remaining super super-power. The world had reached a level of super-confidence in U.S. money and the assets it bought, based on the super-success of the whole range of U.S. institutions—the military, Wall Street, the Fed, corporate leadership, and the "world's most flexible and most dynamic economy."

NOT YOUR GARDEN-VARIETY DOWNTURN

Nothing fails like success we remind readers. In the fall of 2002, foreign investors looked down at the grenade in their hands and began to wonder. What would happen if other foreigners decided they had enough U.S. dollar assets? Or worse, what would happen if they suddenly decided that they had too many?

There is a neat symmetry to all things natural—and markets are natural. No one designs them. No one controls them. Nor can they ever be fully understood or predicted. All we have is intuition . . . and experience. Success is followed by failure as things normally regress to the mean. But investors who have been very successful begin to think that their success knows no limits. They begin to think they deserve outsized success because they are smarter or luckier, or because their economy, their central bankers, or their government is superior.

But nature in her magisterial simplicity goes about her business no matter what people think: The warm, sunny weather of summer gives way to the cold, gray days of winter. Somehow the mean, the average, the long-term trend must be reestablished. People cannot be super-confident forever. They cannot be super-bullish all the time. They cannot be super-anything in perpetuity. Instead, they have to balance out their good days with their bad ones . . . their sense of adventure with their fearfulness . . . and their yin with their yang, so that they come to the happy medium that we know as "real life."

A long time ago, economists noticed that commerce had a certain natural rhythm to it. They illustrated this by describing the pattern of hog farmers.

When the price of pigs rose, rational profit-optimizers that they were, farmers increased production. But it took time to raise the new pigs. About 18 months later, the new hogs arrived on the market. The new supplies caused prices to fall—whereupon, the farmers decided to cut back, which caused prices to rise again.

This pattern of expansion and reduction, magnified across an entire economy, is what economists refer to when they talk of cyclical booms and busts. Since World War II, the Fed has managed these cyclical ups and downs, attempting to control and soften them. Indeed, the Fed appeared so successful at managing these cycles that it began to look as though it had mastered the science of central banking—eliminating the downward part of the cycle altogether.

However there is another type of downward motion that is not merely cyclical, but "structural": It occurs when there is something fundamentally wrong with the structure of the economy. Since 1945, the U.S. economy has suffered many ups and downs. All were cyclical. All downturns, save two, were intentional. These "planned recessions" were deliberately brought about by the Fed in an effort to cool down the economy and lower inflation rates.

"None of the postwar expansions died of old age; they were all murdered by the Fed," or at least that's what Professor Rudi Dornbush of the Massachusetts Institute of Technology used to say. The first exception was the downturn of 1973 to 1974, in which an oil embargo played the Fed's role. The second was the slump of 2001.

This most recent slump was not a normal, garden-variety postwar downturn. It was more like the structural, post-bubble depression of the 1930s. Examples are few. The only other structural downturn in a major economy in the postwar period can be found in Japan beginning in the 1990s. Japan's hysterical boom was followed by a long period of false recovery, bear market, and on-again, off-again recession. America's post-bubble slump, too, might reasonably be expected to resemble Japan's—since both are structural and both have happened amid the mass capitalism of the late twentieth century.

The structural problem is not the same, but the effects may be similar. Japan thought it could export its way to permanent financial growth and prosperity. The United States thought it could do the same with imports. Thanks largely to mass participation, both economies exaggerated their advantages during the boom years . . . and then resisted the inevitable structural adjustments.

"This is no traditional business cycle," explained an *Economist* article from autumn 2002, "but the bursting of the biggest bubble in America's history. Never before have shares been so overvalued. Never before have so many people owned shares. And never before has every part of the economy invested (indeed, overinvested) in new technology with such gusto. All this makes it likely that the hangover from the binge will last longer and be more widespread than is generally expected."[5]

Part of the blame for these long hangovers must be the magnitude of the hullabaloo that preceded them. The world had never seen anything on quite the same scale as Japan's bubble, or the United States'. So many participants exaggerated typical bubble excesses. These people—and institutions—had a keen interest in keeping the good times rolling. Many of them also had the power to influence the economy in a major way.

In the United States, the effects of the collapsing stock market bubble were visible almost immediately on government budgets at every level. The federal government swung from running a surplus of about $94 billion in the first 11 months of fiscal year 2001, to a deficit of $159 billion in 2002, and a projected loss of nearly $500 billion the following year. California announced a budget deficit, at the beginning of 2003, equal to $1,000 for every man, woman, and child in the state; New York said it was looking at a $10 billion shortfall; and the Texas deficit was close to $12 billion.

In Japan, the nation's budget had suffered a similar swing, from a surplus of 2.9 percent of GDP in 1991 to a deficit of 4.3 percent in 1996, as interest rates came down. For, as in the United States 10 years later, Japan's government could not stand by idly as the wealth and economic power of its citizens imploded. Japan Inc. was thought to be invincible. The general belief of the time held that the peculiar characteristics of the Japanese economy made it possible for it to overcome any setback. Now that a setback had appeared, the Japanese had to do something to overcome it. So, they took the action economists urged on them—and made the situation worse.

Keynes had provided no real explanation for why these things happened. He attributed them to a failure of "animal spirits" among investors and businessmen. In the past, animal spirits had even collapsed from time to time, notably in periods before the Great Depression. Typically, a panic in the capital markets would cause havoc, prices would drop sharply, capitalists and speculators would be ruined and disgraced, and then business activity would resume. The boom/bust cycle was a fact of life, with peaks in economic activity occurring in 1887, 1893, 1896, 1900, 1903, 1907, 1910, 1914, 1916, 1920, 1923, 1927, and 1929. In all of these cycles, the bust reached its lowest point less than 16 months after the boom had attained its peak.

Before 1916, it was practically impossible for the U.S. government to affect the macro-economy. Taxes and government spending in the prewar era were too small; they were less than 59.9 percent of GNP until World War I.

After 1915, government spending as a percentage of GNP increased from less than 2 percent to more than 10 percent in the mid-1930s, but really began to soar during World War II. Using its new tools, "increasing government control of aggregate demand in the postwar era has served to dampen many recessions and counteract some shocks entirely," Christina Romer explains. "Thus, the advent of effective aggregate demand management after World War II explains why cycles have become less frequent and less likely to mushroom."[6]

Panics were virtually eliminated—like polio—following the Roosevelt era changes. There was no reason to panic—because banks were now insured! Indeed, although there were major panics in 1890, 1893, 1899, 1901, 1903, and 1907, none occurred after World War II.

"The business cycle is unlikely to be as disturbing or as troublesome to our children as it once was to our fathers," announced Arthur Burns in his 1959 address to the American Economic Association.

Skewed somewhat by the outsized expansion of the 1990s, the average postwar period of growth exceeded the typical prewar expansion by 65 percent, Romer discovered. "The bottom line," she concludes, is that "expansions are noticeably longer after World War II than before World War I, indicating that recession happens less often today than in the past."

Before the Great Depression, there was little public pressure to do something to interrupt the natural course of boom and bust. Those notably busted were usually rich people, entrepreneurs, and speculators . . . and who cared about them? Politically, capitalists in the late nineteenth century were no more popular than smokers in the late twentieth. They were too few to elect even a city councilman.

During and following the Great Depression, however, central banks and governments undertook to soften the busts that had vexed mankind since the beginning of time. Keynes had a theory that told them what to do. Prices fail to adjust quickly enough, he said, because they are "sticky." The government should step in, he said, and provide the economy with a boost, by cutting taxes and spending money. Keynes's idea was simple: Government would run surpluses in the good years and deficits in bad ones. This action would offset the ups and downs of the business cycle.

Years later, Milton Friedman and Anna Schwartz added their own theory. Depressions were caused by too little money in circulation, they said. The Great Depression resulted from the failure of so many banks, which reduced the money supply suddenly. The Fed should have stepped in and replaced the money quickly. Its failure to do so was the biggest policy mistake of the entire era, say the monetarist duo.

The monetarists say a slump can be corrected by printing more money. The Keynesians say the problem can be solved by spending it. Investors do not know one from the other, but they are sure something can be done.

Since our approach is literary and historical, we will not attempt a detailed critique of either of these schools. Instead, we will return to Japan and let the facts speak for themselves.

JAPAN'S LONG, SLOW-MOTION DEPRESSION

In the first major test of mass capitalism since World War II, all of the safety nets, taxes, regulations, central bank intervention, fiscal policies, and the illusion of security only retarded the process of what Schumpeter called "creative destruction." The destruction of bad investments, misdirected capital, and overindebted businesses and consumers took much longer in the late twentieth century than it had before—because such powerful organizations were trying to prevent it. Instead of letting Japanese banks fail, for example, a $514 billion bailout fund was set up in 1998, with about half this sum designated for the government to buy stock in the troubled institutions—thus nationalizing, rather than liquidating, the feeblest banks. Also, the Japanese government set up a 20-trillion-yen credit guarantee fund for loans to zombie companies (those that were losing money and would otherwise go bust). The *Economist* noted dryly that "funds disbursed under the program are often going to companies that are not creditworthy and that would otherwise go bankrupt."

We have already referred to the remarkable spending projects of the Japanese government. In the three-year period from 1992 to 1995, it undertook six spending programs totaling 65.5 trillion yen. In addition, tax rates were cut in 1994. Another 2 trillion yen tax cut was enacted in 1998. Later in the same year, yet another spending program was announced—this one for 16.7 trillion yen. And still later, in November 1998, another 23.9 of fiscal stimulus was added. The following November (in 1999) still another 18 trillion yen spending package was unveiled, to which 11 trillion yen was added the next year. All told, Japan spent more than 100 trillion yen in 10 different spending programs.

What did Japan get for all this spending?

The obvious result was the highest government budget deficit of any G7 nation. In the space of 11 years, Japan went from a budget surplus of roughly 3 percent of GDP (1991) to a budget deficit of nearly 10 percent of GDP in 2002 . . . bringing its national debt to a staggering 150 percent of GDP. But at least the Japanese could afford it; domestic savings in Japan were huge.

It got something else, too—a delayed recovery.

The dominant view among economists is that additional government spending in a slump is a good thing. The burden of proof is clearly on us.

REAL WEALTH AND POVERTY

Wouldn't it be nice if people really could cure their financial troubles by spending more money? Who wouldn't jump at the chance to fix an overdrawn account by going out and buying a new car . . . or salve the pain of bumping into credit card limits by charging a European vacation? If only the world worked that way!

Our intuition tells us it does not. Nothing comes from nothing; adding zeros produces no positive number. We know that in our private lives spending money does not make us wealthy. Forbearance and thrift, not profligacy, lead to prosperity. How could it be any different for an entire economy?

As Adam Smith explains in *An Inquiry into the Nature and Causes of the Wealth of Nations*:

Capitals are increased by parsimony and diminished by prodigality and misconduct.

Whatever a person saves from his revenue, he adds to his capital, and either employs it himself in maintaining an additional number of productive hands, or enables some other person to do so, by lending it to him for an interest, that is, for a share of the profits. As the capital of an individual can be increased only by what he saves from his annual revenue or his annual gains, so the capital of a society, which is the same with that of all the individuals who compose it, can be increased only in the same manner.

Parsimony, and not industry, is the immediate cause of the increase of capital. Industry, indeed, provides the subject which parsimony accumulates.

But that is the marvelous chimera of collective thinking; things we know would not work in our private lives, magnified a million times, suddenly seem possible.

A man could certainly improve his standard of living—at least in the short term. He could just go out and borrow a million dollars and spend it. A nice new car . . . a beach house . . . a new home entertainment system. And, oh yes, take a luxury trip around the world. His standard of living would go up dramatically. Soon, people unaware of the source of his new wealth, would be asking him for financial advice!

If only he did not have to pay the money back! You do not have to be an economist to figure out what happens when he has to repay. Not only does the new spending have to go, but he must also cut expenses below what they were before he borrowed the money.

For an individual, it is obvious that borrowing and spending will not produce enduring wealth. But for an economy, it almost seems possible. Besides, if a hundred million people believe it—it must be true!

Let us imagine a man who is naked and alone on a tropical island. If he spends all his time just trying to get enough to eat, his condition can scarcely be expected to improve; he will live in that savage state until he drops dead. But if he is able to save a little time from his daily maintenance, he may prosper. He might, for example, apply an hour a day to building a shelter, planting a garden, or making better hunting tools. Little by little, he might greatly improve his living standard, for each incremental improvement releases more time with which to make even more progress. Once he has completed his home, he might turn to his garden, which would provide more food in a fraction of the time. Or, better fishing hooks might also produce more fish in less time.

If, however, he were merely to dig holes and then fill them in, or pile up rocks pointlessly, how would he be any better off? Or, imagine that there are two such men on an island and that the two of them go to war. Instead of planting papayas, they build catapults to throw rocks at each other's gardens, thereby reducing yields. They would each be fully employed, no doubt, and each richer in defense capability; but the idea that war would make their economies more prosperous is preposterous.

It is obvious that two elements are essential to material progress—saving and applying the savings to some useful enterprise. Classical economists knew the importance of these things and focused their efforts on how to encourage savings and improve profits. Yet, the corpus of modern economic thinking gives little attention to them. Instead, modern economists focus their intellectual efforts on a fantasy. They imagine that they can "stimulate demand" by decree . . . and that money created out of thin air is as good as the real thing.

Let us return to our island. After a time, a third man washes up on shore. The three decide to specialize, to divide the labor between them so that they will be more efficient and more productive. One gathers coconuts. The other fishes. The third plants banana trees. The coconut gatherer and the fisherman exchange their products with each other.

But what about the banana planter? It will take a couple of years before his bananas are ready to eat; how will he survive?

The other two men recognize the benefit of what he is doing and look forward to eating bananas. They decide to give him coconuts and fish . . . with the understanding that they will get paid back in bananas when they are ready. To effect this transaction, the banana planter issues "money" equal to his entire crop. It is understood that these little shells may be exchanged against his bananas, and thus do the other two men begin amassing their fortunes, feeling wealthier each time they acquire another shell.

But what if the banana planter decided to double the supply of money? What would be the point of it? The fish and coconut suppliers might think they were getting richer—but there would still be only so many bananas, no more.

And yet, most modern economists seem to think that they can create more fishes, more coconuts, and more bananas—just by putting more money in circulation at critical times. The point of it is very simple; the extra money makes people feel as though they have more to spend. They then increase their consumption—which encourages producers to increase output.

The old economists knew that this was too simpleminded to be true. "The encouragement of mere consumption is no benefit to commerce"; wrote Jean-Baptist Say in 1803, "for the difficulty lies in supplying the means, not in stimulating the desire of consumption; and we have seen that production alone furnishes those means. Thus, it is the aim of good government to stimulate production, of bad government to encourage consumption."[7]

CELEBRATING PERVERSITY

Crowds need lies, not truths; they are incapable of living with the infinite complexity, paradoxes, nuances, and gray areas of the truth. Mobs belittle the truth to the point that it no longer resembles itself. From the truth that stocks can rise for long periods of time came the lie that they will always do so. The truth that consumer spending can boost an economy became the lie that consumer spending is all an economy needs. The truth that consumer credit can boost consumer spending became the lie that credit can replace actual savings.

The truth that the Fed can manipulate the economy in the short run became the lie that the Fed could control it over the long run.

The truth that the economy in some ways resembles a giant machine became the lie that the economy functioned mechanically and could be understood statistically.

From the truth that foreigners are generally willing to accept U.S. dollars in exchange for valuable goods and services came the lie that they must always do so.

And from the observation that the U.S. economy—with its emphasis on debt, consumer spending, and stock market investing by the *lumpeninvestoriat*—was a great success in the 1990s, came the fantasy that it represented the end of history.

Taken together, blended and simplified, these notions came to produce a sentiment that was completely at odds with the wisdom of previous generations and contrary to economic reality.

Here we return to Adam Smith:[8]

The prodigal perverts it in this manner. By not confining his expense within his income, he encroaches upon his capital. Like him who perverts the revenues of some pious foundation to profane purposes, he pays the wages of idleness with those funds which the frugality of his forefathers had, as it were, consecrated to the maintenance of industry. By diminishing the funds destined for the employment of productive labor, he necessarily diminishes, so far as it depends upon him, the quantity of that labor which adds a value to the subject upon which it is bestowed, and, consequently, the value of the annual produce of the land and labor of the whole country, the real wealth and revenue of its inhabitants. If the prodigality of some was not compensated by the frugality of others, the conduct of every prodigal, by feeding the idle with the bread of the industrious, tends not only to beggar himself, but to impoverish his country.

Every injudicious and unsuccessful project in agriculture, mines, fisheries, trade, or manufactures, tends in the same manner to diminish the funds destined for the maintenance of productive labor. In every such project, though the capital is consumed by productive hands only, yet, as by the injudicious manner in which they are employed they do not reproduce the full value of their consumption, there must always be some diminution in what would otherwise have been the productive funds of the society.

Consumer spending as a percentage of the entire economy rose for the last four decades of the twentieth century. It could not go on increasing forever. Nor was consumer debt infinitely expandable. Nor would the current account deficit stretch to the edge of the universe. Something had to give sometime. The end-of-the-world-as-we-have-known-it had to come sooner or later. It was just a matter of time.

The United States has always been a high-spending and high-borrowing consumer society. These characteristics were amplified by Reagan-era supply-side policies, so much so that consumerism went into overdrive. Net national savings fell during the 1980s from more than 6 percent of GNP to just over 2 percent, resulting in the lowest net fixed investment ratio in the whole postwar period. These trends got worse in the 1990s. Personal savings continued to fall . . . reaching less than 1 percent in the first quarter of 2002. Business saving (undistributed profits) peaked out in 1997 and then collapsed by about 75 percent in 2001. Total private sector saving fell from about 5 percent of GDP in the first half of the 1990s to less than 0.5 percent at the end.

Still, until March 2000, as stocks rose, Americans thought they were getting richer . . . and spent more money. But could it be true? Could people really get rich by spending instead of saving?

People knew perfectly well that you could not get "something for nothing" in private life, but this bothered them not the least when applied to public life. Something for nothing was exactly what the public and the politicians most wanted. It was the unspoken promise of modern democracy that voters could get something from the system that they had not really earned; the silent promise of mass capitalism was that the common man could get rich by investing in common stocks; and the appeal of credit-based consumerism was that consumers could continue to live beyond their means, forever.

FUNNY MONEY

The Greenspan Fed and the Bush White House moved faster than the Japanese—but in the same direction. Greenspan began cutting rates in January 2001. Fiscal policy cranked up a little later—the Bush Administration announced a $675 billion stimulus plan, stretched out over 10 years. The smell of sushi hung over the entire effort . . . but no one seemed to notice or care. If U.S. consumers stopped spending—as the Japanese had—the government stimulus efforts would do nothing, except waste valuable savings.

When savings rates fall, less money is available for capital investment. Other things being equal, lower savings rates lead to higher interest rates—because there is less money available to borrow. Higher interest rates suppress economic activity because fewer new projects can make it over the "hurdle rate." If an innovation would produce a 10 percent profit, but the cost of the capital to build it is 11 percent, the project will be shelved. At 2 percent, the hurdle may be low enough to make the project worthwhile, for it will still produce an 8 percent profit after the cost of capital.

There is no magic to it. But real savings must be involved . . . and the savings must be used in ways that make people better off. A man cannot lend another what he does not have. It seems obvious enough to two men on an island. But in the hot smoke of public thinking, additional credit from the central bank looks as good as the real thing.

During both bubbles—in Japan as well as the United States—savings rates generally fell, but interest rates fell, too. Interest rates should have gone up—reflecting the fact that there was less capital available and, at least in the boom years, more borrowers who wanted it. Where did the additional capital come from to force down rates? Economists hardly bothered to ask the question. For they had long since given up wondering about how savings worked or where they came from. They knew that central bankers could make as much new credit available as they wanted—creating savings "out of thin air."

But what was this strange money that the central authorities had created out of nowhere? It looked real. You could hold one of the new Federal Reserve notes up to the light and study it carefully; it was indistinguishable from the other notes and bills ginned out by the Bureau of Printing and Engraving. You could take it to the bank and deposit it. You could take it to the grocery store . . . or the haberdasher. You could even take it on a European vacation. All over the world, the new money was as sound as the dollar.

But what really happened when central bankers gave the economy additional credit at a time when actual savings were going down? How was it possible to provide extra savings when there were actually fewer to be had?

Again, modern economists hardly stooped to ask the question, let alone answer it. One Federal Reserve note was as good as another, they believed. Lucre was lucre. Phony savings were as good as real ones. But therein hangs a tale. For what increases production and output is not make-believe savings, but real ones. After all, there are only so many real savings in an economy. Like the man on a deserted island, a hundred million men cannot really increase the amount of free time, or of available capital, just by wishing it were so. Cement factories only produce so much cement. Only so many bricks are held in inventory. Gas tanks and pipelines only hold so much energy—and no more. Of course, they can be increased—but not without the investment of real resources!

Neither the Federal Reserve nor the Bank of Japan have the power to increase the length of time in a day. They might, by decree, increase the number of hours or minutes, but the time it takes for the earth to make its daily rotation remains a constant. Likewise, neither central bank has the power to increase—by proclamation nor by legerdemain— the amount of real savings in a society. All they can do is make believe: Issuing new credit and new notes that look for all the world like the real thing.

Milton Friedman says in response to how to avoid a Japan-like slump, "just print money."[9]

"Don't ask where the money would come from," adds Paul Krugman, "it could and should simply be created . . . the situation offers a perfect opportunity to effect a salutary expansion of the monetary base."[10]

The trouble with these new credits was that they had no real resources behind them—no extra time, no extra materials . . . no nothing. Businessmen, investors, and consumers mistakenly took up the well-made counterfeits because no one could tell the difference. The consumer thought he had more money—didn't his house just go up in value? Weren't his stocks rising every day? He asked few questions and spent more money. The businessman mistook the new spending for more real demand, rather than the temporary fraud it was. He hired extra workers and built new facilities to meet the new demand. And the investor thought he saw a boom. Eager to participate, he bid up the prices of capital assets and thought he had gone to heaven without dying.

It is all too wonderful—while it lasts. But it is a boom built on deceit and cannot continue forever. The trouble is, it can last so long that it begins to look eternal. And the more successful the central bankers are at keeping it going, the greater the embarrassment and dislocation when it eventually falls apart. To keep the whole thing rolling, the central bank provides even more credit at even lower prices. Interest rates come down, inducing even further indebtedness among an already spendthrift population. After stocks collapsed in the United States, beginning in March 2000, borrowing for business expansion, IPOs, mergers and acquisitions, and stock market margin accounts gradually trailed off. But borrowing on real estate—particularly, home refinancing—soared.

Rising real estate prices, lower monthly payments, and cash-out refinancing made homeowners feel as if they were coming out ahead. But even with increasing real estate values, they were getting poorer.

Astonishingly, the net worth of most U.S. households had gone down during the biggest boom in the nation's history. A University of Michigan study released in February 2000 determined that "the net worth of households headed by Americans under the age of 60 actually declined . . ." during the previous 10 years.

Households headed by older Americans got wealthier because those were the people who held most of the stocks and real estate. If the decade of the 1990s did anything, it boosted stock prices. But the next three years knocked down stock prices, which affected the over-60 households more than any others.

Americans did not make nearly as much from the bull market as they thought, either.[11] John Bogle, founder of the Vanguard group, interviewed in *Fortune* magazine at the end of 2002, explained that frequent trading by fund managers and high fees had reduced the average rate of return during the biggest bull market in history—1984 to 2001—to just 4.2 percent per year. This was a period in which the S&P rose 14.5 percent a year. If the results from 2002 had been included, he estimated that the average return from equity funds would have fallen to less than 3 percent per year—or lower than the inflation rate!

If they had bothered to look hard, Americans might have noticed that their economy was not making them as rich as they thought. This, too, was not a cyclical or accidental problem; it was a structural feature of their late, collective capitalism—the consequence of a half century of rising consumption. Instead of saving and investing in profitable new projects, Americans had chosen to live beyond their means. Now, the day of reckoning had come.

ECONOMIC DEAD END

In America, a disturbing feature of the credit-led economy showed itself in the early 1960s: Profits as a percentage of GDP had started heading down and the current account deficit began heading up. Pretax profits, which were more than 9 percent of GDP in 1963, fell to less than 3 percent by the century's end. Why? Because there had been little capital investing that might actually create profits for investors or pay increases for workers. This partly explains why wages for manufacturing workers have gone nowhere in the past 30 years and why the average American has enjoyed only minimal increases in his income. The problem lies at the very deepest structure of the consumerist economy. Spending beyond your means does not produce economic perfection but an economic dead end, just as might have been predicted by a moral philosopher but missed by an economist.

But wasn't there a huge increase in capital spending in the late 1990s? It was widely thought that large amounts of money were being invested in new businesses and new technologies. And they were. But the investments took the peculiar direction dictated by U.S. mass capitalism. Instead of investing in real projects that might produce real profits over the long haul, companies concentrated on financial engineering in order to produce short-term profits that would wow the *lumpeninvestoriat.* "A penny more than forecast" was the ideal earnings report of the last half of the last decade of the twentieth century. It did not seem to matter what was behind the numbers—no one bothered to look. Analysts rarely issued a "sell" signal or even questioned the companies' pro forma footnotes. Wall Street strategists rarely expected prices to go anywhere but up. Economists told investors that whatever price the market assigned to a stock must be the right price—the perfect price. And everyone was too busy making money to worry about it.

After the Nasdaq plummeted and the dust cleared, it became apparent that little actual money had been invested in new plants and equipment, after all. Besides the investments in acquisitions, buybacks, initial public offerings (IPOs), and mergers and so on . . . much of the money actually invested in technology was for projects that would never make a dime of profit. Offices were full of young programmers and dealmakers working for dot-com businesses. On paper, billions had been invested in the new technology—but it was largely worthless.

Also, the Bureau of Labor Statistics came up with an ingenious way of crunching the numbers that distorted them so badly even their own mothers never would have recognized them. As described earlier, the theory was that the Bureau should measure real output—rather than nominal output. But when the concept was applied to information technology, where dramatic advances in computer processing were taking place, these hedonic measurements made it look as if huge amounts of money were being invested.

JUST IN TIME

Actual business investment in plants and equipment was sinking, but one of the many conceits of the New Era was that it needed less capital than traditional business. The new economy was supposed to produce wealth with minimal investment. Businesses had discovered that "just-in time" inventory systems could reduce their capital requirements. They needed faith, of course. Supplies had to be there when they needed them or their factories would shut down.

Likewise, U.S. consumers discovered that just in time worked for other things. They no longer needed to carry much cash in their wallets, because ATM machines delivered currency whenever they needed it. Nor did they need to save money, because what really mattered was cash flow. What point was there in having idle cash earning low rates of interest when the money could be working, either invested in the stock market or spent on something that you could enjoy? There was always cash available . . . from paychecks that came along just in time to pay the bills.

Besides, everybody knew that savings lost value over time. Better to take the money off the shelves and put it to use.

The just-in-time mentality seemed to work for everything. Jobs were plentiful. There would always be one when you needed it. Food, too—who stocked food at home when the supermarkets and convenience stores would do it for you? Even stacks of wood seemed to go out of fashion in the late 1990s: There would always be someone who would deliver wood . . . or oil, gas, or electricity . . . just in time for when you needed it.

Just-in-time thinking encouraged a close look at a person's operating budget, but neglected the balance sheet. It did not seem to matter how much of his house he had mortgaged, or how much he owed, as long as the cash was there to pay the bills. Of course, Americans did not save; there was no need to. Savings rates in the United States declined, not cyclically, but structurally. From a high of 10.9 percent in 1982, Americans stocked fewer and fewer dollar bills on their shelves, until, by the end of the 1990s, the savings rate had declined to less than 3 percent.

This just-in-time economy, at the end of 2001, was still widely saluted as the crown of economic creation. But its thorns were beginning to prick. Consumer debt as a percentage of GDP could not grow larger forever. Nor could a society expect to make economic progress without savings. Running down the savings rate had given the U.S. economy the appearance of growth and prosperity, but how long could that go on? Deprived of real investment and saddled with relatively high labor costs, U.S. businesses were becoming less profitable. How would they pay higher wages? Without higher wages, how could consumers continue spending?

The U.S. economy, once famously rich in profits and growth, now depended on myths and lies—that the trends of the past half century would continue forever and that the U.S. consumer (the consumer of last resort for the entire world) would continue going deeper and deeper into debt indefinitely.

When the slump began in 2001 and jobs were lost, little by little Americans began to ask themselves: Will the cash really be there, just in time, when I need it? The baby boomers in particular, began to wonder if they would have enough money, just in time, to retire on. It was a trend hardly noticed at first, but while no one was looking, consumers began to set aside a little more money.

Against a backdrop of inducements to buy new cars at zero percent financing or new homes with 100 percent mortgages and low monthly payments, savings rates began to rise ever so slightly (to 4 percent in the last quarter of 2002). Having leveraged themselves over a half century, Americans were beginning the long, slow, painful process of deleveraging themselves. "Just in time" was becoming "just in case."

IMPERIAL OVERSTRETCH MARKS

John Quincy Adams, in his Independence Day speech in 1821, said: "America does not go abroad in search of monsters to destroy. She is the well-wisher to the freedom and independence of all. She is the champion only of her own."

But by the end of the following century, Bill Clinton noticed, "We clearly have it within our means . . . to lift billions and billions of people around the world into the global middle class."[12] How the world's largest debtor would do so was not apparent. But the mob of voters, like the great unwashed *lumpeninvestoriat*, asked few questions.

Three years later, the United States was hunting monsters all over the globe. The absurdity of the project seemed to go completely unnoticed.

The general belief that the American Way represented some sort of historical finality took a not-unexpected twist early in the twenty-first century. It was signaled by the use of the word "Homeland" following the Twin Towers disasters. Suddenly, America had outgrown its borders; the empire was about to overstretch itself. Nature abhors both vacuums and monopolies. She detests bubbles of all sorts. Having reached a position of global domination, U.S. policy makers began to look for a pin.

"We have to pursue this thing," said a panelist at a conference in Las Vegas organized by the Foundation for Economic Education in the spring of 2002. Speaking for what may well have been a majority view, he suggested, "The U.S. should launch preemptive strikes at Iraq . . . Syria . . . and even China!"

The logic was solid. These countries may want to do us harm. We have the means to stop them. What's standing in our way? Not much.

"Beginning in 1899," explained Gary North, "the United States has steadily replaced Europe in the expensive, risky business of empire. Our carrier fleet patrols the world's seas. Now we have become the primary target of hatred and revenge. People don't like to be pushed around by foreigners, whether in Greece in the era of the Athenian League, or today."[13]

By 431 B.C., Athens had become an empire, with subject states throughout the Aegean. In that year, the first Peloponnesian War began—between Athens and its allies, and the city of Sparta.

Pericles decided that the best offense was a good defense. He brought the Athenians within the city's walls, hoping that the enemy would become exhausted in futile attacks. But bubonic plague broke out in the besieged city and killed a quarter of the population—including Pericles. A nephew of Pericles, Alcibiades, then stirred the Athenians to an offensive campaign. A great armada was assembled to attack Syracuse, a city in Sicily allied with Athens' foes. The campaign was a complete disaster. The armada was destroyed and the army sold into slavery. Sensing a shift in fortunes, other Greek city-states broke with Athens and went over to Sparta. In 405, the remaining ships in the Athenian fleet were captured at the battle of Aegospotami. Not long after, Athens' walls were breached and the city became a vassal state to Sparta.

We recall this spare history of the Peloponnesian Wars because Athens was probably the first well-known empire in the Western world. Since America seems to be on the march to empire, what happened to Athens might be of interest. Likewise, what was happening in world trade at the beginning of the twenty-first century might be instructive.

Taking the Amtrak from Washington to New York, you will see (we presume it is still there) a large sign in Trenton, New Jersey: "Trenton Makes, the World Takes." But the sign was put up at a different era in American history—when U.S. manufacturing was robust and the nation ran a current account surplus. Those days are long gone. Now it is the rest of the world that makes and Trenton, Sacramento, and every U.S. town, burg, and Middlesex farm that does the taking.

It was obvious that these trends could not continue forever. By 2002, Americans were buying 60 percent of the world's total exports. Of the increase in world trade in the preceding five years, U.S. imports had amounted to 60 percent. Not only did consumers continue to spend more than they could afford . . . government also began running big deficits that needed to be financed. Already, it required 80 percent of the whole world's savings to fill these gaps. How much longer, one might have reasonably asked, would foreigners be willing to finance Americans' consumption? What would happen when they stopped?

Foreign writers—notably Emmanuel Todd in his *Après l'Empire* — were already beginning to refer to the financing gap in U.S. accounts as a form of "Imperial tribute." Trouble was, as Todd pointed out, it was fragile; the foreigners could stop paying anytime they wanted.

The whole system was destined to fail. It was a structure that became weaker and more vulnerable as it grew. Consumer debt rose. The current account deficit widened. Savings shrank. Capital investment—the crucial ingredient for economic progress—shriveled up. And the more successful were Alan Greenspan's efforts to shore it up, the bigger the structural collapse would eventually be.

Every bubble eventually finds its pin. Whether it is a bubble in political power or a bubble in the cotton markets, the thing will expand until, sooner or later, something comes along to let the air out. It can happen with a bang or with a whimper. Sometimes both. As the twenty-first century opened, the United States faced two sharp objects: There was the whimpering dollar on the one side and the cost of empire on the other.

In early April 2002 the *International Herald Tribune* reported that it had become respectable to describe the United States as an empire. "Today," said the paper, "America is no more superpower or hegemon, but a full blown empire in the Roman and British sense."

"No country has been as dominant culturally, economically, technologically, and militarily in the history of the world since the Roman Empire," added columnist Charles Krauthammer.

Paul Kennedy went further, pointing out that the imbalance was even greater than in the Roman era. "The Roman Empire stretched further afield," he noted, "but there was another great empire in Persia and a larger one in China."[14]

In 2002, China was no military competition. It was just another country on America's hit list.

Being a citizen of a Great Empire is not all bad. Most people incline their chins a degree skyward at the mere thought of it. And minding other people's business can be distracting and entertaining. It is easier than arguing with your wife or children, and the chances of victory are higher.

A passage from Robert Kaplan's book, *Warrior Politics: Why Leadership Demands a Pagan Ethos* explained:

> Our future leaders could do worse than be praised for their tenacity, their penetrating intellects and their ability to bring prosperity to distant parts of the world under America's soft imperial influence. The more successful our foreign policy, the more leverage America will have in the world. Thus, the more likely that future historians will look back on the 21st century United States as an empire as well as a republic, however different from that of the Roman and every other empire throughout history.

After all, even after 227 years, America's stock continued to rise. And the modest republic of 1776 had become the great power of 2002—with pretensions to empire that no longer needed to be denied. That its citizens would not be freer was understood. But would they be richer under an empire than they would have been under a humble republic? Would they be safer? Would they be happier?

If so, pity the poor Swiss. In their mountain fastnesses, they have only had themselves to boss around; only their own pastures, lakes, and peaks to amuse their eyes; and only their own industries to provide employment and sustenance. And their poor armed forces! Imagine the boredom . . . the tedious waiting for someone to attack. What glory is there in defense? Oh, for a foreign adventure . . . !

But would the Swiss really be better off if they, too, had an empire to run?

All of the available evidence—from history—suggests one answer: no. If the past is any guide, early military successes are inevitably followed by humiliating defeats, and the good sense of a decent people is soon replaced by a malign megalomania that brings the whole bunch to complete ruin.

But who cares? It is not for us to know the future . . . or to prescribe it. Instead, we get out our field glasses and prepare to watch the spectacle.

A great empire is to the world of geopolitics what a great bubble is to the world of economics. It is attractive at the outset, but a catastrophe eventually. We know of no exceptions. Still, a lot can happen between the beginning of an empire and its end, and it is not all bad.

"There is a crack in everything God made," said Emerson.[15] Who could see the crack in America's apparent triumph?

The U.S. model of human progress depended heavily on the kindness (or naïveté) of strangers: the United States printed money; foreigners made products. The foreigners sent their products to the United States; Americans sent their dollars abroad. The defect here was obvious. What would happen if foreigners changed their minds? Then who would pay so that Americans could continue living beyond their means? And who would finance the U.S. budget deficit, expected to add nearly $5 trillion to the national debt over the next 10 years?

Empires are expensive to build and operate, but at least they are usually self-financing; the imperial power demands tribute from its vassal states to pay its costs. But in the peculiar world of the early twenty-first century, the conquered states—achieved and prospective—were too poor to pay tribute. Instead, it required large inputs of money and materiel to keep them from slipping back into the ranks of renegades and rogues that plagued the new empire.

And yet, the imperial expenses had to be paid.

FIRST PANACEA

In November 2002, when new Fed member, Benjamin Bernanke took up the subject of the threat of Japan-style deflation, he not so much proposed inflation as promised it.[16] The financial press had finally picked up on the Japan example. Fed officials were now routinely asked: "Well, how come the Japanese have been unable to avoid deflation? And how will the Fed do better than the Japanese Central Bank?"

Bernanke didn't wait for the question. The Japanese could have avoided its bouts with deflation if it had targeted higher inflation rates, he maintained.

"Don't worry about that here. Even if we get down to zero rates [real rates were already below zero]," said the Fed governor, there are plenty of other things the central bank can do. Print money, for example. "Sufficient injections of money will always reverse deflation," said Bernanke.

"In the 1930s," he continued, "Roosevelt ended deflation by devaluing the dollar 40 percent against gold." He might have added that deflation ended after the worst depression in America's history had forced 10,000 banks to go bust and left one out of every four workers jobless.

Was it comforting to know that the Fed could beat deflation by destroying the dollar and the economy? Ben Bernanke followed up by saying, "There is virtually no meaningful limit to what we could inject [from the money supply] into the system, were it necessary."

Technically correct, for the Fed could always charter a fleet of helicopters and drop $100 bills over lower Manhattan, but as a monetary policy, printing money is not without its drawbacks.

The essential requirement of money is that it be valuable, which requires that it be of limited supply. But that is also the essential problem with all managed currencies. Its managers may create more of it when it suits them, but they should never create so much that they destroy the illusion of scarcity.

"What the U.S. owes to foreign countries it pays—at least in part," observed Charles de Gaulle in 1965, a full 37 years ahead of Greenspan and Bernanke, "with dollars it can simply issue if it wants to."

De Gaulle was first in line at the "gold window" at the Fed, where he exchanged his dollars for gold and brought the world's monetary system crashing down. Nixon then slammed shut the gold window, and the price of gold began to move upward (30 percent per year from 1968 to the peak in January 1980—exceeding the return on stocks in any 12-year period in history).

Goldbugs were so excited by this that they bought—even as gold reached $800—and regretted it for the next 22 years. But in 2002, the price of gold moved up cautiously; the goldbugs had less money and more sense. Still, on the open market—if no longer at the gold window—the neo-de Gaulles of this world had a way to exchange their dollars for gold. Greenspan and Bernanke must have made them think about it.

So imagine the world's surprise when Fed governor, Ben Bernanke, announced that the Fed would create an almost unlimited supply of new dollars—if it thought necessary—to head off deflation. Dennis Gartman said the speech by Bernanke was "the most important speech on Federal Reserve and monetary policy since the explanation emanating from the Plaza Accord a decade and a half ago."[17]

Bernanke told the world—including foreigners, who held as much as $9 trillion of U.S. assets—that the Fed would not permit a more valuable currency. How would it avoid it? By inflating as much as the situation required. There was effectively "no limit" on how much inflation the Fed could create, or would be willing to create, to avoid deflation, he said.

It was almost like the moment when German central banker, Dr. Rudolf Havenstein, had announced in the early 1920s that Germany intended to destroy the deutschmark in order to skip out of its war reparations. From August 1922 to November 1923, consumer price inflation rose by 10 to the 10th power so that by the end of November, a single dollar was worth 4.2 trillion marks. Now Bernanke proposed a similar feat to finance the United States' imperial and lifestyle ambitions: The United States would take its tribute in the form of an inflated currency.

In the 60 days following Bernanke's speech (on November 21, 2002), the dollar fell 6.4 percent against the euro and 10.1 percent against gold. It continued to slide for another six years . . . that is until the real crisis hit and for a brief period in the fall of 2008 the greenback reasserted itself as the reserve currency of the world.

GIVE WAR A CHANCE

If these inflationary efforts failed, there was always war. The woods and deserts were as full of unreasonable people in 2002 as they had been in the year Emperor Augustus was born. The U.S. military colossus might not be able to win their hearts and minds, but it could sure bomb the hell out of them.

"The shock therapy of a decisive war will elevate the stock market by a couple of thousand points,"[18] Lawrence Kudlow predicted. But Kudlow's record of predicting the future was not without its blemishes. In the gossamer year 1999, he had predicted that the economy would "outperform all expectations. The Dow Jones Industrial Average will reach 15,000, then 30,000 then 50,000 and higher."

He was only partially correct. Wall Street did soon surprise almost everyone—by falling for the next three years. But Kudlow's view that the United States could bomb its way to prosperity was widely shared in the early twenty-first century. The whole promise of the general belief seemed to depend on it. In the popular mind, that is to say the mind of the crowd, subtle distinctions are impossible to make. The United States was not just a great power, but the greatest power the world had ever seen. It seemed unbelievable that the country lacked the power to create the consumer paradise its citizens wanted. And if the force of fiscal programs and cheap money would not work—surely war would.

"Considering we're going to get an uptick in corporate profits and a quick win over Iraq, I think the market will be up 5 percent—10 percent for the year,"[19] opined *Barron's* Roundtable member Scott Black at the beginning of 2003.

It was inconceivable that the war would not be won and that it would not produce economic benefits. But was it so? A man cannot get rich by borrowing and spending, we observed earlier. Can he by killing people? Few people bothered to ask.

Most Americans were probably as sensible as ever, but the currents of popular sentiment were running so strongly in favor of doing something, and there seemed so few choices of what could be done, that war seemed hardly out of the question. In fact, it was tempting to see the United States' new military might as an export industry. Foreigners had financed the United States' spending spree. They had financed the U.S. military machine, too. This was as it should be, Americans began to think; the United States did the work of policing the world. It was only natural that the rest of the world pay protection money. It was a racketeer's logic, of course, but for the great mass of citizen-soldiers of the great Shareholder Nation, it was as good as any other.

"Now we are a mob," Emerson had written, 150 years ahead of his time.

THE BALANCE SHEET RECESSION

As we forecasted in the first edition of this book, the recipe of tax cuts and low interest rates outlined by then Governor Bernanke helped mutate a relatively harmless bubble in the market for tech stocks into a larger, all-encompassing bubble in housing, derivatives, and consumption. Unfortunately, the strategy merely postponed the day of reckoning for six years. Now, in the spring of 2009, the larger, all-encompassing housing and consumption bubble has popped. What's next? Look at Japan!

Richard C. Koo has prepared a remarkable report: "The Age of Balance Sheet Recessions: What Post-2008 U.S., Europe and China Can Learn from Japan 1990–2005."[20] His argument is not far from the one we made six years ago. In the 1980s, Japan ran up stock and property prices in a spree of debt and leverage. Then, when the bubble popped, the usual monetary stimulus didn't work. The Bank of Japan cut rates to almost zero . . . still, few people were willing to borrow.

The economy did not recover; instead, it got worse and worse until 2005—15 years later—when stocks had lost 72 percent of their value, land was down 81 percent, and golf course memberships had sunk 95 percent from their peak.

The problem, Koo explains, was that it was a "balance sheet recession," not a typical business cycle downturn. Companies, banks, and individuals had to pay down the debt that they had accumulated in the boom; they did not want to borrow more money, even at zero interest rates. For seven years, from 1998 to 2005, net business borrowing went negative—meaning, businesses were paying off more debt than they were taking on.

This came as a shock to modern economists. Japanese officials were flummoxed. U.S. economists accused them of not acting swiftly enough . . . or not having the stomach to let the big banks fail. But almost no one seemed to understand what was really going on. They should have. Irving Fisher described it back in 1933, observing that when people who are deeply in debt get into trouble they usually sell assets. Investors dump stocks and property for any price they can get— desperate to pay off their debts before they are dragged into bankruptcy.

This is the phenomenon known to economists as the "fallacy of composition." What is good for every individual investor—cutting expenses, paying off debt—turns out to be bad for the economy itself. Asset prices fall. Sales fall. Unemployment rises. The slump deepens.

In Japan's case, combined capital losses from land and stocks grew from 1990 until 2002, at which time they reached $15 trillion—or three years' worth of Japan's GDP.

You can do the math yourself, dear reader. The United States' GDP is about $14 trillion. Multiply that times three and you get $42 trillion. So far, the United States has lost about $4 or $5 trillion in housing prices . . . and maybe another $6 trillion in stocks, for a total of about $11 trillion, maximum. A long way to go . . .

Within the first few weeks of the election win, Obama was beginning to realize what he's up against. This is no ordinary cyclical downturn. Typically, a slump brings interest rates down. (Usually accompanied by central bank rate cuts.) Cheaper borrowing arouses business and speculative activity . . . which, in turn, tends to get the economy moving again.

This time, that's not happening. In November of 2008, authorities handed out money below the inflation rate and practically begged banks to lend . . . But who wants to lend when there's a danger you might not get your money back? And who wants to borrow when everyone is desperate to get out of debt?

The *Financial Times* announced that another 70,000 jobs could be lost on Wall Street.[21] Who needs so many employees when no one's doing any deals? No one's borrowing . . . no one's lending . . . investors are running scared . . . and private equity is curled up in a cave somewhere . . .

This is what happens in a balance sheet recession. It is not a regular, cyclical downturn. People have lost a lot of money . . . and they're afraid of losing more. So businesses are cutting back as fast as they can. The job losses aren't limited to Wall Street. At the end of 2008 there were 10 million people out of work—the most in 25 years . . . and unemployment was at a 14-year high.

As further proof that this is not your garden-variety recession, we offer exhibit A: a corporate bond from International Paper Company with a yield of nearly 10 percent. Compare that to the yield on U.S. Treasury paper—barely one tenth of one percent on 91-day T-bills. Even the 10-year Treasury notes pay less than the official rate of consumer price inflation. The "spreads" between corporate bonds and U.S. government bonds are wider than at any time since America's Great Depression.

Investors all over the planet are taking a beating. Mr. Market has taken a cudgel to stocks, property, consumer spending, and the economy—just as he did in Japan during the "Lost Decade." People are afraid to lend and afraid to borrow; they worry that the money will be knocked senseless before it finds its way home.

This time, the economy did not overheat . . . nor did labor rates go up. And when the bubble popped, the pin was not higher lending rates. This bust was caused by too much credit, not by too little. Now is the time when businesses, investors, and householders realize that if they don't cut back they could go broke.

And unlike the more typical recession, this is a slump the feds can't control and can't cure. They can offer easier credit; but more debt is just what both lenders and borrowers are most afraid of. The feds can offer more props, more handouts, and more public spending, too, just like Japan. But all they are doing is retarding the correction. Mistakes of the bubble era need to be fixed. Balance sheets need to be brought back into balance. There's no way around it. Japan proved it.

Just a few months ago, investors reached for the highest yields they could get. Now, they fold their arms, clutching to their breasts the lowest-yielding paper on the planet. Once they believed in capitalism and its bonds. Now, they want nothing that does not have the seal of the U.S. government on it. A few months ago, they saw no danger. Now, they see nothing else.

Everywhere, investment portfolios are being trimmed . . . cash is more than king; it has become a demi-god—this despite the fact that there are some great investment bargains around.

Stocks were overpriced for the last 20 years. Now, they're not so overpriced. In fact, by almost any measure you use, they're fairly reasonable. Compared to the yield you get from Treasury bonds, for example—a popular method of gauging the stock market—stocks look like a good deal. P/E ratios, too, are in the "normal" range.

But a balance sheet recession is an unforgiving, mean, and tenacious rascal. After such big losses, businesses, consumers, investors, and banks need to rebuild their balance sheets by paying off, defaulting on, or working out their debt. And then they need to rebuild their confidence . . . with rising asset prices and a growing economy. All that takes years . . . many years.

Worse, a balance sheet recession is like a straightjacket; the harder you fight against it, the tighter it gets. When government tries to prevent assets from being marked to market, for example, it delays and obstructs the process of adjustment. Rather than let the debts and mistakes be flushed out, they remain on balance sheets . . . blocking progress, frustrating change.

If "Change is Nature's delight," as Marcus Aurelius put it, then trying to stop change—at least in a balance sheet recession—is Nature's horror. Balance sheets need to be corrected. Until they are corrected future growth can't happen. So, the whole system is stymied, clogged, stopped up, constipated . . . like the U.S. economy in the 1930s . . . or like Japan's economy in the 1990s.

THE LAND OF THE FREE LUNCH

As the credit crisis began to ramp up in the United States, a flurry of activity occurred: First, the feds bailed out the mortgage industry . . . by nationalizing Fannie and Freddie and promising to put up $200 billion. Congratulations fellow taxpayer; now we own the world's largest source of mortgage finance.

And then, in mid-September of 2008, the big headline was "Fed Takes Control of AIG with $85 Billion Bailout."[22]

Ah yes, dear reader . . . the land of free markets and free men has become the land of the free lunch. Wall Street hustlers can make billions in bonuses—when the sun shines. As soon as it begins to rain, the losses are handed out to the general public. What kind of capitalism is this?

Since AIG was a major financial player—specifically, a major player in the Credit Default Swaps market—and said to be worth about $60 trillion, no one knows what would happen if it went kafooey. But no one wants to find out, either.

And so, AIG was deemed "too big to fail" . . . that if it were to collapse, it might take the whole financial structure down with it.

We've come a long way from when Andrew Mellon was Secretary of the U.S. Treasury in the late 1920s. When Wall Street cracked in 1929, Mellon had the solution: let it happen!

"Liquidate the banks, liquidate the farmers, liquidate Wall Street . . ." Mellon was ready to let the chips fall wherever they might.

But four score years later, the chips are held up . . . cushioned . . . and caught by public nets by officials pretending to labor in the name of the public. Whether it is good or bad, we have no opinion. But it is certainly different. And it recalls to us that we were right about a number of things.

Ten years ago, we began to see a certain parallel between the United States and Japan. The latter was in a terrific slump . . . and U.S. economists thought they knew why: the Japanese refused to let their big banks fail. Instead, they were propped up . . . causing the correction to happen in slow motion. Even today—18 years after the Nikkei Dow collapsed—Japan has still not recovered. You can still buy stocks at 50 percent to 80 percent off!

We thought we saw the handwriting on the wall (in Japanese no less! We couldn't actually read it, but we thought we knew what it said . . .): This shall be your fate, too.

And here we are. Rather than allow the correction to take its natural course—and get it over with—the feds are doing all they can to prevent it. The risk of "systemic failure," is too great, they say.

They must have stolen those words directly from the Japanese. That's what they always said. And so the Japanese hunkered down and stretched out their recovery so long that people gave up on it altogether.

What will be the result of this big bailout of AIG? We don't have to guess. We just have to look across the broad Pacific, at Japan.

If the Japanese model is what we think it is, the bailout—along with all the other props and cushions provided by the feds—will simply delay the inevitable. Stocks will sink. Smaller companies will go broke. Property prices will fall. Consumers will stop spending so much and begin saving.

But where in the U.S. Constitution does it authorize the executive branch of government to go into the insurance business? We don't know . . . but no one cares anyway . . .

But wait. Where do the feds get an extra $300 billion or so? The federal budget was already in deficit, about $400 billion worth. The only choice for the feds is to borrow more. But even the full faith and credit of the U.S. government has its limits. The subprime crisis came about because people borrowed money they couldn't pay back. When investors realized what they had done, they dumped the packaged, AAA subprime credits . . . and ended a 26-year-old credit expansion. And what did they do with the money? They took refuge in the prime credits of the U.S. Treasury. The dollar rose. Bond yields fell.

Now they're having second thoughts. And if they're not . . . they should. The more the economy and financial sector weaken, the more money the feds must put up to rescue them. The more dollars they need, the more they must borrow. And the more they borrow, the more they don't pay back . . . Already the amount unpaid—the official national debt—is almost $12 trillion. The interest alone is nearly $2 billion per day. Meanwhile, tax revenues are falling. Social costs—as people need more unemployment compensation, more free food and medicine, more subsidies and giveaways—are rising. Some economists are predicting budget deficits of $1 trillion . . . others say it could go to $2 trillion . . .

Oh yes . . . dear reader . . . this is where we hear the volcano heating up.

And this is when smart investors take to their golden barks . . . Not that they know what will happen. But they know the safest way to find out—from a distance . . . and, like refugees from time immemorial, with gold coins in their pockets.

Too Small to Bail

AIG was deemed "too big to fail" . . . but Lehman Brothers investment bank was not so lucky.

Ten years ago, the New York Federal Reserve Bank called upon Lehman Bros. and a handful of other major players on Wall Street to rescue a high-flying hedge fund. The firms grumped and whined . . . but they came up with the money, $3.7 billion. The rescue was a success.

LTCM's positions were unwound slowly; there was no panic; Wall Street soon went back to doing what it is supposed to do—separating customers from their money.

Long Term Capital Management was run by a couple of Nobel Prize–winning economists who believed they could use past financial patterns to model the future, just as if price movements were the same as the weather. If a hurricane had hit Houston twice in the last century, they figured the odds that another hurricane would hit the city at 1 in 50. Likewise, if the price of Lehman stock traded between, say, $10 and $30 during its 158-year history, they figured—grosso modo—that it would stay between $10 and $30.

LTCM went bust when the future turned out to be different from the past. Anyone with his eyes open at the time could have told the Nobel laureates why: weather patterns were independent of human decisions; market patterns are not.

One of the big revelations of the 1990s—or was it the 1980s?—was that stocks were traditionally, historically underpriced. Compared to bonds, said a popular financial author, stocks were a better deal. Stock buyers earned a premium over bonds for the risk they undertook, he said. But if you held stocks "for the long run," the risk disappeared. Buying stocks seemed like a no-brainer.

Thus did the *lumpeninvestoriat* begin pumping money into stocks . . . cautiously in the beginning of the 1990s . . . and recklessly at the end of the decade. And by the year 2000, the stock market no longer reflected the "random" movement of prices as predicted by the previous hundred years of stock market history; instead, it reflected the recent and remarkable belief that stocks always went up . . . and that if an investor held stocks long enough the risk disappeared.

From the peak of 2000 until today, stock market investors have earned nothing for their trouble. In nominal terms, stocks are about where they were 10 years ago. Adjusted for inflation, they are down 25 percent to 80 percent, depending on how you measure it.

Wall Street made a fortune selling stocks to naïve investors. When the stock marked topped out, the financial industry might have gone back to sleep. Instead, it got a double dose of caffeine. The Greenspan Fed cut rates in 2001–2002 while the Bush administration boosted spending and cut taxes. All of a sudden, every hand on Wall Street turned to pumping out credit—derivatives, SIVs, CDOs, MBS.

They didn't really have to invent any new theories, they merely recycled the same numbskull ideas that sank LTCM—basically, that you could eliminate risk by modeling historic price movements. If Lehman Bros., for example, had never failed in more than a century and a half, the odds that it would fail this year were so close to zero as to be not worth discussing.

But . . . in the fall of 2008, Lehman was failing. And no consortium of Wall Street banks were willing, or able, to bail it out. Lehman had some $80 billion of dubious credits. These were the products of its own—and many other—whiz kid financial engineers. Lehman hired some of the best talent on Wall Street. It had some of the world's top financial mathematicians on its payroll. It could compute the risk of loss down to 3 . . . 4 . . . heck . . . as many decimal places as you like. But it could do so only as LTCM did—based on past history.

And so, on September 16, 2008, Lehman filed the biggest bankruptcy in Wall Street history with $613 billion in debt.[23]

The handwriting has been on the wall for a long time. Once its collateral began to go down in 2007, the bubble in the financial industry couldn't last long.

But all good things must come to an end . . . especially things that are too good to be true. And now, the great bubble in credit has been popped—and everyone's squawking. The financial industry is in decline—and will probably not recover in our lifetimes. Inflation has given way to deflation. Just look at what happened to Lehman Bros. Hardly more than a year ago, investors had an asset worth $45 billion. Now they have nothing. What happened to that $45 billion? It disappeared.

But what's really new? This is what always happens when boom turns to bust. Asset values disappear. And with them, the money supply itself contracts. People spend less freely. They lend less recklessly. More money stays tucked away for longer periods in pockets and bank accounts. Prices fall. Many assets turn out to be worthless and many people go broke.

Built on Bad Loans

But, of course, lessons are not learned until it is too late. As the housing bubble began to deflate, U.S. financial institutions began to struggle. (See Figure 7.1.)

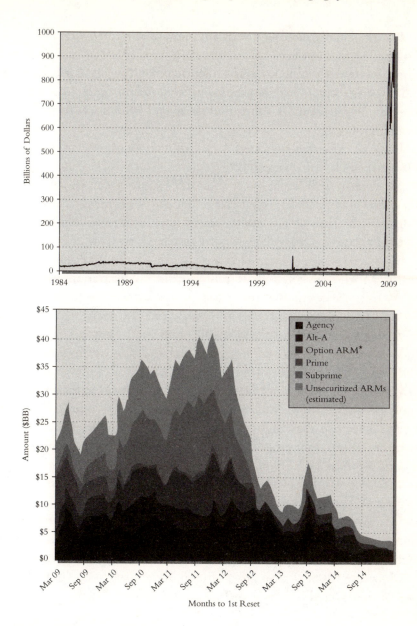

FIGURE 7.1 Lender of Last Resort

In the fall of 2008, the Federal Reserve responded to the banking crisis by buying up mortgage-backed securities, making its own balance sheet balloon with toxic debt. And yet the epicenter of the crisis—bad mortgages of all exotic varieties—were expected to continue defaulting at a breathtaking pace for another 4 years.

*Option ARMs show estimated recast schedule based on current neg-am rate.

Source: Credit Suisse (US Mortgage Strategy), LoanPerformance, FH/FN/GN.

It looked like bankruptcy was imminent for Countrywide Financial. Flourishing only months before, the country's largest mortgage lender found themselves in deep trouble—and lax lending standards were far and away to blame. The lender saw a spike in mortgage defaults and foreclosures especially in subprime mortgages, which was too much to shoulder.

Bank of America swooped in and bought Countrywide for $4.1 billion in stock in January 2008.[24]

More than a full year later, Countrywide was still making head-lines. On June 4, 2009, word came that the Securities and Exchange Commission had filed fraud charges against former Countrywide Chief Executive Officer Angelo Mozilo and two other individuals. Turns out Mozilo et al. misled investors about the mortgage lender's health. Mozilo pocketed $140 million from insider trades.[25]

As the year went on, more and more lenders went the way of Countrywide, buckling under the burden of bad loans. IndyMac, an offshoot of Countrywide, was seized by federal regulators on July 11, 2008. The *New York Times* reported that the debacle could cost the FDIC as much as $8 billion—and shareholders were all but wiped out. What had happened was no big surprise: "Executives at IndyMac, like many people on both Wall Street and Main Street, apparently never dreamed home prices might fall. To the contrary, IndyMac made many loans on terms that implicitly assumed prices would keep rising," reports the *New York Times*.[26]

IndyMac would have been the biggest bank failure in history—that is, until Washington Mutual came along. WaMu is also a prime exam-ple of a bank built on bad loans. The bank fell victim to the subprime fallout. With about $310 billion in assets, WaMu was seized by federal regulators and then acquired by J.P. Morgan Chase for $1.9 billion.[27]

Since the fall of Washington Mutual, there have been 48 bank fail-ures in the United States (as of June 1, 2009).

BASEBALL, HOT DOGS, APPLE PIE, AND CHEVROLET

Banks weren't the only American institutions staggering toward insol-vency during the credit crisis. As of June 2009, General Motors, once the backbone of U.S. manufacturing, is officially bankrupt.[28]

It's a shame, really. The company was set up in 1916. If it had been able to hold together for another seven years, it would have gone 100 years without having to declare bankruptcy.

All people die. All companies die, too. That's why "buy and hold" is wishful thinking. Buy and hold long enough and you are sure to go broke. And die.

Eventually the undertakers and bankruptcy lawyers get you. And business is good in Detroit. What cleared the way for the GM bankruptcy was a deal with the bondholders . . . in which they take equity in exchange for their debt and agree not to contest the bankruptcy filing. Still, the deal—and other deals relating to it . . . including the presence of one very big and very odd shareholder, the government of the United States—is so complicated, it's bound to give bankruptcy lawyers plenty of work for many years.

And since it's 2009, lord knows GM can't be a run-of-the-mill insolvency. The Obama administration has its hands deep in this thing . . . here's the fine print of the second largest industrial bankruptcy in U.S. history:

- Uncle Sam gets a 60 percent stake. The government will pump an additional $30 billion into GM (on top of the $20 billion already squandered). In exchange, the government will be the largest shareholder . . . leverage it will use to usher GM through bankruptcy and convert it to this "leaner, stronger company" we've been promised.
- Half of the UAW's $20 billion health care fund will be converted to GM stock, which will give it a 17.5 percent stake in the company; 12–20 factories will be closed, at the cost of approximately 21,000 union workers. 40 percent of the 6,000 GM dealers will have to close, too.
- The Canadian government gets a 12 percent stake, given all GM's design/manufacturing activity up north.
- Bondholders were bought (bullied?) out. They'll swap their $27.1 billion in unsecured debt for 10 percent of GM, with warrants to own 15 percent more. Surely, they learned from Chrysler's bondholders, who were publicly vilified by President Obama for demanding what was lawfully theirs . . . so much for that hallmark of American capitalism.

- Current shareholders get nada. At least that rule of bankruptcy is still intact. If you were long GM, please consider letting someone else manage your money. Anyone.[29]

The French nationalized their auto companies after the war. Then, when the socialists took control of the government in the 1980s, they nationalized the banks, too. "Silly frogs," said U.S. economists. "Don't they know that a free market works best?" And so you see, dear reader, in all time zones and all languages, people are the same—always hustling up something for nothing, whenever they can get away with it.

CHAPTER 8

THE HARD MATH OF DEMOGRAPHY

Demography is destiny.

—Auguste Compte

The early classical economists—Smith, Ricardo, Malthus, Mill, Marshall, and others—were keenly interested in the role that the young and the aged played in building wealth. Living at a time when birth rates were high and populations were expanding, they wanted to determine how demographic growth changed wages, savings, and output; which classes benefited; and whether a larger population was a long-term blessing.

Two centuries on, Peter Peterson, in his book *Gray Dawn*, warns that we might pose a different question: What happens to the wealth of nations when the populations get old and begin to shrink? In this chapter, we look at the effects of demographic shift . . . not because it is the only trend in place, but because it is one easily missed.

BIG POPULATION SHIFTS DISRUPT POLITICS

In his book *Revolution and Rebellion in the Early Modern World*, the historian Jack Andrew Goldstone argues that the great revolutions of

Europe—the English and French revolutions—had one thing in common with the great rebellions of Asia that destroyed the Ottoman Empire and dynasties in Japan and China. All these crises occurred when inflexible political, economic, and social institutions were faced with the twin pressures of population growth and diminishing available resources.

Across Europe in the early 1700s, populations began to increase as mortality rates from disease (such as plague) and famine declined, and birth rates remained high. A large excess of births over deaths during much of the early modern period produced a baby boom. According to demographer Michael Anderson, the population in Europe doubled in the 100 years between 1750 and 1850. The "age of democratic revolution" in the late 1700s, including the French Revolution, coincided with an expansion in the proportion of young people.

A large, unruly, and youthful rural population was a leading cause of social stress in France prior to and during the Revolution. The population of France grew by 8 to 10 million people in the eighteenth century. By contrast, in the previous century, the population had only increased by a million. Around 1772, Abbé Terray began the first serious survey of demographics in France. Terray pegged the population at 26 million.

By 1789, the eve of the French Revolution, Louis XVI is thought to have had nearly 30 million subjects in his realm—more than 20 percent of the entire population of non-Russian Europe. These numbers, suggests a study published by George Mason University, had to have some effect. Arguably, they changed France both politically and economically. And, we might add, cost Louis his kingdom . . . and his neck.

Likewise, the Russian population doubled between the 1850s and the beginning of World War I. From 1855 until 1913, the population of the Russian Empire increased from about 73 million to about 168 million.[1] The stress of feeding and providing shelter for that many people was too great for the existing order. The principal problem in the countryside was shortage of land. Rapid population growth meant that the size of allotments decreased from an average size of just over five hectares in 1861 to less than three in 1900.

In the West, industry absorbed the swelling population, but Russia could only put about one third of its new population on the assembly line. There was a growing feeling that, unless something was done, the countryside would soon explode. The peasants had a simple solution to their problems—confiscate all private lands owned by the landlords.

In a paper presented at the European Population Conference 2001, the Russian historian Lev Protasov suggested that prior to the Russian Revolution, demographic factors played an important role in stirring up the masses. Curiously, a striking number of the radicals who helped foment the revolution were born in 1880. "The 1880s' generation," says Protasov, "made up almost 60 percent radicals and dominated the left factions: 62 percent of socialist revolutionaries, 58 percent of the Bolsheviks, 63 percent of the 'national' socialists and 47 percent of the Mensheviks. To be sure the powerful showing of young radicals in the early 20th century has been noted by historians."

In rural areas, peasants spit out children like watermelon seeds, leaving villages overwhelmed and "overheated." Infant and child mortality rates fell thanks to better health care, nutrition, and sanitation. "The Russian political cataclysms of 1905 and 1917 were 'prepared' not only by economic or political causes," concludes Protasov, "but by nature acting out its own laws. The demographic bursts in the last decades of the 19th century, not only sharpened modernization problems, but speeded up the marginalization of society and gave abundant 'human material' to the first lines of the future revolution makers."

Population explosions have caused trouble. But now populations are falling. The effect could be equally devastating: As all developed nations rely on taxes paid by young workers to support aging retirees, a declining and aging population will arrive just when the Western societies need more young people most.

THE AGING OF THE WEST

On October 12, 1999, the world saw the birth of citizen number 6 billion. Since the 1970s, with the publication of Paul Ehrlich's *The Population Bomb*, most of the world has been gripped by a neo-Malthusian fear of overpopulation. Yet, in recent years, thanks to books such as *Gray Dawn* and *Agequake*, the metaphor has shifted. Much of the developed world is now shuffling toward old age. At least half of all the people who ever lived to the age of 65 are still alive.[2]

For most of human history, the number of people aged over 65 was roughly 2 percent or 3 percent of the population. When Hammurabi, Julius Caesar, or [even] Thomas Jefferson were alive, observes Peterson, there were low odds (1 person in every 40) of meeting a person aged 65 or over. Today, those odds are about one person in every seven, and in a few decades' time, they will be one person in every four—or in extreme cases (such as Italy) one in every three. According to the Organization for Economic Cooperation and Development (OECD), by 2030 the number of people aged 65 or over across the developed world will have increased by 89 million, whereas the number of working-age adults is projected to have decreased by 34 million.

In 1960, there were nearly seven working-age people for every person over 65. In 2000, that number had dropped to 4.5 working-age people. By 2030, the OECD expects there to be only 2.5 people working for every dependent elderly in the developed world.

In addition to the shift in demography, people across the developed world are retiring younger; thus, the pool of taxpayers supporting retired pensioners is rapidly evaporating. In the highly developed welfare states of Western Europe, the decrease has been striking. In France, Germany, and Italy, fewer than 5 out of 100 men over the age of 65 are working. By 2050, the IMF projects, each of these countries will have only one taxpayer (or fewer in Italy's case) supporting each pensioner.

Dr. Gary North considers that we are living in a "fool's paradise."[3] All citizens of Western industrial democracies (including Japan) have "pay-as-you-go" funding for their government-guaranteed retirement and medical insurance systems. Yet, every Western nation has a birth rate lower than 2.1 children per family. The math is easy. The number of workers coming into the economy is not enough to fund the old-age pension systems.

Again, in the struggle between myth and reality, the masses welcomed the myth that they would all be able to retire at someone else's expense. As in a Ponzi scheme or bubble market, the first to get into the system made a nice profit. They paid in trivial amounts, lived longer than expected, and drew out far more than they had any right to do. Later participants will find it much harder to come out ahead. With longevity increasing and the retirement age decreasing, the financial burden placed on the world's working-age populations may be unbearable.

YOUTH AND ISLAMIC FUNDAMENTALISM

One of the complications of a declining population in the West is a political one. The War on Terrorism, declared on September 13, 2001, promises to be expensive, simply because there are so many potential terrorists to fight. Westerners constitute a decreasing minority of the global population: In 1900, they amounted to 30 percent of humanity; in 1993 that number had dropped to 13 percent and by 2025, following current trends, the percentage will fall to 10 percent. At the same time, the Muslim world is growing younger and increasing in numbers.

In fact, Muslims' market share of the global population has increased dramatically throughout the twentieth century and will continue to do so until the proportion of Westerners to Muslims is inverse that of the 1900 ratio. By 1980, Muslims constituted 18 percent of the world's population and, in 2000, more than 20 percent. By 2025, they are expected to account for 30 percent of world population.

In his *Clash of Civilizations*, Samuel Huntington considers these demographics to have been a major factor in the Islamic resurgence of the late twentieth century. "Population growth in Muslim countries," he says, "and particularly the expansion of the 15- to 24-year-old age cohort, provides recruits for fundamentalism, terrorism, insurgency, and migration . . . demographic growth threatens Muslim governments and non-Muslim societies."[4]

Islamic resurgence began in the 1970s and 1980s, just as the proportion of young people in the 15- to 24-year-old age group in Muslim nations exploded. Indeed this proportion peaked at more than 20 percent of the total population in many Muslim countries during these decades.[5] Muslim youth are a potential supply of members for Islamic organizations and political movements.[6] The Iranian Revolution, for example, in 1979 coincided with a peak in the youth population of Iran.[7]

"For years to come Muslim populations will be disproportionately young populations," Huntington explains, "with a notable demographic bulge of teenagers and people in their 20s."[8] What are we to make of it?

Huntington suggests that the most accurate analogy in Western Society to this youth bulge in Muslim populations is the Protestant Reformation.

Ironically, both the rise of the fundamentalist movement in the Muslim world and the Protestant Reformation came about in reaction "to the stagnation and corruption of existing institutions," says Huntington. Both advocate a "return to a purer and more demanding form of their religion; preach work, order and discipline; and appeal to emerging, dynamic middle-class people." Both challenge the political and economic order of the time; and where the threat of the former is concerned, major defense spending on the part of the West would not seem appropriate.

"The Protestant Reformation," writes Huntington, "is an example of one of the outstanding youth movements in history." Citing Jack Goldstone, Huntington continues, "a notable expansion of the proportion of youth in Western countries coincides with the Age of Democratic Revolution in the last decades of the 18th century. In the 19th century successful industrialization and emigration reduced the political impact of young populations in European societies. The proportion of youth rose again in the 1920s, however, providing recruits to fascist and other extreme movements. Four decades later the post–World War II baby boom generation made its mark in the demonstrations of the 1960s."

Whereas young people generally exhibit a rebellious and revolutionary influence on society, what happens when people grow old? The exact opposite.

Fearfulness and loss of desire commonly accompany aging. Older people tend not to want as many things in life as young people. They lose their desire to impress friends, relatives, and partners. Instead of buying items they don't need, they tend to become fearful that they will not be able to obtain what they do need. There is nothing peculiar about this; it is just nature's way of recognizing diminishing opportunities. A man in his forties can start over. But in his late sixties, he no longer has the energy or the desire to do so. He therefore starts saving everything—tinfoil, money, rags—for fear he will not be able to get them when he needs them. This is how an elderly individual tends to behave. But what does an aging society look like? Again, we need only look across the ocean—to Japan.

THE SETTING SUN AND THE INFLUENCE OF THE AGED

Japan is an "early warning test case" because it has already begun aging so rapidly.[9]

In the early 1980s, Japan was the youngest society in the developed world. But by 2005, it will be the oldest. Japan has 105 aged people (defined here as those over 64 years of age) for every scamp under 15.[10] Marketers around the globe have already cottoned on to the trend. They now study Japan to find out what happens to consumers as they age. Among Japan's declining industries are pediatrics, toys, and education; whereas nursing, leisure cruises, pets, and religious icons are booming.

Japan's newspapers warn of "plunging birth rates" and a "demographic disaster." By the year 2010, Japan's old-age dependency ratio (the number of working-age adults to elders) will be the first of the developed economies to fall below three. With the number of children under 15 in Japan, now only 14.3 percent of the population, estimates show that the population will drop from 127 million to 100 million by 2050. This is not speculation, but extrapolation, as the figures are based on trends currently in place.

Why are these trends so marked compared with other nations in the developed world? Japan, unlike the United States and Europe, experienced a larger baby bust than boom following World War II. In the early 1960s, the birth rate plunged to half the level it had been two decades before. Today, the number of unmarried Japanese women aged 25 to 29 has doubled since 1950, and, not surprisingly, birth rates have continued to slide.

Japan's citizens also live longer than those of other nations. In 1998, Japan became the first country in which life expectancy reached 80 years. In 1950, if a Japanese citizen reached 65 years old he could expect to live another 12 years, on average. Today, he can expect to tack on another 19 years! And, if he reaches 80? The chances are that he will live to see his 89th birthday.

At this rate, by 2015, a full 25 percent of the population will be 65 years or older. By 2050, more than 42 percent of Japan's population will be aged 60 or over, with another 15 percent over 80 years of age. On reviewing these numbers, Toyota Motor Corporation chairman Dr. Shoichiro Toyoda joked that the Japanese race would become extinct in just 800 years. A health and welfare ministry report suggested that if they "dared to make the calculation, Japan's population will be . . . about 500 people in the year 3000 and 1 person in the year 3500."

What is the effect of this aging process? Analyzing data from a U.S. Census Bureau report,[11] analyst Ya-Gui Wei noticed the obvious: "For each individual member of society, no matter which metrics you look at, their ability is likely to increase as they grow up, then peak at a certain age, finally decline as they get older. This is true whether you are measuring their strength, their sexual prowess, or their money earning power."

The Cowles Foundation for Research in Economics at Yale University published a study comparing demographic trends to investor behavior. It corroborated Wei's conclusions: Older people downscale their lives, cut back on their spending, pay down their debts, and add to their savings. As people move from middle age into old age, they increasingly save for retirement and sell any stocks they had during their middle age. This contributed directly to the collapse of the Nikkei in 1989, and has undoubtedly worsened the Japanese economy's slump over the past 12 years.

Japan's consumer society grew in the 1970s and when most of its boomers were entering middle age. It experienced its asset bubble in the latter half of the 1980s at a time when the largest segment of its population reached the peak spending years of 45 to 54. The bust happened soon thereafter . . . just as Mr. and Mrs. Yokohama began preparing for retirement. During the asset bubble, Japanese market indexes increased more than 1,000 percent. By the end of the decade, however, the market had collapsed—losing two thirds of its value.

"Throughout the 1990s, the kernel of the Japanese problem has been the lack of investment opportunities to match the flow of savings," writes Paul Wallace. "The Japanese have been saving prodigiously for their retirement. But because of past fertility declines, the working-age population is starting to decline. That means there are fewer investment opportunities since there are fewer people to equip with capital."[12] Demographics were a "root cause" of Japan's recent economic crisis in the 1990s.

The Japanese baby boom started in 1945 and ended in 1950. Forty-five years later, the Japanese market crashed. Ever since, Japan's stocks and economy have been pulling back as Japanese baby boomers save money for retirement. These demographic patterns are eerily consistent with the boom and bust of the late 1990s in the United States. Meanwhile, whereas the baby boom in Japan was over in 1950, in America, it was just getting started: The real peak in U.S. births took place in the five years between 1955 and 1960—10 years after the Japanese peak.

Old Folks at Home

Citizens in the United States are also aging and living longer. By the year 2040, the Census Bureau expects that the number of fogies (those aged 65 to 74) will grow by 80 percent, and that the over-80 age group will skyrocket by 240 percent. In 1900, Peter Peterson points out, the number of U.S. residents older than 85 was only 374,000. In 2000, that number was nearly 4 million and by 2040 it will exceed 13 million (your authors hope to be among them). By 2040, the number of Americans older than 80 is expected to more than triple—eclipsing the number of school-age children.

Ya-Gui Wei noticed that the average income is highest among the 45 to 54 age group, followed by the 35 to 44 age group. "If you are the average citizen," observes Wei "before you are 46 years old, your income level is likely to continue to go up. During this period, you'll also be thinking about your retirement, and have more and more disposable income to put into retirement and savings funds. After 46 years of age, your income is likely to go down, as will the portion of your money available for savings" (see Figure 8.1).

If age 46, as Harry Dent suggests,[13] is the peak spending and investing age, then the year 2000 was a reasonably predictable market top. Mr. Dent thought we might see a boom through 2008, but the math doesn't hold up. In 1954, we were just under midway through the baby boom period, and 1954 + 46 = 2000, the year when the U.S. stock market peaked. When a baby boomer moves into late middle age (55 to 59) he will, if he is like his neighbors, begin to sell off the stock he bought for retirement. He will spend a little less . . . save a little more.

The experience in Japan suggests that a demographic shift from young to old throughout the developed world is likely to be as challenging "to the existing political and economic structures" as any youth revolution of the past. Imagine millions of people preparing for retirement. They no longer borrow money to finance a bigger home. They no longer buy bigger cars for their family vacations. They have all the time-saving devices and household appliances they need. And they are no longer buying stocks "for the long run."

They bought those stocks 10 or 15 years ago: Now the long run has come.

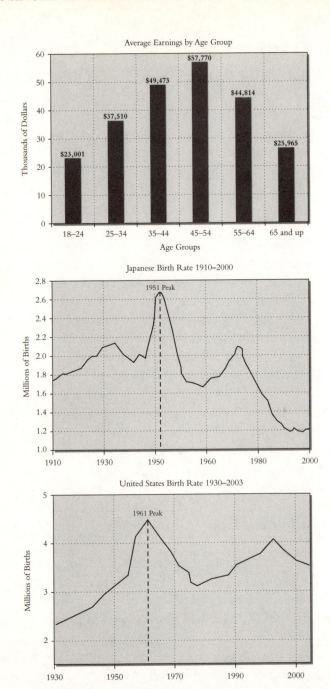

FIGURE 8.1 Demographic Roots of the Bust?
Ages 45 to 54 generally continue the peak "getting and spending" years (top). The Japanese baby boom reached its peak around 1951 (middle). The United States baby boom reached its peak in 1961 (bottom). The respective booms happened roughly 40 years later.

Trendsetters

Seventy-eight million Americans were born between 1946 and 1964—the biggest population boom in U.S. history. The baby boom generation was the largest ever, accounting for a full third of the population by the mid-1980s. Starting with 1.2 billion cans of baby food sold in 1953 and running through the 150 million credit cards issued in 2002, "the boomers" have made their presence known.

Much has been written about the size and influence of the boomer generation. We add this nuance: The history of crowds will reveal none bigger and none more aware of itself than the group of 78 million born after World War II. Never before had such a big group grown up together. Thanks to modern communications—most importantly, television—the boomers were able to keep in touch with each other from coast to coast. They watched each other on the *Mickey Mouse Club*, *Leave It to Beaver*, or *Dick Clark's American Bandstand*. Hours and hours of television showed them not only how to dance, but what music to listen to, how to dress, how to talk, and what to think. The world had never seen anything like it.

It has been commonplace to show how this big mass of people moved through American society and changed it. What has never been fully realized is the extent to which—unlike any previous group in the history of man—the boomers were subject to the madness of crowds on a monumental scale. The boomers adopted every idea that appealed to them and dumbed it down . . . broadcast it . . . vulgarized it . . . and took it up as they would their favorite pop song. Revolutionary in their youth, they became bourgeois in middle age. Then, applying its outsize weight to the stock market, the boomer generation created an outsize boom. To give the reader a quick peek at what's ahead: The boomers are now likely to create an outsize bust.

" 'I am a student! Do not fold, spindle or mutilate!' read the signs of picketers outside Berkeley's Sproul Hall in 1964," write William Strauss and Neil Howe in their book, *The Fourth Turning*. Many of these demonstrators would be working for Silicon Valley firms in a few decades, and yet they were mocking the "computer card" treatment they were supposedly receiving from the university.

Where Allen Ginsberg and the beatniks of the previous generation voiced their protests in tranquil poetry sessions, the boomers took their beef to the streets. What their beef was, and with whom, was never exactly clear, least of all to the boomers. "Boomer hippies megaphoned their 'nonnegotiable demands' without caring much who listened," say Strauss and Howe.

"Tune in, turn on, drop out!" they chanted.

A supercharged economy in the 1960s offered jobs to all who wanted them; the risk of being left out was nil. "Most campus rioters," say Strauss and Howe, "assumed that the instant they deigned to do so, they could drop back into the American Dream machine. Planning for tomorrow was no big deal." A popular song of the time urged boomers to "la, la, la live for today. Don't worry about tomorrow . . . " With long hair, tie-dyed T-shirts and ripped jeans, the emerging boomer deliberately confronted the highly ordered society of the "man in the gray flannel suit." In *The Graduate,* an Academy Award winning movie in 1967, Katherine Ross approached the corporate ladder and heard something inside screaming: "Stop!" The boomers stopped, for a while.

Baby boomers protested the Vietnam War, as a moral issue . . . until the draft was abolished. Many valued instant gratification over patience and expressed rage and petulance if they did not get what they wanted. Whatever they encountered—sex, drugs, rock and roll—they thought that they had invented it.

One elderly senator described the boomers as critical of everything, impossible to please, indifferent to nuance and incapable of compromise. They lauded perfection, but oddly never saw it in anybody but themselves. For the demographer, William Dunn, President Clinton epitomized the lot: "a little self-indulgent and pretty much convinced that he and his generation are smarter than everyone else."

Within a decade, however, the boomers' ability to "drop back in" to the dream machine was challenged for the first time in their lives, when the 1970s brought with them the first major bear market since the crash of 1929.

The Arab oil embargo of 1973 hit the economy hard, causing a recession, after which entry-level jobs became hard to find. "With the economy souring," write Strauss and Howe, "many boomers found new reasons why making money was beneath them. 'I have made no plans because I have found no plans worth making,' a Dartmouth valedictorian declared to the cheers of his peers." Indeed, "there was very little doing," said music promoter Bill Graham, speaking of the young radicals of his generation. As the Beatles song suggested, they were happy to "say" they wanted a revolution. But if it came to actually doing something, the average boomer would chant, "don't you know that you can count me out." Their youth passed like a tantrum.

THE RISE OF CONSUMER SOCIETY

With the 1980s came family life, middle age, and a desire for the material things they had previously eschewed. "It was time to go straight," recalls Todd Gitlin, "from marijuana to white wine, from hip communes to summers in Cape Cod." Snoopy and Woodstock implored the boomers to "Get Met, It Pays!" The boomer generation "couldn't linger forever in a suspended state of animation," say Strauss and Howe. In short, boomers began aspiring to consumption and careerism in a major way.

On March 25, 1984, the *New York Times* declared "The Year of the Yuppie." The yuppies (Young Urban Professionals) began to get married and have children. It became the hip thing to do. "Deferring gratification, has suddenly become fashionable," noticed the *Wall Street Journal,* mid-decade.

There was a problem, however. The generation that had so far managed to get everything its own way through the sheer force of its numbers, suddenly had numbers working against it. In the 1980s, the many boomers in the labor market were driving wages down. "America was awash in fads, diets, and jokes about Perrier drinking sellouts engaged in what *Newsweek* described as 'a state of transcendental acquisition.'" Yet for the first time in U.S. economic history, the boomer generation was unable to live up to the living standards of its parents—let alone surpass them.

In the 1980s, the boomers were turning middle-aged, and they should have been saving for retirement. Instead, they increasingly ran up debts. Given the reality of the earnings picture, the attractiveness of credit proved too strong to resist. Amex touted that the "membership has its privileges." And the boomers signed up by the truckload. According to the Federal Reserve, by 1999, more than 42 percent of the baby boomers averaged $11,616 in credit card debt (see Figure 8.2).

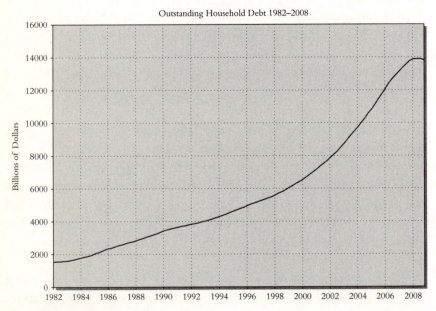

FIGURE 8.2 "La, La, La, Live for Today"

Throughout the 1990s, the savings rate in the United States declined steadily (top). Rapidly increasing credit-card debt (bottom) bolstered consumer spending. By the end of the decade, outstanding household debt threatened to exceed national annual output of goods and services.

Source: Federal Reserve.

Boomers went into debt, en masse. And they carried on their spending spree well into the 1990s, racking up both credit card debt and hefty mortgages. Rather than saving, the average boomer spent. This spending—multiplied over millions of consumers—had a remarkable effect; the whole economy was soon flooded with credit, SUVs, and retail outlets. The nature of the economy had gradually been switching its focus from production to consumption over the lifetime of the boomer generation. By the end of the 1990s, the trend had become grotesque, with 4.8 new dollars worth of credit and debt for every extra dollar's worth of gross domestic product (GDP), 1997 to 2001.

What does it take to create wealth? Time. Work. Imagination. Skill. Forbearance. Instead of spending every sou that comes our way, it's necessary to save a few to invest in capital improvements—new machinery, for example—so that more wealth can be created. But here was a generation on which the hard-wrought tradition of the past had been lost. They had no patience for saving or investing.

No worries. Thanks to the biggest expansion of credit in history, the U.S. economy enjoyed an unprecedented boom. Still, it was a boom of a strange sort. Families were able to maintain their standards of living and enjoy the illusion of financial progress . . . but only by going more deeply into debt and working harder.

Americans confused capital gains with capital accumulation. They could look at their stock portfolios and think themselves rich. But at the same time, debt levels were at record highs. Americans—believing themselves on top of the world (like the Japanese in 1989)—bid up asset prices to absurd levels. But unlike the Japanese, they also allowed themselves to become the world's biggest debtors, owing more money to more people than any nation had ever done.

Were they getting as rich as they thought? The numbers are hard to follow and often misleading, but deconstructing them turns a McMansion into a double-wide.

Paul Krugman, who has since won the Nobel Prize for Economics, took up the task in an article appearing in the *New York Times* magazine on October 20, 2002. "Over the past 30 years," he wrote, "most people have seen only modest salary increases: the average annual salary in America, expressed in 1998 dollars (that is, adjusted for inflation), rose from $32,522 in 1970 to $35,864 in 1999. That's about a 10 percent increase over 29 years—progress, but not much."

"Average family income—total income divided by the number of families—grew 28 percent from 1979 to 1997," Krugman continued. "But median family income—the income of a family in the middle of the distribution, a better indicator of how typical American families are doing—grew only 10 percent. And the incomes of the bottom fifth of families actually fell slightly. . . . Median family income has risen only about 0.5 percent per year—and as far as we can tell from somewhat unreliable data, just about all of that increase was due to wives working longer hours, with little or no gain in real wages."

Phony Boom

What kind of boom was this? How come the most dynamic, most technologically advanced capitalist society ever did not share its bounty with the people who greased its wheels and schlepped its detritus to the dump? There must be more to the story, right? Right.

Krugman goes on to compare the rough-and-tumble free-enterprise United States at the debut of the third millennium to quasi-socialist Sweden, which had barely participated in the Great New Era Boom:

> Life expectancy in Sweden is about three years higher than that of the U.S. Infant mortality is half the U.S. level. . . . Functional illiteracy is much less common than in the U.S. . . . Swedes take longer vacations than Americans, so they work fewer hours per year. . . . The median Swedish family has a standard of living roughly comparable with that of the median U.S. family: wages are if anything higher in Sweden, and a higher tax burden is offset by public provision of health care and generally better public services. And as you move further down the income distribution, Swedish living standards are way ahead of those in the U.S. Swedish families with children that are at the 10th percentile—poorer than 90 percent of the population—have incomes 60 percent higher than their U.S. counterparts. And very few people in Sweden experience the deep poverty that is all too common in the United States. One measure: in 1994 only 6 percent of Swedes lived on less than $11 per day, compared with 14 percent in the U.S.

You can draw many different conclusions from these insights. Typically, Krugman managed to find some absurd ones. But his facts are revealing: the United States' big boom was a fraud.

As a result, for many boomers, career opportunities and salaries failed to live up to their hallucinations. Real hourly wages began leveling off in the 1970s and have barely improved since. "In terms of earning more money," writes economist Gary North, "there was an increase in compensation. But in terms of real wages, there was very little improvement 1973 to 2000."

From 1947 to 1973, the peak earning and spending years of the baby boomers' parents, there was a steady increase in household productivity and compensation. But from 1973 through 1993, the years heralded by the press as "the decade of greed," there was zero family income growth. To stay even, more wives entered the workforce. But it had an unforeseen consequence: The real wages of men fell. As shown in Table 8.1, in 1979 a man earned $677 a week, on average.

TABLE 8.1   Median Weekly Earnings in the United States, 1979–2000 (in year 2000 dollars)

	All ($)	Men ($)	Women ($)
1979	558	677	424
1980	546	653	421
1981	541	648	419
1982	544	656	429
1983	541	654	436
1984	540	648	439
1985	549	650	443
1986	562	658	456
1987	565	656	459
1988	560	654	459
1989	554	650	455
1990	543	634	456
1991	539	623	463
1992	540	615	466
1993	547	608	468
1994	543	607	464
1995	541	608	459
1996	538	611	459
1997	540	621	462
1998	553	632	482
1999	567	639	489
2000	576	646	491

Source: Bureau of Labor Statistics.

In 2000, 21 years later—he earned $33 a week less. Women on the other hand, saw an increase of only $47 per week over the same 20-year period. And their incomes remain lower than those of men.

"The total hours worked by American families increased," North shows, "but family income stagnated," as Table 8.1 reveals. The richest families continued to work more hours as a group throughout the 21-year period, but all other income groups increased their working hours dramatically. Yet family incomes did not increase. "No explanation for this reduction of per capita income has been widely accepted by economists," says North, "the following charts are some of the most discouraging in recent economic history" (see Table 8.1 and Figure 8.3).

Here we offer an explanation: The general belief of the boomer generation was a bit different from that of its parents. Little by little, through mob sentiment rather than using individual logic, it had picked up the credo of the *Whole Earth Catalog*: "We are as gods and might as well get good at it." These gods had created an economy in their own image. A healthy economy needs forbearance, thrift, savings, patience, discipline—the very characteristics the boomers never had. Soon, the economy began to reflect the boomer personality: cocksure, short-sighted, in need of immediate gratification, reckless, and self-indulgent.

Late, Degenerate Capitalism

Nowhere were these traits better illustrated—or with more disastrous results—than in the management of U.S. corporations. Instead of investing in new plants and equipment to produce future profits, U.S. corporations slashed costs and engaged in various forms of financial engineering and accounting legerdemain to bring profits forward at the expense of the balance sheet. Like the new cocksure Americans themselves, companies went deeply into debt, often purchasing their own shares at outrageous prices, in order to provide the illusion of growing current profits.

Phony credits introduced by the Fed encouraged consumption and bad investment decisions, both of which ate into the real savings available for future growth. This, combined with the collapse of earnings, savings, and capital gains, meant that the resources available for growth and development actually shrank during the boom . . . and may well have been smaller in 1999 than when the boom began.

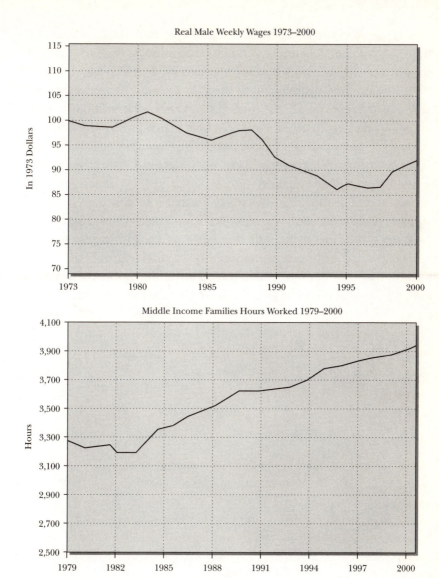

FIGURE 8.3 Decades of Greed

During the 1980s and 1990s, median family income stagnated. Real wages for men fell (top). And the average family was on the clock an increasing amount of time per week (bottom).

According to the late economist Kurt Richebächer, the highly visible result (of the consumption binge) that nobody cares to notice, is a progressive steep rise in consumption as a share of GDP.[14] In the late 1970s the rate of consumption in the U.S. economy as a percentage of GDP was 62 percent. By the end of the 1980s, that number rose by 4 percent to 66 percent; and it rose another 4 percent by the end of the 1990s. But by the end of 2001, consumption as a share of current GDP growth exceeded 70 percent (see Figure 8.4) and stayed there for the balance of the decade.

Increasing consumption was to have a further unpleasant effect. The boomers' twisting of their parents' (relatively) high-saving, high capital-investment and high value-added economy to a low-saving, low capital-investment, consumer economy resulted in changes in its structure. It went from an economy that could give the boomers what they needed in the long run to one that gave them what they wanted in the

FIGURE 8.4 The Rise of the Consumer Society

The baby boomers remade the economy in their own image. Once relatively high saving, high capital investment, and value added, the economy shifted from producing what the boomers needed in the long run to giving them what they wanted short term.

Source: Federal Reserve.

short run. Favoring immediate consumption over long-term investment, the economy was now unable to produce enough earnings and profits to allow average Americans to retire. True, the boom boosted up their stock portfolios, but 79 million of them could not retire on paper capital gains. As soon as they went to sell, the gains would disappear.

They needed earnings, profits, and income to retire on. And for that, they needed an economy with high levels of savings and capital investment.

Why did corporate earnings collapse . . . why did personal earnings stagnate . . . and why did Americans have to work longer and longer just to maintain their standard of living? You can't get something for nothing, is our answer.

Without savings, there can be no real capital investment—because there is nothing to invest. Instead, there is only make-believe investment paid for with credit. Without real capital investment in profit-making new machinery, new plants and equipment, people do not have high-value-added new jobs. Wages cannot increase, for companies are not really producing more and better goods and services. People are forced to work longer hours and go into debt, while their stocks and real estate investments rise in value. This gives them the illusion of financial progress. Then, once they think they are getting rich, they are encouraged to borrow and spend even more—which further distorts the entire economy toward a level of consumption that cannot be maintained. Eventually, the consumers arrive at retirement age and realize that they don't have enough money.

What can they do? Go back to work!

"Everyone, Back in the Labor Pool," suggested a *Time* article in the July 20, 2002, issue. "Eroding pension benefits, longer life-spans and a major meltdown in stocks add up to this: most of us will have to work well into our 70s." At least Americans were used to it. They had been schlepping longer and longer hours since 1982. Now they were preparing to work until they dropped dead.

High on Stocks

Having grown of age during the bull market, there was nothing in the baby boomers' own experience that might make them think twice. An entire generation of investors had come to believe that they had made a discovery as agreeable as sex and as immutable as gravity. They thought they now knew something their forebears had missed: Stocks always went up. The new metaphor was like a gift from heaven that had gone unnoticed.

According to James K. Glassman's 1998 book *Dow 36,000,* stocks had been mispriced for two centuries. Investors had required a "risk premium" from stocks—in effect, demanding a higher rate of return from their investments in stocks than from their investments in bonds—because stocks were riskier. Now, Glassman revealed the shocking discovery: Stocks were not riskier after all; there was no need for a risk premium. Take away the risk premium, jiggle the figures a bit, and stocks should be much more expensive—say, 36,000. Why not?

Trouble is, the average investor in 2001 had never put a penny into stocks before the Great Bull Market of 1982 to 2000 began.

But in October 2001, none of this was apparent to the average baby boomer—turned "investor"—looking at the Dow chart, unadjusted for inflation. He must have looked at the chart as a climber looks at a mountain. His eye would have drifted over the right-hand side and there it was, the Everest of the Great Bull Market of 1982 to 2000. It would have seemed to him that he should ignore the gullies, streams, rivers, and depressions in between. The important thing was to get up there. And for that, all he had to do was just start walking.

In the 1990s, gussied up by low interest rates and a consumer-oriented society, the U.S. bull market went from strength to strength. Then, following the patterns of booms and busts throughout history, a bubble formed at the end of the period of prosperity. During the period from 1982 to 1999, the S&P 500 gained 19 percent per year, dividends included. In the later period—1994 to 1999—stocks did even better. The S&P 500 rose at 20 percent per year. Boomers were euphoric.

But it was only a dream. In the spring of 2000, Richard Russell began charting the end of the bubble and the commencement of a long, difficult, confusing bear market using what he called the "Top Out Parade": "Daily new highs topped out on Oct. 3, 1997 . . . the Advance/Decline ratio topped out on April 3, 1998 . . . transportation stocks topped out on May 12, 1999 . . . the NYSE Financial Average hit its peak the next day. Utilities topped out on June 16, 1999 . . . NYSE Composite topped out a month later. The Dow itself hit its all-time high on Jan. 14, 2000, at 11,722.98. The Nasdaq have peaked on March 10 at 5,048.62. And the S&P topped out on the 24th of March at 1,527."[15]

The bubble had popped. Market after market, sector after sector, stock after stock—all hit their highs and began a permanent reversal. Yet investors still could not imagine anything but rising stocks. Encouraged by TV, books, magazines, cocktail chatter, and the Internet, they became convinced that they need not worry about stock prices going down. Not that the stock market was necessarily immune from downturns, but that "over the long run stocks always go up." Jeremy Siegel had argued this point persuasively in his book, *Stocks for the Long Run.*

Few seemed to recall that, in the past, periods of falling stock prices had lasted for many years. A Mr. Kurt Leln of St. Paul, Minnesota, tried to warn his fellow investors. In a letter to *Barron's,* he explained that in 1954 the Dow was still 27 percent lower than it had been 25 years earlier. And, in 1982, the Dow was actually 22 percent lower than it had been in 1966. "I suspect that many of today's investors would consider it a disaster if the Dow fell to 8500 next year," wrote Mr. Leln, "I can only imagine their reaction if history were to repeat itself, leaving the Dow still hovering around the 8500 level in the year 2025."[16]

The Dow did indeed fall to 8,500 . . . 8,567.39 to be exact on September 26, 2001 . . . and farther still to 7,997.12 the same date, the following year. But the United States' new investors did not consider it a disaster. Not quite. They were doomed by the "success" of the 18-year bull market. The more seriously they believed that buy and hold really worked, the more certain they all were to lose money.

The average boomer came of prime "stock-buying" age in the year when all good things seemed not just possible, but inevitable. At the height of the boom, "buy and hold," "don't fight the Fed," "in the market for the long-term" were taken as truths. Why not take some of that extra income and let it ride in the market? A man could even imagine himself retiring young. He did not need to crunch numbers, he just had to tote them up. At 18 percent per year compounded growth in common shares, a 47-year-old with $100,000 in a 401(k) could see himself retiring at age 59 with a $1 million retirement account.

With so much imaginary wealth coming his way, he saw no reason to hold back on the little real spending power he actually had.

But just a few years later, the math got harder. He could not expect 18 percent . . . or 15 percent . . . or even 12 percent per year on his stock investments. Warren Buffett said he could expect only 6 percent to 7 percent from his stocks over the next 5 to 10 years. PIMCO's Bill Gross said the number would be about 6 percent. Jeremy Grantham told *Barron's* that 5 percent is the most reasonable number. And given the demographic shift about to take place in the United States, even those numbers are wishful thinking.

Bad Moon Rising

Three little numbers at the end of the world:

1. Average age of American baby boomers on January 1, 2009: 54.
2. Average amount in retirement plan: $50,000 or less.
3. Number of years at 6 percent growth to reach comfortable retirement income: 63.

But wait, there is one more number that may be important:

4. Amount of money in U.S. Social Security "Trust" Fund: $0. Or less.

We do not believe in crunching numbers. Nor do we flatten them, twist them, inflate them, or torture them into more appealing shapes. We just take them as they are, however disagreeable.

Painting by the preceding numbers produces no great work of art . . . rather a monstrous futuristic tableau. Something Goya might have done on a bad day . . . or Andre Serano on a good one. The scene is much the same all over the Western world: More and more people are getting older and older. And, as discussed earlier, Japan is the trend-setter. Its people are about 10 years older than most of those of most Western nations. So, we now wonder, what happens when whole populations get old? We look to Japan for an answer . . . and do not like what we see. And then we remember something worse: The average Japanese householder never invested heavily in stocks . . . and never stopped saving. The picture in the United States may be even uglier.

What would happen, we wonder, if the great U.S. baby boomer turned a little Japanese in the coming years? What if he figured he could not wait 49 more years to build his nest egg? What if he decided to cut back on his spending, pay down his debts, and add to his savings?

What happens to corporate profits when their products stop selling? What happens to consumer prices when the world's consumers of last resort stop consuming? And what happens if stocks do not bottom out in the next few months . . . and then do not begin a slow recovery—5 percent to 7 percent per year—as everyone expects? What if the New York Dow tracks its distant Tokyo cousin and closes at 2,700 in the year 2012? In short, what happens to the world economy when aging baby boomers start to act their age?

The Cowles Foundation study gives us a pretty good indication: Based on demographics alone, you can expect U.S. stocks to decline for the next 18 years. And you can expect consumers to start saving. The importance of this study is not that it gives us a startling conclusion; rather, it gives us an expected one. Nature corrects everything, sooner or later: the boomers and their stock market along with everything else.

The study shows a strong correlation between age and P/E ratios. "The results that we obtain," say the authors of the study in their introduction, "strongly support the view that changes in demographic structure induce significant changes in security prices—and in a way that is robust to variations in the underlying parameters." Buying patterns of investors as they age can explain the 20-year bull market . . . and portend an extended decline for the foreseeable future. "We obtain variations in the price-earnings ratios which approximate those observed in the U.S. over the last 50 years," the authors explain, "and in line with recent work of Campbell and Shiller (2001), the model supports the view that a substantial fall in the price-earnings ratio is likely in the next 20 years."

"Income of an individual is small in youth, high in middle age and small or nonexistent in retirement," they explain, and these results are consistent with findings by Harry Dent and Ya-Gui Wei. Further according to the study, demographics are the most critical factor in determining long-term market trends, as investment behavior largely depends on age-related patterns. The report finds that younger adults, from 20 to 39, tend to be consumers, that middle-aged people, 40 to 59, generally invest in shares, and that retirees (60+) are more likely to sell shares than buy them: "They seek to borrow in youth, invest in equity and bonds in middle age, and live on this middle-age investment in their retirement." The study also holds that the relative numbers of people in each of these three life stages strongly affects market performance.

How does this explain stock market performance in the United States since the 1970s? The 1970s and 1980s were periods of high consumption and high spending. The boomers were young adults; that is what you would expect from them. Share prices began to rise in the 1980s through 1999, exactly the period when boomers were middle-aged. Predictably, as was the case in Japan, the stock market peaked in 2000, the year when the ratio of middle-aged to younger adults was at its peak. Accordingly, sales of stocks by boomers as they enter retirement should continue to outweigh the purchases being made by the next generation as they approach middle age. The study predicts that while the market may rally periodically, its overall direction will be downward until around 2018.[17]

One of the sustaining rumors of the boom on Wall Street was that these millions of baby boomers were pouring billions of dollars into 401(k)s and other stock market investment programs in anticipation of retirement. This gush of money was supposed to carry the Dow to 36,000 in what Harry Dent called "the greatest boom in history." Dent may have guessed high, but it was, in fact, the greatest boom in history.

Which is also why it should be followed by history's greatest bust.

The New Math Catches Up

By all measures, the Dow at 11,722 was overpriced. At 14,279 it was absurd. Nobel Prize-winning economist, James Tobin, developed something known as "q" to determine just how overpriced the market was.

The idea is simple. A company should be worth what it would cost to replace it. The q ratio, which has the market price as the numerator of a fraction and the replacement cost as the denominator, should, therefore, be 1. Smithers and Wright, applied the concept of q to the entire stock market, and discovered that if the market were to follow the example of the 1973 to 1974 bear market, it would fall below 4,000. Whereas, if it were to follow the pattern of the post-1929 bust, the Dow would have to fall below 2,000.

The new math is catching up with the boomer generation. As Buffett and many others pointed out, since 1792, American financial markets have suffered at least eight major bear markets that have lasted, on average, about 14 years: 1802 to 1829, 1835 to 1842, 1847 to 1859, 1872 to 1877, 1881 to 1896, 1902 to 1921, 1929 to 1942, and 1966 to 1982.

The average loss of these eight bear markets would have cost investors nearly 6 percent per year for more than 14 years. If this bear market were to follow the pattern of its predecessors, prices might not stop falling for another dozen years. If it were to follow the pattern of the two bear markets that kicked off the two preceding centuries— 1802, 1902—it would not be over for another 20 years.

An investor, who bought at the top in 2007 at 35 years of age, might be 55 before his investments return to their original value. Arguably, an investor who still wears his baseball cap backward can wait out the down cycles. Over the long run, he can say to himself, I'll come out ahead. But an investor approaching retirement looks at his finances with a greater sense of alarm. Usually, he will forgo the incremental gains from stocks, if there are any, in favor of the surer returns from bonds, mortgage lending, or rents.

People are not idiots, not even baby boomers. They know they need to set money aside for the future. So, when capital gains disappear, they have to compensate somehow. For a while, of course, they can tell themselves that the market will come back and that the capital gains will return. And, maybe the market will cooperate—for a while. But the arithmetic is unrelenting.

PENSION PLAN POISON

After the stock market began to fall in 2000, private pension benefits became increasingly vulnerable. Having invested in stocks with the same reckless confidence as the individual investors, corporate pension plans are in trouble.

For example, Eric Fry, then chief of Apogee Research, pointed out that during the fiscal year ending October 31, 2001, Deere & Company, the tractor manufacturing company, expected its pension plan and post-retirement benefit plans to produce investment gains of $657 million. Instead, these plans had losses of $1.4 billion, a difference of more than $2 billion, bringing Deere's underfunded pension liability to more than $3 billion.

Likewise, General Motors reported that assets in its U.S. pension plan had dropped by 10 percent in 2002, meaning that the company's after-tax pension expense could rise by about $1 billion, or $1.80 a share, in 2003. Standard & Poor's promptly downgraded GM's credit rating because "poor pension investment portfolio returns have contributed to a huge increase in GM's already-large unfunded pension liability." Today, GM is in a whole different category of hurt, as we'll see in the next chapter.

During the bull market of the 1990s, outsized investment returns created a "cookie jar" full of excess earnings. One way or another, America's creative CFOs made sure these excesses found their way onto the income statement, helping to flatter the reported earnings results—including the returns on pension funds invested in the market.

Alas, just as stocks go up, so they go down. The bear market in the early part of the twenty-first century brought the practice of pension fund investment to a screeching halt. Most of the corporate pension plans that once enjoyed a plump surplus now find themselves badly underfunded. According to David Zion, an accounting analyst at CSFB, of the 360 companies in S&P's 500 Index with defined pension-benefit plans, 240 had underfunded schemes at the end of 2001.

In a bear market, corporations can no longer take a portion of their pension plans' stock market gains and book it as profit. Many companies will have to contribute cash to make up the pension deficits as a priority *before* investing in their business, paying down debt, repurchasing shares, or making other moves to benefit investors. Here again, supposedly capitalist companies end up working for retired workers rather than for shareholders.

By 2002, the S&P 500 companies' pension-fund deficits totaled more than $300 billion. Many of these funds managed to dig themselves out of a giant hole between 2002 and 2007. As long as the reflation trade was at play in the stock market, corporate pension systems looked as though they would be able to carry out their mandate. At the end of 2007, companies in the S&P 500 had a combined pension-plan surplus of about $60 billion, according to David Zion, accounting analyst at Credit Suisse. The market sell-off in the nine months to late

September 2008 turned that into a combined deficit of about $75 billion, he estimated.[18]

Merrill Lynch, meanwhile, estimated in a recent report that pension hits could cut expected 2009 earnings at General Motors (GM) by 79 percent, while leading to a 35 percent reduction at Con Edison (ED) and a 24 percent decline at New York Times Co.[19]

The upending of the financial system could also force companies to rethink long-term return assumptions, which now average about 8 percent; all too rosy given that over the past 10 years, the S&P 500 has actually lost about 12 percent, for an annual return of about negative 0.6 percent.

If the stock market isn't going to provide retirement security, what will?

SOCIAL SECURITY? NOT EXACTLY

The first public retirement pension scheme was created by Otto von Bismarck in 1880 Germany. Fifty years later, during the Great Depression, Franklin Roosevelt followed suit in the United States. As we've seen, the number of people expected to reach the retirement age of 65 was not considered to pose a threat to future funding. Life expectancy in 1935, in the United States, for example, was 76.9 for men. Workers relying on the plan for retirement would not receive much each month and were not expected to live long enough to drain the system.

When Social Security was founded, the typical U.S. worker at age 65 could expect to live another 11.9 years. But if today's official projections are right, by the year 2040 the typical 65-year-old worker can expect to live at least another 19.2 years. If the normal retirement age had been indexed to longevity since 1935, today's worker would be waiting until age 73 to receive full benefits and tomorrow's workers even longer.[20]

In a report called "Demographics and Capital Markets Returns," Robert Arnott and Anne Casscells argue that the crisis is not in Social Security, but in demographics. "When an entire society ages," suggest Arnott and Casscells, ". . . the thing that matters most is the ratio between the workers to retirees. Unfortunately, the aging of the baby boom generation, which is a significant bulge in population, will cause a dramatic increase in the ratio between workers to retirees, one that will put enormous strain on society and cause friction between generations."

In the United States, as in other developed countries, the unfunded benefit liability for public pensions amounts to 100 percent to 250 percent of GDP. It is a "hidden debt" far greater than official public debt. Unlike in the private sector, these debts are not amortized as expenses over 30 to 40 years.[21] And it may be worth pointing out that under normal conditions economies do not run such crushing deficits. They only do so in crisis mode.

The annual cost of Social Security benefits represented 4.4 percent of GDP in 2008 and is projected to increase to 6.2 percent of GDP in 2034, and then decline to about 5.8 percent of GDP by 2050 and remain at about that level.[22]

A Bubble in Health Care

And to the retiring boomers' other doubts and insecurities, we might add that U.S. health care costs are expected to rise by 7 percent of GDP over the next 40 years—a rate that is more than twice as fast as other developing nations. The "old old,"—those aged 80 and over—are predicted to rise sharply through 2050 and will dramatically increase long-term care costs as well as disability, dependence, and health care expenses.

In fact, by official projections, in 2030, the U.S. government will be spending more on nursing homes than it spends on Social Security today. "Although people justifiably worry about Social Security," says Victor Fuchs, an economist who studies the health care industry, "paying for old folks' health care is the real 800-pound gorilla facing the U.S. economy."[23] Adding projections for Medicare and Medicaid's expenditures to those of Social Security could raise the total cost to more than 50 percent of payroll taxes.[24]

The fiscal kickers of health cost inflation and political demand for more long-term care benefits threaten to raise public spending dramatically in the United States. Between 2005 and the fall of 2008, we spent two and a half years chronicling the efforts of David Walker, the former comptroller general of the United States, and Bob Bixby, executive director of the Concord Coalition, to reign in reform and shore up the Social Security and Medicare systems. The project yielded a feature length documentary film, which earned us a trip to the Sundance Film Festival in January of 2008 and another to the Critic's Choice Awards in Los Angeles a year later. We published a best-selling companion book of the same title in late 2008. You're encouraged to delve into the numbers we presented in the film and book. They're truly mindboggling. But in many ways the project was dated the moment we released it to the public.

The credit crisis that reached a fever pitch developed in 2008 pushed the date of insolvency of these programs ever closer. On May 13, 2009, the Medicare Trustees warned that the fund they tap to pay for beneficiaries' hospital care will be insolvent by 2017—two years earlier than trustees had predicted the year before. The program has been paying out more than it collects in taxes and interest since last year, in part due to a recession well underway.[25]

Medicare would have to deposit $13.4 trillion—$1 trillion higher than last year's estimate—into an interest-earning account today in order for the hospital fund to pay its scheduled benefits over the next 75 years.[26]

The program's total unfunded obligation, which includes doctor and prescription drug benefits, is $37.8 trillion. The trustees estimated that in coming years, Medicare spending will rise faster than workers' earnings or the economy as a whole.[27]

Trustees say that while the financial standing of Social Security decreased more sharply than Medicare last year, the health program remains at greater risk of insolvency. The financial difficulties facing Social Security and Medicare pose serious challenges, the report concluded.[28]

For Social Security, the reform options are relatively well understood but the choices are difficult. Medicare is a bigger challenge. Its cost growth can be contained without sacrificing quality of care only if health care cost growth more generally is contained. But despite the difficulties—indeed, because of the difficulties—it is essential that action be taken soon, particularly to control health care costs.

After the revised Social Security and Medicare announcement the world began to wonder: Can the United States hold onto its AAA credit rating?

"The U.S. government has had a triple-A credit rating since 1917," David Walker, now president and CEO of the Peterson G. Peterson Foundation, commented in the *Financial Times* following the release of the Trustees report, "but it is unclear how long this will continue to be the case. In my view, either one of two developments could be enough to cause us to lose our top rating.

"First, while comprehensive health care reform is needed, it must not further harm our nation's financial condition. Doing so would send a signal that fiscal prudence is being ignored in the drive to meet societal wants, further mortgaging the country's future.

"Second, failure by the federal government to create a process that would enable tough spending, tax and budget control choices to be made after we turn the corner on the economy would send a signal that our political system is not up to the task of addressing the large, known and growing structural imbalances confronting us."[29]

Of course, we must note that the whole credit rating biz is . . . well . . . corrupt. The agencies that are responsible for dishing out sovereign credit ratings (S&P, Fitch, and Moody's) are the same ones that left us all out to dry in 2007. (Of course, mortgage-backed securities get a AAA . . . housing prices never fall!) Rest assured, if Wall Street can buy its way into AAA, Uncle Sam surely can, too.

But even Moody's is starting to hedge their bets. They've since created three subdivisions within their AAA rating: resistant, resilient, and vulnerable . . . a corporate way of saying the good, the bad, and the ugly. While the United States isn't in the worst of the bunch, it's certainly not the best.

THE PANIC OF 2008

The ratings agencies were complicit in the making of the crisis that spooked the credit markets in the fall of 2008. But it was capitalism itself that bore the brunt of the abuse. "Bankruptcy of Neo-Capitalism," shouted a headline in the French press on September 26, 2008, barely a week after Lehman Brothers declared bankruptcy. Scarcely since Hitler blew his brains out has the type been bigger or the contentment broader.

Almost everyone everywhere was enjoying the show. Each headline brought more laughs. The financial markets give people neither what they expect nor what they want, but what they deserve. What a treat it was to see people getting it—good and hard. That galling "millionaire next door"? Many will take pleasure in seeing his portfolio of

The Case-Shiller Index of House Prices: 1988–2008

— U.S. National, index level (left)
---- U.S. National, % change (right)

Nationally, home prices are back
to their late 2002 levels

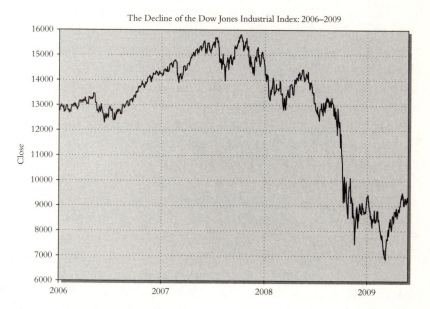

The Decline of the Dow Jones Industrial Index: 2006–2009

FIGURE 8.5 Hard New Math

Beginning with housing market collapse, as indicated here by the Case-Shiller Index of house prices (top), and the plunge in stock values, seen here in the decline of the Dow Jones Industrial Index (below), many planners began to question the security of their formerly pristine retirements. Seemingly, all at once, the "wealth effect" was thrown into reverse.

Source: Standard & Poor's and Fiserv.

stocks marked down. "Stocks for the long run," he used to say, smugly; the silly old coot will be dead before his stocks come back! He'll have to work until he drops dead, just like the rest of us.

On Wall Street, the masters of the universe—who had the pay slips to prove it!—began getting blown up by their own debt bombs. The top five firms on Wall Street were thought to be "too big to fail." But Bear Stearns had been blown to smithereens. Lehman exploded into small pieces. Merrill ducked and missed the blast. Then, the last big capitalist desperadoes—J.P. Morgan and Goldman—waved the white flag. They petitioned the government to allow them to become regulated, deposit-taking banks!

The takeover of Fannie and Freddie alone left half the country living in what are effectively government-subsidized housing projects. Meanwhile, the coordinated takeover of Wall Street, put together by his apparatchiks, left even the hardened socialists at France's Liberation in shock and awe: "This enormous statist intervention . . . is the work of the most ideological and extremist administration that the U.S. has ever had."

How heartwarming to see that the meddlers and world-improvers get a second wind. It was like driving around in a 1933 Lincoln . . . or throwing rocks at the gendarmes in 1968. The old, gray Bolshies feel young again! Impetuous! Brainless!

All the capitalists were behind the bailout program, too. All over the world, markets are out—state-sponsored meddling is in. Free market principles are fine, until prices start going down!

And there was the breathtaking chutzpah of it! After proposing a $700 billion program, in which the government buys up Wall Street's mistakes—otherwise known as "cash for trash"—Henry Paulson claimed he had no choice. "We did this to protect the taxpayer," said the former Goldman chief.[30]

Even Russia got into the act. New to counterfeit capitalism, it's getting the hang of it fast, pledging $20 billion in the fight to keep stock prices from falling to what they are really worth.

Then, not to be left behind in general hysterical absurdity, SEC honcho Christopher Cox announced a list of 799 financial stocks on which shorting was banned until October 2. In Britain, the FSA's ban on shorting financial shares lasted until January 16. But Pakistan got the King Canute Memorial Prize; by law in that benighted land, stocks can't go below their August 27 close.[31]

And what a bunch of numbskulls—Greenspan, Paulson, and Bernanke! Every word they've said so far has been financial poison. Greenspan relaxed about house prices in 2005, then decided that most negatives in housing were probably behind us in October 2006.

In April 2007, Paulson said of the subprime woes: It's "not a serious problem . . . I think it's going to be largely contained."[32] "We believe the effect of the troubles in the subprime sector . . . will be likely limited . . . ," said Bernanke in May 2007.[33]

But these are the same numbskulls who now say they are saving capitalism from itself. Ah, there's the rub . . . amid all this giddy merriment is a serious threat. The feds have bailed out the bankers, the insurers, the mortgage lenders, and half of Wall Street. But who will bail out the feds?

Since 1971, the world's money system rests on the dollar. And the dollar rests on nothing but faith, hope, and the kindness of strangers. And while the full faith and credit of the United States of America is elastic, it can snap.

For the last 15 years, the U.S. money supply has grown about twice as fast as GDP. Federal government liabilities, meanwhile, have grown three times as fast. As a result, the United States now has more financial obligations than assets. It is, effectively, broke. Nevertheless, the debit side of its ledgers grow heavier and heavier. This year's U.S. government deficit in 2009 will reach an estimated $1.8 trillion. Deficits, we have been warned, will run in the trillion-plus range for several years to come. The U.S. trade deficit is about $700 billion. The U.S. bailout plan will probably cost at least $1 trillion more.

Where will the government get that kind of money? There are only two possibilities—one honest and depressing, the other corrupt and alarming. Whether it borrows the money, or prints it up, the world enjoys no net increase in financial resources. Borrowing takes resources from projects that might have been worthwhile and diverts them to the losers. Interest rates rise, as a consequence of the extra borrowing; higher rates generally worsen the economic picture. And while the United States borrows, long term at almost 5 percent, it lends at barely 2 percent. It's like a bank that has gotten its business model badly mixed up. The more it borrows and lends, the faster it goes broke.

If, on the other hand, it merely prints the money—or if it creates it "out of thin air," to use Lord Keynes' handy phrase—the results are even worse. Inflating the money supply with new currency, à la Argentina or Zimbabwe, wipes out debts. But it destroys faith in the dollar and brings down the whole world's money system.

Sooner or later, this is just what will probably happen. Not because capitalism doesn't work, but because it does. Capitalism is doing just what it should do—it is separating fools from their money. But the fools vote. After a big bubble, there are more fools than sages . . . and, in the United States, more debtors than creditors. Sooner or later, Americans will realize that they are better off destroying their own money than preserving it . . . and that they would prefer to stiff their creditors rather than pay their bills.

That is when deflation will give way to inflation . . . and the world's post-1971 dollar-based money system comes to an end.

CROWDING OUT

The run-up of deficits and debt poses an even greater threat to the prospect of recovery itself. If consumers can't spend and corporations can't borrow, the conventional wisdom goes, government must spend to make up the difference. But that act "crowds out" productive investment in the real economy. Patrick Cox, editor of *Breakthrough Technology Report* explained the concept in an e-mail to us early in May of 2009:

> There is, at any time, a finite amount of capital available for investment. When government borrows, creating debt, it does two things. First, it ties up existing capital that would otherwise be invested in new businesses and technologies. This is, using economists' jargon, the "crowding out" effect. Second, because taxpayers are liable for this debt, it reduces future disposable incomes as well as capital.
>
> The crowding out effect means that there [is] less capital available for the new businesses and technologies that are responsible for economic growth and job creation. If government creates enough debt, growth falters and fails. In recent decades, we've seen it happen over and over again outside the United States. Many Americans, though, don't believe or care, apparently, that it can happen here.

The current government is involved in an unprecedented program of instant gratification; shopaholic politics. The very purpose of the stimulus bill is to avoid paying the price for expanding debt irresponsibly in the past. The most relevant example is the Community Reinvestment Act that made taxpayers liable for almost unimaginably massive subprime mortgages that were bound to fail as soon as the housing bubble popped. The cure for this banking collapse, however, is more of the same debt that sent the economy into the doldrums initially.

The great irony is that the only people who can reduce the pain that politicians have inflicted on us all are wealthy investors. Pension funds don't invest in the transformational breakthrough technologies that can fuel the growth we need now. That's the domain of "the rich" investors who are demonized by the class warriors in the current administration. As far as I'm concerned, those who deny or do not understand this simple fact are disqualified from adult status.

Like a lot of us who did our best to steer America from our current crisis, I'm tired of arguing and I'm tired of explaining to people whose tribal partisanship trumps all reason. The most moral and heroic activity today is the placement of capital into the technologies that can save our collective glutes from the wealth-destroying shopaholic politicians and their tax-recipient supporters. A lot of people don't deserve to be saved but that's always been the downside of capitalism. Wasn't it JFK who said, a rising tide lifts all boats . . . even those loaded with envy-driven class warriors and self-righteous leaches?

WHAT ABOUT AUSTERITY?

"Within the billions of sentences about the financial bailout," Juan Enrique and Jorge Dominguez wondered in the *Boston Globe* opinion editorial on October 1, 2008, "there is one word notably absent, austerity. All talk is of payments, supports, subsidies, incurring more debt, stimulus packages. The thesis seems to be: If only we spend more the party can go on. True, only if the financial meltdown is a temporary mismatch and dislocation in housing and credit markets. But suppose there is something fundamentally wrong with the U.S. economy. Then spending more will not fix it. Getting the diagnosis right means getting the treatment right. It may save us a trillion or two."[34]

Enriquez is a Harvard-trained MBA, an entrepreneur, and a scientist. He's concerned that government bailouts and stimulus spending might permanently damage the U.S. economy and prevent the development of programs, therapies, and treatments that would reign in health care costs . . . averting the largest portion of the entitlement crisis bearing down on the West. As an alternative Enriquez suggests:

> The United States requires a massive restructuring to address its debt, cutting back on its borrowing, spending, and wars. The bailout package is essential to keep the credit markets open. But absent sentences that include the word austerity all the bailout will accomplish is a temporary postponement. Bailout and stimulus are a stopgap.
>
> A solution requires the country to begin to spend what it earns, reduce its mountainous debt, and address massive liabilities, restructure Social Security, pension deficits, military, and Medicare. No wonder politicians would rather spend more of your money now rather than address these problems. Because we have been spending 5 to 7 percent more each year than we earn, a forced restructuring, triggered by a currency collapse, would have the same effect on wages and purchasing power that the housing collapse had on housing prices.[35]

People do not choose to grow old—neither individually nor collectively. But that is what happens to them. As near as we can tell, a person, like an entire economy, can only prevent a natural decline by making things unnaturally worse. A man can always stop the aging process by blowing himself up, for example, just as a central bank can avoid deflation by destroying its currency, and an economy can defer a debt correction by inducing people to borrow more.

In the long run, the Social Security system will blow up, too. For it is founded on a lie—that you can get something for nothing; that a person can get more out of the system than he put into it. And while this may be true for some people, it cannot be true in the aggregate. The illusion depends on ever-larger groups of workers to pay for retirees' benefits. In fact, that hope is at the heart of the whole baby boomer illusion: Not only do they expect the next generation to support them through the Social Security system, they also expect to sell their homes and their stocks to the younger group, at a profit. But sooner or later, the next generation will balk. It will not be big enough or rich enough to give the boomers what they expect.

In this respect, as in so many others, Americans think they have an edge on the Japanese. Unlike Japan, the United States still allows immigrants the privilege of coming in and working their duffs off to support the aging, indigenous population.

Immigration, it is widely believed, will save the day. But, Arnott and Casscells suggest that it would take 4 million new immigrants a year—or an increase of 1.5 percent of the U.S. population per year to protect the system. That is roughly double the figures for current immigration levels, which is not likely to happen.

The boomers in the vanguard are now 63 years old. Behind them trail 80 million Americans, few of whom have taken the challenge of retirement planning seriously: 80 percent of the population has no more than eight months' worth of financial reserves. The "50-Plus Population Not Prepared for Retirement" says an AARP Report. And the number of those not prepared for retirement is swelling faster than their lower extremities. Bank in 2000, about 76 million Americans—or 28 percent—were older than 50. By 2020, projections still show 40 million more in that group, amounting to 36 percent of the population.

Approaching retirement, we suspect that very soon baby boomers will discover savings as they once discovered sex, drugs, and rock and roll. They may even come to like the idea . . . and think they invented it. And perhaps they will even do it (like everything else they do) to excess.

Even a small dose of thrift could have a dramatic effect on the overall economy. Every one percent change of the savings rate equals roughly 0.6 percent of GDP. Writing for the American Enterprise Institute, John Makin figured that if boomers were to save, rather than spend, at only one third the prevailing real rate of the 1990s—that is, at 5 percent—they would have to forgo $350 billion of spending each year. This would subtract 3.5 percent from the GDP—effectively guaranteeing recession for many years to come.

Personal Savings as a Percentage of Disposable Income 1929–2009

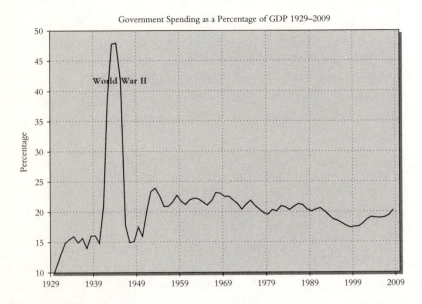

Government Spending as a Percentage of GDP 1929–2009

FIGURE 8.6 America in Crisis

During the 1930s and 1940s, the last time the U.S. economy faced a housing crisis, collapsing stock market and war, the personal savings rate skyrocketed to more than 25 percent (top); government spending increased to nearly one-half of the GDP (middle); and deficits increased to nearly 13 percent of the GDP (bottom). If the savings rate in the United States today were to revert to only half the postwar average, it would plunge the nation "into the deepest longest recession since WW II." And so it goes.

Source: BEA.

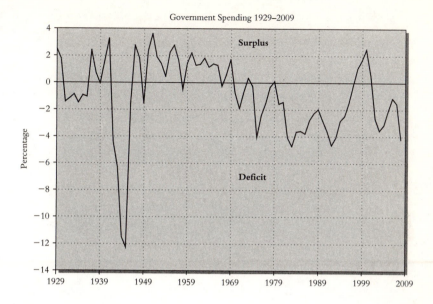

FIGURE 8.6 *(continued)*

The late Kurt Richebächer did the math, too. He found that if the savings rate were to revert to only half the postwar average it would make for the deepest and longest recession since WWII[36] (see Figure 8.6). Sure enough, looks like his projections were accurate.

CHAPTER 9

MORAL HAZARDS

We cannot guarantee success, but we can deserve it.

—George Washington

Not infrequently, governments "shoot themselves in the foot." But in 2009, they have brought out the biggest cannon in history. We look on with amusement as they blow their fool heads off.

Readers are reminded of our Daily Reckoning dicta: "The force of a correction is equal and opposite to the deception that preceded it." Now, we offer a corollary: "The greatness of a depression is commensurate to the government's efforts to prevent it."

Since these iron laws seem to contradict almost everything one hears on the subject, the burden of proof is on us. So, to the witness stand, we call our first expert, Angela Merkel. Alone among the world leaders, she seems to have kept her head:

"The crisis did not come about because we issued too little money but because we created economic growth with too much money, and it was not sustainable," explains Germany's chancellor. She went on to suggest that maybe we shouldn't repeat the errors of the past.[1]

As a proxy for "deception" in our handy dictum, substitute "money." And now consider it in its two misleading forms—credit and deficit spending. "Credit not backed by real savings is a fraud," the great economist, Kurt Richebächer, used to say. It is a fraud when it comes not from willing lenders, but from central banks, artificially reducing lending rates in order to spur the economy. Deficit spending by government is a flimflam, too. Governments rarely have extra funds to spare; they have to borrow the money. Eventually, that debt will have to be paid.

During the entire last half century, leading Western economists imagined a world that couldn't exist for one minute—where consuming wealth makes people wealthier . . . and where simply making more credit available can stimulate consumption. Each time the economy slowed down, the authorities induced people to buy more of what they didn't need with more money they didn't have. This produced "growth." But it was an ersatz growth. Every dollar of borrowed money would one day have to be paid back. Every step forward would have to be followed, eventually, by another one to the rear.

In the first four U.S. recessions after the Great Depression, from the mid-1930s through the mid-1950s, the total amount of monetary stimulus was actually negative. Instead of lowering rates, the feds—witless, as usual—often increased them or left them alone. But deficit spending went up an average of 2.2 percent of GDP each time. Later, the feds began to get the hang of it; every recession after 1958 was met with both more credit and more spending.

As the feds put in more money and credit, they found that more money and credit was needed. At the beginning of the period an extra $2 of credit would result in $1 of extra GDP. By the time the lights went out in 2007, it took about $6 of additional credit to produce a single extra dollar of output. Each new dollar of credit had to support not only the new growth the feds were after, but all the accumulated debt and mistakes from previous stimulus programs.

In the recession of 1973, Brookings Institution economist George Perry told Congress that "we should be pulling out all the stops" to fix it. The resulting fiscal and monetary stimulus program cost the United States 4 percent of GDP, according to an estimate by Jim Grant. Future generations of Fed governors and Treasury secretaries found more stops . . . and, of course, pulled them out, too. In the micro recession of 2001, for example, the combined fiscal and monetary boost amounted to 7.2 percent of GDP, according to Grant.[2]

The deceptions of the bubble epoque, 2001–2007, were enormous. The correction has been enormous, too. And here are the same economists who mismanaged the economy, offering advice to governments who mismanaged their regulatory roles, about how to keep mismanaged companies alive, so that bondholders who mismanaged their investments might not go broke. That this will result in more misery is a foregone conclusion—at least, here at the Daily Reckoning. The measure of that misery, if our iron law holds, is how adamantly governments fight to keep their mismanagement going. Just looking at the numbers, the toll will be monstrous. All over the world, interest rates have been cut and budgets padded. France's deficit is running at 8 percent of GDP. England is running a deficit of more than 12 percent of GDP. And the United States is mobilizing as if it had been attacked by Martians. On the credit side, the feds have cut rates more than ever before, for a monetary boost equivalent to 18 percent of GDP, according to Grant. As to spending, $13 trillion has been pledged . . . an amount equivalent to a full year's annual output of the United States. This response is three times more (adjusted to today's dollars) than the United States spent to fight WWII. It is 12 times more (relative to GDP) than the total committed to fight the Great Depression.

What will happen next?

In this chapter, we turn our attention to the future—not that we get to peek at tomorrow's newspapers. We know no more about what will happen than the forecasters at the Federal Reserve or at the Dial-A-Psychic Hotline. Recently, a news item told us that the Dial-A-Psychic business was doing so well, the companies needed to hire new people to take the phone calls. "Will Train" said their help wanted ads. We thought about answering the ad. For as hard as we have tried, we have never been able to master the skill on our own.

Lacking clairvoyance, we take a guess.

THE AGE OF UNCERTAINTY

Early in the twentieth century, Albert Einstein upset the world with his Relativity Theory. All of a sudden, there were no fixed positions; everything seemed unhinged . . . loose. It is all relative, people said. Nothing was absolutely this or that, right or wrong, here or there. And then Heisenberg's Indeterminacy Principle came along, and even Einstein had had enough. Not only are there no absolutes, said

Heisenberg, but you could not know it even if there were. Everything is in motion, he pointed out; you can figure out where an object is, or its speed, but not both. And the process of trying to figure it out cannot help but change the readings! "God does not play dice," Einstein protested. After Einstein and Heisenberg, the world had begun to look like a giant crap game. You throw the dice and hope for the best; what else can you do?

The idea of an uncertain, unknowable universe did not please Einstein; he spent the rest of his life trying to prove it was not so. But Einstein and Heisenberg proved the latter's point. Trying to describe the world, they changed it. "A kind of madness gained hold . . . " wrote Stefan Zweig of Germany in the 1930s. The whole nation seemed to come unhinged by the realization that nothing was quite what they thought it was.

Today, we hear the rattle of dice everywhere. People warm up the dice for another throw. What are the odds of this . . . or that . . . they wonder.

The odds of a huge meteorite destroying lower Manhattan, we assume, are fairly low—as remote as the odds of Osama bin Laden winning a Nobel Peace Prize. Anything can happen, but some things are more likely than others. As Heisenberg warns us, however, as soon as we try to figure these things out, we distort the odds.

That is the strange perversity of the marketplace. As people come to believe that something will happen, the odds of making any money at it go down. Herein lies the difference between hard science and human science. When humans realize that a market event is forthcoming, likely as not, it has already happened. As people come to believe they can get rich by buying stocks, for example, they disturb the universe—they buy stocks and run up prices. Then, the higher the stock prices go, the more people believe in them, and prices go still higher. At some point, because this cannot go on forever, stocks eventually reach their peaks—at almost precisely the point when people are most sure they can get rich by buying them.

This point was reached in the United States somewhere between fall 1999 and March 2000. A kind of madness had taken hold.

Almost all market forecasters were wrong over the next three years; they overwhelmingly thought stocks would go up, not down—especially in 2002, as stocks "almost never go down three years in a row."

Abby Cohen, Ed Yardeni, Louis Rukeyser, James Glassman, Jeremy Siegel, Peter Lynch—all the big names from the 1990s—still believed that stocks would go up, if not last year or this year . . . certainly the next. They seemed completely unaware that their own bullishness had tilted the odds against them. Talking up the bull market year after year, they had helped convince Mom and Pop that stocks for the long run were an almost foolproof investment. Now, the fools were having their way—proving that nothing fails like success.

In the last quarter of the twentieth century, nothing seemed to succeed better than U.S. consumer capitalism. Stocks began rising in 1975 . . . and continued, more or less, until March 2000. By then, all doubt had been removed. Americans had become believers in the stock market.

"To believe that stocks will be rotten again . . . ," wrote James Glassman, the unashamed author of *Dow 36,000* early in 2002, "is to believe that they will buck a strong tide that has been running in the same direction for more than 60 years."[3]

Glassman did not seem to notice that tides do not run in a single direction forever. They ebb and flow in equal amounts and opposite directions. Glassman was like a weather forecaster who never looked out the window. "It rains, but the sun comes out again. Stocks fall, but they always recover to a higher ground," he wrote. And then, he failed to mention, it rains again!

And if the sun shines long enough, people stop noticing clouds on the horizon. Who noticed, on those perfect days of early 2000, that the odds had changed; that the stock market had become very different from the stock market of 1975 and that the few investors who bought shares in 1975 were very different from the many Moms and Pops who put their money into stocks in 2000? Who noticed, as Buffett put it, that these people might have bought for the right reason in 1975—but that they bought for the wrong ones in 2000?

Millions of new investors entered the stock market in the last 25 years of the twentieth century, lured by Buffett's example, Rukeyser's spiel, and the appeal of getting something for nothing. Hardly a single one of them carried an umbrella.

When the market crashed, the little guys got wet, but they did not panic. They still believed—at least at the beginning of 2003—in the promise of U.S. consumer capitalism and its gurus. They believed the reasons given for why stocks were likely to rise . . . because they hardly ever go down four years in a row!

Stocks rarely go down four years in a row because, usually, after 36 months, they have almost always hit bottom. But at the beginning of 2003, stocks were still selling at prices more typical of a top than a bottom. Based on core earnings, S&P stocks were priced at 40 times earnings. Or, as *Barron's* calculated it, based on reported earnings in 2002, they sold at a P/E of 28. Either way, they were expensive.

While earnings were subject to interpretation, dividend yields were not; stocks yielded only 1.82 percent in dividends at the end of 2002. The number is important, partly because dividends do not lie, and partly because so much of the promise of the stock market actually reposes on earnings. For a hundred years, according to popular interpretation, stocks gained ground at a rate of 7 percent per year—beating bonds, real estate, old masters' paintings, everything. Little-noticed was the fact that five of those seven percentage points came from compounded earnings, not stock market appreciation. Take that away, and stocks would have underperformed several other asset classes, including bonds.

Dividends depend on earnings. As noted, earnings have been falling for the entire consumer capitalist period—since the 1960s. With falling earnings, it became more and more difficult for companies to maintain their dividend payments. As a percentage of earnings, dividends actually increased in the boom years, from about 35 percent in 1981 to more than 50 percent in 2001. And after 1997, profits took their worst dive since the Great Depression. How could investors reasonably expect dividends to increase? And without higher dividend payouts, how could they expect to match the returns of the past 100 years, let alone the returns of the last 25 years of the twentieth century? A retiree looking to live on 1.82 percent dividends would need $2 million invested in stocks to give him a $36,000 income. Yet, at the end of 2002, the average baby boomer had a grand total of $50,000 to invest.

The patsies hardly considered the issue. And who knows; maybe they will get lucky. Maybe stocks will go up. Maybe it is just luck, after all. Imagine the roar of laughter when Einstein arrived in heaven and God explained, "I don't have any plan . . . I just roll the damned dice!"

God can do what he wants, of course. We do not presume to know God's plan or his method.

But so what? As the existentialists tell us, we still have to get up in the morning and make decisions. Recognizing that we cannot know whether stocks will go up or down in the year ahead, what do we do?

We take a guess . . . and try to do the right thing. We might try to do the smart thing, but we are not that smart. All we can do is to try to protect ourselves from madness by following the most ancient and venerable traditions: the distilled wisdom of previous generations.

We guess that stocks are a bad investment, for very simple reasons: "The place to find a safe and remunerative investment is usually where others aren't looking for it,"[4] writes James Grant. Everybody is looking on Wall Street. So we will look elsewhere.

"Buy low, sell high," the old chestnut practically pops out of the pan toward us; the rule tells us the right thing to do. For the past 100 years or so, the average stock has sold for less than 15 times earnings (which used to be calculated more honestly). Almost any measure you take puts them at about twice that price today.

"A bear market continues until it comes to its end—at real values," says long-time observer Richard Russell. Stocks are real values when they sell for 8 to 10 times earnings, not 28 to 40 times. If stocks are destined to sell for 10 times earnings at some time in the future, why would we want to buy them today?

Of course, stocks could go up. And maybe they will. But we are not smart enough to know. So rather than roll the dice, we will follow the rule. And cross our fingers.

THE SCHOOL OF "OUGHT"

Your authors have a forecasting approach all their own. We do not try to figure out what will happen, for it is impossible to know. Instead, we look at what *ought* to happen. Without "will," we have only "ought" to do the work of forecasting. "People ought to get what they've got coming," we say to ourselves.

In the markets, they usually do.

A reasonable man expects things to happen that ought to happen. A fool ought to be separated from his money. A thief ought to go to jail. A man who abuses a child or double-crosses a friend ought to roast in hell. Whether they do or not is not up to us, of course . . . but we can hope. And what better way has a man of running his own life than figuring out what ought to happen and then making his decisions as if it really will? Of all the systems, secrets, formulas, charts, and graphs, and models that help a man invest, we have found none more rewarding than this: Assume what ought to happen will happen: Buy low, sell high . . . and don't worry about it too much.

But what ought to happen? Alas, it is not always easy to know . . .

"The great judge of the world," wrote Adam Smith in his *Theory of Moral Sentiments*, "has, for the wisest reasons, thought proper to interpose, between the weak eye of human reason, and the throne of his eternal justice, a degree of obscurity and darkness . . . [which] . . . renders the impression of it faint and feeble in comparison of what might be expected from the grandeur and importance of so mighty an object."

If "Ought" were a person, Ought would not be a bartender or a good-hearted prostitute. Ought is not the kind of word you would want to hang out with on a Saturday night, or relax with at home for it would always be reminding you to take out the trash or fix the garage door.

If it were a Latin noun, Ought would be feminine, but more like a shrewish wife than a willing mistress. For Ought is judgmental—a nag, a scold. Even the sound of it is sharp; it comes up from the throat like a dagger and heads right for soft tissue, remembering the location of weak spots and raw nerves for many years.

Ought is neither a good-time girl nor a boom-time companion, but more like the I-told-you-so who hands you aspirin on Sunday morning, tells you what a fool you were, and warns you what will happen if you keep it up. "You get what you deserve," she reminds you.

A man who lets himself be bossed around by Ought is no man at all, in our opinion. He is a dullard, a wimp, and a wuss—a logical, rational, reasonable lump. Thankfully, most men, most of the time, will not readily submit. Instead, they do not do what they ought to do, but what they want to do. Stirred up by mob sentiments or private desires, they make fools of themselves regularly. They cannot help themselves.

Of course, Ms. Ought is right; they get what they deserve. But sometimes it is worth it.

Modern economists no longer believe in Ought. They do not appreciate her moral tone and try to ignore her. To them, the economy is a giant machine with no soul, no heart . . . no right and no wrong. It is just a matter of finding the accelerator.

The nature of the economist's trade has changed completely in the past 200 years. Had he handed out business cards, Adam Smith's would have borne the professional inscription "Moral Philosopher," not "Economist." Smith saw God's "invisible hand" in the workings of the marketplace. Trying to understand how it worked, he looked for the Oughts everywhere. Everywhere and always people get what they deserve, Smith might have said. And if not . . . they ought to!

Today, the "Ought to" school of economics has few students and fewer teachers. Most economists consider it only one step removed from sorcery. But here at our offices on the rue de la Verrerie in Paris, the flame is still alive, flickering.

"Call it the overinvestment theory of recessions of 'liquidationism,' or just call it the 'hangover theory,'" Paul Krugman began his critique of the "Ought to" school. "It is the idea that slumps are the price we pay for booms, that the suffering the economy experiences during a recession is a necessary punishment for the excesses of the previous expansion . . .[5]

"Deep economic problems are supposed to be a punishment for deep economic sins," Krugman continued in June 1998.[6]

Krugman elaborated the concept in December of the same year. The "hangover theory," he called it—referring to the way a man feels after he has been on a drinking binge. The hangover theory is "disastrously wrongheaded," Krugman explains. "Recessions are not necessary consequences of booms. They can and should be fought, not with austerity but with liberality—with policies that encourage people to spend more, not less."[7]

What kind of world is it? Is it one in which a man can cure a hangover by getting drunk or get out of debt by borrowing more? Or is there a price to be paid for foolishness, collectively as well as individually?

Is the world just a fine-tuned machine where a capable public servant can simply turn a screw or tighten a knob to make history turn out the way he wants? Or is it an infinitely complicated, natural thing as prone to error as a mob of teenage delinquents.

"The hangover theory is perversely seductive—not because it offers an easy way out, but because it doesn't," Krugman continued in his December 1998 attack. "Powerful as these seductions may be, they must be resisted, for the hangover theory is disastrously wrongheaded," he concluded.

In Krugman's mechanistic world, there is no room for Ought. If the monetary grease monkeys after the Great Depression of the 1930s or in Japan of the 1990s had failed to get their machines working, it was not because there were invisible hands at work or that there were nagging moral principles to be reckoned with . . . but because they had not managed to turn the right screws!

It is completely incomprehensible to Krugman that there may be no screws left to turn or that the mechanics might inevitably turn the wrong screws as they play out their roles in the morality spectacle.

THE TRIUMPH OF MORAL HAZARD

Krugman is hardly alone. As the twentieth century developed, mass democracy and mass markets gradually took the Ought out of both politics and markets. In the nineteenth century, a man would go bust and his friends and relatives would view it as a personal, moral failing. They would presume he did something he oughtn't have. He gambled. He drank. He spent. He must have done something.

But as economies collectivized, the risk of failure was removed from the individual and spread among the group. If a man went broke in the 1930s, it wasn't his fault; he could blame the Crash and Great Depression. If people were poor, it wasn't their fault; it was society's fault, for it had failed to provide jobs. And if investors lost money, that, too, was no longer their own damned faults . . . but the fault of the Fed . . . or the government. If consumers spent too much money, whose fault was it? Perhaps the Fed had set rates too low. In any case, the masses recognized no personal failing. Instead, the failure was collective and technical—the mechanics had failed to turn the right screws. Ought had disappeared.

In politics, the masses recognized no higher authority than the will of the sacred majority. No matter what lame or abominable thing they decided to do, how could it be wrong?

Likewise, in markets, economists won a Nobel Prize for pointing out that mass markets could never be wrong. The Perfect Market Hypothesis demonstrated that the judgment of millions of investors and spenders must always be correct. The whole method of modern economics shifted from exploring what a man ought to do to statistical analysis.

"There is more than a germ of truth in the suggestion that, in a society where statisticians thrive, liberty and individuality are likely to be emasculated," wrote M.J. Moroney in *Fact from Figures*. "Historically, statistics is no more than 'State Arithmetic,' a system by which differences between individuals are eliminated by the taking of an average. It has been used—indeed, still is used—to enable rulers to know just how far they may safely go in picking the pockets of their subjects."

Economists attached sensors to various parts of the great machine, as if they were running diagnostics on an auto engine. Depending on the information, they twisted up interest rates or suggested opening up the throttle to let in more new money. Of course, it was absurd. Had not the perfect market already set rates exactly where they needed to be?

We note, ominously, that even though modern economists took the moral ought out of their calculations, they could not take the moral hazard out of the market. The masses, the *lumpeninvestoriat*, scarcely noticed; but the more economists and investors ignored the ought, the more the hazard grew.

In a small town in the Midwest, a man would have to sneak around under the eyes of his neighbors in order to get up to something. Then, word would get around . . . and soon the whole thing would be over.

But here in Paris, there are moral hazards on every street corner, which is what we like about the place. Here, a man can get into trouble and stay there for a long time before it catches up with him. And if he had no vice when he arrived in town, he can pick one up quickly and develop it into a lifelong companion.

After work, your authors could sit across the street at the Paradis Bar, have a few drinks, a cigarette or two, and then wander over to the infamous rue St. Denis and enjoy ourselves with Brigitte or Françoise for a modest outlay. If we were more ambitious about picking up vices, we could take up gambling, stock market speculating, or even theft.

We might begin picking pockets on the metro and work our way up: First, we could rob our partners or defraud investors—and then, moving on to the big time, we could go into politics.

But there is a certain rhythm to moral hazards. Whether petty or great, all are exhilarating at the beginning and heartbreaking at the end. For there is always a price to pay.

"All the universe is moral," wrote Emerson early in the nineteenth century. Now, no one seems to believe it . . . except us. And yet, the cycle is the same for market booms, empires, and even an individual life. What tickles the fancy so much at the debut saddens it at the finale.

"Whatever is your weakness," says Richard Russell, "the market will find it."

Greedy investors wait too long to sell—and lose their money. Fear keeps others from ever buying in the first place. Laziness gets others who fail to do their homework and get carried along by mob sentiments into buying the most popular stocks at their most absurd prices.

"I ought to have sold at the top," says the one. "I ought to have bought at the bottom," says the other. "I ought to have looked at the balance sheet," says the third. "I ought not to have drunk that last bottle," says the fourth.

But modern economists act as if the story had no moral . . . as if there were no "oughts." Everything happens according to cause and effect, they believe. There is no such thing as a stock that is too expensive or too cheap: The stock market is perfect. It finds the exactly ideal price every minute of every day. There is no such thing as moral failing either. A man cannot be faulted for buying a stock at its perfect price.

And prices would indeed be perfect if, as economists seem to think, men carefully weighed the available information and calculated the odds as coldly as a sniper. But real men rarely weigh anything carefully—except perhaps sirloin steaks when they buy them by the pound. Many have never met a moral hazard they did not like. And when they participate in collective undertakings—such as politics, war, football games, or stock market booms—they immediately become even bigger boobs.

Economists imagine that the economy functions as a sort of machine, too, with rational men popping up and down like valve lifters.

No moral hazards present themselves, for a machine is as indifferent to larceny as it is to a short skirt.

You can put a pack of cards or a fifth of whiskey in front of a machine, come back an hour later, and the machine still will not have touched them. Not so a human being. All he needs is an opportunity, and he is on his way to hell!

BOOM, BUBBLE, BUST . . . AND BEYOND

The term *moral hazard* has a special meaning as well as a general one. "The idea is simple," explains Jeffrey Tucker, in an article published by the Mises Institute in December 1998. "If you are continually willing to protect people from the consequences of their own errors, your benevolence will be factored into the future decisions of the persons rescued. In the long run, they will make even more errors. The principle exists at all levels. The teacher who changes grades when students plead hardship isn't helping in the long run. The teacher is rewarding and thereby encouraging poor study habits. He is creating moral hazard."[8]

The new, collectivized world of the late twentieth century was full of accommodating teachers and forgiving wives. Investors paid too much for stocks. Businesses and consumers borrowed too much. And the whole world seemed to believe what could not be true—that the dollar was more valuable than gold. For nearly 20 years, gold went down, while the dollar went up.

Gold ought to have gone up. Since the beginning of Alan Greenspan's term to the end of 2002, the monetary base almost tripled. In the most recent few years of Mr. Greenspan's term, short-term interest rates were driven down to barely a fifth of what they had been two years before.

"[L]owering rates or providing ample liquidity when problems materialize, but not raising them as imbalances build up, can be rather insidious in the longer run," conceded a working paper from the Bank of International Settlements. "They promote a form of moral hazard that can sow the seeds of instability and of costly fluctuations in the real economy."

By the beginning of 2003, as much as $9 trillion of U.S. dollar assets were in foreign hands and three times as many were in circulation as there had been in 1987. The hazards had never been greater . . . nor ever harder to discern.

In the late 1990s, even after Alan Greenspan noted that investors had become irrationally exuberant, they seemed to become even more irrationally exuberant. And then, when recession and bear market threatened, these irrational investors were sure that the very same central banker, who could not prevent a bubble from forming, could nevertheless stop it from springing a leak.

Alas, this proved a vain hope; a bear market beginning in March 2000 had reduced the nation's stock market wealth by $7 trillion as of January 2003. But another remarkable thing happened at the same time—nothing much.

"The 2000 to 2002 stock market slump failed to produce a financial crisis," wrote David Hale, chairman of Prince Street Capital hedge fund, in an early 2003 issue of *Barron's*. "Wealth losses in the U.S. equity market since March 2002 have been unprecedented. They have been equal to 90 percent of GDP, compared with 60 percent during the two years after the 1929 stock-market crash. But during the past two years, only eleven banks failed in the United States, compared with nearly 500 [from] 1989 to 1991 and thousands during the 1930s."

And in the economy, there was the same remarkable lack of anything special. Unemployment lines grew longer, but not so long as you might reasonably expect. And consumer borrowing and spending did not fall, as could have been expected, but rose. "In 2002, mortgage refinancing shot up to $1.5 trillion compared with a previous peak of $750 billion in '98," Hale tells us.

Following a mild economic downturn in 2001—and after the opening shots in the War Against Terror—"it is difficult to imagine a more benign scenario than the 3 percent growth in output that the economy actually enjoyed during the past year," Hale concluded.

What bothered us about this situation was precisely what delighted Mr. Hale—we could not reasonably expect it. What ought to follow a spectacularly absurd boom is a spectacularly absurd bust.

But the Japanese bubble wasn't completely destroyed in a year or two, either. Economists were still reluctant to cast their eyes toward Japan—because they could not explain it. Neither monetary nor fiscal stimuli seemed to have done the trick. But if you could grab their heads and turn them toward the Land of the Rising Sun, they would see that after a mild recession, GDP growth continued in Japan following the stock market peak in 1989—at about 2 percent to 3 percent per year. This went on for several years. But then the economy went into a more prolonged slump. By 2000, GDP per person was back to 1993 levels.

In both cases—Japan and the United States—there ought to have been a correction worthy of the preceding boom. In Japan, eventually, there was. In the United States, we presume, there will be.

Japan's example, we are told, does not apply anywhere outside Japan because the Japanese created a form of capitalism that was almost unrecognizable to Westerners. It was a system of cross-holdings, state intervention, cronyism, and a stock market that had become a popular sensation. In the financial frenzy of the late 1980s, Japanese companies ceased to act like capitalist enterprises altogether, for they ignored the capitalists. Profits no longer mattered. Assets per share had become an illusion. All that seemed to count was growth, market share, and big announcements to the press.

What kind of capitalism could it be when the capitalists did not require a return on their investment? Was it so different from the U.S. model? U.S. businesses in the late 1990s seemed to care even less about their capitalists than Japanese ones had. As stock prices peaked out on Wall Street in early 2000, profits had already been falling for three years. They continued to fall, sharply, for the first two years of the slump. Executive salaries soared, first as profits fell, and later as many of the biggest companies in the country edged into insolvency. Plus, the managers gave away the store in options to key employees—further disguising the real costs of business.

Despite all the hullabaloo about investing in New Economy technology, actual investment in plants, equipment, and things-that-might-give-investors-higher-profits-in-the-future declined. In the late 1990s, net capital investment dropped to new postwar lows.

As described earlier, instead of paying attention to the business, U.S. corporate executives focused on deal making, acquisitions, and short-term profits—anything that would get their names in the paper.

You'd think an owner would get upset. But none of this mattered to the capitalists—because they had ceased to exist. Old-time capitalists who put money into businesses they knew and understood—with the reasonable hope of earning a profit—had been replaced by a new, collectivized *lumpeninvestoriat*, whose expectations were decidedly unreasonable. The patsies and chumps expected impossible rates of return from stocks about which they had no clue. Management could run down the balance sheet all it wanted. It could make extravagant compensation deals with itself. It could acquire assets for preposterous prices; it could borrow huge sums and then wonder how it would repay the money. It could cut dividends . . . or not pay them at all; the little guys would never figure it out.

The *lumpeninvestoriat* in Japan, as in the United States, ought to have jumped away from stocks, debt, and spending immediately following the crash in the stock market. The market should have plunged and then recovered. But government policy makers and central bankers were soon out in force—spreading so many safety nets, there was scarcely a square foot of pavement on which to fall.

Of course, the little guys never knew what they were doing in the first place. Was it such a surprise that they did the wrong thing again; resisting change by holding on, dragging out the pain of the correction, and postponing a real recovery? In Japan, analysts got weary waiting. Then, the slump continued, slowly and softly, like a man drowning in a beer tank.

THE U.S. DOLLAR AS RESERVE CURRENCY

Having looked at what ought to have happened to the stock market and the economy and what really did happen, we now peek under the hood of the imperial currency, the U.S. dollar. What ought it do, we ask ourselves? To make it easy for readers, we give our verdict before presenting any evidence: It ought to go down.

The *lumpeninvestoriat*, that is, the hoi polloi of common investors, tend to believe things that are not true. In the heydays of the great boom, they believed they could get 18 percent return on their money invested in stocks—even though they had no idea what the companies really did or how they operated. They believed they could trust corporate executives to make investors rich, rather than just making themselves rich. They believed that stocks always went up and that Alan Greenspan would not permit a major bear market. They believed that the U.S. system of participatory capitalism, open markets, and safety nets was the finest ever devised; and that it represented some sort of perfection that would remain on top of the world . . . if not forever, at least for a very long time.

They believed also that the U.S. dollar was as real as money gets, and that it would be destroyed in an orderly, measured way. A little inflation, they had been told, was actually good for an economy.

Of all the lies that the new *investoriat* took up, none was more provocative than the dollar. In order for anything to retain any value—particularly a currency—it must be in limited supply. If there were millions of paintings by Monet or Rembrandt, for example, they would be worth a lot less than they are today. Back in the nineteenth century, currencies were backed by gold. This had the effect of limiting the quantity of money, for there was only so much gold available.

After getting into the habit of accepting paper backed by gold, people barely noticed when the paper no longer had any backing at all. Government still printed and distributed the new, managed currencies. Governments would make sure that they did not print too much, or so people assumed.

But while central bank reserves increased only 55 percent between 1948 and 1971 (the Bretton Woods period), they rose more than 2,000 percent during the next 30 years. This explosive growth in money and credit can also be measured by the increase in the bond market. Worth $776 billion in 1970, the global bond market had grown to $40 trillion by the end of the century. But who complained? The money found its way first into stock prices . . . and later into real estate. People looked at the house that just sold down the street and felt richer, not poorer—just as the Japanese had, 10 years before.

And yet, since John Law first test-drove the idea in 1719, it has not been possible for a central bank to create trillions in new money—out of thin air—without driving the currency itself into the ground. "The dollar ought to fall," economists began saying as the 1990s passed. Finally, in 2002, the dollar did fall—against other currencies, particularly the euro and gold, against which it went down about 20 percent in 2002 alone.

What ought it do next, we ask again?

Here we add two complicating details. First, as described in previous chapters, for as much as the American *lumpeninvestoriat* was deceived by the dollar's apparent strength, foreigners were even bigger dupes. They could not get enough of them.

How could a country balance its books when it was buying more from foreigners than it was selling? It had to make up the difference by bringing the money back home as investment funds. Foreigners did not dump their dollars for their home currencies; instead, they used the money to buy dollar assets—U.S. stocks, real estate, businesses. By the end of 2002, the total of foreign holdings of dollar assets had risen to a Himalayan high. With the dollar now falling and U.S. stocks also falling, foreigners ought to want to lighten up on their dollar holdings.

Even tossing off a small percentage of these holdings could have a devastating effect on the dollar's price. On average, the dollar fell only 10 percent against foreign currencies in 2002. In the 1980s, with far less provocation, it dropped nearly 50 percent.

The other complication is that in addition to the $9 trillion worth of existing foreign holdings, the current account deficit grew by $1.5 billion every day. However successful the United States has been as a military superpower, this power pales against its success as a monetary super superpower. Every day, Americans struck a bargain with foreigners in which the latter traded valuable goods and services for little pieces of paper with green ink on them. They had no intrinsic value and their own custodians had pledged to create an almost infinite supply of them, if need be, to make sure they did not gain value against consumer goods!

"There is a crack in everything God made," Emerson keeps reminding us. The crack in this bargain is that it undermined the profitability of U.S. companies. Spurred by the Fed, consumers spent their money at full gallop. They even spent money they did not have. But profits at U.S. companies continued to fall. In fact, as a percentage of GDP, profits had been falling ever since the early 1960s, not coincidentally as the percentage of the economy devoted to consumer spending and the current account deficit increased.

What was happening was obvious. Americans were spending money, but the funds ended up in the coffers of foreign businesses. U.S. companies had the expense of employing U.S. workers, but the money did not come back to them; it went to their overseas competitors. At the beginning of 2003, U.S. profits were already at a post–World War II low. This was not a trend that could go on forever. And as Herbert Stein pointed out, if it can't, it won't.

PERILS OF SUCCESS

In December 2002, Alan Greenspan spoke to the New York Economic Club and sounded, for a while, like the Randian acolyte he was circa 1963:

> Although the gold standard could hardly be portrayed as having produced a period of price tranquility, it was the case that the price level in 1929 was not much different, on net, from what it had been in 1800. But, in the two decades following the abandonment of the gold standard in 1933, the consumer price index in the United States nearly doubled. And, in the four decades after that, prices quintupled. Monetary policy, unleashed from the constraint of domestic gold convertibility, had allowed a persistent overissuance of money. As recently as a decade ago, central bankers, having witnessed more than a half-century of chronic inflation, appeared to confirm that a fiat currency was inherently subject to excess.

Of course, Mr. Greenspan was setting the stage. He might have added that no central banker in all history had ever succeeded in proving the contrary. Every fiat currency the world had ever seen had shown itself "subject to excess" and then subject to destruction. Circa 2002, against this epic background, central banker Mr. Greenspan strutted out, front and center.

Each métier comes with its own hazards. The baker burns his fingers . . . the psychiatrist soon needs to have his own head examined. The moral hazard of central banking is well documented. Given the power to create money out of thin air, the central banker almost always goes too far. And if one resists, his successor will almost certainly succumb.

There are some things at which succeeding is more dangerous than failing. Running a central bank—like robbing one—is an example. The more successful the central banker becomes and the more people come to believe in the stability of his paper money, the more hazardous the situation becomes.

Warren Buffett's father, a congressman from Nebraska, warned in a 1948 speech: "The paper money disease has been a pleasant habit thus far and will not be dropped voluntarily any more than a dope user will without a struggle give up narcotics . . . I find no evidence to support a hope that our fiat paper money venture will fare better ultimately than such experiments in other lands . . . ."[9]

In all other lands, at all other times, the story was the same. Paper money had not worked; the moral hazard was too great. Central bankers could not resist; when it suited them, they overdid it, increasing the money supply far faster than the growth in goods and services that the money could buy.

When we went looking for a list of the world's defunct of failing paper money, we were soon overwhelmed. We found a good long list, in alphabetical order . . . but gave up when at number 318 we were still in the Bs.

Against this sorry record of managed currencies is the exemplary one of gold. No matter whose face adorns the coin, or what inscription it bears, or when it was minted, an unmanaged gold coin today is still worth at least the value of its gold content, and it will generally buy as much in goods and services today as it did the day it was struck.

Gold is found on earth in limited amounts—only 3.5 parts per billion. Had God been less niggardly with the stuff, gold might be more ubiquitous and less expensive. But it is precisely because the earth yields up its gold so grudgingly that it is so valuable. Paper money, on the other hand, can be produced in almost infinite quantities. When central bankers reach the limits of modern printing technology, the designers have only to add a zero, and they will have increased the speed at which they inflate by a factor of 10. In today's electronic world, a man no longer measures his wealth in stacks of paper money. It is now just "information." A central banker does not even have to turn the crank on the printing press; electronically registered zeros can be added at the speed of light. Given the ease with which new paper money is created, is it any wonder the old paper money loses its value?

For a while, Mr. Greenspan seemed to have God's light shining on him. His paper dollars rose in value against gold for two decades, when they ought to have gone down.

Mr. Greenspan explains how this came about:[10]

The adverse consequences of excessive money growth for financial stability and economic performance provoked a backlash. Central banks were finally pressed to rein in overissuance of money even at the cost of considerable temporary economic disruption. By 1979, the need for drastic measures had become painfully evident in the United States. The Federal Reserve, under the leadership of Paul Volcker and with the support of both the Carter and the Reagan Administrations, dramatically slowed the growth of money. Initially, the economy fell into recession and inflation receded. However, most important, when activity staged a vigorous recovery, the progress made in reducing inflation was largely preserved. By the end of the 1980s, the inflation climate was being altered dramatically.

The record of the past 20 years appears to underscore the observation that, although pressures for excess issuance of fiat money are chronic, a prudent monetary policy maintained over a protracted period can contain the forces of inflation.

Until 2001, Greenspan's genius was universally acclaimed. Central banking looked, at long last, like a great success. But then the bubble burst. People began to wonder what kind of central bank would do such a dumb thing.

"Evidence of history suggests that allowing an asset bubble to develop is the greatest mistake that a central bank can make," wrote Andrew Smithers and Stephen Wright in *Valuing Wall Street*, in 2000. "Over the past five years or so the Federal Reserve has knowingly permitted the development of the greatest asset bubble of the 20th century."

When the stock market collapsed, Mr. Greenspan's policies began to look less prudent. During his tour of duty at the Fed, the monetary base tripled, at a time when the gross domestic product rose only 50 percent. More new money came into being than under all previous Fed chairmen—roughly $6,250 for every new ounce of gold brought up from the earth.

All this new money created by the Greenspan Fed had the defect of excess paper money; it had no resources behind it. Though taken up by shopkeepers and dog groomers as if it were the real thing, it represented no increase in actual wealth. The retailer and the groomer thought they had more money, but there was really nothing to back it up.

The new money was issued, light on value, but heavy on consequences. It helped lure the *lumpeninvestoriat* into their own moral hazard; they no longer needed to save—because the Greenspan Fed always seemed to make new money available, at increasingly attractive rates.

And it misled suppliers into believing there was more demand than there really was. Consumers were buying; there was no doubt about that. But how long could they continue to spend more than they actually earned?

The effects of this moral hazard are just now being felt. The consumer is more heavily in debt than ever before and seems to need increased credit just to stay afloat. State and federal governments have gone from modest surplus to flagrant deficit. Where is the money going to come from?

Americans have very little in savings; so as previously mentioned, the money must be imported from abroad. But in 2001, the current account was already in deficit by $450 billion annually. Stephen Roach estimates that new capital demands will push the deficit to $600 billion—or $2.5 billion every working day in 2003. Foreigners may be willing to finance the new U.S. spending binge. Then again, with the dollar already falling, they may not.

We cannot know what will happen, but we can take a guess: They will not be willing to do so at the same dollar price.

A CLASSIC SUCKER'S RALLY

After months of the markets in a free-fall, in the spring of 2009, something remarkable happened: the money began flowing again. People thought they saw a bottom.

"Cramer: The Depression is over," says a headline.[11] Mad Money's Jim Cramer says the bottom has come and gone. That's all we need to know. If Cramer thinks the worst is over . . . well, it must be so.

Even Nouriel Roubini, according to *Forbes*, thinks there is "light at the end of the tunnel."[12]

"Bernanke Sees Hopeful Signs," read the headline in the *New York Times*.

"Ben S. Bernanke, the chairman of the Federal Reserve, said the economic free fall of the last nine months was nearing an end and that the United States should begin a fragile recovery by the end of this year."[13]

Is this good news? Or what? "Or what" is our bet.

Can the feds now fix the trouble they never saw coming? Can the people who ran banks into the ground now run the banks that will help finance the recovery? Can the investors who bought trashy investments with borrowed money now recognize the good investments that are put in front of them?

Neither Ben Bernanke, Tim Geithner, Hank Paulson, nor Alan Greenspan could see it—but there was something clearly wrong with the Bubble Economy of 2001–2007. We said so many times.

"Good riddance," we celebrated, when it keeled over.

But now they struggle to revive it. Like a brain-dead codger on life support, they are bankrupting the next generation trying to keep it alive.

"We expect that the recovery will only gradually gain momentum," Ben Bernanke forecast, trying to manage expectations, "and that the economic slack will diminish slowly."[14]

Really? Oh, the wonders of modern medicine. Now, with 20/20 vision, the Fed chief can look ahead and tell us what will happen next. If only he'd gone to the doctor two years ago!

Stocks are rallying all over the world. Economists are putting on their spectacles and looking to the future. Bankers are cashing their checks and laughing all the way home from work.

"That sense of unremitting free fall we had a month or two ago is not present today," says White House economic advisor Larry Summers.[15]

Barron's Big Money Poll shows professional portfolio managers are bullish again. They're looking for the Dow to gain 7 percent this year . . . and 17 percent by the middle of next year.[16]

This is good news for us. We were beginning to look around and notice that too many stupid people agreed with us. But now that we see the pros are in the opposite camp . . . we can sleep more soundly.

The proximate cause of all this optimism is the vigor with which the people who didn't see the problem coming have gone about fighting it. Mr. Market may taketh away . . . but Mr. Federal Official putteth back. At least, that's the logic of it. So far, in the United States alone, they've earmarked a sum nearly three times the cost of fighting World War II. Not all of that is direct cash outlays. Much of it is in the form of financial "guarantees" and "investments" (such as buying up Wall Street's smelly derivatives). Still, it's a lot of money.

Normally, in a correction, the supply of money—M1—falls. Asset values are destroyed . . . borrowers default . . . money disappears into vaults and mattresses. But this time, so vigorous has been the authorities' response that M1 is actually increasing at about a 14 percent annual rate. The money's got to go somewhere . . .

Japan announced another $100 billion stimulus program in April.[17] That should do the trick. After 17 years of bailouts and stimulus programs, the Japanese should be getting good at them. But it's a little like a guy who's getting good at suicide—if he's so good at it, you'd think he'd be dead by now.

But no . . . the Japanese economy is still one of the worst performers in the world; their bailouts and stimuli have done no good . . . maybe they've even made the situation worse.

No matter, there's a rally on . . . this is not the time to ask questions. Our instinct tells us this rally is going to carry the Dow back above 9,000 . . . possibly above 10,000. Why? Because people do not go directly from believing nothing can go wrong to believing that nothing can go right. (See Figure 9.1.)

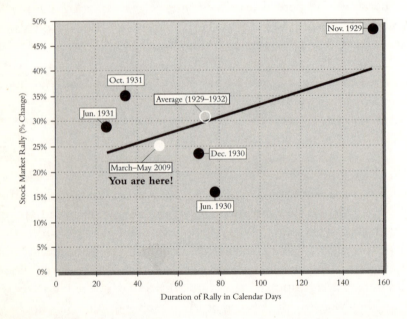

FIGURE 9.1 A Classic Sucker's Rally

Markets don't go smoothly in any one direction—up or down. During the Great Depression the Dow rallied 15% or more at least 5 times. The rallies lasted as many as 180 days. Some even longer. After a long slow trudge—and a world war—the market finally began rising again in the 1950s.

Source: chartoftheday.com.

The kind of delusional optimism that took stocks up over 14,000 on the Dow . . . and doubled property prices . . . and had sober bankers buying billions' worth of ticking debt bombs doesn't disappear overnight. It has to be killed like Rasputin—many times. Stab it. Shoot it. And then douse it with gasoline and set it on fire. Maybe then, it will finally die.

That's why this rally is just a trap for the unwary . . . a suckers' rally. Investors are getting back on their feet just so Mr. Market can whack them again. So, if you're playing this rally . . . be sure to keep those stops moving up behind your stocks.

So far, this rally has recovered less than 20 percent of the previous losses. Typically, at least one good rally in a bear market will recover more than half of the losses. Looking at the long term, the Dow rose from the low in the early 1930s of only 41 points to the high in 2007, when it was over 14,000 points. This bear market wiped out more than half of the capital gains made by investors during that whole 76-year period. A 50 percent bounce from the January 2009 low would put the Dow back up close to 10,000.

Our forecast? Bulls, bears, spenders, savers—our guess is that Mr. Market intends to paddle them all.

The bulls will be whacked when the Dow falls another 50 percent from its low—down to, say, below 4,000. The bears will be whacked when the Fed seems unable to stop deflation . . . and the prices in the mining and commodities sectors collapse. Then, the spenders will be trapped in a burning house of debt—with the door barred by deflation. Later, the roof will fall on the savers, too—when the feds finally manage to get an inflation backfire going. The fire will get away from them immediately, we predict, burning up trillions worth of savings overnight.

So, we see, the feds are on the case. Investors are coming back into the market. The banks have money again. What could go wrong?

Why . . . everything . . . of course!

HEARTS AND MINDS

The sucker's rally itself is a part of a larger battle between two contradictory body parts—the heart and the mind. The heart wants to believe that the worst is over. It reacts sentimentally, remembering the glory days of the great bubble era and wishing they were back. For example, higher consumer confidence readings will send the stock market higher—in this case, the heart ruled.

But then comes the head's turn. The head looks at the facts: housing and employment are still going down. People will spend less money. Businesses will make less money. Ergo, no reason to expect stocks to go up. Instead, they're more likely to go down.

The head noticed, too, that the Treasury market is getting slammed by higher yields. The long bond yielded 4.56 percent in the final days of May 2009—up from well below 3 percent at the end of the previous year.

"Treasury yields give cause for concern," says the *Financial Times*.[18]

"Rising Treasury yields threaten to stifle economic recovery," continues another article.[19]

But has the top of the bond market really passed? Is the credit cycle now in full retreat? Will homeowners and businessmen be tortured with higher interest rates?

Those are the questions the head was asking yesterday. And it didn't like the answers. If there were any "green shoots" of recovery, it reasoned, higher interest rates could crush them.

And then at least a few heads began thinking about what this meant to the big strategic issues . . . and how this all will turn out.

At the end of 2008, America's great buddy, China, changed its policy. Instead of buying long-dated U.S. debt, China began buying the short stuff. China's top man openly wondered whether the United States would be able to protect the value of the dollar and keep its promises to foreign lenders.

"We have a huge amount of money in the United States," said China's premier. He reminded the United States that China had entrusted a lot of its wealth to U.S. paper and went on to request that the United States respect its obligations to bond buyers. Obviously, the Chinese must wonder if the United States is capable of protecting its currency while still funding its war against deflation.[20]

Tim Geithner promptly responded. "Yes we can!" But the Chinese cogitated on the matter . . . "No they can't," they began to think.

FIGURE 9.2   A Bubble in Bonds

At one point during the fall of 2008, investors were willing to take a negative yield on U.S. Treasuries, meaning they were willing to pay the government to keep their money safe from carnage in the stock market. This overinvestment in treasuries will unwind itself in as dramatic a fashion as it wound up.

Then, they switched to buying short-term U.S. debt, leaving the longer-term bonds to other buyers. (See Figure 9.2.) Since the Chinese were the biggest buyers at U.S. Treasury debt auctions, this switch in policy had a quick and noticeable effect. Bills rose. Bonds fell. The yield on bills fell to below zero, while the yield on the 30-year bond has gone steadily up. On June 1, 2009, when he told a group of students at Peking University that the Chinese investment in U.S. Treasuries was safe, the auditorium erupted in laughter. The event was barely mentioned in the U.S. press.[21]

Still, if U.S. supply lines to cheap credit have been cut, she is at a great strategic disadvantage. Or rather, her preexisting strategic disadvantage is becoming more apparent: she depends on foreigners just to be able to continue living in the style to which she has become accustomed. As Barack Obama acknowledged:

"We're out of money now."[22]

HEGEMONY IN QUESTION

Watch out, the greenback is going into the toaster oven . . . here's what Nouriel Roubini had to say in the *New York Times*:[23]

> We may now be entering the Asian century, dominated by a rising China and its currency. This decline of the dollar might take more than a decade, but it could happen even sooner if we do not get our financial house in order. The United States must rein in spending and borrowing, and pursue growth that is not based on asset and credit bubbles. For the last two decades America has been spending more than its income, increasing its foreign liabilities and amassing debts that have become unsustainable.

Yes, it could take more than a decade. But investors could take a big loss any day. All it would take would be a sudden move by China . . . or a shocking inflation figure in the United States . . . or a Treasury bond auction that doesn't go as planned.

Everyone is watching the United States . . . carefully. And foreigners hold trillions' worth of dollar-based assets outside the United States. These are dollars that people hold, not to pay their bills or buy gasoline, but as a speculation. They're speculating the greenback will hold its value as well or better than the other things they might do with their money.

Europeans hedge their bets against the euro—with dollars. Asians hedge their bets against falling stock prices. Russians hedge their bets against the ruble. Latin Americans hedge their bets against their own pesos, bolivars, and cordobas. Everybody likes dollars because they are the most trusted money in the world. For the last 50 years, nothing could compete with the dollar. (Even though the dollar lost value against a number of other currencies over long periods of time.)

These foreign holders are already nervous. They've seen the mess the United States has gotten itself into. They read the headlines. They watch the news. They know that the United States is running a budget deficit this year equal to four times the biggest budget deficit ever—a record set just last year. It is as if a runner broke the record in the 100-yard dash . . . and then ran the course four times faster a year later. This is not progress. This is spooky.

The Chinese already let the United States know they are worried. "We trust you to protect the value of our assets," they in essence said to the U.S. Treasury Secretary.

And in the middle of May 2009, from the *Financial Times* comes news that Brazil and China are working toward using their own currencies in trade transactions rather than the U.S. dollar.[24]

This comes on the heels of the news that China's central bank governor Zhou Xiaochuan proposed to create a reserve currency "that is disconnected from individual nations." What Mr. Zhou would like is to replace the U.S. dollar as the world's leading currency with a new international reserve currency, possibly in the form of special drawing rights (SDRs), a unit of account used by the International Monetary Fund.[25]

Then in June, Russian President Dmitry Medvedev questioned the U.S. dollar's future as a global reserve currency and said using a mix of regional currencies would make the world economy more stable. Russia may consider ruble-yuan swaps.

The dollar "is not in a spectacular position, let's be frank, and its prospects cause various questions as do the prospects for the global currency system," Medvedev said in an interview published by the Moscow-based *Kommersant* newspaper. Regarding the global financial system, "therefore our task is to make it more mobile and at the same time more balanced."[26]

But for now, as long as these countries trust the United States to keep its promises and protect its money, they continue to hold U.S. dollar investments—notably, U.S. Treasury bonds. But just wait until the United States loses their trust. In a matter of minutes, China could dump enough U.S. dollars to set off alarms all over the world. All of a sudden dollar holders would rush for the exits—each one trying to get out before the others. In minutes, the dollar market could collapse . . . taking down U.S. Treasury bonds with it.

THE TRADE OF THE DECADE(S)

Investors do not need to make many decisions. Studies have shown that allocation decisions are what make or lose the most money. Individual choices—selecting individual stocks or bonds—do not seem to make much difference in the long run. But deciding which market to be in and when—makes all the difference in the world.

An investor would have done well, over the past 30 years, to pay attention to his investments on the first day of each decade . . . and otherwise ignore the whole subject. He could have made three simple decisions and turned an original grubstake of $10,000 into $268,300.

Think how his life would have been better! Instead of spending hours with CNBC, *Money*, the Internet, and all the other enticements of the financial press, he could have gone fishing or read the classics. Think how much better off he would have been without the noise and information of the mass media.

All he had to do was recognize that in cutting the link to gold in the early 1970s, the Nixon administration practically guaranteed inflation and a higher gold price. Gold traded at an average of $36 per ounce in 1970. Ten years later, the same ounce of gold sold for $615. With no leverage, no stocks, no research, no headaches, and little risk, he would have made a profit of 1,708 percent. And he would have paid not a penny of tax on his investment during the entire period.

But then, on January 1, 1980, things changed. Our investor should have taken note that nothing lasts forever and that there was a new man at the Fed. Paul Volcker meant business. He would drive down inflation rates—and gold—one way or another. It was time to sell. But where to put the money?

He might not have noticed—they do not advertise these things—but Japan, Inc., was extremely energetic in the early 1980s. He could not have known at the time, but had he bought Japanese stocks, he would have seen his fortune multiply again. The Nikkei 225 index rose from 5,994 at the end of January 1980 to 38,916 at the end of 1989—an increase of 549 percent.

It was important not to open a paper to the financial section during the last years of the 1980s. The news from Japan was so absurd, a U.S. investor would have wanted to sell too soon. But, if he had looked at the facts on New Year's Day, 1990, he would have seen it was time for a change.

On that day, he should have brought his money home to the United States and invested it in U.S. stocks. At 12.4 times earnings, with the Dow at 2,586, American equities were a good deal. Besides, there were 78 million baby boomers ready to spend and invest as never

FIGURE 9.3 The Trade of the Decade

Priced in ounces of gold the Dow has historically reverted to the mean following periods of intense speculation in stocks. The trade of the decade—sell stocks, buy gold—still has some legs in it yet.

before . . . and a friend at the Fed, Alan Greenspan, ready to make sure they had the money to do it with. Over the next 10 years, the Dow rose to 11,041, for another 426 percent profit.

By January 2000, that trend, too, had run its course. What would be the Trade of the Decade for the next 10 years? For all the reasons given in this book, we think it will be to sell the Dow and buy gold. In the first three years—2000 to 2003—gold rose from $282 to $342. The Dow, meanwhile, fell—from 11,522 on January 7, 2000, to 8,740 three years later. An investor was already ahead 2,683 percent. (See Figure 9.3.)

As we pointed out earlier, too, the day of reckoning we thought was coming during "the recession that wasn't" in 2001–2002, was merely postponed six years. Should you stay with our trade of the decade? Should we go for two? We honestly don't know. But gold as it stands is more of an insurance policy against financial collapse. And at no other time have we edged up to that precipice like we have today.

HOW TO RELAX AND ENJOY THE END OF THE WORLD

The world as we have known it is coming to an end. But what do we care? We smile and vow to enjoy it. It took the Roman Empire hundreds of years to fall. During that time, most people did not even know their world was coming to an end. Most must have gone about their business, planting their crops, drinking their wine, and bouncing their children on their knees, as if the empire were eternal. Of course, the mobs in Rome may have reeled and wailed with every news flash: The barbarians had crossed the river Po and were headed South—soon, they would be at the gates!

But others lived quiet lives of desperation and amusement—as if nothing had happened. And what could they have done about it anyway . . . except get out of harm's way and tend to their own affairs?

Plenty of people enjoyed the Great Depression. If you had a well-paying job, it must have been paradise—no waiting in lines, no need for a reservation at good restaurants. Keeping up with the Joneses had never been easier—because the Joneses were in reverse. So much of the satisfaction in life comes from feeling superior to other people. What better time than a depression to enjoy it?

The secret to enjoying all mass movements is to be a spectator, not a participant. How much better it would have been to wave at the passing of the Grande Armée on its way to destruction in Russia than to march along with them. Perhaps you could have sold them earmuffs and mittens!

Likewise, what better way to enjoy the great boom on Wall Street of the 1990s than by tuning in to CNBC from time to time just to see what absurd thing analysts would say next? And now that it is over, how better to enjoy it than from a safe distance, standing well clear of the exits?

Readers are urged to be suspicious of headlines in the news and opinions on the editorial pages. Almost all mass movements that they stir up will one day be regarded with regret and amazement.

But that is the way of the world; one madness leads to the next. A man feels excited and expansive because the economy is said to be in the midst of a New Era . . . and then he feels a little exhausted when he discovers that the New Era has been followed by a New Depression. And all the while, his life goes on exactly as it had before. His liquor is no better, his wife no prettier or uglier, his work every bit as insipid or inspiring as it was before. We have no complaint about it. Still, "the world is too much with us," wrote Emerson:

> Most men have bound their eyes with one or another handkerchief, and attached themselves to some one of these communities of opinion. This conformity makes them not false in a few particulars, authors of a few lies, but false in all particulars. Their every truth is

not quite true. Their two is not the real two, their four not the real four; so that every word they say chagrins us, and we know not where to begin to set them right. Meantime nature is not slow to equip us in the prison-uniform of the party to which we adhere. We come to wear one cut of face and figure, and acquire by degrees the gentles' asinine expression . . .

What better time to shut out the world and wipe that silly grin off our face than now—when the world that we have known for at least three decades, the Dollar Standard period, is coming to an end?

U.S. consumer capitalism is doomed, we think. If not, it ought to be. The trends that could not last forever seem to be coming to an end. Consumers cannot continue to go deeper into debt. Consumption cannot continue to take up more and more of the GDP. Capital investment and profits cannot go down much further. Foreigners will not continue to finance Americans' excess consumption until the Second Coming—at least not at the current dollar price. And fiat paper money will not continue to outperform the real thing—gold—forever.

The United States will have to find a new economic model, for it can no longer hope to spend and borrow its way to prosperity. This is not a cyclical change, but a structural one that will take a long time. Structural reforms—that is, changing the way an economy functions—do not happen overnight. The machinery of collectivized capitalism resists change of any sort. The Fed tries to buoy the old model with cheaper and cheaper money. Government comes forward with multibillion-dollar spending programs to try to simulate real demand. And the poor *lumpeninvestoriat*—bless their greedy little hearts—will never give up the dream of U.S. consumer capitalism; it will have to be crushed out of them.

As Paul Volcker put it, "It will all have to be adjusted someday." Why not enjoy it?

AN AVALANCHE OF CLAPTRAP

Illusions pile up . . . They're sure to come down sooner or later.

Like snow at high altitudes, the central banks' new money is piling up. At the end of May 2009, all the world's major central banks turned on their snow machines. The Federal Reserve was authorized to "print" $1.75 trillion worth of new money in order to buy Treasury bonds. The Bank of England began its own program—worth 75 billion pounds, so far. Even Switzerland was printing money—so much that its money supply, as measured by M2, was growing at 30 percent per year. In addition, the European Central Bank announced that it too would begin creating money in order to buy corporate bonds.

This, you recall, is referred to as "Quantitative Easing"—how central banks describe what is essentially an act of counterfeiting. They buy bonds with money created—electronically—specifically for that purpose. Abracadabra—"money" comes into being.

The feds aim to provide liquidity for the cities and farms. But so far, only a trickle is coming down. Instead, chilly weather in the upper reaches of the financial sector holds it frozen in place. Hundreds of billions comes down from central banks, but there it stays . . . waiting for spring.

The feds' counterfeit money does such a good imitation of the real thing, you can't tell them apart. But the problem with all money is that it is as fickle and unreliable as a bad girlfriend. One minute she goes along with the flow. The next minute she turns silly and bubbly. And then, she gives you the cold shoulder.

According to theory, an increase in the supply of something leads directly to a decrease in the price of it . . . That is, if other things remain constant. Despite the credit crunch, the banking freeze-up, and the economic recession, the money supply in the United States as measured by M1 is actually rising at 14 percent per year. Yet consumer prices are not keeping pace. The latest report shows them actually going down slightly in the spring of 2009.

Turns out, causing inflation is not as easy as it looked; controlling it probably will be even harder. It's not enough to manage the quantity of money; you also need to be able to control its behavior. Money can be a solid, a liquid, or a gas depending upon the temperature of the economy. At normal temperatures, money runs freely, watering the economy. And when things really get hot, it vaporizes, creating gaseous bubbles such as those of the late Bubble Period. But when the temperature falls, money shivers in wallets and bank accounts—reluctant to go out into the cold. Economists refer to the "velocity of money" to describe the magnifying effects of motion. When the same dollar bill appears in three different places in the same day, it is as if the money supply had been multiplied threefold. In a freeze, on the other hand, it comes to a dead stop.

When the thaw will come, we don't know. But the authorities are ready for it. When consumer prices begin to rise, they'll stop adding to the money supply. Then, they'll withdraw liquidity, as need be, to keep it under control.

They know that runaway inflation would cause problems—the collapse of the dollar . . . and the U.S. Treasury bond market, for example. So, at the first signs of inflation, they will move quickly to remove excess liquidity from the system. How? Their emergency plan is simple enough. Now, they are buying bonds. When their inflation targets are met, they will begin selling them.

We thought the Bubble Epoch was the peak in claptrap and illusions. But we were only in the foothills. The feds now pretend to bail out the economy by giving money to companies that pretend to be concerned, run by people who pretend to know what they are doing. And when they run short of money, they create more of it, pretend it is real . . . and pretend they can tell it what to do.

What is likely is that money will have a mind of its own. First, the markets will react . . . and the authorities will not. They will remember their own critiques of Japanese and Roosevelt-era monetary policy. In both cases, they believe central banks removed the punch bowl too early—before the party really got rolling. In both cases, the recovery was cut off.

Then, while they are hesitating, money will turn on them. Inflation rates will rise further. The velocity of money will pick up. And investors, including foreign governments, will become eager sellers of government debt. Suddenly, it will be too late. In order to remove the monetary inflation they previously added, central banks will have to sell bonds instead of buying them, trying to reabsorb money from the economy. The extra cash would then disappear back into the central banks. But in order to bring inflation under control, the biggest bond buyers in the world must turn into the world's biggest sellers. Bond prices, already falling as investors feared the worst, will collapse immediately. An avalanche of dollars will fall upon the world markets—as dollar holders all over the world become desperate to get rid of them.

We don't know what day it will happen. But we have a good idea as to what time of day central bankers will realize that they are doomed. About 4 A.M. is our guess. That is the moment when Ben Bernanke and other central bankers begin to feel like members of the Donner Party. That is, like imbeciles.

ADVICE TO THE CLASS OF 2009

So far, not a single major university has asked us to make the commencement address. Nor a minor college. Not even a school of cosmetology or taxidermy. But as we write from London, protected by a broad ocean and a narrow reading of the First Amendment, we will give them advice no one asked for.

"Plastics," was the advice given to college graduates in Mike Nichols' 1967 film *The Graduate*. But that was when there was still hope for the United States' manufacturing sector. Even then, it was too late. The percentage of GDP from the manufacturing sector fell for the next four decades, from more than 20 percent in the last 1960s to barely 12 percent in 2008. Better advice would have been "derivatives." They stank just as bad, but they were much more profitable. Although only 8 percent of GDP, finance accounted for 40 percent of corporate profits in 2007. And derivatives grew from nothing to a face value of 16 times the GDP of the entire planet.

But your elders are always giving you bum advice.

"You cannot decline the burdens of empire and still expect to share its honors," said Pericles to the class of 430 B.C. He lived during a time not unlike your parents' era in the United States—when Athens was on top of the world. But vanity got the better of him. He launched an attack on Sparta that backfired badly. He soon died of plague and Athens was not only ruined, but enslaved. Athens' "golden age" turned to lead. Young Athenians should have shrugged off the burden rather than accept it. You should do the same.

When you were born 20-some years ago, the nation's total debt per person was less than $90,000—adjusted to 2009 dollars, of course. Although that was a lot of money, it was nothing compared to what was coming. Now it's $186,717 per person—more than twice as much, in real terms. Fortunately, private debt is not inheritable. But it comes to you as a lien against property. Instead of paying off their mortgages and leaving you a house, free and clear, the baby boomer generation spent the "equity" in their houses even faster than they got it. House prices rose. But mortgage debt rose faster. Although your grandparents owned 80 percent of their houses, by 2007, the typical homeowner only really owned four rooms of an eight-room house. And then, when house prices fell, so did his remaining equity . . . to the point where one out of six homeowners in the United States is now underwater. You could still eventually inherit a house, but you may have to scrape the barnacles off the front porch.

But that's not even the half of it. Although your parents had control of the U.S. government, they allowed themselves a little larceny. Add the unfunded retirement and health care benefits they voted for themselves to the official national debt, and together they are scheduled to cost your generation four times the total annual output of the United States. This is over and above the private debt they accumulated.

Some of this debt can be carried. Some will have to paid down. But as it stands, as much as $77 trillion of post-2009 earnings must be stolen from the future in order to pay for the liquor your parents drank . . . the bombs they dropped on god-forsaken foreigners . . . and the interest on their debts. So, forget about saving for a European vacation or a house of your own. Even if every penny of your savings—and every other American's savings—are put to the task you will still be paying for your parents' expenses all your life.

But wait, there's more! The burden is getting heavier. Federal budget projections show an additional $7 trillion in deficits over the next 10 years. Described as the cost of fighting recession, the present generation buries its own mistakes under cash that the next generation hasn't even earned yet. Today's bankers, businessmen, and speculators are being bankrolled by you—tomorrow's bankers, businessmen, and speculators. Today's homeowners get a helping hand . . . from whom? Tomorrow's homeowners—you. Today's employees get a boost, too. Same story. Where do you think the money came from to pay Wall Street bonuses? How do you think GM stays in business . . . and Fannie Mae . . . and AIG . . . Who pays those salaries? Who pays to keep troops all over the world and keep old people supplied with new drugs? Who pays for hundreds of billions' worth of "shovel-ready" boondoggles? You will. At least, that's the plan.

The luck of one generation is the curse of the next. Like Pericles, your parents inherited a dollar; they leave you a peso. They took over the strongest, richest, most competitive nation in the world. And like Pericles they minded everyone's business but their own. Now, not only does the United States owe money all over town, its government puts out trillions more in IOUs every year—each one with your name on it. You're not even out in the real world yet, and you're getting the bill for 50 cents of every dollar the feds spend—almost none of it earmarked for you. But that is the thing about the real world your teachers probably forgot to tell you about. It is more unreal and fantastical than anything you studied.

Here's what's real: You've been dealt a bad hand. From the bottom of the deck . . . your parents have slipped you some nasty cards. Our advice? Fold 'em. Get up from the table before they clean you out.

NOTES

CHAPTER 1: THE GILDERED AGE

1. See article by Fred Barbash, "Market Guru Put Acolytes on Wild Ride," *Washington Post* (March 5, 2000): H01.
2. Tom Brokaw, "Examination of how and why big CEOs have made millions while investors lost everything," *NBC News* transcript (July 28, 2002).
3. See article by George Gilder and Bret Swanson, "Metcalfe's Exaflood," *Shalom Equity Fund Newsletter* (June 26, 2001). Available from www.imakenews.com/shalomequityfund/e_article000030389.cfm.
4. Rodes Fishburne and Michael Malone, in an interview with Gordon Moore and Bob Metcalfe titled "Laying Down the Law," *Forbes ASAP* (February 21, 2000). Available from www.forbes.com/asap/2000/0221/096.html.
5. See note 4.
6. See article by Bill Bonner, "The Digital Man," *Daily Reckoning* (August 15, 2000). Available from www.dailyreckoning.com.
7. See note 6.
8. See article by David Denby, "The Quarter of Living Dangerously: How Greed Becomes a Way of Life," *New Yorker* (April 24, 2000/May 1, 2000).
9. See note 8.
10. See article by Mark Leibovich, "MicroStrategy's CEO Sped to the Brink," *Washington Post* (January 6, 2002): A01.
11. See article by Larissa MacFarquar, "A Beltway Billionaire and His Big Ideas," *New Yorker* (April 3, 2000): 34.

12. See note 10.

13. See article by Bill Bonner, "A River Runs through It," *Daily Reckoning* (June 7, 2000). Available from www.dailyreckoning.com.

14. "Playboy Interview: Jeff Bezos," *Playboy*, vol. 47, no. 2 (February 1, 2000): 59.

15. See article by Joshua Cooper Ramo, "Jeffrey Preston Bezos; 1999 Person of the Year. The Fast-Moving Internet Economy Has a Jungle of Competitors and Here's the King," *Time* (December 27, 1999): 50.

16. See article by Gretchen Morgenson, "A Year Underachievers Everywhere Can Be Proud Of," *New York Times*, sec. 3 (December 31, 2000): 1.

17. See article by George Gilder, "The Coming Boom," *American Spectator*, vol. 34, no. 4 (May 2001): 45–52.

18. See article by Bill Bonner, "End of the Gildered Age," *Daily Reckoning* (June 20, 2002). Available from www.dailyreckoning.com.

19. David Shenk, *Data Smog: Surviving the Information Glut* (San Francisco: Harper, 1998).

20. *American Economic Review* (May 1978).

21. See note 19.

22. See article by David Serchuk, "Spooked by the Federal Reserve," *Forbes*, (January 13, 2009).

23. See article by Robert Shiller, "Infectious Exuberance," *The Atlantic* (July/August 2008).

24. www.loanperformance.com/pressreleases/LoanPerformance_HPIDec 08v1_021809.pdf.

25. Anonymous. "Buffalo Most Affordable Metro Area, L.A. Least Affordable." *Mortgage Banking*. October 1, 2005. www.allbusiness.com/finance/ 3596603-1.html.

26. See article by Kelly Zito, "How Do They Afford It?," *San Francisco Chronicle*, (August 18, 2005).

27. See article by Eric Fry, "Housing Bubble: In the Beginning," *The Rude Awakening* (2005). Available from www.agorafinancialpublications/ RudeAwakening.

28. CNN online survey, November 17, 2008.

29. From Barack Obama's Inaugural Address, January 20, 2009.

CHAPTER 2: PROGRESS, PERFECTIBILITY, AND THE END OF HISTORY

1. Paul Johnson, *Intellectuals* (New York: HarperTrade, 1992).

2. Available from www.firstworldwar.com/features/casualties.htm.

3. *Porter Stansberry's Investment Advisory* (Summer 2001).

4. See note 3.

5. See article by Bill Bonner, "The Wild Charge," *Daily Reckoning* (September 28, 2001). Available from www.dailyreckoning.com.

6. See note 5.
7. See article by Bill Bonner, "Pearl Harbor," *Daily Reckoning* (December 7, 2001). Available from www.dailyreckoning.com.
8. See article by Leah Nathans Spiro, "Dream Team," *BusinessWeek* (August 29, 1994): 50.
9. See article by Edmund Sanders, "A Renewed Call to Redo Accounting," *Los Angeles Times*, pt. 3 (January 25, 2002): 1.
10. Charles J. Whalen, "Integrating Schumpeter and Keynes: Hyman Minsky's Theory of Capitalist Development," *Journal of Economic Issues*, vol. 35, no. 4 (December 2001): 805–823.
11. Remarks by Governor Ben S. Bernanke at the Sandridge Lecture, Virginia Association of Economics, Richmond, Virginia. March 10, 2005. www.federalreserve.gov/boarddocs/speeches/2005/200503102/default.htm.
12. *Global Financial Stability Report*, April 2006, Chapter 2: The Influence on Credit Derivative and Structured Credit Markets on Financial Stability.
13. Henry Paulson, interview on CNBC Television, March 13, 2007.
14. Ben Bernanke, Semiannual Monetary Policy Report to the Congress Before the Committee on Financial Services, U.S. House of Representatives. July 19, 2007.
15. Countrywide Financial June 2007 operational data.
16. See article by Bill Bonner, "The Housing Market's Stray Puppy," *Daily Reckoning* (July 18, 2007). Available from http://dailyreckoning.com.
17. See article by Chris Wilson, "What Is a Mortgage-Backed Security?" Slate.com (March 17, 2008).
18. See article by Julie Creswell and Vikas Bajaj, "$3.2 Billion Move by Bear Stearns to Rescue Fund," *New York Times* (June 23, 2007).
19. See note 16.
20. A letter from Bear Stearns to investors, July 18, 2007. Full text here: www.telegraph.co.uk/finance/2812345/Bear-Stearns-letter-sent-to-investors-last-night.html.
21. See article by Dina El Boghdady, "No Money Down Disappearing as Mortgage Option," *Washington Post* (August 5, 2007).
22. See article by Gretchen Morgenson, "Rescue Me—Fed Bailout Crosses a Line," *New York Times* (March 16, 2008).
23. Remarks by Chairman Alan Greenspan, "Financial Derivatives," before the Futures Industry Association, Boca Raton, Florida. March 19, 1999. www.federalreserve.gov/boarddocs/speeches/1999/19990319.htm.
24. Berkshire Hathaway's annual report for 2002. www.fintools.com/docs/Warren%20Buffet%20on%20Derivatives.pdf.
25. See article by Nelson D. Schwartz and Julie Creswell, "Who Created this Monster?" *New York Times* (March 23, 2008).
26. See note 25.
27. See article by Charles Duhigg, "Doubts Raised on Big Backers of Mortgages," *New York Times* (May 6, 2008).

28. See article by Steven Pearlstein, "In Crisis, Paulson's Stunning Use of Federal Power," *Washington Post* (September 8, 2008).
29. See article by Andrew Ross Sorkin, "Lehman Files for Bankruptcy; Merrill Is Sold," *New York Times* (September 14, 2008).

CHAPTER 3: JOHN LAW AND THE ORIGINS OF A BAD IDEA

1. Antoin E. Murphy, *John Law: Economic Theorist and Policymaker* (Oxford, UK: Clarendon Press, 1997).
2. Paul Strathern, *Dr. Strangelove's Game* (London: Penguin Books, 2001).
3. Charles Mackay, "The Mississippi Scheme," *Extraordinary Popular Delusions and the Madness of Crowds* (London: Wordsworth Editions, 1995).
4. Marc Faber, *Tomorrow's Gold* (CLSA, 2002).
5. See article by Bill Bonner, "A Freer Place?" *Daily Reckoning* (May 31, 2001). Available from www.dailyreckoning.com.
6. Quote from Ferdinand Lips' lecture "Why Gold-Backed Currencies Help Prevent Wars," delivered at the Humanitarianism at the Crossroads Congress in Feldkirch, Austria (August 30–September 1, 2002).
7. See article by Dan Denning, "Life After the Credit Depression," *Daily Reckoning – Australian Edition* (January 9, 2009). Available at http://daily reckoning.com/au.
8. David Ricardo, *On the Principles of Political Economy and Taxation* (London: John Murray, 1817).
9. Quote from a speech by William Poole, President of the Federal Reserve Bank of St. Louis, given to the Cato Institute, Washington, D.C., on November 30, 2007. www.allbusiness.com/government/government-bodies-offices-government/8897429-1.html.
10. Irving Fisher, "A Statistical Relationship between Unemployment and Price Changes," *International Labour Review* 13(6), 785–792 (1926).
11. See article by Edmund S. Phelps, "Our Uncertain Economy," *Wall Street Journal* (March 14, 2008).
12. Franklin Folsom, *America Before Welfare*, (New York: New York University Press, 1996).
13. Rik W. Hafer, Scott E. Hein, *The Stock Market* (Greenwood Publishing Group, 2007).
14. Samuel Butler, *The Note Books* (Echo Library, June 19, 2006).
15. Ludwig von Mises, *Human Action: A Treatise on Economics* (Laissez Faire Books; 4th Rev. Edition, January 9, 2008).
16. See note 15.
17. Taken from a *60 Minutes* interview on May 15, 2009.

CHAPTER 4: THE ERA OF CROWDS

1. See article by Bill Bonner, "Traditional Values," *Daily Reckoning* (June 10, 2002). Available from www.dailyreckoning.com.
2. See note 1.
3. See article by Bill Bonner, "Beyond Nietzche," *Daily Reckoning* (April 9, 2002). Available from www.dailyreckoning.com.
4. See article by Zbigniew Brzezinski, "Moral Duty, National Interest," *New York Times*, sec. 4 (April 7, 2002): 15.
5. See article by Jeffrey E. Garten, "The World Economy Needs Help," *International Herald Tribune* (January 13, 2003): 8.
6. Alfred N. Whitehead and Bertrand Russell, *Principia Mathematica* (New York: Cambridge University Press, 1927).
7. See article by James Sloan Allen, "Newspeak: Orwell's Most Prophetic Idea," *Christian Science Monitor* (June 8, 1984): 23.
8. Gustave Le Bon, *The Crowd* (Mineola, NY: Dover Publications, 2002).
9. See note 8.
10. Joseph Conrad, *Nostromo* (Mineola, NY: Dover Publications, 2002).
11. Robert A. Peterson, "A Tale of Two Revolutions," *Advocates for Self-Government's Freeman Archives* (August 1989). Available from www.self-gov .org/freeman/8908pete.html.
12. See note 11.
13. See note 11.
14. See article by Bill Bonner, "The Age of Chic," *Daily Reckoning* (June 27, 2002). Available from www.dailyreckoning.com.

CHAPTER 5: TURNING JAPANESE

1. Japanese word for outsiders.
2. See article by Doug Struck, "U.S. Urgings Perplex Japanese; Talk of Raising Standard of Living Falls on Affluent Ears," *Washington Post* (February 7, 2001): A12.
3. See note 2.
4. Ezra Vogel, *Japan as Number One: Lessons for America* (Cambridge, MA: Harvard University Press, 1979).
5. See article by Frank Gibney Jr., "Time for Hardball?" *Time* (February 18, 2002): 42.
6. Alex Kerr, *Dogs and Demons: The Rise and Fall of Modern Japan* (London: Penguin Books, 2001).
7. See note 6.
8. Japanese untouchables (lowest level in caste system).
9. "Terrible Twins?" *The Economist* (June 15, 2002).

10. See article by Peronet Despeignes and Abigail Rayner, "Data on Economy Ease Recession Fears," *Financial Times* (February 23, 2001).
11. David Leonhardt, "Japan and U.S.: Bubble, Bubble, Toil and Trouble," *New York Times*, sec. C (October 2, 2002): 1.
12. Bill Powell, "We're Not Turning Japanese," *Fortune* (September 15, 2002).
13. Japan's central bankers during the 1990s.
14. See article by Paul Krugman, "Fear Itself," *New York Times*, sec. 6 (September 30, 2001): 36.
15. Justin Lahart, "How Bad Could It Get? Think Japan," *CNN/Money.com* (July 23, 2002).
16. The 26th governor of the Bank of Japan.
17. See article by Martin Fackler "Japan's Big-Works Stimulus is Lesson," *New York Times* (February 5, 2009).
18. See note 17.
19. See article by Alaina Varvaloucas, "I See the World Crying," *Newsweek* (January 31, 2009).
20. See article by Nelson Banya, "Zimbabwe Knocks 12 Zeroes Off Inflation-Hit Dollar," *Reuters* (February 2, 2009).
21. See article on BBCNews.com "Zimbabwe Prices 'Begin to Fall' " (March 25, 2009).
22. See entry on Steve Keen's DebtWatch, "Can The U.S. Debt-Spend Its Way Out?" (November 29, 2008). www.debtdeflation.com/blogs/2008/11/29/can-the-usa-debt-spend-its-way-out/.
23. Ben Bernanke, "Deflation: Making Sure 'It' Doesn't Happen Here," speech before the National Economists Club, Washington, D.C. (November 21, 2002).
24. Ben Bernanke speech at ceremonial swearing in by President Bush (February 6, 2006).

CHAPTER 6: THE FABULOUS DESTINY OF ALAN GREENSPAN

1. See article by Bill Bonner, "Species by Decree," *Daily Reckoning* (July 16, 2001). Available from www.dailyreckoning.com.
2. Jeffrey R. Hummel, *Emancipating Slaves, Enslaving Free Men: A History of the American Civil War* (Chicago: Open Court Publishing, 1996).
3. See article by Dan Atkinson and Graeme Beaton, "Greenspan's Move to Cut Rates Dampened by Speculative Market," *Daily Mail* (January 7, 2001).
4. See article by Thomas Easton, "8 Investing Rules That Have Stood the Test of Time," *Forbes* (December 27, 1999): 174.

5. Knox is better remembered as America's Secretary of War in World War II, and for his remark to TV. Tsoong, the Chinese Ambassador, in which he proclaimed his confidence in the American war against the Japanese: "Don't worry, TV, we'll lick those yellow bastards yet."

6. See article by Julian E. Zelizer, "The Forgotten Legacy of the New Deal: Fiscal Conservatism and the Roosevelt Administration, 1933–1938," *Presidential Studies Quarterly*, vol. 30, no. 2 (June 1, 2000): 331.

7. R.W. Bradford, "Alan Greenspan—Cultist? The Fascinating Personal History of Mr. Pinstripe" (September 9, 1997). Available from www.theamericanenterprise.org/taeso97a.htm.

8. See article by William Powers, "Ayn Rand Was Wrong: It Turns Out There Is an Afterlife after All," *Washington Post* (August 25, 1996): F01.

9. Thom Calandra, "30 Years Later, Gold Solution for Dollar Is Examined," for *CBS MarketWatch* (August 17, 2001).

10. Alan Greenspan, "Gold and Economic Freedom," reprinted in *Capitalism: The Unknown Ideal* by Ayn Rand (New York: NAL, 1986).

11. See note 10.

12. See article by David McWilliams, "Investors Own the Third World," *Global News Wire* (August 12, 2001).

13. See article by Gregory Nokes, "Miller Blames Gold Price Rise on Unsettled Conditions," Associated Press (January 15, 1980).

14. See article by Bob Woodward, "In '87 Crash, All Eyes on Greenspan," *Washington Post* (November 13, 2000): A01.

15. See article by John Cassidy, "The Fountainhead," *New Yorker* (April 24, 2000/May 1, 2000): 162.

16. See article by Bob Woodward, "Behind the Boom," *Washington Post* (November 12, 2000): W08.

17. See article by Richard W. Stevenson, "Inside the Head of the Fed," *New York Times*, sec. 3 (November 15, 1998): 1.

18. See article "Uncharted Waters," *Upside,* vol. 13, no. 1 (January, 2001): 178–184.

19. See article by Rob Norton, "In Greenspan We Trust," *Fortune* (March 18, 1996): 38.

20. See article by Bill Bonner, "End of an Era," *Daily Reckoning* (May 5, 2000). Available from www.dailyreckoning.com.

21. See article by Sharon Reier, "5 Years Later, Greenspan's 'Irrational Exuberance' Alert Rings True," *International Herald Tribune* (December 1, 2001): 13.

22. See article by Joseph N. DiStefano, "Worst of Times for an Internet Apostle," *Philadelphia Inquirer* (December 6, 2000): A01.

23. See article by David Hendricks, "Economist Says Looming War with Iraq Has Slowed Rebound," *San Antonio Express-News* (December 12, 2002).

24. See article by Thom Calandra, "Defying Naysayers, Tiny Gold Stocks Thrive," *CBS MarketWatch* (March 1, 2002).

25. "Hearing of the Senate Banking, Housing and Urban Affairs Committee," Federal News Service, Inc., Senator Paul Sarbanes chaired. (July 16, 2002).

26. See article by Mike Clowes "Monday Morning: Bad Time for Rise in Personal-Saving Rate," *Investment News* (September 2, 2002): 2.

27. See article by Brendan Murray and Craig Torres, "Not So Green for Greenspan," *Pittsburgh Post-Gazette* (October 27, 2002): D10.

28. See note 27.

29. See article by Murray N. Rothbard, "Alan Greenspan: A Minority Report," *Free Market* (August 1987).

30. See article by Reed V. Landberg and Paul George, "Greenspan 'Mess' Risks US Recession, Stiglitz Says," Bloomberg (November 16, 2007).

31. See article by Martin T. Sosnoff, "Blame Greenspan," *Forbes* (August 7, 2007).

32. See article by Greg Ip and Jon E. Hilsenrath, "How Credit Got So Easy and Why It's Tightening," *Wall Street Journal* (August 8, 2007).

33. See article by Brian Swint and Jennifer Ryan, "King, BOE Face 'Crisis of Confidence' After Rescue," Bloomberg (September 17, 2007).

34. See article "Bush Signs Economic Stimulus Package," Associated Press (February 13, 2008).

CHAPTER 7: RECKONING DAY: THE DELEVERAGING OF AMERICA

1. See article by Warren Vieth, "Consumer Spending Spree May Be Ending," *Los Angeles Times*, pt. 3 (September 10, 2001): 1.

2. See article by Sam Zuckerman, "People are Borrowing to Maintain Lifestyles," *San Francisco Chronicle* (June 3, 2001): E1.

3. See note 2.

4. See article by Thomas E. Ricks, "For U.S. Troops, It's Personal," *Washington Post* (March 24, 2002): A01.

5. See article "The Unfinished Recession," *The Economist* (September 28, 2002).

6. See article by Christina Romer, "Changes in Business Cycles: Evidence and Explanations," *Journal of Economic Perspectives*, vol. 13, no. 2 (Spring 1999): 23–44.

7. See article by Kurt Richebächer, "Bubble Aftermath," *Daily Reckoning* (November 13, 2002). Available from www.dailyreckoning.com.

8. From *An Inquiry into the Nature and Causes of the Wealth of Nations* (Book Two: *The Nature, Accumulation, and Employment of Stock;* Chapter 3, of the

Accumulation of Capital, or of Productive and Unproductive Labour); first published 1776.

9. See article "More Answers for Japan," *Investor's Business Daily* (September 11, 1998): A6.

10. See article by Paul Krugman, "Japan Heads for the Edge," *Financial Times* (January 20, 1999): 18.

11. See article by Justin Fox, "Saint Jack on the Attack," *Fortune* (January 20, 2003): 112.

12. From "Remarks by President Bill Clinton to the Council on Foreign Relations," White House Briefing in Federal News Service (September 14, 1998).

13. See article by Bill Bonner, "Empire Strikes Out," *Daily Reckoning* (May 14, 2002). Available from www.dailyreckoning.com.

14. See Emily Eakin's, "All Roads Lead to D.C.," *New York Times*, sec. 4 (March 31, 2002).

15. Ralph Waldo Emerson, "Compensation," from *Essays: First Series* (first published 1841).

16. For more information on Bernanke's speech, see Chapter 4.

17. See article by John Mauldin, "What the Fed Believes," *Daily Reckoning* (December 3, 2002). Available from www.dailyreckoning.com.

18. See article by Larry Kudlow, "Taking Back the Market—By Force," *National Review* (June 26, 2000).

19. See article by Lauren R. Rublin, "Smiling Again?" *Edge Singapore* (February 3, 2003).

20. See a research report by Richard Koo, "The Age of Balance Sheet Recessions: What Post-2008 U.S., Europe and China Can Learn from Japan 1990–2005," Nomura Research Institute (March 2009).

21. See article by Francesco Guerra and Aline van Duyn, "Wall Street Jobs Axe Threatens 70,000," *The Financial Times* (November 9, 2008).

22. See article by Hugh Son and Erik Holm, "Fed Takes Control of AIG with $85 Billion Bailout," Bloomberg (September 17, 2008).

23. See article by Sam Mamudi, "Lehman Folds With Record $613 Debt," *MarketWatch* (September 15, 2008).

24. See AP article, "Bank of America to Acquire Countrywide," Associated Press (January 11, 2008).

25. See article by Tami Luhby, "Countrywide's Mozilo Accused of Fraud," CNNMoney.com (June 4, 2009).

26. See article by Vikas Bajaj, "Lax Lending Standards Led to IndyMac's Downfall," *New York Times* (July 29, 2008).

27. See article by John Letzig, "WaMu Seized, Sold to JP Morgan Chase," *MarketWatch* (September 26, 2008).

28. See article by Neil King Jr. and Sharon Terlep, "GM Collapses Into Government's Arms," *Wall Street Journal* (June 2, 2009).

29. See article by David E. Sanger, Jeff Zeleny, and Bill Vlasic, "G.M. to Seek Bankruptcy and a New Start," *New York Times* (May 31, 2009).

CHAPTER 8: THE HARD MATH OF DEMOGRAPHY

1. Walter Moss, *A History of Russia* (New York: McGraw-Hill, 1997).
2. Peter G. Peterson, *Gray Dawn* (New York: Three Rivers Press, 2000), p. 28.
3. See article by Bill Bonner, "The NEW New Economy," *Daily Reckoning* (June 26, 2001). Available from www.dailyreckoning.com.
4. Samuel P. Huntington, *Clash of Civilizations* (New York: Free Press, 2002).
5. See note 4.
6. See note 4.
7. See note 4.
8. See note 4.
9. See note 2.
10. See *Investor's Business Daily*, Aging Index chart.
11. Census Bureau Data, 1996.
12. Paul Wallace, *Agequake* (London: Nicholas Brealey, 2001).
13. Harry S. Dent Jr., *The Roaring 2000s Investor* (New York: Touchstone Books, 1999), p. 25. The author considers the peak of spending of the average family today in the United States to be age 46.5.
14. Kurt Richebächer, "Letters to the Editor," *Financial Times* (September 5, 2000): 16.
15. "Erdman's World: Growling Bears," *CBC MarketWatch* transcript (June 13, 2000).
16. See article by Bill Bonner, "Disgraceful Wallowing in the Misery of Others: Enjoy It While You Can," *Daily Reckoning* (November 21, 2000). Available from www.dailyreckoning.com.
17. Mark Hulbert writing in *New York Times* (December 1, 2002). His article is based on a report by John Geanokoplos, Michael Magill, and Martine Quinzii, *Demography and the Long-Run Predictability of the Stock Market* (New Haven, CT: Yale University Press, 2002).
18. See article by David Reilly, "Trouble is Brewing for Pension Plans," *Wall Street Journal* (October 30, 2008).
19. See note 18.
20. See note 2 (p. 40).
21. See note 2 (p. 73).
22. See "A Summary of the 2009 Annual Reports" by Social Security and Medicare Boards of Trustees. www.ssa.gov/OACT/TRSUM/index.html.
23. See note 2 (p. 85).
24. See note 2 (p. 85).
25. See note 22.
26. See Kaiser Daily Health Policy Report, "Medicare/Medicare Hospital Fund Will Be Insolvent by 2017, Two Years Earlier Than Expected, Trustees Say" (May 13, 2009).

27. See note 26.
28. See note 22.
29. See article by David Walker, "America's Triple A Rating is at Risk," *Financial Times* (May 12, 2009).
30. See *Meet the Press* transcript for September 21, 2008.
31. See article by Kara Scannell, "Short Sale Ban Spreads Across the Globe," *Wall Street Journal* (September 22, 2008).
32. See Reuters article, "Treasury's Paulson—Subprime Woes Likely Contained," Reuters (April 20, 2007).
33. See article by Jane Padgham, "Bernanke Plays Down Effect of US Subprime Mortgage Crisis," *The Independent* (May 18, 2007).
34. See article by Juan Enriquez and Jorge Dominguez, "What About Austerity?" The *Boston Globe* (October 1, 2008).
35. See note 34.
36. See article by Murray Rothbard, "Rethinking the Legacy of the 80's," *Washington Times*, pt. B (March 22, 1992): B4.

CHAPTER 9: MORAL HAZARDS

1. See article by Karoline Durr, "The German Perspective," *Global Post* (April 1, 2009).
2. See article by James Grant, *Grant's Interest Rate Observer*, vol. 27, no. 07 (April 3, 2009).
3. See article by James K. Glassman, "Stocks Won't Fall Forever," *Washington Post* (January 6, 2002): H01.
4. See article by Bill Bonner, "Great Expectations," *Daily Reckoning* (January 9, 2003). Available from www.dailyreckoning.com.
5. Paul Krugman, "The Hangover Theory," *Slate* (December 4, 1998). Available from http://slate.msn.com/?querytext=krugma n+hangover+theory&id =3944&action=fulltext.
6. Paul Krugman, "Setting Sun," *Slate* (June 11, 1998).
7. See note 3.
8. Jeffrey Tucker, "Mr. Moral Hazard," *Free Market*, vol. 16, no. 12 (December 1998). Available from www.mises.org/freemarket_detail.asp?control=48.
9. See article by Bill Bonner, "The Perils of Success," *Daily Reckoning* (January 13, 2003). Available from www.dailyreckoning.com.
10. Alan Greenspan, "Remarks by Chairman Alan Greenspan," remarks before the Economic Club of New York on the Federal Reserve Board's web site (December 19, 2002). Available from www.federalreserve.gov/boarddocs/ speeches/2002/ 20021219/.
11. See article by Nick Sabloff, "Jim Cramer Declares the Depression 'Over,' " *Huffington Post* (April 4, 2009).

12. See article by Nouriel Roubini, "Light at the End of the Tunnel," *Forbes* (April 2, 2009).

13. See article by Edmund L. Andrews, "Bernanke Sees Hopeful Signs, but No Quick Recovery," *New York Times* (May 5, 2009).

14. See note 13.

15. See article by Sean Lengell, "Summers Sees End to Free Fall," *Washington Times* (April 27, 2009).

16. See article by Jack Willoughby, "Back in the Pool," *Barron's* (April 28, 2009).

17. See article by Takashi Nakamichi, "Japan Sets $100 Billion Stimulus Plan," *Wall Street Journal* (April 6, 2009).

18. See article by Michael Mackenzie, "Treasury Yields Give Cause for Concern," *Financial Times* (May 27, 2009).

19. See article by Michael Mackenzie, "Rising Treasury Yields Threaten to Stifle US Economic Recovery," *Financial Times* (May 28, 2009).

20. See article by Dexter Roberts, "China Worried After Lending 'Huge Amount' to US," *BusinessWeek* (March 13, 2009).

21. See article by Augusta Chronicle Editorial Staff, "No Laughing Matter," *Augusta Chronicle* (June 3, 2009).

22. See C-SPAN interview with Barack Obama (May 23, 2009).

23. See article by Nouriel Roubini, "The Almighty Renminbi," *New York Times* (May 13, 2009).

24. See article by Jonathan Wheatly, "Brazil and China Eye Plan to Axe Dollar," *Financial Times* (May 18, 2009).

25. See note 24.

26. See article by Lyubov Pronina, "Medvedev Questions Dollar as World Currency, Open to Yuan Swaps," Bloomberg (June 5, 2009).

BIBLIOGRAPHY

Ahearne, Alan, Joseph Gagnon, Jane Haltmaier, and Steve Kamin. *Preventing Deflation: Lessons from Japan's Experience in the 1990s* (Report—International Finance discussion papers no. 729). Washington, DC: Federal Reserve Board, June 2002.

Alexander, Bevin. *How Hitler Could Have Won World War II*. New York: Three Rivers Press, 2001.

Arnott, Robert D. and Anne Casscells. "Demographics and Capital Markets Return." *Financial Analysts Journal*, vol. 59, no. 2 (March–April 2003).

Asher, David, and Andrew Smithers. *Japan's Key Challenges for the 21st Century* (Report—SAIS Policy Forum Series Report). Washington, DC: March 1998.

Bernstein, Peter L. *The Power of Gold: The History of an Obsession*. New York: John Wiley & Sons, 2000.

Bloom, David E., A. K. Nandakumar, and Manjiri Bhawalkar. *The Demography of Aging in Japan and the United States* (written for the American Academy of Arts and Sciences Aging and Health Symposium), March 2001. An earlier version of this paper was presented at the American Academy of Arts and Sciences, Cambridge, MA in September 2000, at a conference entitled Aging and Health: Environment, Work, and Behavior.

Boia, Lucien. "The Myth of Democracy." *Les Belles Lettres* (April 19, 2002).

Browning, Christopher. *Ordinary Men*. New York: Perennial, 1993.

Cargill, Thomas, Michael Hutchison, and Takatoshi Ito. *The Political Economy of Japanese Monetary Policy*. Cambridge, MA: MIT Press, 1997.

Chancellor, Edward. *Devil Take the Hindmost: A History of Financial Speculation*. New York: Farrar, Straus and Giroux, 1999.

Chang, Iris. *The Rape of Nanking*. New York: Penguin, 1998.

Cogley, Timothy and Heather Royer. "The Baby Boom, the Baby Bust, and Asset Markets." San Francisco: Federal Reserve Bank of San Francisco Economic Letter 98–20 (June 26, 1998).

Dent, Harry S. *The Great Boom Ahead*. New York: Hyperion, 1993.

Dent, Harry S. *The Roaring 2000s Investor*. New York: Touchstone Books, 1999.

de Tocqueville, Alexis. *Democracy in America*. Signet Classic, 2001.

"Dicing with Debt." *The Economist* (January 24, 2002).

Ehrlich, Paul R. *The Population Bomb*. Cutchogue, New York: Buccaneer Books, 1997.

Emerson, Ralph Waldo. "Compensation" from *Essays First Series* (first published 1841).

Ezrati, Milton. "Seeking the Will to Act." *Barron's* (December 2, 2002).

Friedman, Milton and Anna Schwartz. *A Monetary History of the United States, 1867–1960*. Princeton, NJ: Princeton University Press, 1963.

Friedman, Robert, ed. "The Baby Boom Turns 50." *LIFE* (Special Issue), (June 1996).

Friedrich, Otto. *Before the Deluge—A Portrait of Berlin in the 1920s*. New York: Perennial, 1995.

Fukuyama, Francis. "The End of History" (article appearing in the *National Interest*). (Summer 1989).

Garrett, Garet. *Where the Money Grows and Anatomy of the Bubble*. New York: John Wiley & Sons, 1997.

The Gartman Letter (Financial Newsletter). (October 23, 2002; November 20, 2002).

Geanokoplos, Jean, Michael Magill, and Martine Quinzii. *Demography and the Long-Run Predictability of the Stock Market*. New Haven, CT: Yale University, Cowles Foundation for Research in Economics, 2002.

Gilder, George. *Microcosm*. New York: Touchstone Books, 1990.

Gilder, George. *Telecosm*. New York: Touchstone Books, 2002.

Glassman, James K. and Kevin A. Hassett. *Dow 36,000*. New York: Times Business, 1999.

Goldstone, Jack A. *Revolution and Rebellion in the Early Modern World*. Berkeley: University of California Press, 1990.

Goubert, Pierre. *The Course of French History*. London: Routledge, 1999.

Grant, James. *The Trouble with Prosperity*. New York: Times Books, 1996.

"Half a Billion Americans?" *The Economist* (August 22, 2002).

"How Japan Will Survive Its Fall." *The Economist* (Special Issue, July 11, 1992).

Hummel, Jeffrey Rogers. *Emancipating Slaves, Enslaving Free Men: A History of the American Civil War*. Chicago: Open Court Publishing Company, 1996.

Huntington, Samuel P. *Clash of Civilizations*. New York: Free Press, 2002.

Hurd, Micheal D. and Naohiro Yashiro, eds. *The Economic Effects of Aging in the United States and Japan*. Chicago: National Bureau of Economic Research Conference Report. University of Chicago Press, January 1997.

Kaplan, Robert D. *Warrior Politics:Why Leadership Demands a Pagan Ethos.* New York: Random House, 2001.

Kerr, Alex. *Dogs and Demons: The Rise and Fall of Modern Japan.* London: Penguin Books, 2001.

Kindleberger, Charles P. *Manias, Panics and Crashes: A History of Financial Crises.* 4th ed. New York: John Wiley & Sons, 2000.

Krugman, Paul. "The Fear Economy." *New York Times* (September 30, 2001).

Krugman, Paul. *Japan's Trap.* Retrieved May 1998, from http://web.mit.edu/krugman/www/.

Larimer, Tim. "The Sun Also Sets." *Time* (May 2002).

Le Bon, Gustave. *The Crowd.* Mineola, NY: Dover Publications, 2002.

Lee, Ronald and Jonathon Skinner. "Will Aging Baby Boomers Bust the Federal Budget?" *Journal of Economic Perspectives*, vol. 13, no. 1 (Winter 1999).

Locke Christopher, Levine Rick, Doc Searls, and David Weinberger. *The Cluetrain Manifesto: The End of Business as Usual.* New York: Perseus Publishing, 2001.

Lowenstein, Roger. *When Genius Failed.* New York: Random House Trade Paperbacks, 2000.

Mackay, Charles. *Extraordinary Popular Delusions & the Madness of Crowds.* London: Wordsworth Editions, 1995.

Macunovich, Diane J. *The Baby Boomers.* New York: Macmillan Encyclopedia of Aging, 2002.

Malkiel, Burton. *A Random Walk Down Wall Street.* New York: W.W. Norton, 2000.

Miller, Geoffrey P. *The Role of a Central Bank in a Bubble Economy.* Geoffrey P. Miller, Professor of Law and Director, Center for the Study of Central Banks, New York University Law School, 1997.

Minsky, Hyman P. *The Financial Instability Hypothesis* (working paper no. 74, May 1992). The Jerome Levy Economics Institute of Bard College (prepared for *Handbook of Radical Political Economy*, edited by Philip Arestis and Malcolm Sawyer). Edward Elgar Publishing, 1993.

Moroney, M. J. *Fact from Figures.* New York: Viking Press, 1952.

Moss, Walter G. *A History of Russia*, vol. II. New York: McGraw-Hill, 1997.

Murphy, Antoin E. *John Law: Economic Theorist and Policymaker.* Oxford, UK: Clarendon Press, 1997.

OECD Economic Survey of Japan, vol. 2002. Paris: Organisation for Economic Co-operation and Development, 2002.

Ogura, Seiritsu, Toshiaki Tachibanaki, and David Wise, eds. *Aging Issues in the United States and Japan.* Chicago: National Bureau of Economic Research Conference Report, University of Chicago Press, January 2001.

Okina, Kunio, Masaaki Shirakawa, and Shigenori Shiratsuka. *The Asset Price Bubble and Monetary Policy: Japan's Experience in the Late 1980s and the Lesson* (IMES discussion paper no. 2000-E-12). Tokyo: Bank of Japan, May 2000.

Parker, Thornton. *What if Boomers Can't Retire?* San Francisco: Berrett-Koehler Publishers, 2000.

"Perspective, 'False Charges?'" *Investor's Business Daily* (April 3, 1997).

Peterson, Peter G. *Gray Dawn*. New York: Three Rivers Press, 2000.

Posen, Adam S. and Ryoichi Mikitani, eds. *Japan's Financial Crisis and Its Parallels to U.S. Experience*. Washington, DC: Institute for International Economics, 2000.

Powell, Benjamin. *Explaining Japan's Recession*. Auburn, AL: Mises Institute, December 3, 2002.

Rand, Ayn. *Atlas Shrugged*. New York: Dutton/Plume, 1999.

Rand, Ayn. *Capitalism: The Unknown Ideal*. New York: NAL, 1986.

Rand, Ayn. *The Fountainhead*. New York: Dutton/Plume, 2002.

Schumpeter, Joseph. *The History of Economic Analysis*, rev. ed. Oxford University Press, 1996.

Seismic Shifts: The Economic Impact of Demographic Change. Boston: Federal Reserve Bank of Boston, 2001; following the Federal Reserve Bank of Boston's June 2001 conference of the same name. "Foreword" by Cathy E. Minehan (President and CEO of the FRBB) and "Overview" by Jane Sneddon Little and Robert K. Triest.

Shiller, Robert. *Irrational Exuberance*. New York: Broadway Books, 2001.

Siebel, Thomas and Michael Malone. *Virtual Selling*. New York: Free Press, 1996.

Siegel, Jeremy J. *Stocks for the Long Run*. 3rd ed. New York: McGraw-Hill Trade, 2002.

Smith, Adam. *An Inquiry into the Nature and Causes of the Wealth of Nations*. First published 1776. More recent edition, Modern Library, 1994.

Smith, Adam. *Theory of Moral Sentiments*. First published 1759. More recent edition: Prometheus Books, 2000.

Smithers, Andrew and Stephen Wright. *Valuing Wall Street: Protecting Wealth in Turbulent Markets*. New York: McGraw-Hill Trade, 2000.

Spencer, Herbert. *The Man versus the State: With Six Essays on Government, Society, and Freedom*. First published 1884. Indianapolis, IN: Liberty Fund, 1982.

Strathern, Paul. *Dr. Strangelove's Game*. London: Penguin Books, 2001.

Strauss, William and Neil Howe. *The Fourth Turning*. New York: Broadway Books, 1997.

"A Tale of Two Bellies." *The Economist* (August 22, 2002).

"Tales of Youth and Age." *The Economist* (December 21, 2000).

"Terrible Twins: America's Economy Looks Awfully Like Japan's After Its Bubble Burst." *The Economist* (June 13, 1992).

Tindall, George Brown. *America: A Narrative History*. 2nd ed. New York: W.W. Norton, 1988.

Todd, Emmanuel. *Après l'Empire*. Paris: Gallimard, 2002.

Tuccille, Jerome. *Alan Shrugged*. Hoboken, NJ: John Wiley & Sons, 2002.

Tvede, Lars. *Business Cycles: The Business Cycle Problem from John Law to Chaos Theory*. New York: Penguin, Harwood Academic, 1997.

Vogel, Ezra F. *Japan as Number One: Lessons for America*. Cambridge, MA: Harvard University Press, 1979.

Wallace, Paul. *Agequake*. London: Nicholas Brealy Publishing, 2001.

Wei, Ya-Gui. *Demographic Reasons for Market Bubbles and Crashes—From Baby Boom to Market Bust*. Retrieved March 17, 2001, from www.comwerx.net/users/yawei/stock/a031701.htm.

Weldon's Money Monitor (Financial Newsletter). (October 7, 2002; October 9, 2002).

Whitehead, Alfred N. and Bertrand Russell. *Principia Mathematica*. New York: Cambridge University Press, 1927.

Wood, Christopher. *The Bubble Economy*. London: Sidgwick and Jackson, 1992.

Woodward, Bob. *Maestro: Greenspan's Fed and the American Boom*. New York: Simon & Schuster, 2000.

INDEX